WEBSTER'S
RHYMING
DICTIONARY ALPHABETICAL GUIDE TO
RHYMING SOUNDS

WEBSTER'S RHYMING DICTIONARY

ALPHABETICAL GUIDE TO RHYMING SOUNDS

CREATED IN COOPERATION WITH THE EDITORS OF

MERRIAM-WEBSTER

Dalmatian Press

This 2011 Edition published by arrangement with Federal Street Press,
a division of Merriam-Webster, Incorporated

Distributed by: **Dalmatian Press**
118 Seaboard Lane, Franklin, TN 37067
CE13844/1110

ISBN 1-40377-644-0

Printed in Fort Wayne, IN, USA
11 12 13 14 CLI 5 4 3 2 1

Contents

How to Use This Book

Welcome to this new rhyming dictionary, where you'll find over 40,000 rhyming words—enough to last you the rest of your life.

We've tried to make this book as easy as possible to use. However, it works quite differently from an ordinary dictionary, so please read these brief instructions to be sure you make the best use of it you can.

All the entries in this book are for *rhyming sounds*. All rhyming sounds begin with a vowel, so every entry begins with *A*, *E*, *I*, *O*, *U*, or *Y*.

All rhyming sounds also begin with an accented syllable. The rhyming sounds listed here all have one syllable, two syllables, or three syllables.

If a word has only one syllable, that syllable is always accented (as in *bee* and *sea*). A two-syllable word may be accented on either its first syllable (as in *beta* and *data*) or its second syllable (as in *agree* and *must-see*). A three-syllable word may be accented on its first syllable (*attitude*, *gratitude*), its middle syllable (*illusion*, *seclusion*), or its last syllable (*anymore*, *tug-of-war*).

Though the rhyming sounds in this dictionary are never more than three syllables long, the words themselves may have six or more syllables. In every entry, the words are divided into sections according to number of syllables; each section begins with a small bullet (•). So, for instance, the **y**[1] entry starts with a group of one-syllable words, which is followed by five more bulleted sections, the last one consisting of six-syllable words.

Some words have two accented syllables, with one of them almost always stronger than the other. Notice that when you say the word "middle," you put no accent at all on the second syllable, but when you say "schoolkid," you put a strong accent on its first syllable and a weaker accent on its second syllable. In this book, the rhyming sound always begins with the *last* accented syllable, whether or not that syllable is the one with the strongest accent. So *schoolkid* is shown at the **id**[1] entry—that is, the entry for its weakly accented syllable.

Many rhymes can be spelled in several different ways. For example, the rhyming sound that is often spelled -*eek* (as in *creek*) can also be spelled -*eak* (as in *peak*), -*ique* (*mystique*), -*ic* (*chic*), or -*ik* (*batik*). So how do you find a rhyme for a particular word? Just look up the spelling of its rhyming sound.

Let's suppose you need a rhyme for *equator*. All you need to do is notice how its rhyming sound is spelled. Since the rhyming sound always begins with the last accented syllable and always begins with a vowel, the rhyming sound of *equator* is obviously spelled -*ator*. And sure enough, the entry **ator** shows all the rhymes for *equator*, no matter how their endings are spelled: *crater, freighter, creator*, etc.

But suppose you had instead wanted a rhyme for *later*, and had looked up the spelling for its rhyming sound, *-ater*. There you would have found two separate entries, **ater**[1] and **ater**[2]. Next to **ater**[1] you would have seen the pronunciation \ȯt-ər\, and next to **ater**[2] you would have seen the pronunciation \āt-ər\. Looking at the Pronunciation Symbols table on page viii, you would have seen that only the second pronunciation matched the pronunciation of *later*. But you might not have even needed to look up the pronunciation symbols, since you would have noticed immediately that the words listed at **ater**[1]—words such as *daughter* and *water*—didn't rhyme with *later*. Moving on to **ater**[2], you would have seen that no words are listed there at all, but that it instead simply contains the direction "see ATOR." Turning to **ator**, you would have found all the words that rhyme with *later*, regardless of how they were spelled.

Now suppose you need a word to rhyme with *dance*, and you've found the list you were looking for at **ance**[3]. But maybe none of the words there is quite what you want. This time you're in luck: there are some other possibilities. At the end of the entry, you'll see the following note: "—*also* -s, -'s, *and* -s' *forms of nouns and* -s *forms of verbs listed at* ANT[5]." In other words, at **ant**[5] you can find some nouns and verbs that might do the trick. Turning to **ant**[5], you see that it lists such nouns as *aunt* and *confidant*, which would rhyme with *dance* in their plural form (*aunts, confidants*), in their possessive form (*aunt's, confidant's*), or in their plural possessive form (*aunts', confidants'*). You would also see such verbs as *enchant* and *gallivant*, which in the first-person singular (*enchants, gallivants*) would also rhyme with *dance*.

Not everyone pronounces all words the same way. So, for example, you will see words like *drawn, gone*, and *yawn* at both **on**[1] and **on**[3]. Usually only one pronunciation will seem right for you.

These few instructions should be all you need to make the best use of the dictionary. We hope you'll keep it close at hand to jog your memory, enlarge your lyrical vocabulary, and expand your poetic ambitions.

Pronunciation Symbols

ə	banana, collide, **abut**
ᵊ	preceding \l\ and \n\, as in bat**tle**, mit**ten**, and eat**en**; following \l\, \m\, \r\, as in French tab**le**, pris**me**, tit**re**
ər	fu**r**ther, me**r**ger, bi**rd**
a	m**a**t, g**a**g, s**a**p
ā	d**ay**, f**a**de, **ao**rta
ä	b**o**ther, c**o**t, f**a**ther
au̇	n**ow**, l**ou**d, F**au**st
b	**b**a**b**y, ri**b**
ch	**ch**in, na**t**ure \'nā-chər\
d	**d**i**d**, a**dd**er
e	b**e**t, p**e**ck, h**e**lp
ē	f**ee**, **ea**sy, med**ia**
f	**f**i**f**ty, **ph**one, rou**gh**
g	**g**o, bi**g**
h	**h**at, a**h**ead
i	t**i**p, ban**i**sh, act**i**ve
ī	s**i**te, b**uy**, den**y**
j	**j**ob, **g**em, ju**dge**
k	**k**in, coo**k**, a**ch**e
k̲	German i**ch**, Bu**ch**
l	**l**i**l**y, poo**l**
m	**m**ur**m**ur, di**m**
n	**n**o, ow**n**
ⁿ	preceding vowel or diphthong is pronounced with the nasal passages open, as in French *un bon vin blanc* \œⁿ-bōⁿ-vaⁿ-bläⁿ\
ŋ	si**ng** \'siŋ\, fi**ng**er \'fiŋ-gər\, i**n**k \'iŋk\
ō	b**o**ne, kn**ow**, b**eau**
ȯ	s**a**w, **a**ll, c**au**ght
ȯi	c**oi**n, destr**oy**
p	**p**e**pp**er, li**p**
r	**r**ed, ca**r**, ra**r**ity
s	**s**ource, le**ss**
sh	**sh**y, mi**ss**ion, ma**ch**ine, spe**c**ial
t	**t**ie, a**tt**ack, la**t**e
th	**th**in, e**th**er
t̲h̲	**th**en, ei**th**er
ü	r**u**le, f**oo**l, **u**nion \'yün-yən\, few \'fyü\
u̇	p**u**ll, w**ou**ld, b**oo**k
v	**v**i**v**id, gi**v**e
w	**w**e, a**w**ay
y	**y**ard, c**u**e \'kyü\, m**u**te \'myüt\
z	**z**one, rai**s**e
zh	vi**s**ion, a**z**ure \'a-zhər\

A

a¹ \ä\ aah, ah, baa, bah, blah, bra, fa, ha, la, ma, moi, nah, pa, rah, shah, ska, spa • aha, Allah, blah-blah, Casbah, chutzpah, Degas, faux pas, feta, gaga, goombah, grandma, grandpa, ha-ha, hoopla, hurrah, huzzah, oompah, pooh-bah, ta-ta, Utah, voilà • Akita, aloha, baklava, brouhaha, Chippewa, coup d'état, guarana, la-di-da, ma-and-pa, Mardi Gras, Omaha, Ottawa, panama, Panama, polenta, Shangri-la, tempura • ayatollah, je ne sais quoi, phenomena

a² \ā\ see AY¹

a³ \ȯ\ see AW¹

aa¹ \a\ see AH³

aa² \ä\ see A¹

aag \äg\ see OG¹

aal¹ \āl\ see AIL

aal² \ȯl\ see ALL¹

aal³ \äl\ see AL¹

aam \äm\ see OM¹

aan \an\ see AN⁵

aans¹ \äns\ see ANCE²

aans² \änz\ see ONZE

aard \ärd\ see ARD¹

aari \är-ē\ see ARI¹

aaron \ar-ən\ see ARON²

aarten \ärt-ᵊn\ see ARTEN

aas \äs\ see OS¹

aatz \ätz\ see OTS

ab¹ \äb\ see OB¹

ab² \äv\ see OLVE²

ab³ \ab\ blab, cab, crab, dab, drab, fab, flab, gab, grab, jab, lab, Lab, nab, scab, slab, stab, tab • Ahab, backstab, confab, prefab, rehab, smack-dab • baobab, taxicab

aba \äb-ə\ casaba • Ali Baba

abah \äb-ə\ see ABA

abard \ab-ərd\ clapboard, scabbard —also -ed forms of verbs listed at ABBER²

abbard \ab-ərd\ see ABARD

abbas \ab-əs\ see ABBESS

abbat \ab-ət\ see ABIT

abbed¹ \ab-əd\ crabbed, rabid

abbed² \abd\ blabbed, stabbed —also -ed forms of verbs listed at AB³

abber¹ \äb-ər\ see OBBER

abber² \ab-ər\ blabber, crabber, gabber, grabber, jabber, stabber • backstabber, land-grabber

abbess \ab-əs\ abbess • Barabbas

abbet \ab-ət\ see ABIT

abbey \ab-ē\ see ABBY

abbie¹ \äb-ē\ see OBBY

abbie² \ab-ē\ see ABBY

abbit \ab-ət\ see ABIT

abbitt \ab-ət\ see ABIT

abble¹ \äb-əl\ bauble, cobble, gobble, hobble, Kabul, squabble, wobble

abble² \ab-əl\ Babel, babble, dabble, gabble, rabble, scrabble, Scrabble • hardscrabble • psychobabble, technobabble

abbler \ab-lər\ babbler, dabbler, scrabbler

abbly \ab-lē\ see ABLY

abbot \ab-ət\ see ABIT

abby \ab-ē\ abbey, Abby, blabby, cabbie, crabby, flabby, gabby, grabby, scabby, shabby, tabby

abe¹ \āb\ babe, nabe

abe² \ab\ see AB³

abe³ \ä-bə\ see ABA

abel \ā-bəl\ see ABLE

aben \äb-ən\ see OBIN

aber¹ \ā-bər\ see ABOR
aber² \äb-ər\ see OBBER
abes \ā-bēz\ see ABIES
abi¹ \äb-ē\ see OBBY
abi² \əb-ē\ see UBBY
abi³ \ab-ē\ see ABBY
abid \ab-əd\ see ABBED¹
abies \ā-bēz\ rabies, scabies • antirabies
  —also -s, -'s, and -s' forms of nouns listed at ABY
abile \ab-əl\ see ABBLE²
abit \ab-ət\ abbot, habit, rabbit • cohabit, inhabit, jackrabbit
able \ā-bəl\ Abel, able, Babel, cable, fable, gable, label, Mabel, sable, stable, table • disable, enable, round table, timetable, turntable, unable, unstable, worktable
abled \ā-bəld\ fabled, gabled
  —also -ed forms of verbs listed at ABLE
ablis \ab-lē\ see ABLY
ably \ab-lē\ chablis, drably
abor \ā-bər\ labor, neighbor, saber • belabor
abot \ab-ət\ see ABIT
abre \äb\ see OB¹
abul \äb-əl\ see ABBLE¹
abulous \ab-yə-ləs\ fabulous • fantabulous
aby \ā-bē\ baby, maybe • crybaby
ac¹ \ak\ see ACK²
ac² \äk\ see OCK¹
ac³ \o̅\ see AW¹
aca¹ \äk-ə\ see AKA¹
aca² \ak-ə\ alpaca • Strait of Malacca
acable \ak-ə-bəl\ see ACKABLE
acao \ō-kō\ see OCO
acas \ak-əs\ fracas • Caracas
acca¹ \ak-ə\ see ACA²
acca² \äk-ə\ see AKA¹
accent \ak-sənt\ accent • relaxant
acchus \ak-əs\ see ACAS
accid \as-əd\ see ACID

acco¹ \ak-ə\ see ACA¹
acco² \ak-ō\ see AKO²
ace¹ \ās\ ace, base, bass, brace, case, chase, face, grace, Grace, lace, mace, Mace, pace, place, race, space, Thrace, trace, vase • abase, airspace, backspace, birthplace, boldface, bookcase, bootlace, briefcase, crankcase, debase, deface, disgrace, displace, dogface, efface, embrace, encase, erase, fireplace, footrace, lactase, misplace, nutcase, outpace, outrace, paleface, replace, retrace, shoelace, showcase, showplace, slipcase, someplace, staircase, suitcase, typeface, unlace, wheelbase, workplace, worst-case • about-face, aerospace, anyplace, commonplace, cyberspace, database, double-space, everyplace, hyperspace, interface, interlace, interspace, lowercase, marketplace, pillowcase, single-space, steeplechase, triple-space, uppercase
ace² \ā-sē\ see ACY
ace³ \äs\ see OS¹
ace⁴ \as\ see ASS³
ace⁵ \äch-ē\ see OTCHY
ace⁶ \äs-ə\ see ASA¹
aceable \ā-sə-bəl\ placeable, traceable • embraceable, erasable, replaceable, untraceable • irreplaceable
acean \ā-shən\ see ATION¹
aced \āst\ based, baste, chaste, faced, haste, laced, paste, taste, waist, waste • bald-faced, barefaced, bold-faced, distaste, foretaste, lambaste, moonfaced, rad waste, shamefaced, snailpaced, slipcased, stone-faced, straight-faced, straitlaced, toothpaste, two-faced • aftertaste, poker-faced • scissors-and-paste
  —also -ed forms of verbs listed at ACE¹

aceless \ā-sləs\ baseless, faceless, graceless

aceman \ā-smən\ baseman, spaceman

acement \ā-smənt\ basement, casement, placement • displacement, replacement • bargain-basement

acency \ās-ᵊn-sē\ adjacency, complacency

acent \ās-ᵊnt\ adjacent, complacent

aceor \ā-sər\ see ACER¹

aceous \ā-shəs\ see ACIOUS

acer¹ \ā-sər\ pacer, racer, spacer, tracer • defacer, eraser • steeplechaser

acer² \as-ər\ see ASSER

acet \as-ət\ asset, facet, tacit

acewalking \ās-wȯ-kiŋ\ racewalking, spacewalking

acey \ā-sē\ see ACY

ach¹ \äk\ see OCK¹

ach² \ak\ see ACK²

ach³ \ach\ see ATCH³

acha \äch-ə\ cha-cha, gotcha

ache¹ \āk\ see AKE¹

ache² \ash\ see ASH³

ache³ \äch-ē\ see OTCHY

ache⁴ \ach-ē\ see ATCHY

ached \acht\ attached, detached • unattached
—*also* -ed *forms of verbs listed at* ATCH³

acher \ā-kər\ see AKER¹

achet \ach-ət\ see ATCHET

achi \äch-ē\ see OTCHY

achian \ā-shən\ see ATION¹

achm \am\ see AM²

achment \ach-mənt\ see ATCHMENT

acho \äch-ō\ macho, nacho • gazpacho

acht \ät\ see OT¹

achtsman \ät-smən\ see OTSMAN

achy \ā-kē\ see AKY

acia \ā-shə\ geisha • acacia, Croatia, Dalmatia

acial \ā-shəl\ facial, glacial, racial, spatial • biracial, palatial • interracial, multiracial

acian \ā-shən\ see ATION¹

acias \ā-shəs\ see ACIOUS

acid \as-əd\ acid, flaccid, placid • antacid, nonacid

acie \ā-shə\ see ACIA

acier¹ \ā-shər\ see ASURE¹

acier² \ā-zhər\ see AZIER

acile \as-əl\ see ASSEL²

acing \ā-siŋ\ bracing, casing, facing, lacing, racing, spacing, tracing • all-embracing, self-effacing
—*also* -ing *forms of verbs listed at* ACE¹

acious \ā-shəs\ gracious, spacious • audacious, bodacious, capacious, curvaceous, fallacious, flirtatious, Ignatius, loquacious, mendacious, pugnacious, rapacious, sagacious, tenacious, ungracious, vivacious, voracious • disputatious, efficacious, ostentatious, perspicacious

acis \as-ē\ see ASSY

acist \ā-səst\ see ASSIST

acit \as-ət\ see ACET

acity¹ \as-tē\ see ASTY²

acity² \as-ət-ē\ audacity, capacity, pugnacity, rapacity, sagacity, tenacity, veracity, vivacity • incapacity • overcapacity

acive \ā-siv\ see ASIVE

ack¹ \äk\ see OCK¹

ack² \ak\ back, black, Braque, clack, crack, flak, hack, jack, Jack, knack, lack, Mac, Mack, pack, plaque, quack, rack, sac, sack, shack, slack, smack, snack, stack, tach, tack, thwack, track, wack, whack, wrack, yak • aback, Amtrak, attack, backpack, backtrack, Balzac, bareback, blackjack, blowback, bushwhack, buyback, callback, carjack, coatrack, cognac, come back, comeback, cossack, cut back, cutback,

drawback, fall back, fallback,
fastback, fast-track, fatback,
feedback, flapjack, flashback,
fullback, greenback, halfback,
half-track, hardback, hatchback,
hayrack, haystack, hijack, hold
back, horseback, humpback,
hunchback, Iraq, jam-pack, jet-
black, kayak, Kazak, kickback,
knapsack, knickknack, laid-back,
macaque, Muzak, one-track,
outback, payback, pitch-black,
play back, playback, racetrack,
ransack, restack, roll back, roll-
back, runback, sad sack, set back,
setback, shellac, sidetrack, six-
pack, skyjack, slapjack, Slovak,
smokestack, snap back, snow-
pack, softback, sumac, swayback,
swept-back, switchback, tarmac,
throwback, thumbtack, ticktack,
touchback, unpack, wisecrack,
wolf pack • almanac, applejack,
back-to-back, bivouac, bric-a-
brac, canvasback, cardiac, crack-
erjack, cul-de-sac, diamondback,
gunnysack, Kodiak, lumberjack,
maniac, medevac, mommy track,
moneyback, multitrack, off-the-
rack, paperback, piggyback,
Pontiac, quarterback, running
back, single-track, Union Jack,
zodiac • Adirondack, biofeed-
back, counterattack, demoniac,
insomniac • egomaniac,
hypochondriac, pyromaniac, sal
ammoniac • megalomaniac

ackable \ak-ə-bəl\ packable, stack-
able

ackal \ak-əl\ see ACKLE

acked \akt\ see ACT

acken \ak-ən\ blacken, slacken

ackened \ak-ənd\ blackened,
slackened

acker \ak-ər\ backer, clacker,
cracker, hacker, jacker, lacquer,
packer, slacker, stacker, tracker

• attacker, backpacker, bush-
whacker, carjacker, firecracker,
graham cracker, hijacker,
kayaker, linebacker, nutcracker,
safecracker, skyjacker,
wisecracker • soda cracker
—also -er forms of adjectives listed
at ACK^2

acket \ak-ət\ bracket, jacket,
packet, racket • dust jacket, flak
jacket, life jacket, straitjacket
• bomber jacket, dinner jacket,
yellowjacket

ackey \ak-ē\ see ACKY

ackguard \ag-ərd\ see AGGARD

ackie \ak-ē\ see ACKY

acking \ak-iŋ\ backing, blacking,
cracking, packing, smacking,
tracking, whacking • bushwhack-
ing, kayaking, meatpacking,
nerve-racking, safecracking,
skyjacking
—also -ing forms of verbs listed at
ACK^2

ackish \ak-ish\ blackish, brackish

ackle \ak-əl\ cackle, crackle,
grackle, jackal, shackle, tackle
• debacle, ramshackle • block and
tackle, tabernacle

ackly \ak-lē\ blackly, slackly • ab-
stractly, compactly, exactly • in-
exactly • matter-of-factly

acko \ak-ō\ see AKO^2

ackson \ak-sən\ see AXON

acky \ak-ē\ Jackie, khaki, lackey,
tacky, wacky • Nagasaki, ticky-
tacky

acle^1 \ik-əl\ see ICKLE

acle^2 \äk\ see OCK^1

acle^3 \äk-əl\ see OCKLE

acle^4 \ak-əl\ see ACKLE

aco \äk-ō\ see OCCO

acon^1 \ā-kən\ see AKEN

acon^2 \ak-ən\ see ACKEN

acque^1 \ak\ see ACK^2

acque^2 \äk\ see OCK^1

acquer \ak-ər\ see ACKER

acques \äk\ see OCK[1]
acre[1] \ā-kər\ see AKER[1]
acre[2] \ak-ər\ see ACKER
act \akt\ act, backed, bract, cracked, fact, packed, pact, stacked, tact, tracked, tract • abstract, attract, class act, compact, contact, contract, crookbacked, detract, distract, enact, exact, extract, humpbacked, hunchbacked, impact, intact, outact, playact, protract, react, refract, retract, subtract, swaybacked, transact • artifact, cataract, counteract, eye contact, inexact, interact, noncontact, overact, reenact, subcompact, subcontract, vacuum-packed • matter-of-fact, overreact, ultracompact
— also -ed *forms of verbs listed at* ACK[2]
actable \ak-tə-bəl\ compactible, contractible, distractible, exactable, extractable, intractable, retractable
acte[1] \äkt\ see OCKED
acte[2] \akt\ see ACT
acted \ak-təd\ abstracted, impacted
—*also* -ed *forms of verbs listed at* ACT
acter \ak-tər\ see ACTOR
actery \ak-trē\ see ACTORY
actible \ak-tə-bəl\ see ACTABLE
actic \ak-tik\ tactic • climactic, didactic, galactic • chiropractic • anticlimactic, intergalactic
actical \ak-ti-kəl\ practical, tactical • impractical
actice \ak-təs\ cactus, practice • malpractice
actics \ak-tiks\ tactics
—*also* -s, -'s, *and* -s' *forms of nouns listed at* ACTIC
actile \ak-t°l\ tactile • pterodactyl
acting \ak-tiŋ\ acting • exacting, self-acting

—*also* -ing *forms of verbs listed at* ACT
action \ak-shən\ action, faction, fraction, traction • abstraction, attraction, contraction, diffraction, distraction, extraction, inaction, infraction, live-action, reaction, refraction, retraction, subtraction, transaction • benefaction, chain reaction, counteraction, interaction, satisfaction • dissatisfaction, overreaction, self-satisfaction • affirmative action
actional \ak-shnəl\ factional, fractional
active \ak-tiv\ active • attractive, inactive, proactive, reactive • hyperactive, interactive, overactive, psychoactive, retroactive, unattractive • radioactive
actly \ak-lē\ see ACKLY
actor \ak-tər\ actor, factor, tractor • contractor, detractor, fudge factor, protractor, reactor, subtracter • benefactor, chiropractor, malefactor, subcontractor
actory \ak-trē\ factory • olfactory, refractory • satisfactory • unsatisfactory
actous \ak-təs\ see ACTICE
actress \ak-trəs\ actress • benefactress
actual \ak-chəl\ actual, factual • contractual
acture \ak-chər\ fracture • compound fracture, manufacture, simple fracture
actus \ak-təs\ see ACTICE
actyl \ak-t°l\ see ACTILE
acular \ak-yə-lər\ oracular, spectacular, vernacular • unspectacular
acy \ā-sē\ Basie, lacy, racy, spacey, Stacy, Tracy • prima facie
acyl \as-əl\ see ASSEL[2]
ad[1] \ä\ see A[1]

ad² \äd\ see OD¹

ad³ \ad\ ad, add, bad, bade, brad, cad, Chad, clad, dad, fad, gad, glad, grad, had, lad, mad, pad, plaid, rad, sad, scad, shad, tad, trad • Baghdad, Belgrade, comrade, Conrad, crash pad, crawdad, doodad, dryad, egad, footpad, forbade, gonad, granddad, ironclad, keypad, launchpad, maenad, mouse pad, naiad, nomad, notepad, reclad, scratch pad, Sinbad, touch pad, triad • armorclad, Galahad, Iliad, legal pad, Leningrad, lily pad, Stalingrad, Trinidad, undergrad, Volgograd • jeremiad, olympiad, Upanishad

ada¹ \äd-ə\ nada • armada, cicada, Granada, Masada, Nevada, tostada • empanada, enchilada, yada yada • Sierra Nevada

ada² \äd-ə\ Ada • armada, cicada, Granada

adable \äd-ə-bəl\ gradable, tradable • persuadable, upgradable • biodegradable

adah \äd-ə\ see ADA²

adal \ad-ᵊl\ see ADDLE

adam \ad-əm\ Adam, madam • macadam

adan¹ \ad-n\ see ADDEN

adan² \äd-n\ see ODDEN

add \ad\ see AD³

adden \ad-ᵊn\ gladden, madden, sadden • Aladdin

adder \ad-ər\ adder, bladder, gladder, ladder, madder, sadder • air bladder, fish ladder, gallbladder, puff adder, stepladder • Jacob's ladder

addie \ad-ē\ see ADDY¹

addik \äd-ik\ see ODIC

addin \ad-ᵊn\ see ADDEN

adding \ad-iŋ\ padding
—also -ing forms of verbs listed at AD³

addish¹ \äd-ish\ see ODDISH

addish² \ad-ish\ see ADISH

addle \ad-ᵊl\ addle, paddle, saddle, straddle • astraddle, dog paddle, sidesaddle, skedaddle, unsaddle

addler¹ \äd-lər\ see ODDLER

addler² \ad-lər\ paddler, straddler

addock¹ \ad-ik\ see ADIC

addock² \ad-ək\ haddock, paddock

addy¹ \ad-ē\ baddie, caddie, caddy, daddy, faddy, laddie, paddy • granddaddy, tea caddy

addy² \äd-ē\ see ODY¹

ade¹ \äd\ aid, aide, bade, blade, braid, fade, glade, grade, jade, laid, made, maid, paid, raid, rayed, shade, spade, staid, suede, they'd, trade, wade • abrade, afraid, air raid, arcade, Band-Aid, barmaid, Belgrade, blockade, bridesmaid, brigade, brocade, cascade, Cascade, charade, clichéd, cockade, crusade, decade, degrade, dissuade, downgrade, evade, eyeshade, fair-trade, first aid, grenade, handmade, handmaid, homemade, housemaid, inlaid, invade, limeade, low-grade, man-made, mermaid, milkmaid, nightshade, nursemaid, old maid, parade, persuade, pervade, postpaid, repaid, sacheted, self-made, stockade, sunshade, switchblade, tirade, unbraid, unmade, unpaid, upbraid, upgrade, waylaid • accolade, Adelaide, aquacade, balustrade, barricade, cannonade, cavalcade, centigrade, chambermaid, colonnade, custom-made, dairymaid, escapade, esplanade, everglade, foreign aid, hearing aid, legal aid, lemonade, marinade, marmalade, masquerade, Medicaid, meter maid, motorcade, orangeade, palisade, promenade, ready-made, renegade, retrograde, serenade, tailor-made, unafraid, underlaid, visual aid

—*also* -ed *forms of verbs listed at* AY[1]

ade[2] \äd\ see OD[1]

ade[3] \ad\ see AD[3]

ade[4] \äd-ə\ see ADA[2]

adely \ad-lē\ see ADLY

aden[1] \ād-ᵊn\ laden, maiden • handmaiden • overladen

aden[2] \äd-ən\ Aden • Baden-Baden

ader \ād-ər\ aider, blader, grader, Nader, nadir, raider, seder, trader • crusader, day trader, evader, fair trader, free trader, horse trader, invader • masquerader, serenader

ades[1] \ād-ēz\ ladies, Hades

ades[2] \ādz\ AIDS • Cascades • Everglades • jack-of-all-trades —*also* -s, -'s, *and* -s' *forms of nouns and* -s *forms of verbs listed at* ADE[1]

adge \aj\ badge, cadge, hajj, Madge

adger \aj-ər\ badger, cadger

adh \äd\ see OD[1]

adhe \äd-ē\ see ODY[1]

adian \ād-ē-ən\ Acadian, Arcadian, Barbadian, Canadian, circadian • French Canadian, Trinidadian

adic \ad-ik\ haddock • nomadic, sporadic • seminomadic

adie \ād-ē\ see ADY

adies \ād-ēz\ see ADES[1]

ading \ād-iŋ\ braiding, shading • degrading, unfading —*also* -ing *forms of verbs listed at* ADE[1]

adir \ād-ər\ see ADER

adish \ad-ish\ faddish, radish • horseradish

adium \ād-ē-əm\ radium, stadium • palladium

adle \ād-ᵊl\ cradle, dreidel, ladle

adley \ad-lē\ see ADLY

adly \ad-lē\ badly, Bradley, gladly, madly, sadly • comradely

adness \ad-nəs\ badness, gladness, madness, sadness

ado[1] \äd-ō\ bravado, mikado • avocado, Colorado, Coronado, desperado, El Dorado • aficionado • incommunicado, Llano Estacado

ado[2] \ād-ō\ credo • Alfredo, Laredo, tornado • desperado, El Dorado

ados \ā-dəs\ see ADUS

adrate \äd-rət\ see ODERATE

adrian \ā-drē-ən\ Adrian, Adrienne, Hadrian

adrienne \ā-drē-ən\ see ADRIAN

adt \ät\ see OT[1]

adual \aj-əl\ see AGILE

adus \ā-dəs\ Barbados —*also* -s, -'s, *and* -s' *forms of nouns listed at* ADA[2]

ady \ād-ē\ lady, Sadie, shady • bag lady, first lady, landlady, milady, old lady, saleslady • dragon lady, leading lady, painted lady

ae[1] \ā\ see AY[1]

ae[2] \ē\ see EE[1]

ae[3] \ī\ see Y[1]

aea \ē-ə\ see IA[1]

aean \ē-ən\ see EAN[1]

aedal \ēd-ᵊl\ see EEDLE

aedile \ēd-ᵊl\ see EEDLE

aegis[1] \ā-jəs\ see AGEOUS

aegis[2] \ē-jəs\ see EGIS

ael \āl\ see AIL

aeli \ā-lē\ see AILY

aelic \al-ik\ see ALLIC

aemon \ē-mən\ see EMON[1]

aen \äⁿ\ see ANT[1]

aena \ē-nə\ see INA[2]

aenia[1] \ē-nē-ə\ see ENIA[1]

aenia[2] \ē-nyə\ see ENIA[2]

aens \äⁿs\ see ANCE[1]

aeon \ē-ən\ see EAN[1]

aera \ir-ə\ see ERA[2]

aere[1] \er-ē\ see ARY[1]

aere[2] \ir-ē\ see EARY

aerial[1] \er-ē-əl\ see ARIAL

aerial[2] \ir-ē-əl\ see ERIAL

aerie[1] \ā-rē\ airy, fairy
aerie[2] \er-ē\ see ARY[1]
aerie[3] \ir-ē\ see EARY
aero[1] \er-ō\ see ERO[2]
aero[2] \ar-ō\ see ARROW[2]
aeroe[1] \ar-ō\ see ARROW[2]
aeroe[2] \er-ō\ see ERO[2]
aery[1] \ā-rē\ see AERIE[1]
aery[2] \er-ē\ see ARY[1]
aesar \ē-zər\ see EASER[2]
aestor \ē-stər\ see EASTER
aet \āt\ see ATE[1]
aetor \ēt-ər\ see EATER[1]
aeum \ē-əm\ see EUM[1]
aeus \ē-əs\ see EUS[1]
af \af\ see APH
afe[1] \āf\ chafe, safe, strafe, waif
• fail-safe, unsafe, vouchsafe
• supersafe
afe[2] \af\ see APH
afel \äf-əl\ waffle • falafel • Belgian
waffle
afer \ā-fər\ strafer, wafer
aff \af\ see APH
affable \af-ə-bəl\ affable, laughable
affe \af\ see APH
affed \aft\ see AFT[2]
affer[1] \äf-ər\ see OFFER[1]
affer[2] \af-ər\ laugher, staffer
affic \af-ik\ see APHIC
affick \af-ik\ see APHIC
affir \af-ər\ see AFFER[2]
affle[1] \äf-əl\ see AFEL
affle[2] \af-əl\ baffle, raffle
affy \af-ē\ daffy, taffy
afic \af-ik\ see APHIC
afir \af-ər\ see AFFER[2]
aft[1] \äft\ waft
—*also* -ed *forms of verbs listed at*
OFF[1]
aft[2] \aft\ aft, craft, daft, draft, graft,
haft, raft, shaft, Taft, waft • abaft,
aircraft, campcraft, camshaft,
crankshaft, downdraft, driveshaft,
handcraft, life raft, redraft, skin
graft, spacecraft, stagecraft, state-
craft, updraft, witchcraft, wood-

craft • fore-and-aft, handicraft,
hovercraft, landing craft, under-
staffed, watercraft • antiaircraft
—*also* -ed *forms of verbs listed at*
APH
after \af-tər\ after, crafter, drafter,
grafter, laughter, rafter • here-
after, thereafter • handicrafter
aftsman \af-smən\ craftsman,
draftsman, raftsman • handcrafts-
man • handicraftsman
afty \af-tē\ crafty, drafty
ag \ag\ bag, brag, crag, drag, fag,
flag, gag, hag, jag, lag, mag, nag,
rag, sag, shag, slag, snag, stag,
swag, tag, wag • air bag, beanbag,
brown-bag, dirtbag, dishrag, dog
tag, do-rag, fleabag, flight bag,
gasbag, grab bag, handbag, ice
bag, jet lag, mailbag, mixed bag,
outbrag, phone tag, price tag,
ragtag, red flag, sandbag, school-
bag, sight gag, sleazebag, tea bag,
time lag, tote bag, washrag, wind-
bag, zigzag • carpetbag, doggie
bag, duffel bag, garment bag,
litterbag, lollygag, punching bag,
saddlebag, scalawag, shopping
bag, shoulder bag, sleeping bag
• capture the flag, overnight bag
aga[1] \ä-gə\ bodega, omega
• rutabaga
aga[2] \eg-ə\ see EGA[1]
agan \ā-gən\ see AGIN
agar[1] \äg-ər\ see OGGER[1]
agar[2] \ag-ər\ see UGGER[1]
agate \ag-ət\ see AGGOT
age[1] \äj\ dodge, lodge, raj • barrage, collage, corsage, dislodge,
garage, hodgepodge, massage
• camouflage • espionage
age[2] \äzh\ barrage, collage, corsage, dressage, garage, massage,
mirage, montage, portage • as-
semblage, bon voyage, camouflage, decoupage, fuselage,
sabotage • espionage

age³ \āj\ age, cage, gage, gauge, page, rage, sage, stage, wage • assuage, backstage, birdcage, engage, enrage, front-page, ice age, Iron Age, new age, offstage, onstage, Osage, outrage, rampage, rib cage, road rage, school age, soundstage, space-age, teenage, uncage, upstage • batting cage, center stage, disengage, legal age, mental age, middle age, multistage, underage • coming-of-age, minimum wage

age⁴ \āg\ see EG¹

age⁵ \äg-ə\ see AGA¹

aged \ājd\ aged, gauged • engaged • middle-aged
—*also* -ed *forms of verbs listed at* AGE³

agel \ā-gəl\ bagel, Hegel • finagle, inveigle

ageless \āj-ləs\ ageless, wageless

agen¹ \ā-gən\ see AGIN

agen² \ā-gən\ see OGGIN

ageous \ā-jəs\ aegis • courageous, contagious, outrageous • advantageous, noncontagious • disadvantageous

ager¹ \ā-jər\ major, pager, sager, wager • New Ager, teenager • golden-ager, middle-ager, pre-teenager, Ursa Major

ager² \äg-ər\ see OGGER¹

agey \ā-jē\ see AGY

agga \äg-ə\ see AGA¹

aggar \äg-ər\ see OGGER¹

aggard \ag-ərd\ blackguard, haggard, laggard

agged \ag-əd\ cragged, jagged, ragged

agger \ag-ər\ bagger, dagger, lagger, stagger, swagger, • threebagger, two-bagger • carpetbagger, cloak-and-dagger

aggie \ag-ē\ see AGGY²

agging \ag-iŋ\ bagging, flagging, lagging, nagging • unflagging • carpetbagging
—*also* -ing *forms of verbs listed at* AG

aggle \ag-əl\ gaggle, haggle, straggle, waggle

aggly \ag-lē\ scraggly, straggly

aggot \ag-ət\ agate, maggot

aggy¹ \äg-ē\ see OGGY¹

aggy² \ag-ē\ baggy, craggy, scraggy, shaggy

agh \ä\ see A¹

agi¹ \äg-ē\ see OGGY¹

agi² \ag-ē\ see AGGY²

agian \ā-jən\ see AJUN

agic \aj-ik\ magic, tragic

agile \aj-əl\ agile, fragile, gradual

agin \ā-gən\ pagan, Reagan • Copenhagen

aging \ā-jiŋ\ aging, raging, staging • unaging
—*also* -ing *forms of verbs listed at* AGE³

agion \ā-jən\ see AJUN

agious \ā-jəs\ see AGEOUS

agm \am\ see AM²

agman \ag-mən\ bagman, flagman

agne \ān\ see ANE¹

ago¹ \äg-ō\ Chicago, farrago • Santiago

ago² \ā-gō\ farrago, Tobago, virago • San Diego • Tierra del Fuego

ago³ \äŋ-gō\ see ONGO

agon \ag-ən\ dragon, flagon, wagon • bandwagon, chuck wagon, Pendragon, snapdragon • covered wagon, paddy wagon, station wagon

agonal \ag-ən-ᵊl\ diagonal, hexagonal, octagonal, pentagonal

agoras \ag-ə-rəs\ Protagoras, Pythagoras

agot \ag-ət\ see AGGOT

agrance \ā-grəns\ flagrance, fragrance

agrant \ā-grənt\ flagrant, fragrant, vagrant

agster \ag-stər\ dragster, gagster

agua \äg-wə\ Managua
• Aconcagua, Nicaragua

ague[1] \āg\ see EG[1]

ague[2] \äg\ see OG[1]

aguey \eg-ē\ see EGGY

agy \ā-jē\ cagey, stagy

ah[1] \ä\ see A[1]

ah[2] \ȯ\ see AW[1]

ah[3] \a\ baa, nah

aha \ä-hä\ aha, Baja

aham \ā-əm\ see AHUM

ahd \äd\ see OD[1]

ahdi \äd-ē\ see ODY[1]

ahdom \äd-əm\ see ODOM

ahib \äb\ see OB[1]

ahl \äl\ see AL[1]

ahler \äl-ər\ see OLLAR

ahlia \ā-lē-ə\ see ALIA

ahma[1] \äm-ə\ see AMA[1]

ahma[2] \am-ə\ see AMA[2]

ahman[1] \äm-ən\ see OMMON

ahman[2] \am-ən\ see AMMON

ahn \än\ see ON[1]

ahms \ämz\ see ALMS

ahnda \än-də\ see ONDA

ahr \är\ see AR[3]

aht \ät\ see OT[1]

ahua \ä-wə\ see AWA[1]

ahum \ā-əm\ Graham, mayhem

ahveh \ä-vā\ see AVE[1]

ai[1] \ā\ see AY[1]

ai[2] \ē\ see EE[1]

ai[3] \ī\ see Y[1]

ai[4] \ȯi\ see OY

a'i \ī\ see Y[1]

aia[1] \ā-ə\ Hosea, Isaiah, Judea
• Himalaya, Mauna Kea

aia[2] \ī-ə\ see IAH[1]

aiad \ī-əd\ see YAD

aiah \ā-ə\ see AIA[1]

aic \ā-ik\ archaic, Hebraic, Judaic, mosaic, prosaic • algebraic, formulaic

aice \ās\ see ACE[1]

aiche \esh\ see ESH[1]

aid[1] \ād\ see ADE[1]

aid[2] \ed\ see EAD[1]

aid[3] \ad\ see AD[3]

aida \ī-də\ see IDA[2]

aide[1] \ād\ see ADE[1]

aide[2] \īd-ē\ see IDAY

aiden \ād-ᵊn\ see ADEN[1]

aider \ād-ər\ see ADER

aiding \ād-iŋ\ see ADING

aido \ī-dō\ see IDO[1]

aids \ādz\ see ADES[2]

aiety \ā-ət-ē\ see AITY

aif \āf\ see AFE[1]

aig \āg\ see EG[1]

aight \āt\ see ATE[1]

aighten \āt-ᵊn\ see ATEN[1]

aightly \āt-lē\ see ATELY[1]

aign \ān\ see ANE[1]

aigne \ān\ see ANE[1]

aignment \ān-mənt\ see AINMENT

aik \īk\ see IKE[2]

aika \ī-kə\ see ICA[1]

ail \āl\ ail, ale, bail, bale, braille, Braille, dale, Dale, fail, flail, frail, gale, Gale, Gayle, grail, hail, hale, jail, kale, mail, male, nail, pail, pale, quail, rail, sail, sale, scale, shale, snail, stale, tail, tale, they'll, trail, vale, veil, wail, whale, Yale • airmail, assail, avail, bake sale, betrayal, bewail, blackmail, bobtail, broadtail, bud scale, cattail, chain mail, Clydesdale, coattail, cocktail, contrail, curtail, derail, detail, dovetail, downscale, ducktail, e-mail, entail, exhale, fan mail, female, fire sale, fishtail, folktale, full-scale, guardrail, handrail, hangnail, impale, inhale, junk mail, mainsail, outsail, passfail, pigtail, portrayal, presale, prevail, renail, resale, retail, right whale, Scottsdale, shirttail, slop pail, small-scale, snail mail, sperm whale, strong gale, tag sale, telltale, thumbnail, timescale, toenail, toothed whale, topsail, travail, unveil, upscale, voice mail, wage scale, wassail, white sale, white whale, wholesale, yard sale • Abigail, altar rail, antimale, Chippendale, Chisholm Trail, coffin nail, cottontail, express mail, fairy tale, fingernail, garage sale, ginger ale, Holy Grail, humpback whale, killer whale, monorail, nightingale, old wives' tale, paper trail, pilot whale, ponytail, Richter scale, rummage sale, supersale, swallowtail, tattletale, tooth and nail, vapor trail • certified mail, Fort Lauderdale, Oregon Trail, registered mail, Santa Fe Trail, self-betrayal, sixpenny nail, tenpenny nail

ailable \ā-lə-bəl\ mailable, sailable, salable, scalable • available, resalable, unsalable • unassailable, unavailable

ailand \ī-lənd\ see IGHLAND

aile \ī-lē\ see YLY

ailed \āld\ mailed, nailed, sailed, scaled, tailed, veiled • detailed, pigtailed, unveiled • ponytailed
—*also* -ed *forms of verbs listed at* AIL

ailer \ā-lər\ bailer, baler, jailer, mailer, sailor, scaler, tailor, Taylor, trailer, wailer, whaler • blackmailer, derailleur, detailer, e-mailer, house trailer, retailer, self-mailer, wholesaler • semitrailer
—*also* -er *forms of adjectives listed at* AIL

ailey \ā-lē\ see AILY

ailie \ā-lē\ see AILY

ailiff \ā-ləf\ bailiff, caliph

ailing \ā-liŋ\ failing, mailing, railing, sailing, veiling, whaling • boardsailing, prevailing, retailing, unfailing • parasailing
—*also* -ing *forms of verbs listed at* AIL

aille¹ \āl\ see AIL

aille² \ī\ see Y¹

aille³ \īl\ see ILE¹

aille⁴ \ä-yə\ see AYA¹

ailles \ī\ see Y¹

ailleur \ā-lər\ see AILER

ailment \āl-mənt\ ailment • derailment

ailor \ā-lər\ see AILER

ails \ālz\ see ALES¹

aily \ā-lē\ daily, gaily, scaly • Israeli • ukulele

aim \ām\ see AME¹

aimable \ā-mə-bəl\ see AMABLE

aiman \ā-mən\ see AMEN¹

aimant \ā-mənt\ see AYMENT

aiment \ā-mənt\ see AYMENT

aimer \ā-mər\ framer, gamer, lamer, tamer • disclaimer, proclaimer • Hall of Famer

aimless \ām-ləs\ see AMELESS

ain¹ \ä-ən\ see AYAN¹

ain² \än\ see ANE¹

ain³ \en\ see EN¹

ain⁴ \in\ see IN¹

ain⁵ \īn\ see INE¹

ain⁶ \aⁿ\ see IN⁴

aina \ī-nə\ see INA¹

ainable \ā-nə-bəl\ stainable, trainable • attainable, containable, explainable, obtainable, restrainable, sustainable • unattainable, uncontainable, unobtainable

aine¹ \än\ see ANE¹

aine² \en\ see EN¹

ained \ānd\ brained, caned, craned, drained, grained, pained, stained, strained, veined • birdbrained, bloodstained, coarsegrained, contained, harebrained, ingrained, lamebrained, restrained, tearstained, unfeigned, unstained, untrained • featherbrained, multipaned, scatterbrained, self-contained, unexplained, unrestrained
—*also* -ed *forms of verbs listed at* ANE¹

ainer \ā-nər\ drainer, gainer,

planer, stainer, strainer, trainer
• abstainer, campaigner, complainer, container, explainer, nobrainer, obtainer, retainer
• aquaplaner, entertainer
—*also* -er *forms of adjectives listed at* ANE[1]

ainful \ān-fəl\ baneful, gainful, painful • disdainful

aininess \ā-nē-nəs\ braininess, graininess

aining \ā-niŋ\ complaining, sustaining, weight training • selfsustaining, uncomplaining
—*also* -ing *forms of verbs listed at* ANE[1]

ainless \ān-ləs\ brainless, painless, stainless

ainly \ān-lē\ mainly, plainly, sanely, vainly • humanely, insanely, profanely, ungainly • inhumanely

ainment \ān-mənt\ arraignment, attainment, containment, detainment • edutainment, entertainment, infotainment, self-containment

aino \ī-nō\ see INO[1]

ains \ānz\ reins • cremains, Great Plains, remains
—*also* -s, -'s, *and* -s' *forms of nouns and* -s *forms of verbs listed at* ANE[1]

aint \ānt\ ain't, faint, feint, mayn't, paint, quaint, saint, taint • acquaint, complaint, constraint, greasepaint, oil paint, repaint, restraint, war paint • head restraint, patron saint, plaster saint, self-restraint • Latter-Day Saint, luminous paint

ain't \ānt\ see AINT

ainting \ān-tiŋ\ oil painting, wall painting • finger painting
—*also* -ing *forms of verbs listed at* AINT

aintly \ānt-lē\ faintly, quaintly, saintly

ainy \ā-nē\ brainy, grainy, rainy, zany • Khomeini • Allegheny

ainz \īnz\ see INES[3]

aipse \āps\ see APES

air[1] \er\ see ARE[4]

air[2] \īr\ see IRE[1]

aira \ī-rə\ see YRA

aird \erd\ see AIRED

aire[1] \er\ see ARE[4]

aire[2] \ir\ see EER[2]

aire[3] \īr\ see IRE[1]

aired \erd\ laird • fair-haired, impaired, long-haired, prepared, shorthaired, unpaired, wirehaired
• multilayered, underprepared, unimpaired
—*also* -ed *forms of verbs listed at* ARE[4]

airer \er-ər\ see EARER[1]

aires[1] \er\ see ARE[4]

aires[2] \ar-ēs\ see ARES[2]

airess[1] \er-əs\ see ERROUS

airess[2] \ar-əs\ see ARIS[2]

airie \er-ē\ see ARY[1]

airing \er-iŋ\ see ARING[1]

airish \er-ish\ see ARISH[1]

airist \er-əst\ see ARIST

airly \er-lē\ barely, fairly, rarely, squarely

airn \ern\ see ERN[1]

airo \ī-rō\ see YRO[1]

airs \erz\ theirs • downstairs, nowheres, somewheres, upstairs • foreign affairs, musical chairs
—*also* -s, -'s, *and* -s' *forms of nouns and* -s *forms of verbs listed at* ARE[4]

airy[1] \er-ē\ see ARY[1]

airy[2] \ā-rē\ see AERIE[1]

ais \ā\ see AY[1]

aisal[1] \ā-zəl\ see ASAL

aisal[2] \ī-səl\ see ISAL[1]

aisant \ās-ᵊnt\ see ACENT

aise[1] \āz\ see AZE[1]

aise[2] \ez\ see AYS[1]

aiser[1] \ā-zər\ see AZER

aiser² \ī-zər\ see IZER
aisian \ā-zhən\ see ASION
aisin \āz-ᵊn\ see AZON
aising \ā-ziŋ\ blazing, glazing, hazing, phrasing • amazing, appraising, fund-raising, hair-raising, stargazing, trailblazing • crystal gazing
—*also* -ing *forms of verbs listed at* AZE¹
aisle \īl\ see ILE¹
aisley \āz-lē\ paisley, nasally
aisne \ān\ see ANE¹
aisse \ās\ see ACE¹
aisson \ās-ᵊn\ see ASON¹
aist¹ \ā-əst\ see AYEST
aist² \āst\ see ACED
aist³ \äst\ see OST¹
aisy \ā-zē\ see AZY
ait¹ \ā\ see AY¹
ait² \āt\ see ATE¹
ait³ \īt\ see ITE¹
ait⁴ \at\ see AT⁵
aite \īt\ see ITE¹
aited \āt-əd\ see ATED
aiten \āt-ᵊn\ see ATEN¹
aiter \āt-ər\ see ATOR
aith \āth\ eighth, faith, Faith, wraith • good faith
aithe \āth\ see AITH
aiti \āt-ē\ see ATY
aitian \ā-shən\ see ATION¹
aiting \āt-iŋ\ see ATING
aitly \āt-lē\ see ATELY¹
aitor \āt-ər\ see ATOR
aitour \āt-ər\ see ATOR
aity \ā-ət-ē\ deity, gaiety • spontaneity
aius \ī-əs\ see IAS¹
aiva \ī-və\ see IVA¹
aive \āv\ see AVE²
aix \ā\ see AY¹
aize \āz\ see AZE¹
aj \äj\ see AGE¹
aja¹ \ä-hä\ see AHA
aja² \ī-ə\ see IAH¹
ajan \ā-jən\ see AJUN

ajj \aj\ see ADGE
ajor \ā-jər\ see AGER¹
ajun \ā-jən\ Cajun • contagion
ak¹ \äk\ see OCK¹
ak² \ak\ see ACK²
aka¹ \äk-ə\ Dhaka, Oaxaca, Osaka • Lake Titicaca
aka² \ak-ə\ see ACA²
akable \ā-kə-bəl\ breakable, shakable • mistakable, nonbreakable, unbreakable • unmistakable
akan \ak-ən\ see ACKEN
akar \äk-ər\ see OCKER
ake¹ \āk\ ache, bake, Blake, brake, break, cake, drake, Drake, fake, flake, Jake, lake, make, quake, rake, sake, shake, sheikh, slake, snake, spake, stake, steak, take, wake • air brake, awake, backache, beefsteak, caretake, cheesecake, cheesesteak, clambake, cupcake, daybreak, disc brake, earache, earthquake, fast break, firebreak, fish cake, forsake, fruitcake, green snake, hand brake, handshake, headache, heartache, heartbreak, hotcake, housebreak, intake, jailbreak, keepsake, king snake, milk snake, mistake, muckrake, namesake, opaque, outbreak, outtake, pancake, partake, pound cake, prebake, rat snake, remake, retake, rewake, seaquake, sea snake, shortcake, snowflake, sponge cake, toothache, uptake, windbreak • bellyache, coffee break, coral snake, Crater Lake, double take, garter snake, give-and-take, Great Salt Lake, Great Slave Lake, griddle cake, hognose snake, johnnycake, make-or-break, minute steak, overtake, parking brake, patty-cake, piece of cake, plumber's snake, rattlesnake, station break, stomachache, undertake, water snake,

wedding cake • Salisbury steak, tension headache, upside-down cake • emergency brake, Lady of the Lake, potato pancake

ake² \ak\ see ACK²

ake³ \äk-ē\ see OCKY

aked \ākt\ awaked, half-baked, sunbaked
—*also* -ed *forms of verbs listed at* AKE¹

aken \ā-kən\ bacon, Macon, shaken, taken, waken • awaken, forsaken, mistaken, retaken, unshaken • godforsaken, overtaken, undertaken

aker¹ \ā-kər\ acre, baker, breaker, faker, maker, Quaker, shaker • backbreaker, caretaker, carmaker, dressmaker, filmmaker, gill raker, glassmaker, heartbreaker, homemaker, housebreaker, icebreaker, jawbreaker, kingmaker, lawbreaker, lawmaker, mapmaker, matchmaker, muckraker, noisemaker, pacemaker, peacemaker, printmaker, sailmaker, saltshaker, shirtmaker, shoemaker, snowmaker, steelmaker, strikebreaker, tiebreaker, toolmaker, watchmaker, windbreaker, winemaker, wiseacre • automaker, bellyacher, circuit breaker, coffee maker, moviemaker, papermaker, pepper shaker, troublemaker, undertaker • cabinetmaker, policymaker

aker² \ak-ər\ see ACKER

akery \ā-krē\ bakery, fakery

akes \āks\ cornflakes, Great Lakes, sweepstakes
—*also* -s, -'s, *and* -s' *forms of nouns and* -s *forms of verbs listed at* AKE¹

ake-up \ā-kəp\ break up, breakup, make up, makeup, rake up, shake-up, shake up, take up, wake-up

akey \ā-kē\ see AKY

akh \äk\ see OCK¹

aki¹ \äk-ē\ see OCKY

aki² \ak-ē\ see ACKY

akian \äk-ē-ən\ see OCKIAN

aking \ak-iŋ\ see ACKING

ako¹ \äk-ō\ see OCCO

ako² \ak-ō\ wacko • tobacco

aky \ā-kē\ achy, cakey, flaky, shaky, snaky • headachy

al¹ \äl\ doll, loll, sol • atoll, Baikal, cabal, chorale, Nepal, real • aerosol, femme fatale, parasol, Portugal, protocol, Senegal • Neanderthal

al² \el\ see EL¹

al³ \ȯl\ see ALL¹

al⁴ \al\ gal, pal, Val • canal, chorale, corral, decal, locale, morale • femme fatale, rationale • Guadalcanal

ala¹ \äl-ä\ à la, Allah, gala

ala² \äl-ə\ Allah, gala • Kampala, koala, Valhalla • ayotollah, Guatemala

ala³ \ā-lə\ gala • Venezuela

ala⁴ \al-ə\ Allah, gala • Valhalla

alable \ā-lə-bəl\ see AILABLE

alace \al-əs\ see ALIS²

alad \al-əd\ see ALID²

alam \äl-əm\ see OLUMN

alan \al-ən\ see ALLON

alance \al-əns\ balance, valance • imbalance, rebalance • counterbalance, overbalance, platform balance

alap \al-əp\ see ALLOP²

alar \ā-lər\ see AILER

alary \al-ə-rē\ calorie, gallery, salary, Valerie • rogues' gallery

alas \al-əs\ see ALIS²

alate \al-ət\ see ALLET²

ald¹ \ȯld\ bald, scald, walled • socalled • Archibald, Buchenwald, coveralled
—*also* -ed *forms of verbs listed at* ALL¹

ald² \ȯlt\ see ALT
alder \ȯl-dər\ alder, balder
ale¹ \ā-lē\ see AILY
ale² \āl\ see AIL
ale³ \āl\ see AL¹
ale⁴ \al\ see AL⁴
ale⁵ \äl-ē\ see OLLY¹
ale⁶ \al-ē\ see ALLY⁴
alea \ā-lē-ə\ see ALIA
aleck¹ \el-ik\ see ELIC
aleck² \al-ik\ see ALLIC
aled \āld\ see AILED
aleigh¹ \äl-ē\ see OLLY¹
aleigh² \ȯl-ē\ see AWLY
alement \āl-mənt\ see AILMENT
alen \ä-lən\ see OLLEN⁵
alent \al-ənt\ see ALLANT
alep \al-əp\ see ALLOP²
aler¹ \ā-lər\ see AILER
aler² \äl-ər\ see OLLAR
alerie \al-ə-rē\ see ALARY
ales¹ \ālz\ sales, Wales • entrails
• New South Wales, Prince of
Wales • cat-o'-nine-tails
—*also* -s, -'s, *and* -s' *forms of
nouns and* -s *forms of verbs listed
at* AIL
ales² \äl-əs\ see OLIS
alet \al-ət\ see ALLET²
alette \al-ət\ see ALLET²
aley \ā-lē\ see AILY
alf \af\ see APH
alfa \al-fə\ see ALPHA
algia \al-jə\ neuralgia, nostalgia
ali¹ \äl-ē\ see OLLY¹
ali² \al-ē\ see ALLY⁴
ali³ \ȯ-lē\ see AWLY
ali⁴ \ā-lē\ see AILY
alia \ā-lē-ə\ Australia, azalea, re-
galia • bacchanalia • paraph-erna-
lia
alian¹ \ā-lē-ən\ alien • Australian,
mammalian • bacchanalian
• Episcopalian
alian² \al-yən\ see ALLION
alic \al-ik\ see ALLIC
alice \al-əs\ see ALIS²

alid¹ \äl-əd\ see OLID
alid² \al-əd\ ballad, pallid, salad,
valid • invalid • Caesar salad,
Waldorf salad
alien \ā-lē-ən\ see ALIAN¹
aling \ā-liŋ\ see AILING
alinist \äl-ə-nəst\ see OLONIST
alinn \al-ən\ see ALLON
alion¹ \ā-lē-ən\ see ALIAN¹
alion² \al-yən\ see ALLION
aliph \ā-ləf\ see AILIFF
alis¹ \ā-ləs\ see AYLESS
alis² \al-əs\ Alice, callous, callus,
chalice, Dallas, malice, palace
• aurora borealis
alist \al-əst\ ballast, callused
ality¹ \äl-ət-ē\ jollity, quality
• equality, frivolity • coequality,
inequality
ality² \al-ət-ē\ brutality, fatality,
finality, formality, frugality, legal-
ity, locality, mentality, morality,
mortality, neutrality, rascality,
reality, totality, vitality • abnor-
mality, actuality, amorality, cor-
diality, factuality, functionality,
generality, geniality, hospitality,
illegality, immorality, immortal-
ity, informality, joviality, logical-
ity, musicality, nationality,
personality, practicality, punctu-
ality, rationality, sensuality, sexu-
ality, technicality, triviality,
unreality • congeniality, eventual-
ity, impartiality, impracticality,
irrationality, municipality, origi-
nality, sentimentality, spirituality,
split personality, theatricality,
universality • artificiality, confi-
dentiality, constitutionality, indi-
viduality, unconventionality,
virtual reality
alk \ȯk\ balk, caulk, chalk, gawk,
hawk, squawk, stalk, talk, walk
• back talk, Black Hawk, board-
walk, cakewalk, catwalk, corn-
stalk, crosswalk, eyestalk, fish

hawk, jaywalk, leafstalk, marsh
hawk, Mohawk, moonwalk,
nighthawk, Norfolk, outtalk, pep
talk, racewalk, ropewalk,
shoptalk, sidewalk, sleepwalk,
small talk, space walk, sweet-talk,
trash talk • baby talk, double-
talk, Kitty Hawk, pillow talk,
power walk, sparrow hawk, toma-
hawk

alker \ȯ-kər\ gawker, hawker,
squawker, stalker, walker • jay-
walker, sleepwalker, spacewalker
• double-talker

alkie \ȯ-kē\ balky, chalky, gawky,
gnocchi, stalky, talky • Milwau-
kee • walkie-talkie

alking \ȯ-kiŋ\ caulking, walking
• racewalking, spacewalking
—*also* -ing *forms of verbs listed at*
ALK

alkland \ȯk-lənd\ see AUCKLAND

alky \ȯ-kē\ see ALKIE

all¹ \ȯl\ all, awl, ball, bawl, brawl,
call, crawl, doll, drawl, fall, gall,
hall, haul, mall, maul, pall, Paul,
Saul, scrawl, shawl, small, sprawl,
squall, stall, tall, trawl, wall, y'all,
yawl • and all, appall, air ball, at
all, atoll, AWOL, baseball, Baikal,
beach ball, beanball, befall, bird-
call, blackball, brick wall, catcall,
cell wall, close call, cornball,
cure-all, curveball, de Gaulle,
dodgeball, downfall, drywall,
duck call, eight ball, enthrall,
eyeball, fair ball, fastball, fireball,
fire wall, foosball, football, fore-
stall, foul ball, free-fall, game
ball, golf ball, goofball, googol,
hair ball, handball, hardball,
holdall, house call, install, John
Paul, jump ball, landfall, meat-
ball, menthol, mess hall, moth-
ball, Nepal, nightfall, oddball,
paintball, pinball, pitfall, pratfall,
prayer shawl, puffball, rainfall,

rainsquall, recall, roll call, Saint
Paul, screwball, seawall, short-
haul, shortfall, sidewall, sleaze-
ball, slimeball, snowball, snowfall,
softball, sour ball, spitball, stick-
ball, stonewall, stone wall, strip
mall, tell-all, toll call, town hall,
U-Haul, windfall, withdrawal,
you-all • above all, aerosol, after
all, alcohol, all in all, basketball,
borough hall, butterball, cannon-
ball, carryall, caterwaul, city hall,
climbing wall, conference call,
coverall, crystal ball, curtain call,
Donegal, ethanol, free-for-all,
gasohol, judgment call, know-it-
all, knuckleball, methanol, music
hall, Montreal, off-the-wall, over-
all, overhaul, paddleball, parasol,
protocol, racquetball, reinstall,
Senegal, shopping mall, study
hall, superball, tetherball, unin-
stall, urban sprawl, volleyball,
wake-up call, wall-to-wall, warts-
and-all, waterfall, wherewithal
• cholesterol, hole-in-the-wall,
medicine ball, Neanderthal, total
recall

all² \äl\ see AL¹

all³ \al\ see AL⁴

alla¹ \äl-ə\ see ALA²

alla² \al-ə\ see ALLOW⁴

allace \äl-əs\ see OLIS

allad \al-əd\ see ALID²

allage \al-ə-jē\ see ALOGY²

allah¹ \äl-ä\ see ALA¹

allah² \äl-ə\ see ALA²

allah³ \al-ə\ see ALLOW⁴

allan \al-ən\ see ALLON

allant \al-ənt\ gallant, talent

allas \al-əs\ see ALIS²

allast \al-əst\ see ALIST

alle¹ \al\ see AL⁴

alle² \al-ē\ see ALLY⁴

alle³ \äl-ē\ see OLLY¹

alled \ȯld\ see ALD¹

allee \al-ē\ see ALLY⁴

allen \al-ən\ see ALLON

aller[1] \ȯ-lər\ bawler, brawler, caller, crawler, drawler, hauler, mauler, scrawler, smaller, squaller, taller, trawler • installer, night crawler • melon baller

aller[2] \al-ər\ pallor, valor

alles \ī-əs\ see IAS[1]

allet[1] \äl-ət\ see OLLET

allet[2] \al-ət\ ballot, mallet, palate, palette, pallet, valet • secret ballot

alley \al-ē\ see ALLY[4]

alli \al-ē\ see ALLY[4]

allic \al-ik\ Gaelic, italic • metallic, smart aleck • nonmetallic

allid \al-əd\ see ALID[2]

allie \al-ē\ see ALLY[4]

alling \ȯ-liŋ\ calling, drawling, falling, galling, hauling, mauling, Pauling, stalling • appalling, name-calling
—*also* -ing *forms of verbs listed at* ALL[1]

allion \al-yən\ scallion, stallion • battalion, Italian, medallion, rapscallion

allis[1] \al-əs\ see ALIS[2]

allis[2] \al-ē\ see ALLY[4]

allis[3] \äl-əs\ see OLIS

allish \ȯ-lish\ smallish, tallish

allit \ä-lət\ see OLLET

allith[1] \äl-əs\ see OLIS

allith[2] \äl-ət\ see OLLET

allo \äl-ō\ see OLLOW[1]

allon \al-ən\ Alan, Allen, gallon, talon

allop[1] \äl-əp\ see OLLOP

allop[2] \al-əp\ gallop, scallop • bay scallop, sea scallop

allor \al-ər\ see ALLER[2]

allory \al-ə-rē\ see ALARY

allot \al-ət\ see ALLET[2]

allous \al-əs\ see ALIS[2]

allow[1] \el-ō\ see ELLO

allow[2] \al-ə\ see ALA[2]

allow[3] \äl-ō\ see OLLOW[1]

allow[4] \al-ō\ callow, fallow, hallow, shallow, tallow • marsh-mallow

allows \al-ōz\ gallows
—*also* -s, -'s, *and* -s' *forms of nouns listed at* ALLOW[4]

alls \ȯlz\ Angel Falls • Niagara Falls, Yellowstone Falls • Victoria Falls, Yosemite Falls
—*also* -s, -'s, *and* -s' *forms of nouns and* -s *forms of verbs listed at* ALL[1]

allused \al-əst\ see ALIST

ally[1] \ā-lē\ see AILY

ally[2] \äl-ē\ see OLLY[1]

ally[3] \ȯ-lē\ see AWLY

ally[4] \al-ē\ alley, dally, galley, rally, Sally, tally, valley • blind alley, Death Valley, finale, Nepali • Central Valley, dillydally, Great Rift Valley, Mexicali, shilly-shally, Tin Pan Alley • lily of the valley, Yosemite Valley

allyn \al-ən\ see ALLON

alm \äm\ see OM[1]

almar \äm-ər\ see OMBER[1]

almer \äm-ər\ see OMBER[1]

almily \äm-ə-lē\ see OMALY

almish \äm-ish\ see AMISH[1]

almist \äm-ist\ psalmist • Islamist

almon \am-ən\ see AMMON

alms \ämz\ alms, Brahms, Psalms
—*also* -s, -'s, *and* -s' *forms of nouns and* -s *forms of verbs listed at* OM[1]

almy \äm-ē\ see AMI[1]

alo \äl-ō\ see OLLOW[1]

aloe \al-ō\ see ALLOW[4]

alogist \äl-ə-jəst\ see OLOGIST

alogy[1] \äl-ə-jē\ see OLOGY

alogy[2] \al-ə-jē\ analogy • mineralogy

alom \äl-əm\ see OLUMN

alon \al-ən\ see ALLON

alop \al-əp\ see ALLOP[2]

alor[1] \äl-ər\ see OLLAR

alor[2] \al-ər\ see ALLER[2]

alorie \al-ə-rē\ see ALARY

alory \al-ə-rē\ see ALARY

alp \alp\ alp, scalp
alpha \al-fə\ alpha • alfalfa
alque \ók\ see ALK
alsa \òl-sə\ balsa, salsa
alse \òls\ false, waltz
alt \òlt\ fault, halt, malt, salt, vault,
  volt, Walt • asphalt, assault,
  basalt, cobalt, default, exalt, no-
  fault, pole vault, rock salt • garlic
  salt, somersault, table salt • San
  Andreas Fault
alta \äl-tə\ Malta, Yalta
altar \òl-tər\ see ALTER
alter \òl-tər\ altar, alter, falter,
  halter, vaulter, Walter • Gibraltar,
  pole-vaulter
alti \òl-tē\ see ALTY
alting \òl-tiŋ\ halting, salting,
  vaulting
  —also -ing *forms of verbs listed at*
  ALT
altless \òlt-ləs\ faultless, saltless
alto \al-tō\ alto • contralto • Palo
  Alto
alty \òl-tē\ faulty, salty
altz \òls\ see ALSE
alus¹ \ā-ləs\ see AYLESS
alus² \al-əs\ see ALIS²
alve¹ \äv\ see OLVE²
alve² \alv\ salve, valve • bivalve
  • safety valve, univalve
alve³ \av\ calve, halve, have, salve
alvin \al-vən\ Alvin, Calvin
aly \al-ē\ see ALLY⁴
alysis \al-ə-səs\ analysis, dialysis,
  paralysis
am¹ \äm\ see OM¹
am² \am\ am, clam, cram, dam,
  damn, damned, Graham, gram,
  ham, jam, jamb, lam, lamb,
  ma'am, Pam, ram, Sam, scam,
  scram, sham, slam, spam, swam,
  yam • exam, grand slam, imam,
  logjam, madame, Mailgram, program, webcam • Abraham, Ams-
  terdam, Boulder Dam, cablegram,
  centigram, cryptogram, diagram,

diaphragm, epigram, giant clam,
hard-shell clam, hexagram, holo-
gram, Hoover Dam, kilogram,
milligram, Minicam, monogram,
pentagram, pictogram, repro-
gram, Rotterdam, self-exam, soft-
shell clam, Suriname, telegram,
Uncle Sam • Grand Coulee Dam,
ideogram, Virginia ham • parallel-
ogram
ama¹ \äm-ə\ Brahma, comma,
  drama, lama, llama, mama,
  momma • pajama • Dalai Lama,
  diorama, docudrama, Fujiyama,
  melodrama, panorama, Suriname,
  Yokohama
ama² \am-ə\ Brahma, drama,
  gamma, mamma • da Gama,
  Miami, pajama • Alabama, diorama, docudrama, melodrama,
  panorama
amable \ā-mə-bəl\ blamable,
  claimable, framable, nameable,
  tamable
aman¹ \ā-mən\ see AMEN¹
aman² \am-ən\ see OMMON
amant \ā-mənt\ see AYMENT
amash \äm-ish\ see AMISH¹
amateur \am-ət-ər\ see AMETER
amba \äm-bə\ mamba, samba
ambar¹ \äm-bər\ see OMBER²
ambar² \am-bər\ amber, Amber,
  clamber, timbre
amber¹ \am-bər\ see AMBAR²
amber² \am-ər\ see AMMER
ambia \am-bē-ə\ Gambia, Zambia
amble¹ \äm-bəl\ see EMBLE
amble² \am-bəl\ amble, bramble,
  gamble, ramble, scramble • un-
  scramble
ambler \am-blər\ gambler, ram-
  bler, scrambler • unscrambler
ambol \am-bəl\ see AMBLE²
ame¹ \ām\ aim, blame, came,
  claim, dame, fame, flame, frame,
  game, lame, maim, name, same,
  shame, tame • A-frame, acclaim,

aflame, airframe, ball game, became, big game, big-name, board game, brand name, code name, declaim, defame, disclaim, exclaim, first name, inflame, last name, mainframe, mind game, misname, nickname, no-name, pen name, place-name, postgame, pregame, proclaim, reclaim, reframe, rename, selfsame, surname, time frame, trade name, war game • all the same, arcade game, counterclaim, domain name, family name, given name, Hall of Fame, just the same, maiden name, overcame, singing game, waiting game • baptismal name, name of the game, video game

ame² \äm\ see OM¹

ame³ \am\ see AM²

ame⁴ \äm-ə\ see AMA¹

ameable \ā-mə-bəl\ see AMABLE

amed \āmd\ named • ashamed • unashamed
—also -ed forms of verbs listed at AME¹

amel \am-əl\ see AMMEL

ameless \ām-ləs\ aimless, blameless, nameless, shameless

amely \ām-lē\ gamely, lamely, namely, tamely

amen¹ \ā-mən\ caiman, Cayman, Haman, layman, shaman, stamen, Yemen • Grand Cayman, highwayman

amen² \äm-ən\ see OMMON

ameness \ām-nəs\ lameness, sameness, tameness • selfsameness

ament \ā-mənt\ see AYMENT

amer \ā-mər\ see AIMER

ames \āmz\ James • fun and games • Olympic Games
—also -s, -'s, and -s' forms of nouns and -s forms of verbs listed at AME¹

ameter \am-ət-ər\ amateur • diam-

eter, hexameter, parameter, pentameter, tetrameter

amfer \am-pər\ see AMPER²

ami¹ \äm-ē\ balmy, mommy, palmy, swami, Tommy • pastrami, salami, tsunami • origami

ami² \am-ə\ see AMA²

ami³ \am-ē\ see AMMY

amic¹ \ō-mik\ see OMIC²

amic² \am-ik\ ceramic, dynamic • panoramic, undynamic • aerodynamic, thermodynamic

amics \äm-iks\ see OMICS

amie¹ \ā-mē\ Amy, Jamie, Mamie • cockamamy

amie² \am-ē\ see AMMY

amil¹ \äm-əl\ see OMMEL¹

amil² \am-əl\ see AMMEL

amin \am-ən\ see AMMON

amine \am-ən\ see AMMON

aming \ā-miŋ\ flaming, framing, gaming
—also -ing forms of verbs listed at AME¹

amish¹ \äm-ish\ Amish • schoolmarmish

amish² \am-ish\ Amish, famish

amist \äm-əst\ see ALMIST

amity \am-ət-ē\ amity • calamity

amma \am-ə\ see AMA²

ammable \am-ə-bəl\ flammable • inflammable, nonflammable, programmable • diagrammable

ammal \am-əl\ see AMMEL

ammar \am-ər\ see AMMER

amme \am\ see AM²

ammel \am-əl\ camel, mammal • enamel

ammer \am-ər\ clamber, clamor, crammer, glamour, grammar, hammer, jammer, scammer, slammer, spammer, stammer, yammer • clawhammer, enamor, jackhammer, programmer, sledgehammer • ball-peen hammer, yellowhammer

ammes \äm-əs\ see OMISE

ammie \am-ē\ see AMMY

amming \am-iŋ\ damning • programming
—also -ing forms of verbs listed at AM[2]

ammon \am-ən\ famine, salmon • backgammon, examine • cross-examine

ammy \am-ē\ chamois, clammy, Grammy, jammy, mammy, Sammy, whammy • Miami • double whammy

amn \am\ see AM[2]

amned \am\ see AM[2]

amning \am-iŋ\ see AMMING

amois \am-ē\ see AMMY

amon[1] \ā-mən\ see AMEN[1]

amon[2] \äm-ən\ see OMMON

amor \am-ər\ see AMMER

amorous \am-rəs\ amorous, clamorous, glamorous

amos \ā-məs\ see AMOUS

amour \am-ər\ see AMMER

amous \ā-məs\ Amos, famous • ignoramus, Nostradamus

amp[1] \ämp\ see OMP[1]

amp[2] \ä[n]\ see ANT[1]

amp[3] \amp\ amp, camp, champ, clamp, cramp, damp, lamp, ramp, scamp, stamp, tamp, tramp, vamp • arc lamp, boot camp, break camp, C-clamp, death camp, floor lamp, food stamp, off-ramp, on-ramp, revamp, sunlamp, tax stamp, time-stamp, unclamp • labor camp, postage stamp, rubber-stamp, writer's cramp

amper[1] \äm-pər\ see OMPER

amper[2] \am-pər\ camper, damper, hamper, pamper, scamper, tamper • happy camper

amphor \am-fər\ see AMFER

ampi[1] \äm-pē\ see OMPY

ampi[2] \am-pē\ see AMPY

ample \am-pəl\ ample, sample, trample • example • for example

ampy \am-pē\ crampy, scampi

amus[1] \ā-məs\ see AMOUS

amus[2] \äm-əs\ see OMISE

amy \ā-mē\ see AMIE[1]

an[1] \ä[n]\ see ANT[1]

an[2] \än\ see ON[1]

an[3] \ən\ see UN[1]

an[4] \aŋ\ see ANG[2]

an[5] \an\ an, Ann, ban, bran, can, clan, Dan, fan, Jan, man, Nan, pan, plan, ran, scan, span, Stan, tan, van, Van • adman, afghan, Afghan, ape-man, Batman, bedpan, began, best man, Bhutan, birdman, boss man, caftan, caiman, CAT scan, caveman, Cayman, Cèzanne, chessman, Cheyenne, Chopin, deadpan, Diane, dishpan, divan, doorman, dustpan, flight plan, frogman, game plan, G-man, Greenspan, headman, he-man, Iran, Japan, jazzman, Joanne, Koran, life span, Luanne, madman, mailman, Milan, milkman, newsman, oilcan, oilman, oil pan, old man, oneman, outran, pecan, plowman, point man, postman, Queen Anne, Qur'an, rattan, Roseanne, routeman, Roxanne, Ruthann, Saipan, sandman, saucepan, sedan, snowman, spaceman, Spokane, spray can, straight man, strongman, stuntman, Sudan, suntan, Suzanne, Tarzan, tin can, toucan, trainman, trashman, vegan, Walkman, wingspan, wise man, yes-man • also-ran, anchorman, bogeyman, boogeyman, businessman, cameraman, caravan, cattleman, countryman, defenseman, family man, frying pan, garageman, garbageman, handyman, Julianne, Kazakhstan, Ku Klux Klan, Kurdistan, Kyrgyzstan, leading man, man-to-man, Marianne, master plan, middleman, minivan, minuteman, mountain man, muscleman, ombudsman, overran, Pakistan, Parmesan, partisan, Peter Pan, plainclothesman, Ramadan, rather than, repairman, selectman, serviceman, spick-and-span, superman, Superman, Teheran, Turkistan, weatherman, workingman, Yucatan • Afghanistan, attention span, bipartisan, catamaran, cavalryman, committeeman, deliveryman, medicine man, newspaperman, orangutan, radioman, Raggedy Ann, Tajikistan, Turkmenistan, Uzbekistan, watering can

an⁶ \äng\ see ONG¹

an⁷ \änt\ see ANT²

ana¹ \än-ə\ Anna, Donna, fauna, Ghana, Lana • Botswana, iguana, Madonna, mañana, nirvana, piranha, Tijuana • French Guiana, prima donna, Rosh Hashanah • Americana

ana² \ā-nə\ Dana, Lana

ana³ \an-ə\ Anna, Ghana, Hannah, Lana • banana, bandanna, cabana, Diana, Guiana, Guyana, gymkhana, Havana, hosanna, Joanna, Montana, savanna, Susanna • French Guiana, Indiana, Juliana, Mariana, poinciana, Pollyanna, Santa Ana • Americana, Louisiana

anacle \an-i-kəl\ see ANICAL

anagh \an-ə\ see ANA³

anah¹ \ō-nə\ see ONA¹

anah² \än-ə\ see ANA¹

analyst \an-ᵊl-ist\ analyst, panelist • psychoanalyst

anan \an-ən\ see ANNON

anary \an-rē\ see ANNERY

anate \an-ət\ see ANNET

anc¹ \aⁿ\ see ANT¹

anc² \aŋ\ see ANG²

anc³ \aŋk\ see ANK

anca \aŋ-kə\ Sanka • Casablanca

ance¹ \äⁿs\ nuance, Provence, séance • diligence, renaissance • insouciance • pièce de résistance
—*also* -s, -'s *and* -s'*forms of nouns and* -s *forms of verbs listed at* ANT¹

ance² \äns\ Hans • nuance, response, séance • nonchalance, renaissance

ance³ \ans\ chance, dance, France, glance, lance, Lance, prance, stance, trance • advance, askance, barn dance, break-dance, by chance, enhance, entrance, expanse, finance, freelance, line dance, outdance, romance, sideglance, snake dance, square dance, sun dance, sweatpants, tap dance, war dance • at first glance, ballroom dance, belly dance, circumstance, fighting chance, game of chance, happenstance, in advance, Port-au-Prince, refinance, smarty-pants, song and dance, underpants
—*also* -s, -'s, *and* -s' *forms of nouns and* -s *forms of verbs listed at* ANT⁵

ancement \an-smənt\ advancement, enhancement • selfadvancement

ancer \an-sər\ answer, cancer, dancer • break-dancer, freelancer, line dancer, lung cancer, nondancer, square dancer, tap dancer • anticancer, ballroom dancer, belly dancer • Tropic of Cancer

ances \an(t)-səs\ see ANCIS

anch¹ \änch\ see AUNCH¹

anch² \ȯnch\ see AUNCH²

anch³ \anch\ blanch, Blanche, branch, ranch, stanch • dude ranch • avalanche, olive branch

anche¹ \anch\ see ANCH³

anche² \an-chē\ see ANCHY

anchi \an-chē\ see ANCHY

anchion \an-chən\ see ANSION

anchor \aŋ-kər\ see ANKER

anchy \an-chē\ branchy
• Comanche
ancial \an-chəl\ see ANTIAL
ancis \an(t)-səs\ Frances, Francis
• Aransas
—*also* -s, -'s, *and* -s' *forms of
nouns and* -s *forms of verbs listed
at* ANCE³
anck \änk\ see ONK¹
anco \äŋ-kō\ see ONCO
ancor \aŋ-kər\ see ANKER
ancre \aŋ-kər\ see ANKED
anct \aŋt\ see ANKED
ancy \an-sē\ chancy, fancy, Nancy
and¹ \äⁿ\ see ANT¹
and² \änd\ see OND¹
and³ \and\ and, band, bland,
brand, canned, gland, grand,
hand, land, manned, sand, stand,
strand • armband, at hand, back-
hand, badland, bandstand, brass
band, broadband, brushland,
cabstand, coastland, command,
cowhand, crash-land, cropland,
deckhand, demand, disband,
dockhand, dreamland, expand,
farmhand, farmland, field hand,
firebrand, firsthand, forehand,
freehand, gangland, grandstand,
grassland, handstand, hatband,
headband, headstand, heartland,
homeland, hour hand, Iceland,
inland, kickstand, Lapland, left-
hand, longhand, mainland, marsh-
land, newsstand, nightstand,
offhand, oil gland, old hand, on
hand, parkland, playland, quick-
sand, rangeland, right-hand,
shorthand, stagehand, swamp-
land, sweatband, sweat gland,
Thailand, thirdhand, waistband,
washstand, wasteland, watchband,
wetland, withstand, wristband
• baby grand, beforehand, belly-
land, borderland, contraband,
countermand, Dixieland, fairy-
land, fatherland, Ferdinand,
forestland, garage band, hand in
hand, helping hand, high command, Holy Land, meadowland,
minute hand, motherland, nar-
rowband, no-man's-land, on demand, one-man band, out of
hand, overhand, pastureland,
promised land, public land, repri-
mand, Rio Grande, rubber band,
Samarkand, secondhand, sleight
of hand, taxi stand, timberland,
try one's hand, understand, won-
derland • misunderstand, multi-
plicand, to beat the band,
vacationland • never-never land
• Alice-in-Wonderland
—*also* -ed *forms of verbs listed at*
AN⁵
and⁴ \än\ see ON¹
and⁵ \änt\ see ANT²
anda¹ \an-də\ panda • Amanda,
Miranda, Uganda, veranda • giant
panda, memoranda, propaganda
anda² \än-də\ see ONDA
andable \an-də-bəl\ expandable
• understandable
andaed \an-dəd\ see ANDED
andal \an-dᵊl\ see ANDLE
andaled \an-dᵊld\ handled • well-
handled
—*also* -ed *forms of verbs listed at*
ANDLE
andall \an-dᵊl\ see ANDLE
andam \an-dəm\ see ANDUM
andar \ənd-ər\ see UNDER
ande¹ \ən\ see UN¹
ande² \an\ see AN⁵
ande³ \an-dē\ see ANDY
ande⁴ \and\ see AND³
ande⁵ \än-də\ see ONDA
anded \an-dəd\ banded, branded,
candid, handed, landed, stranded
• backhanded, bare-handed, high-
handed, left-handed, one-handed,
red-handed, right-handed, short-
handed, two-handed • empty-
handed, evenhanded,

heavy-handed, singlehanded, underhanded
—*also* -ed *forms of verbs listed at* AND³

andel \an-d³l\ see ANDLE
andem \an-dəm\ see ANDUM
ander¹ \en-dər\ see ENDER
ander² \än-dər\ see ONDER¹
ander³ \an-dər\ blander, brander, candor, gander, grander, grandeur, pander, sander, slander • bystander, commander, demander, left-hander, meander, right-hander • Alexander, coriander, salamander, wing commander
anders \an-dərz\ Flanders
—*also* -s, -'s, *and* -s' *forms of nouns and* -s *forms of verbs listed at* ANDER³
andes \an-dēz\ Andes
—*also* -s, -'s, *and* -s' *forms of nouns and* -s *forms of verbs listed at* ANDY
andeur \an-dər\ see ANDER³
andhi \an-dē\ see ANDY
andi \an-dē\ see ANDY
andible \an-də-bəl\ see ANDABLE
andid \an-dəd\ see ANDED
anding \an-diŋ\ branding, standing • commanding, crash landing, freestanding, long-standing, outstanding, upstanding • belly landing, mind-expanding, notwithstanding, pancake landing, understanding • instrument landing, misunderstanding
—*also* -ing *forms of verbs listed at* AND³
andish \an-dish\ blandish, brandish • outlandish
andist \an-dəst\ blandest, grandest • propagandist
andle \an-d³l\ candle, Handel, handle, Randall, sandal, scandal, vandal • manhandle, mishandle, panhandle • Roman candle, votive candle

andled \an-d³l\ see ANDALED
andly \an-lē\ see ANLY
ando \an-dō\ Brando • commando, Fernando, Orlando • San Fernando
andom \an-dəm\ see ANDUM
andor \an-dər\ see ANDER³
andra \an-drə\ Sandra • Cassandra • Alexandra
andrea \an-drē-ə\ see ANDRIA
andres \an-dərz\ see ANDERS
andria \an-drē-ə\ Andrea, Alexandria
andsome \an-səm\ see ANSOM
andum \an-dəm\ random, tandem • memorandum
andy \an-dē\ Andy, bandy, brandy, Brandy, candy, dandy, handy, Randy, sandy, Sandy • ear candy, eye candy, hard candy, jim-dandy, rock candy, unhandy • cotton candy, Rio Grande
ane¹ \ān\ bane, brain, Cain, cane, chain, crane, Crane, Dane, deign, drain, Duane, feign, gain, grain, Jane, lane, main, Maine, mane, pain, pane, plain, plane, rain, reign, rein, sane, Seine, skein, slain, Spain, sprain, stain, strain, train, vain, vane, vein, wane, Wayne, Zane • abstain, again, air lane, airplane, attain, Bahrain, biplane, birdbrain, bloodstain, brain drain, campaign, champagne, Champlain, choke chain, chow mein, cocaine, complain, constrain, contain, detain, disdain, domain, Elaine, explain, eyestrain, fast lane, floodplain, food chain, germane, Great Dane, Helene, humane, Hussein, inane, ingrain, insane, lamebrain, left brain, lo mein, Lorraine, maintain, membrane, methane, midbrain, migraine, mundane, New Spain, obtain, octane, ordain, pertain, plain-Jane, profane,

propane, ptomaine, raise Cain, refrain, remain, restrain, retain, retrain, right brain, sea-lane, seaplane, sustain, tearstain, terrain, Ukraine, unchain, urbane, warplane • acid rain, aeroplane, aquaplane, Aquitaine, ascertain, bullet train, cell membrane, cellophane, Charlemagne, down the drain, entertain, featherbrain, free throw lane, high-octane, hurricane, inclined plane, inhumane, Mary Jane, memory lane, monoplane, multigrain, multilane, Novocain, novocaine, overtrain, pollen grain, preordain, reattain, sandhill crane, scatterbrain, Spanish Main, sugarcane, Tamerlane, toilet train, wagon train, water main, weather vane, whooping crane, windowpane • Serengeti Plain

ane² \an\ see AN⁵
ane³ \än-ə\ see ANA¹
ane⁴ \än\ see ON¹
anea \ā-nē-ə\ see ANIA
anean \ā-nē-ən\ see ANIAN
aned \ānd\ see AINED
anee \an-ē\ see ANNY
aneful \ān-fəl\ see AINFUL
anel \an-ᵊl\ see ANNEL
anelist \an-ᵊl-əst\ see ANALYST
aneous \ā-nē-əs\ extraneous, spontaneous • instantaneous, miscellaneous, simultaneous • contemporaneous, extemporaneous
aner¹ \ā-nər\ see AINER
aner² \än-ər\ see ONOR¹
anet \an-ət\ see ANNET
aneum \ā-nē-əm\ see ANIUM
aney \ȯ-nē\ see AWNY¹
ang¹ \äŋ\ see ONG¹
ang² \aŋ\ bang, clang, dang, fang, gang, hang, rang, sang, slang, sprang, tang, twang • bang-bang, big bang, chain gang, ginseng,

harangue, meringue, mustang, shebang, slam-bang • antigang, boomerang, give a hang, intergang, overhang • orangutan
ang³ \ȯŋ\ see ONG²
anga \äŋ-gə\ see ONGA
angar \aŋ-ər\ see ANGER²
ange \änj\ change, mange, range, strange • arrange, chump change, derange, estrange, exchange, freerange, long-range, short-range, shortchange, small change • Cascade Range, disarrange, driving range, interchange, post exchange, prearrange, rearrange, stock exchange, Teton Range, Wasatch Range • Alaska Range, Aleutian Range
angel \aŋ-gəl\ see ANGLE
angell \aŋ-gəl\ see ANGLE
angement \änj-mənt\ arrangement, derangement, estrangement • prearrangement, rearrangement
anger¹ \ān-jər\ changer, danger, manger, ranger, stranger • arranger, endanger, exchanger, lone ranger, shortchanger • forest ranger, money changer, Texas Ranger • dog in the manger
anger² \aŋ-ər\ hangar, hanger • cliff-hanger, coat hanger, headbanger • paperhanger
anger³ \aŋ-gər\ anger, clangor
angi \aŋ-ē\ see ANGY²
angie \aŋ-ē\ see ANGY²
anging¹ \ān-jiŋ\ unchanging, wideranging
—*also* -ing *forms of verbs listed at* ANGE
anging² \aŋ-iŋ\ hanging • paperhanging
—*also* -ing *forms of verbs listed at* ANG²
angle \aŋ-gəl\ angle, bangle, dangle, jangle, mangle, spangle, strangle, tangle, wangle, wrangle • entangle, quadrangle, rectangle,

right angle, triangle, untangle,
wide-angle • disentangle
• Bermuda Triangle
angled \aŋ-gəld\ angled, tangled
• newfangled, right-angled, star-
spangled
—*also* -ed *forms of verbs listed at*
ANGLE
angler \aŋ-glər\ angler, strangler,
wrangler
angling \aŋ-gliŋ\ angling, gangling
—*also* -ing *forms of verbs listed at*
ANGLE
angly \aŋ-glē\ gangly, jangly
ango \aŋ-gō\ mango, tango • fan-
dango
angor[1] \aŋ-ər\ see ANGER[2]
angor[2] \aŋ-gər\ see ANGER[3]
angour \aŋ-ər\ see ANGER[2]
angster \aŋ-stər\ gangster,
prankster
angue \aŋ\ see ANG[2]
anguer \aŋ-ər\ see ANGER[2]
anguish \aŋ-gwish\ anguish, lan-
guish
anguor \aŋ-ər\ see ANGER[2]
angy[1] \ān-jē\ mangy, rangy
angy[2] \aŋ-ē\ tangy, twangy
anha \än-ə\ see ANA[1]
ani[1] \än-ē\ Bonnie, bonny, Connie,
Donnie, Ronnie, tawny • afghani,
Irani • Modigliani, Pakistani
• mulligatawny
ani[2] \an-ē\ see ANNY
ania \ā-nē-ə\ mania • Tasmania
• egomania, kleptomania, Lithua-
nia, Mauritania, Oceania, Penn-
sylvania, pyromania, Transylvania
• megalomania
anian \ā-nē-ən\ Albanian, Iranian,
Jordanian, Romanian, Ukrainian
• Lithuanian, Pennsylvanian,
subterranean • Mediterranean
aniard \an-yərd\ lanyard, Spaniard
anic \an-ik\ manic, panic • Ger-
manic, Hispanic, mechanic, or-
ganic, satanic, titanic, volcanic
• aldermanic, inorganic, mes-
sianic, oceanic, pre-Hispanic
• transoceanic
anical \an-i-kəl\ manacle • botani-
cal, mechanical, tyrannical • puri-
tanical
anice \an-əs\ see ANISE
anicle \an-i-kəl\ see ANICAL
anics \an-iks\ annex, panics • me-
chanics
aniel[1] \an-ᵊl\ see ANNEL
aniel[2] \an-yəl\ see ANUAL[1]
anion \an-yən\ banyan, canyon
• Bryce Canyon, companion,
Grand Canyon, Hells Canyon
anis \an-əs\ see ANISE
anise \an-əs\ anise, Janice, Janis
• Johannes • Scipio Africanus
anish \an-ish\ banish, clannish,
mannish, Spanish, tannish, vanish
anister \an-ə-stər\ banister, canis-
ter
anite \an-ət\ see ANNET
anity \an-ət-ē\ sanity, vanity • hu-
manity, insanity, profanity
• Christianity, inhumanity
anium \ā-nē-əm\ cranium • gera-
nium, titanium, uranium
ank \aŋk\ bank, blank, clank,
crank, dank, drank, flank, franc,
frank, Frank, hank, lank, plank,
prank, rank, sank, shank, shrank,
spank, stank, swank, tank, thank,
yank, Yank • gangplank, out-
flank, outrank, point-blank, sand-
bank, snowbank, state bank,
think tank, West Bank • antitank,
data bank, draw a blank, Georges
Bank, national bank, piggy bank,
riverbank, walk the plank • clink-
ety-clank
anka \aŋ-kə\ see ANCA
anked \aŋt\ tanked • sacrosanct
—*also* -ed *forms of verbs listed at*
ANK
ankee \aŋ-kē\ see ANKY
anker \aŋ-kər\ anchor, banker,

canker, flanker, hanker, rancor,
tanker, thanker • supertanker
—*also* -er *forms of adjectives listed
at* ANK
ankh \äŋk\ see ONK[1]
ankie \aŋ-kē\ see ANKY
ankish \aŋ-kish\ crankish, prank-
ish
ankle \aŋ-kəl\ ankle, rankle
ankly \aŋ-klē\ blankly, frankly
anks \aŋs\ see ANX
ankster \aŋ-stər\ see ANGSTER
anky \aŋ-kē\ cranky, hankie,
lanky, skanky, swanky, Yankee
• hanky-panky
anley \an-lē\ see ANLY
anli \an-lē\ see ANLY
anly \an-lē\ blandly, grandly,
manly, Stanley • unmanly
ann[1] \an\ see AN[5]
ann[2] \än\ see ON[1]
anna[1] \än-ə\ see ANA[1]
anna[2] \an-ə\ see ANA[3]
annah \an-ə\ see ANA[3]
annalist \an-ᵊl-əst\ see ANALYST
annan \an-ən\ see ANNON
anne \an\ see AN[5]
anned \and\ see AND[3]
annel \an-ᵊl\ channel, Daniel,
flannel, panel • impanel • English
Channel
anner \an-ər\ banner, canner,
manner, manor, planner, scanner,
tanner • city planner
annery \an-rē\ cannery, granary,
tannery
annes \an-əs\ see ANISE
annet \an-ət\ granite, Janet, planet
• pomegranate
annexe \an-iks\ see ANICS
annibal \an-ə-bəl\ cannibal, Hanni-
bal
annic \an-ik\ see ANIC
annie \an-ē\ see ANNY
annin \an-ən\ see ANNON
annish \an-ish\ see ANISH
annon \an-ən\ cannon • Buchanan

annous \an-əs\ see ANISE
anns \anz\ see ANS[4]
annual \an-yəl\ see ANUAL[1]
anny \an-ē\ Annie, canny, cranny,
Danny, fanny, granny, Lanny,
nanny • afghani, uncanny • Hin-
dustani, hootenanny
ano[1] \än-ō\ guano • Chicano, piano, soprano • grand piano
• mezzo-soprano, player piano,
upright piano
ano[2] \an-ō\ piano, soprano
• mezzo-soprano
anon \an-ən\ see ANNON
anor \an-ər\ see ANNER
anous \an-əs\ see ANISE
anqui \aŋ-kē\ see ONKY
ans[1] \äns\ see ANCE[2]
ans[2] \änz\ see ONZE
ans[3] \ans\ see ANCE[3]
ans[4] \anz\ Hans
—*also* -s, -'s, *and* -s' *forms of
nouns and* -s *forms of verbs listed
at* AN[5]
ans[5] \aⁿ\ see ANT[1]
ansard \an-sərd\ see ANSWERED
ansas \an(t)-səs\ see ANCIS
anse \ans\ see ANCE[3]
anser \an-sər\ see ANCER
ansion \an-chən\ mansion • expan-
sion
ansom \an-səm\ handsome, ransom • king's ransom
answer \an-sər\ see ANCER
answered \an-sərd\ answered,
mansard • unanswered
ansy \an-zē\ pansy, tansy • chimpanzee
ant[1] \äⁿ\ croissant, Mont Blanc,
Rouen, savant • aide-de-camp,
denouement
ant[2] \änt\ aunt, can't, flaunt, font,
fount, gaunt, taunt, want • gallant, grandaunt, piedmont, savant, Vermont • commandant,
confidant, debutante, dilettante,
nonchalant, restaurant

ant³ \ənt\ see ONT¹
ant⁴ \ônt\ see AUNT¹
ant⁵ \ant\ ant, aunt, can't, chant, grant, Grant, pant, plant, rant, scant, shan't, slant • eggplant, enchant, extant, fire ant, gallant, grandaunt, houseplant, implant, jade plant, land grant, recant, replant, savant, seed plant, supplant, transplant, white ant • adamant, commandant, confidant, confidante, cormorant, covenant, dilettante, gallivant, pitcher plant, power plant, rubber plant, spider plant, sycophant • flowering plant
anta \ant-ə\ Fanta, manta, Santa • Atlanta
antal \änt-ᵊl\ see ONTAL¹
antam \ant-əm\ bantam, phantom
antar \ant-ər\ see ANTER²
ante¹ \än-tā\ Brontë, Dante • andante
ante² \änt\ see ANT²
ante³ \ant\ see ANT⁵
ante⁴ \änt-ē\ see ANTI¹
ante⁵ \ant-ē\ ante, chantey, pantie, scanty, shanty • andante • vigilante
anted \an-təd\ disenchanted
—also -ed forms of verbs listed at ANT⁵
anter¹ \änt-ər\ see AUNTER¹
anter² \ant-ər\ banter, canter, granter, grantor, planter • decanter, enchanter, implanter • tam-o'-shanter
antes \an-tēz\ antes • Cervantes
antey \ant-ē\ see ANTE⁵
anther \an-thər\ anther, panther • Black Panther
anti¹ \änt-ē\ Brontë, jaunty • andante
anti² \ant-ē\ see ANTE⁵
antial \an-chəl\ substantial • circumstantial, insubstantial, nonfinancial, unsubstantial

antic \ant-ik\ antic, frantic • Atlantic, gigantic, pedantic, romantic • North Atlantic, transatlantic, unromantic
antie \ant-ē\ see ANTE⁵
anting¹ \ant-iŋ\ planting • enchanting
—also -ing forms of verbs listed at ANT⁵
anting² \ənt-iŋ\ see UNTING
antis \ant-əs\ mantis • Atlantis
anto \än-tō\ Squanto • Toronto
antom \ant-əm\ see ANTAM
antor \ant-ər\ see ANTER²
antos \an-təs\ see ANTIS
antre \ant-ər\ see ANTER²
ants \ans\ see ANCE³
antus \ant-əs\ see ANTIS
anty \ant-ē\ see ANTE⁵
anual¹ \an-yəl\ annual, Daniel, spaniel • biannual, field spaniel, Nathaniel • cocker spaniel, semiannual, springer spaniel, water spaniel
anual² \an-yə-wəl\ annual, manual, Manuel • biannual, Emmanuel, Immanuel • semiannual • Victor Emmanuel
anuel \an-yəl\ see ANUAL²
anus¹ \ā-nəs\ see AYNESS
anus² \an-əs\ see ANISE
anx \aŋs\ thanks • Fairbanks, Grand Banks, phalanx • Outer Banks
—also -s, -'s, and -s' forms of nouns and -s forms of verbs listed at ANK
any¹ \ā-nē\ see AINY
any² \en-ē\ see ENNY
anyan \an-yən\ see ANION
anyard \an-yərd\ see ANIARD
anyon \an-yən\ see ANION
anz \ans\ see ANCE³
anza \an-zə\ stanza • bonanza • Sancho Panza • extravaganza
anzee \an-zē\ see ANSY
ao¹ \ā-ō\ see EO¹

ao² \ō\ see OW¹

ao³ \aů\ see OW²

aoighis \ash\ see ECHE¹

aole \aů-lē\ see OWLY²

aône \ōn\ see ONE¹

aori \aůr-ē\ see OWERY

aos¹ \aůs\ see OUSE²

aos² \ä-äs\ chaos, Laos

aotian \ō-shən\ see OTION

aow \aů\ see OW²

ap¹ \äp\ see OP¹

ap² \əp\ see UP

ap³ \ap\ cap, chap, clap, flap, gap, gape, hap, lap, Lapp, map, nap, nape, pap, rap, sap, scrap, slap, snap, strap, tap, trap, wrap, yap, zap • bootstrap, burlap, catnap, cell sap, claptrap, death cap, death trap, dunce cap, dewlap, dognap, earflap, entrap, enwrap, firetrap, gift wrap, hubcap, ice cap, jockstrap, kidnap, kneecap, madcap, mishap, mousetrap, mud flap, nightcap, on tap, pace lap, recap, remap, road map, sand trap, shrink-wrap, skullcap, skycap, snowcap, speed trap, stopgap, unsnap, unstrap, unwrap, whitecap, wiretap • baseball cap, beat the rap, blasting cap, booby trap, gangsta rap, giddyap, gingersnap, handicap, leghold trap, on the map, overlap, photomap, rattletrap, relief map, shoulder strap, stocking cap, thinking cap, thunderclap, tourist trap, weather map • Venus flytrap

apable \ā-pə-bəl\ capable • escapable, incapable • inescapable

apal \ā-pəl\ see APLE

apboard \ab-ərd\ see ABARD

ape¹ \āp\ ape, cape, crape, crepe, drape, gape, grape, nape, scrape, shape, tape • agape, cloudscape, duct tape, escape, great ape, landscape, man ape, misshape, moonscape, North Cape, red tape, reshape, Scotch tape, sea grape, seascape, shipshape, snowscape, take shape, townscape, undrape • Barbary ape, cityscape, fire escape, masking tape, ticker tape, waterscape • audiotape, adhesive tape, anthropoid ape, bent out of shape, magnetic tape, videotape

ape² \ap\ see AP³

ape³ \äp-ē\ see OPPY

ape⁴ \ap-ē\ see APPY

apel \ap-əl\ see APPLE

apelin \ap-lən\ see APLAIN

apen \ā-pən\ capon • misshapen

aper \ā-pər\ caper, draper, gaper, paper, scraper, shaper, taper, tapir, vapor • crepe paper, flypaper, graph paper, landscaper, newspaper, notepaper, reshaper, sandpaper, skyscraper, tar paper, term paper, wallpaper, wastepaper, waxed paper • butcher paper, carbon paper, funny paper, tissue paper, toilet paper, tracing paper, writing paper

apery \ā-prē\ drapery, papery, vapory

apes \āps\ traipse
—also -s, -'s, and -s' forms of nouns ending and -s forms of verbs listed at APE¹

aph \af\ calf, chaff, gaffe, graph, half, laugh, staff, staph • bar graph, behalf, carafe, Falstaff, flagstaff, giraffe, half-staff, horselaugh, line graph, riffraff • autograph, bathyscaphe, circle graph, epigraph, epitaph, half-and-half, lithograph, paragraph, phonograph, photograph, polygraph, seismograph, telegraph, understaff • choreograph

aphe¹ \āf\ see AFE¹

aphe² \af\ see APH

apher \af-ər\ see AFFER²

aphic \af-ik\ graphic, traffic • autographic, biographic, demographic,

geographic, lithographic, phono-
graphic, photographic, seismo-
graphic, telegraphic, typographic
• choreographic

api \äp-ē\ see OPPY

apid \ap-əd\ rapid, vapid

apir \ā-pər\ see APER

apist \ā-pist\ rapist • escapist,
landscapist

aplain \ap-lən\ chaplain, Chaplin,
sapling

aple \ā-pəl\ maple, papal, staple
• red maple, rock maple • antipa-
pal, sugar maple

aples \ā-pəlz\ Naples, staples

apless \ap-ləs\ hapless, strapless

aplin \ap-lə-n\ see APLAIN

aply \ap-lē\ see APTLY

apo \äp-ō\ capo • da capo, gestapo

apon \ā-pən\ see APEN

apor \ā-pər\ see APER

apory \ā-prē\ see APERY

apour \ā-pər\ see APER

app \ap\ see AP³

appable \ap-ə-bəl\ mappable • re-
cappable, unflappable

appalli \äp-ə-lē\ see OPOLY

appe \ap\ see AP³

apped \apt\ see APT

apper¹ \äp-ər\ see OPPER

apper² \ap-ər\ clapper, dapper,
flapper, mapper, rapper, snapper,
tapper, trapper, wrapper, yapper,
zapper • backslapper, catnapper,
dognapper, dust wrapper, kidnap-
per, knee-slapper, red snapper,
thigh slapper, wiretapper
• gangsta rapper, whippersnapper

apphic \af-ik\ see APHIC

appie \äp-ē\ see OPPY

appily \ap-ə-lē\ happily, snappily
• unhappily

appiness \ap-ē-nəs\ happiness,
sappiness, snappiness • unhappi-
ness

apping \ap-iŋ\ capping, mapping,
strapping, trapping, wrapping

—*also* -ing *forms of verbs listed at*
AP³

apple \ap-əl\ apple, chapel, dapple,
grapple, scrapple • crab apple,
mayapple, pineapple, thorn apple
• Adam's apple

apps \aps\ see APSE

appy \ap-ē\ gappy, happy, sappy,
scrappy, snappy • serape,
slaphappy, unhappy • trigger-
happy

aps \aps\ see APSE

apse \aps\ chaps, lapse, taps, traps
• collapse, elapse, perhaps, re-
lapse, time-lapse
—*also* -s, -'s, *and* -s' *forms of
nouns and* -s *forms of verbs listed
at* AP³

apt \apt\ apt, rapt • adapt, snow-
capped, untapped
—*also* -ed *forms of verbs listed at*
AP³

apter \ap-tər\ captor, chapter,
raptor • adapter • oviraptor • ve-
lociraptor

aption \ap-shən\ caption • adap-
tion, contraption, miscaption

aptive \ap-tiv\ captive • adaptive

aptly \ap-lē\ aptly, raptly

aptor \ap-tər\ see APTER

apture \ap-chər\ rapture • enrap-
ture, recapture

apy \ap-ē\ see APPY

aq¹ \äk\ see OCK¹

aq² \ak\ see ACK²

aqi \äk-ē\ see OCKY

aque¹ \āk\ see AKE¹

aque² \ak\ see ACK²

aqui \äk-ē\ see OCKY

ar¹ \er\ see ARE⁴

ar² \ȯr\ see OR¹

ar³ \är\ are, bar, car, char, czar, far,
gar, jar, mar, noir, our, par, R,
scar, spar, star, tar, tsar, tzar • afar,
ajar, all-star, bazaar, bizarre,
boudoir, boxcar, Bronze Star, cash
bar, cigar, costar, cougar, crossbar,

crowbar, disbar, Dog Star, feldspar, film noir, five-star, fixed star, flatcar, four-star, guitar, Gunnar, Hagar, handcar, horsecar, hussar, Ishtar, jaguar, Jaguar, Kevlar, leaf scar, lounge car, lumbar, Lamar, lodestar, Magyar, memoir, Mylar, NASCAR, North Star, pace car, pine tar, polestar, prowl car, pulsar, Qatar, quasar, radar, railcar, raw bar, rebar, Renoir, roll bar, sandbar, scout car, shofar, sidecar, slot car, snack bar, solar, sonar, sports bar, sports car, stock car, streetcar, tank car, T-bar, toolbar, town car, unbar • air guitar, arctic char, au revoir, avatar, blazing star, Bolívar, bumper car, cable car, caviar, coffee bar, color bar, command car, commissar, dining car, double star, evening star, exemplar, falling star, giant star, handlebar, Indy car, insofar, isobar, jaguar, Jaguar, Kandahar, Leyden jar, mason jar, megastar, millibar, minibar, minicar, Miramar, morning star, motorcar, multicar, muscle car, Myanmar, neutron star, open bar, registrar, rent-a-car, repertoire, reservoir, rising star, salad bar, samovar, scimitar, seminar, shooting star, Silver Star, sleeping car, steel guitar, superstar, touring car, turbocar, VCR, Zanzibar • anti-roll bar, Doppler radar, Madagascar, Mount Palomar, radio car, radio star • Hawaiian guitar, horizontal bar

ara[1] \är-ə\ Laura • Guevara, Gomorrah, saguaro, tiara • capybara, sayonara • Guadalajara

ara[2] \er-ə\ see ERA[1]

ara[3] \ar-ə\ see ARROW[1]

ara[4] \òr-ə\ see ORA

arab \ar-əb\ Arab, Carib, carob, scarab • pan-Arab • anti-Arab

arable \ar-ə-bəl\ arable, bearable, parable, shareable, wearable • declarable, nonarable, unbearable

aracen \ar-ə-sən\ see ARISON

aracin \ar-ə-sən\ see ARISON

arage \ar-ij\ see ARRIAGE

aragon \ar-ə-gən\ paragon, tarragon

arah[1] \er-ə\ see ERA[1]

arah[2] \ar-ə\ see ARROW[1]

aral[1] \ar-əl\ see ARREL[2]

aral[2] \ər-əl\ see ERRAL

aralee \er-ə-lē\ see ARILY

aran[1] \er-ən\ see ARON[1]

aran[2] \ar-ən\ see ARON[2]

arant[1] \er-ənt\ see ARENT[1]

arant[2] \ar-ənt\ see ARENT[2]

araoh[1] \er-ō\ see ERO[2]

araoh[2] \ar-ō\ see ARROW[2]

aras \är-əs\ see ORRIS[1]

arass \ar-əs\ see ARIS[2]

arat \ar-ət\ carat, caret, carrot, karat, parrot • disparate

arate \ar-ət\ see ARAT

arative[1] \er-ət-iv\ declarative, imperative

arative[2] \ar-ət-iv\ narrative • comparative, declarative

arb \ärb\ barb, carb, garb • rhubarb

arbel \är-bəl\ see ARBLE

arber \är-bər\ see ARBOR

arble \är-bəl\ barbel, garble, marble

arboard \är-bərd\ barbered, larboard, starboard

arbor \är-bər\ arbor, barber, harbor • Ann Arbor, Pearl Harbor

arc[1] \äk\ see OCK[1]

arc[2] \ärk\ see ARK[1]

arce \ärs\ see ARSE[1]

arch \ärch\ arch, larch, march, March, parch, starch • cornstarch, dead march • Gothic arch, horseshoe arch, on the march, wedding march

archal \är-kəl\ sparkle • monarchal, outsparkle • hierarchal, matriarchal, patriarchal

arche \ärsh\ see ARSH

arched \ärcht\ arched, parched
—*also* -ed *forms of verbs listed at* ARCH

archer \är-chər\ archer, marcher • departure

archic \är-kik\ anarchic, monarchic • hierarchic, oligarchic

archical \är-ki-kəl\ monarchical • oligarchical

archon \är-kən\ see ARKEN

archy \är-kē\ snarky • anarchy, malarkey, monarchy • hierarchy, matriarchy, patriarchy, oligarchy

arck \ärk\ see ARK[1]

arct \ärkt\ see ARKED

arctic \ärt-ik\ see ARTIC

ard[1] \ärd\ bard, barred, card, chard, guard, hard, lard, shard, yard • Asgard, backyard, bankcard, barnyard, Bernard, blackguard, blowhard, boatyard, bombard, brickyard, charge card, churchyard, coast guard, courtyard, die-hard, diehard, discard, dockyard, dooryard, face card, farmyard, flash card, Gerard, graveyard, green card, ill-starred, junkyard, lifeguard, mudguard, noseguard, off guard, old guard, on guard, phone card, placard, point guard, postcard, punch card, rear guard, rearguard, regard, retard, safeguard, scorecard, shipyard, smart card, sound card, steelyard, stockyard, switchyard, time card, unbarred, vanguard, wild card • Abelard, avant-garde, bodyguard, boulevard, business card, calling card, Christmas card, color guard, credit card, debit card, disregard, greeting card, honor guard, ID card, leotard, lumberyard, MasterCard, national guard, navy yard, no-holds-barred, playing card, postal card, report card, Saint Bernard, Scotland Yard, self-regard, union card, unitard • picture-postcard, video card • identity card
—*also* -ed *forms of verbs listed at* AR[3]

ard[2] \är\ see AR[3]

ard[3] \ȯrd\ see OARD

ardant \ärd-ᵊnt\ ardent • flame-retardant

arde \ärd\ see ARD[1]

arded[1] \ärd-əd\ guarded • retarded, unguarded
—*also* -ed *forms of verbs listed at* ARD[1]

arded[2] \ȯrd-əd\ corded, sordid
—*also* -ed *forms of verbs listed at* OARD

arden[1] \ärd-ᵊn\ garden, harden, pardon • rock garden, roof garden, tea garden • kitchen garden, water garden

arden[2] \ȯrd-ᵊn\ cordon, Gordon, Jordan, warden • churchwarden

ardener \ärd-nər\ gardener, pardner, partner • landscape gardener

ardent \ärd-ᵊnt\ see ARDANT

arder[1] \ärd-ər\ ardor, guarder, larder

arder[2] \ȯrd-ər\ see ORDER

ardi \ärd-ē\ see ARDY

ardian[1] \ärd-ē-ən\ guardian • Edwardian

ardian[2] \ȯrd-ē-ən\ see ORDION

ardine \ärd-ⁿ\ see ARDEN[1]

arding \ȯrd-iŋ\ see ORDING[1]

ardom \ärd-əm\ czardom, stardom • megastardom, superstardom

ardon \ärd-ᵊn\ see ARDEN[1]

ardoner \ärd-nər\ see ARDENER

ardor \ärd-ər\ see ARDER[1]

ardy \ärd-ē\ hardy, tardy • Bacardi, foolhardy

are[1] \er-ē\ see ARY[1]

are[2] \är\ see AR[3]

are³ \är-ē\ see ARI¹

are⁴ \er\ air, bare, bear, Blair,
blare, care, chair, Claire, dare,
e'er, ere, err, fair, fare, flair, flare,
glare, hair, hare, Herr, heir, lair,
mare, ne'er, pair, pare, pear,
prayer, rare, rear, scare, share,
snare, spare, square, stair, stare,
swear, tear, their, there, they're,
ware, wear, where • affair, aglare,
airfare, antbear, armchair, aware,
bakeware, barware, beachwear,
beware, big hair, black bear,
bricklayer, brown bear, bugbear,
carfare, cave bear, clayware,
cochair, coheir, compare, cook-
ware, courseware, day-care, deck
chair, declare, despair, éclair,
elsewhere, ensnare, eyewear,
fanfare, flatware, footwear, for-
bear, forebear, forswear,
foursquare, freeware, giftware,
glassware, Great Bear, groupware,
hardware, health care, hectare,
high chair, horsehair, hot air,
impair, knitwear, life-care, long-
hair, loungewear, menswear,
midair, mohair, neckwear, night-
mare, no fair, nonglare, outstare,
out-there, outwear, playwear,
plowshare, Poor Clare, premiere,
prepare, rainwear, repair, self-
care, shareware, shorthair, Sin-
clair, skiwear, sleepwear, sloth
bear, software, somewhere,
sportswear, stemware, stoneware,
sun bear, swimwear, threadbare,
tinware, unfair, Voltaire, warfare,
welfare, wheelchair • aftercare,
air-to-air, antiglare, anywhere,
arctic hare, Asian pear, billion-
aire, bill of fare, boutonniere,
camel hair, Camembert,
chinaware, compressed air,
county fair, debonair, Delaware,
derriere, dinnerware, disrepair,
doctrinaire, earthenware, easy

chair, étagère, everywhere, germ
warfare, get somewhere, grizzly
bear, here and there, hide or hair,
in one's hair, in the air, ironware,
kitchenware, laissez-faire, legion-
naire, lion's share, Little Bear,
love affair, managed care, market
share, Medicare, metalware,
millionaire, on the square, open-
air, outerwear, overbear, perfect
square, plasticware, polar bear,
potty-chair, prickly pear, ques-
tionnaire, rocking chair, savoir
faire, science fair, self-aware, self-
despair, silverware, snowshoe
hare, solar flare, solitaire, swivel
chair, tableware, tear one's hair,
teddy bear, then and there,
thoroughfare, trench warfare,
Tupperware, unaware, under-
wear, vaporware, wash-and-wear,
wear and tear, woodenware,
world premiere, zillionaire
• breath of fresh air, concession-
aire, devil-may-care, director's
chair, electric chair, enamelware,
hyperaware, intensive care, Kodiak bear, lighter-than-air, out of
one's hair, primary care, ready-to-
wear, social welfare, spectacled
bear, surface-to-air, up in the air
• castle in the air, middle of
nowhere

area \er-ē-ə\ see ARIA

areable¹ \er-ə-bəl\ see EARABLE¹

areable² \ar-ə-bəl\ see ARABLE

areal \er-ē-əl\ see ARIAL

arean¹ \er-ē-ən\ see ARIAN¹

arean² \ar-ē-ən\ see ARIAN²

ared \erd\ see AIRED

aredness \ar-əd-nəs\ see ARIDNESS

arel \ar-əl\ see ARREL²

arely¹ \er-lē\ see AIRLY

arely² \är-lē\ see ARLIE

arem \er-əm\ see ARUM

arence¹ \er-əns\ Clarence, Terence
• forbearance

arence[2] \ar-ən(ts)\ see ARENTS

arent[1] \er-ənt\ daren't, errant, parent • aberrant, apparent, god-parent, grandparent, house parent, knight-errant, nonparent, stepparent, transparent • heir apparent

arent[2] \ar-ənt\ daren't, parent • apparent, godparent, grandparent, stepparent, transparent • heir apparent

aren't[1] \er-ənt\ see ARENT[1]

aren't[2] \ar-ənt\ see ARENT[2]

arents \ar-ən(t)s\ Clarence —also -s, -'s, and -s' forms of nouns listed at ARENT[2]

arer \er-ər\ see EARER[1]

ares[1] \erz\ see AIRS

ares[2] \ar-ēz\ Buenos Aires —also -s, -'s, and -s' forms of nouns and -s forms of verbs listed at ARRY[3]

ares[3] \är-əs\ see ORRIS[1]

aret \ar-ət\ see ARAT

arey[1] \ar-ē\ see ARRY[3]

arey[2] \er-ē\ see ARY[1]

arez \är-əs\ see ORRIS[1]

arf[1] \ärf\ barf, scarf

arf[2] \òrf\ see ORPH

argain \är-gən\ bargain, jargon • outbargain, plea-bargain • in the bargain

arge \ärj\ barge, charge, large, Marge, sarge • at-large, depth charge, discharge, enlarge, recharge, surcharge, take-charge • by and large, countercharge, cover charge, overcharge, service charge, undercharge • carrying charge

arger \är-jər\ charger • enlarger, recharger • turbocharger

arget \är-gət\ argot, target • off target, on target

argo \är-gō\ argot, cargo, Fargo, largo, Margot • embargo, Key Largo • supercargo

argon \är-gən\ see ARGAIN

argot[1] \är-gət\ see ARGET

argot[2] \är-gō\ see ARGO

arh \är\ see AR[3]

ari[1] \är-ē\ quarry, sari, scarry, sorry, starry • curare, safari • calamari, Kalahari, Stradivari

ari[2] \er-ē\ see ARY[1]

ari[3] \ar-ē\ see ARRY[3]

aria \er-ē-ə\ area • Bavaria, Bulgaria, hysteria, malaria, planaria, Samaria

arial \er-ē-əl\ aerial, burial • malarial • adversarial, secretarial

arian[1] \er-ē-ən\ Marian, Marion • agrarian, Aquarian, barbarian, Bavarian, Bulgarian, Cancerian, cesarean, grammarian, Hungarian, librarian, Maid Marian, ovarian, Rotarian, sectarian, Sumerian • antiquarian, centenarian, libertarian, nonsectarian, Presbyterian, proletarian, Rastafarian, Sagittarian, seminarian, Unitarian, vegetarian • Austro-Hungarian, authoritarian, disciplinarian, egalitarian, humanitarian, octogenarian, parliamentarian, totalitarian, utilitarian, veterinarian

arian[2] \ar-ē-ən\ carrion, clarion, Marian, Marion, agrarian, Aquarian, barbarian, Bavarian, Bulgarian, cesarean, Hungarian, ovarian, Rastafarian, Austro-Hungarian

ariat[1] \er-ē-ət\ lariat • commissariat, proletariat, secretariat

ariat[2] \ar-ē-ət\ chariot, lariat • commissariat, proletariat • Judas Iscariot

ariate \er-ē-ət\ see ARIAT[1]

arib \ar-əb\ see ARAB

arice \ar-əs\ see ARIS[2]

aridness \ar-əd-nəs\ aridness • preparedness

aried[1] \er-ēd\ see ERRIED

aried[2] \ar-ēd\ see ARRIED

ariel \er-ē-əl\ see ARIAL

arier¹ \er-ē-ər\ see ERRIER
arier² \ar-ē-ər\ see ARRIER²
aries \ar-ēz\ see ARES²
arilee¹ \ar-ə-lē\ see ARALEE
arilee² \er-ə-lē\ see ARILY
arily \er-ə-lē\ merrily, scarily, warily • primarily • arbitrarily, customarily, legendarily, militarily, momentarily, monetarily, necessarily, ordinarily, secondarily, temporarily, voluntarily • extraordinarily, involuntarily, unnecessarily
arin \är-ən\ foreign, Lauren, Orin, warren, Warren
arinate \ar-ə-nət\ see ARONET
arinet \ar-ə-nət\ see ARONET
aring¹ \er-iŋ\ airing, bearing, Bering, daring, fairing, flaring, glaring, herring, paring, raring, sparing, tearing, wearing • ball bearing, childbearing, seafaring, time-sharing, unerring, unsparing, wayfaring • overbearing, profit sharing
—*also* -ing *forms of verbs listed at* ARE⁴
aring² \er-ən\ see ARON¹
ario \er-ē-ō\ stereo • Ontario
arion¹ \ar-ē-ən\ see ARIAN²
arion² \er-ē-ən\ see ARIAN¹
ariot \ar-ē-ət\ see ARIAT²
arious \er-ē-əs\ Darius, various • Aquarius, gregarious, hilarious, nefarious, precarious, vicarious • Stradivarius, Sagittarius
aris¹ \är-əs\ see ORRIS¹
aris² \ar-əs\ Clarice, harass, Harris, Paris • coheiress, embarrass, Polaris • plaster of paris
arish¹ \er-ish\ bearish, cherish, garish, perish, squarish • nightmarish
arish² \ar-ish\ garish, parish • vinegarish
arison \ar-ə-sən\ garrison, Garrison, Harrison, Saracen • comparison

arist \er-əst\ scenarist
—*also* -est *forms of adjectives listed at* ARE⁴
aritan \er-ət-ᵊn\ see ERATIN
arity¹ \er-ət-ē\ see ERITY
arity² \ar-ət-ē\ charity, clarity, parity, rarity • barbarity, disparity, hilarity, polarity, vulgarity • angularity, circularity, familiarity, muscularity, peculiarity, popularity, regularity, similarity, singularity, solidarity • dissimilarity, irregularity, unfamiliarity, unpopularity
arium \er-ē-əm\ aquarium, herbarium, solarium, terrarium, vivarium • honorarium, oceanarium, planetarium, sanitarium
arius \er-ē-əs\ see ARIOUS
ark¹ \ärk\ arc, ark, bark, Clark, dark, hark, lark, Marc, mark, Mark, narc, nark, park, quark, shark, spark, stark • aardvark, airpark, ballpark, benchmark, birchbark, birthmark, Bismarck, blue shark, bookmark, check mark, debark, Denmark, earmark, embark, hallmark, hash mark, landmark, monarch, Ozark, pitch-dark, pockmark, postmark, remark, shagbark, skylark, theme park, tidemark, trademark, whale shark • basking shark, disembark, double-park, Estes Park, great white shark, Joan of Arc, make one's mark, mako shark, matriarch, meadowlark, oligarch, patriarch, question mark, thresher shark, tiger shark, toe the mark, watermark, water park • amusement park, high-water mark, in the ballpark, shot in the dark, vest-pocket park • whistle in the dark
ark² \ȯrk\ see ORK²
ark³ \ərk\ see ORK¹
arke \ärk\ see ARK¹

arked \ärkt\ marked • ripple-marked
—*also* -ed *forms of verbs listed at* ARK[1]
arken \är-kən\ darken, hearken
arker \är-kər\ barker, darker, marker, Parker, starker • book-marker, Ozarker, skylarker • Magic Marker, nosey parker
arkey \är-kē\ see ARCHY
arkic \är-kik\ see ARCHIC
arking \är-kiŋ\ barking, marking, parking • loan-sharking • valet parking
—*also* -ing *forms of verbs listed at* ARK[1]
arkle \är-kəl\ see ARCHAL
arks \ärks\ Marx • Ozarks
—*also* -s, -'s, *and* -s' *forms of nouns and* -s *forms of verbs listed at* ARK[1]
arky \är-kē\ see ARCHY
arl \ärl\ Carl, gnarl, Karl, quarrel, snarl • ensnarl, unsnarl
arla \är-lə\ Carla, Darla, Marla
arlan \ä-lən\ see ARLINE
arlay \är-lē\ see ARLIE
arle \ärl\ see ARL
arlen \är-lən\ see ARLINE
arler \är-lər\ see ARLOR
arless \är-ləs\ Carlos, starless
arlet \är-lət\ Charlotte, harlot, scarlet, starlet, varlet
arley \är-lē\ see ARLIE
arlie \är-lē\ barley, Charlie, gnarly, Harley, parlay, parley, snarly • bizarrely
arlin \är-lən\ see ARLINE
arline \är-lən\ Harlan, marlin, Marlin • blue marlin, white marlin
arling \är-liŋ\ darling, starling
—*also* -ing *forms of verbs listed at* ARL
arlor \är-lər\ parlor, quarreler
arlos \är-ləs\ see ARLESS
arlot \är-lət\ see ARLET

arlotte \är-lət\ see ARLET
arlous \är-ləs\ see ARLESS
arly \är-lē\ see ARLIE
arlyn \ä-lən\ see ARLINE
arm[1] \ärm\ arm, charm, farm, harm • alarm, disarm, firearm, fish farm, forearm, nonfarm, rearm, schoolmarm, sidearm, strong-arm, tree farm, unarm, wind farm • arm in arm, buy the farm, false alarm, overarm, twist one's arm, underarm • collective farm, shot in the arm
arm[2] \äm\ see OM[1]
arm[3] \ȯrm\ see ORM[2]
arma[1] \är-mə\ karma, Parma
arma[2] \ər-mə\ see ERMA
armed \ärmd\ armed, charmed • unarmed
—*also* -ed *forms of verbs listed at* ARM[1]
arment \är-mənt\ garment, varmint • disbarment • undergarment, overgarment
armer[1] \är-mər\ armor, charmer, farmer • snake charmer • tenant farmer
armer[2] \ȯr-mər\ see ORMER
armic \ər-mik\ see ERMIC
arming[1] \är-miŋ\ charming, farm-ing • alarming, disarming, Prince Charming
—*also* -ing *forms of verbs listed at* ARM[1]
arming[2] \ȯr-miŋ\ see ORMING
armint \är-mənt\ see ARMENT
armless \ärm-ləs\ armless, charm-less, harmless
armoir \är-mər\ see ARMER[1]
army \är-mē\ army, smarmy • standing army • Salvation Army
arn[1] \ärn\ barn, darn, yarn
arn[2] \ȯrn\ see ORN[1]
arna \ər-nə\ see ERNA
arnate \är-nət\ garnet • incarnate
arne[1] \ärn\ see ARN[1]
arne[2] \är-nē\ see ARNY

arner \òr-nər\ see ORNER
arness \är-nəs\ harness
• bizarreness
arnet \är-nət\ see ARNATE
arney \är-nē\ see ARNY
arning \òr-niŋ\ see ORNING
arnish \är-nish\ garnish, tarnish,
varnish
arny \är-nē\ Barney, blarney, carny
• Killarney • chili con carne
aro[1] \er-ō\ see ERO[2]
aro[2] \ar-ō\ see ARROW[2]
aro[3] \är-ə\ see ARA[1]
aro[4] \är-ō\ see ORROW[1]
arob \ar-əb\ see ARAB
aroe[1] \ar-ō\ see ARROW[2]
aroe[2] \er-ō\ see ERO[2]
arol \ar-əl\ see ARREL[2]
arold \er-əld\ see ERALD
arole \ar-əl\ see ARREL[2]
arom \er-əm\ see ARUM
aron[1] \er-ən\ Aaron, baron,
Charon, Erin, heron, raring,
Sharon • sub-Saharan
aron[2] \ar-ən\ Aaron, baron, barren,
Charon, Sharon • sub-Saharan
aronet \ar-ə-nət\ baronet, clarinet
arous[1] \er-əs\ see ERROUS
arous[2] \ar-əs\ see ARIS[2]
arp[1] \ärp\ carp, harp, sharp, tarp
• Jew's harp • Autoharp, super-
sharp
arp[2] \òrp\ see ORP
arpen \är-pən\ sharpen, tarpon
arper \är-pər\ carper, sharper
arpie \är-pē\ see ARPY
arpon \är-pən\ see ARPEN
arpy \är-pē\ harpy, sharpie
arque \ärk\ see ARK[1]
arqui \är-kē\ see ARCHY
arrable \ar-ə-bəl\ see ARABLE
arrage \är-ij\ see [1]orage
arragon \ar-ə-gən\ see ARAGON
arrant[1] \ar-ənt\ see ARENT[2]
arrant[2] \òr-ənt\ see ORRENT
arras \ar-əs\ see ARIS[2]
arrass \ar-əs\ see ARIS[2]

arrative \ar-ət-iv\ see ARATIVE[2]
arre \är\ see AR[3]
arred \ärd\ see ARD[1]
arrel[1] \òr-əl\ see ORAL
arrel[2] \ar-əl\ Aral, barrel, carol,
Carol, Darryl • apparel • cracker-
barrel
arreler \är-lər\ see ARLOR
arrell \ar-əl\ see ARREL[2]
arrely \är-lē\ see ARLIE
arren[1] \ar-ən\ see ARON[2]
arren[2] \òr-ən\ see ORIN[1]
arren[3] \är-ən\ see ARIN
arrener \òr-ə-nər\ see ORONER
arreness \är-nəs\ see ARNESS
arret \ar-ət\ see ARAT
arrett \ar-ət\ see ARAT
arrh \är\ see AR[3]
arriage \ar-ij\ carriage, marriage
• disparage, miscarriage, mixed
marriage • baby carriage, horse-
less carriage, intermarriage, un-
dercarriage
arrie \ar-ē\ see ARRY[3]
arried \ar-ēd\ harried, married,
varied • unmarried
arrier[1] \òr-ē-ər\ see ARRIOR
arrier[2] \ar-ē-ər\ barrier, carrier
• ballcarrier, mail carrier, noncar-
rier, sound barrier, spear-carrier
• aircraft carrier, letter carrier
arrion \ar-ē-ən\ see ARIAN[2]
arrior \òr-ē-ər\ sorrier, warrior
• weekend warrior
arris \ar-əs\ see ARIS[2]
arrison \ar-ə-sən\ see ARISON
arro \är-ō\ see ORROW[1]
arroll \ar-əl\ see ARREL[2]
arron \ar-ən\ see ARON[2]
arrot \ar-ət\ see ARAT
arroty \ar-ət-ē\ see ARITY[2]
arrow[1] \ar-ə\ Clara, Kara, Sarah,
Tara • mascara, Sahara, tiara
• capybara, marinara, Santa Clara
arrow[2] \ar-ō\ arrow, barrow, har-
row, marrow, narrow, pharaoh,
sparrow, taro, tarot, yarrow

• bone marrow, house sparrow, Point Barrow, song sparrow, straight-arrow, tree sparrow, wheelbarrow • straight and narrow • Kilimanjaro

arry[1] \är-ē\ see ARI[1]

arry[2] \òr-ē\ see ORY

arry[3] \ar-ē\ Barry, Carrie, carry, Cary, chary, Gary, Harry, Larry, marry, nary, parry, Shari, tarry • miscarry, safari • cash-and-carry, hari-kari, intermarry, Stradivari • Tom, Dick, and Harry

arryl \ar-əl\ see ARREL[2]

ars \ärz\ Lars, Mars, ours • behind bars, Stars and Bars
—also -s, -'s, and -s' forms of nouns and -s forms of verbs listed at AR[3]

arse[1] \ärs\ farce, sparse

arse[2] \ärz\ see ARS

arsh \ärsh\ harsh, marsh • salt marsh

arshal \är-shəl\ see ARTIAL

arshall \är-shəl\ see ARTIAL

arsle \äs-əl\ see OSSAL

arson \ärs-ᵊn\ arson, Carson, parson

art[1] \ärt\ art, Art, Bart, cart, chart, Chartres, dart, hart, heart, kart, mart, part, smart, start, tart • apart, at heart, bar chart, Bogart, by heart, clip art, depart, dogcart, Earhart, eye chart, false start, fine art, folk art, go-cart, golf cart, handcart, head start, Hobart, impart, in part, jump-start, kick-start, mouthpart, Mozart, outsmart, oxcart, pie chart, pop art, pushcart, rampart, restart, street-smart, Stuttgart, sweetheart, take heart, take part, upstart, voice part • à la carte, applecart, bleeding heart, Bonaparte, change of heart, counterpart, fall apart, flying start, for one's part, heart-to-heart, martial

art, mini-mart, multipart, on one's part, open-heart, poles apart, Purple Heart, running start, set apart, take apart, underpart • for the most part, performance art, state-of-the-art

art[2] \òrt\ see ORT[1]

arta \är-tə\ Marta, Sparta • Jakarta • Magna Carta

artan \ärt-ᵊn\ see ARTEN

artar \ärt-ər\ see ARTER[1]

arte[1] \ärt-ē\ see ARTY[1]

arte[2] \ärt\ see ART[1]

arted[1] \ärt-əd\ see EARTED

arted[2] \òrt-əd\ see ORTED

arten \ärt-ᵊn\ carton, hearten, Martin, smarten, Spartan, tartan • dishearten, Saint Martin • kindergarten

arter[1] \ärt-ər\ barter, Carter, charter, garter, martyr, starter, tartar • nonstarter, self-starter, snail darter
—also -er forms of adjectives listed at ART[1]

arter[2] \òt-ər\ see ATER[1]

arter[3] \òrt-ər\ see ORTER

artes \ärt\ see ART[1]

arth \ärth\ Garth, hearth • open-hearth

arti \ärt-ē\ see ARTY[1]

artial \är-shəl\ marshal, Marshal, Marshall, martial, partial • court-martial, earl marshal, field marshal, grand marshal, impartial, sky marshal

artic \ärt-ik\ arctic, Arctic • antarctic, Antarctic, cathartic

article \ärt-i-kəl\ article, particle • alpha particle, beta particle, microparticle

artile \òrt-ᵊl\ see ORTAL

artily \ärt-ᵊl-ē\ artily, heartily

artin \ärt-ᵊn\ see ARTEN

arting \ärt-iŋ\ carting, charting, karting, parting, starting • self-starting

—also -ing *forms of verbs listed at*
ART[1]

artisan \ärt-ə-zən\ artisan, partisan
• bipartisan, nonpartisan

artizan \ärt-ə-zən\ see ARTISAN

artless \ärt-ləs\ artless, heartless

artly[1] \ärt-lē\ partly, smartly, tartly

artly[2] \órt-lē\ see ORTLY

artner \ärt-nər\ partner • kinder-
gartner, secret partner

arton \ärt-ᵊn\ see ARTEN

artre \ärt\ see ART[1]

artres \ärt\ see ART[1]

artridge \är-trij\ cartridge, par-
tridge

arts[1] \är\ see AR[3]

arts[2] \ärts\ street smarts • private
parts • master of arts, principal
parts
—also -s, -'s, *and* -s' *forms of nouns
and* -s *forms of verbs listed at* ART[1]

arture \är-chər\ see ARCHER

arty[1] \ärt-ē\ arty, hearty, party,
smarty • block party, Havarti, tea
party, war party • cocktail party,
slumber party

arty[2] \órt-ē\ see ORTY

artyr \ärt-ər\ see ARTER[1]

artz[1] \órts\ see ORTS

artz[2] \ärts\ see ARTS[2]

arum \er-əm\ harem • harum-
scarum

arus \ar-əs\ see ARIS[2]

arval \är-vəl\ see ARVEL

arve \ärv\ carve, starve

arvel \är-vəl\ larval, marvel

ary[1] \er-ē\ aerie, airy, berry, bury,
Carey, Cary, Cherie, cherry,
Cherry, dairy, Derry, fairy, ferry,
Gary, Gerry, hairy, Jerry, Kerry,
Mary, marry, merry, Merry, nary,
Perry, prairie, query, scary, Shari,
sherry, terry, Terry, vary, very,
wary • barberry, bayberry, bear-
berry, bing cherry, blackberry,
black cherry, blueberry, canary,
chokeberry, chokecherry, con-

trary, cranberry, dewberry, goose-
berry, hackberry, Hail Mary,
library, mulberry, nondairy,
primary, raspberry, rosemary,
Rosemary, soapberry, strawberry,
summary, tooth fairy, unwary
• actuary, adversary, antiquary,
apiary, arbitrary, aviary, beriberi,
black raspberry, boysenberry,
budgetary, Canterbury, capillary,
cautionary, cemetery, centenary,
chinaberry, commentary, com-
missary, corollary, coronary,
culinary, customary, dictionary,
dietary, dignitary, dromedary,
dysentery, elderberry, emissary,
estuary, February, fragmentary,
functionary, honorary, huckle-
berry, intermarry, January, lec-
tionary, legendary, legionary,
lingonberry, literary, loganberry,
luminary, mercenary, military,
millinery, missionary, momen-
tary, monastery, monetary, mor-
tuary, necessary, ordinary,
partridgeberry, planetary, pul-
monary, red mulberry, reliquary,
salivary, salmonberry, salutary,
sanctuary, sanitary, secondary,
secretary, sedentary, seminary,
serviceberry, solitary, sour
cherry, stationary, stationery,
statuary, Stradivari, temporary,
Tipperary, Tom and Jerry, tribu-
tary, Typhoid Mary, unitary,
urinary, Virgin Mary, visionary,
voluntary, winterberry • bicentenary, confectionery, contempo-
rary, deflationary, disciplinary,
discretionary, extemporary, ex-
traordinary, hereditary, illusion-
ary, imaginary, incendiary,
inflationary, insanitary, interli-
brary, involuntary, itinerary,
judiciary, lending library, nonmil-
itary, obituary, on the contrary,
pituitary, precautionary, prelimi-

nary, probationary, reactionary,
subsidiary, uncustomary, unnec-
essary, unsanitary, veterinary,
vocabulary • beneficiary, evolutionary, intermediary, interplane-
tary, paramilitary, penitentiary,
revolutionary
ary² \ar-ē\ see ARRY³
ary³ \är-ē\ see ARI¹
aryan¹ \er-ē-ən\ see ARIAN¹
aryan² \ar-ē-ən\ see ARIAN²
aryl \ar-əl\ see ARREL²
as¹ \ash\ see ASH³
as² \as\ see ASS³
as³ \az\ see AZZ
as⁴ \ä\ see A¹
as⁵ \äsh\ see ASH¹
as⁶ \äz\ see OISE¹
as⁷ \əz\ see EUSE¹
as⁸ \äs\ see OS¹
as⁹ \o̊\ see AW¹
asa¹ \äs-ə\ Lhasa, Ossa • kielbasa
asa² \äz-ə\ see AZA¹
asable \ā-sə-bəl\ see ACEABLE
asal \ā-zəl\ Basil, hazel, Hazel,
nasal, phrasal • appraisal, witch
hazel
asally \āz-lē\ see AISLEY
asca \as-kə\ see ASKA
ascal \as-kəl\ paschal, rascal
ascar \as-kər\ see ASKER
ascent \ās-ᵊnt\ see ACENT
asch¹ \ask\ see ASK
asch² \äsh\ see ASH¹
asch³ \o̊sh\ see ASH²
aschal \as-kəl\ see ASCAL
ascia \ā-shə\ see ACIA
ascible \as-ə-bəl\ see ASSABLE
ascicle \as-i-kəl\ see ASSICAL
asco¹ \äs-kō\ see OSCOE
asco² \as-kō\ fiasco, Tabasco
ascot \as-kət\ see ASKET
ascus \as-kəs\ Damascus,
Velázquez
ase¹ \ās\ see ACE¹
ase² \āz\ see AZE¹
ase³ \äz\ see OISE¹

asel \äz-əl\ see OZZLE
ased \āst\ see ACED
aseless \ā-sləs\ see ACELESS
aseman \ā-smən\ see ACEMAN
asement \ās-mənt\ basement,
casement • abasement, debase-
ment • bargain-basement, self-
abasement
aser¹ \ā-sər\ see ACER¹
aser² \ā-zər\ see AZER
asey \ā-sē\ see ACY
ash¹ \äsh\ gosh, josh, mosh, nosh,
posh, quash, slosh, squash, swash,
wash • awash, backwash, eyewash, galosh, goulash, kibosh,
mishmash, mouthwash, whitewash • acorn squash, hubbard
squash, mackintosh, summer
squash, winter squash
ash² \o̊sh\ gosh, quash, slosh,
squash, swash, wash • awash,
backwash, brainwash, car wash,
eyewash, hogwash, mouthwash,
prewash, whitewash • acorn
squash, hubbard squash, summer
squash, winter squash
ash³ \ash\ ash, bash, brash, cache,
cash, clash, crash, dash, flash,
gash, gnash, hash, lash, mash,
rash, sash, slash, smash, splash,
stash, thrash, thresh, trash
• abash, backlash, backslash, cold
cash, eyelash, gate-crash, goulash,
green flash, heat rash, hot flash,
mishmash, moustache, mustache,
potash, rehash, slapdash, tongue-
lash, unlash, Wabash, whiplash,
white ash • balderdash, calabash,
diaper rash, mountain ash, nettle
rash, petty cash, prickly rash,
succotash • settle one's hash
ashan \ash-ən\ see ASSION
ashed¹ \o̊sht\ sloshed
• stonewashed, unwashed • acid-
washed
—*also* -ed *forms of verbs listed at*
ASH²

ashed² \asht\ dashed, smashed
• unabashed
—*also* -ed *forms of verbs listed at* ASH³

ashen \ash-ən\ see ASSION

asher¹ \äsh-ər\ josher, mosher, nosher, squasher, washer • dishwasher

asher² \ósh-ər\ washer • brainwasher, dishwasher, whitewasher

asher³ \ash-ər\ basher, crasher, rasher, slasher, smasher • gatecrasher • atom-smasher, haberdasher

ashi¹ \äsh-ē\ see ASHY¹

ashi² \ash-ē\ see ASHY²

ashing \ash-iŋ\ crashing, dashing, flashing, mashing, slashing, smashing • tongue-lashing
—*also* -ing *forms of verbs listed at* ASH³

ashion \ash-ən\ see ASSION

asht \asht\ see ASHED²

ashy¹ \äsh-ē\ squashy • wishy-washy

ashy² \ash-ē\ ashy, flashy, splashy, trashy

asi¹ \äs-ē\ see OSSY¹

asi² \äz-ē\ see AZI¹

asi³ \äsh-ē\ see ASHY¹

asia \ā-zhə\ Asia • Caucasia, Eurasia, fantasia, Malaysia • Anastasia, Australasia, euthanasia

asian¹ \ā-shən\ see ATION¹

asian² \ā-zhən\ see ASION

asic \ā-zik\ phasic • euthanasic, multiphasic

asid \as-əd\ see ACID

asie \ā-sē\ see ACY

asil¹ \as-əl\ see ASSEL²

asil² \az-əl\ see AZZLE

asil³ \āz-əl\ see ASAL

asil⁴ \äz-əl\ see OZZLE

asin \ās-ᵊn\ see ASON¹

asing¹ \ā-siŋ\ see ACING

asing² \ā-ziŋ\ see AISING

asion \ā-zhən\ Asian • abrasion, Caucasian, dissuasion, equation, Eurasian, evasion, invasion, occasion, persuasion • Amerasian, anti-Asian, Australasian, on occasion

asis \ā-səs\ basis • oasis • homeostasis

asive \ā-siv\ abrasive, evasive, invasive, persuasive, pervasive

ask \ask\ ask, bask, Basque, cask, flask, mask, task • death mask, face mask, gas mask, ski mask, unmask • multitask, take to task, vacuum flask • oxygen mask

aska \as-kə\ Alaska, Nebraska

asked \ast\ see AST²

asker \as-kər\ masker • Madagascar

asket \as-kət\ ascot, basket, casket, gasket • breadbasket, handbasket, wastebasket • blow a gasket

asking \as-kiŋ\ multitasking
—*also* -ing *forms of verbs listed at* ASK

asm \az-əm\ chasm, plasm, spasm • phantasm, sarcasm • ectoplasm, protoplasm • enthusiasm

asma \az-mə\ asthma, plasma • miasma

asn't \əz-ᵊnt\ doesn't, wasn't

aso¹ \as-ō\ see ASSO¹

aso² \äs-ō\ see ASSO²

ason¹ \ās-ᵊn\ basin, caisson, chasten, hasten, Jason, mason, Mason • Freemason, Great Basin, stonemason, washbasin

ason² \āz-ᵊn\ see AZON

asp \asp\ asp, clasp, gasp, grasp, hasp, rasp • handclasp, last-gasp, unclasp

asque \ask\ see ASK

asquer \as-kər\ see ASKER

ass¹ \ās\ see ACE¹

ass² \äs\ see OS¹

ass³ \as\ ass, bass, brass, class, crass, gas, glass, grass, has, lass, mass, pass, sass • air mass, alas,

Alsace, amass, art glass, beach grass, bear grass, bent grass, black bass, Black Mass, bluegrass, bunchgrass, bypass, crabgrass, crevasse, cuirass, cut glass, degas, eelgrass, en masse, eyeglass, first-class, folk mass, ground glass, harass, high-class, high mass, hourglass, impasse, jackass, jump pass, landmass, Madras, milk glass, morass, oat grass, outclass, plate glass, quack grass, rock bass, ryegrass, salt grass, sand-glass, saw grass, screen pass, sea bass, sheet glass, shortgrass, smart-ass, spun glass, spyglass, stained glass, striped bass, sub-class, sung mass, surpass, sweet-grass, switchgrass, sword grass, tallgrass, teargas, third-class, trespass, turfgrass, wheatgrass, white bass, wineglass, wire grass, wiseass, witchgrass, world-class, yard grass • bottled gas, Brenner Pass, Cajon Pass, channel bass, cocktail glass, come to pass, demitasse, Donner Pass, fiber-glass, forward pass, Khyber Pass, largemouth bass, laughing gas, lemongrass, looking glass, lower-class, middle-class, opera glass, overpass, Plexiglas, safety glass, sassafras, second-class, Simplon Pass, smallmouth bass, solemn mass, tourist class, underclass, underpass, upper-class, water glass, working-class • atomic mass, critical mass, laughing jackass, snake in the grass

assable \as-ə-bəl\ passable • im-passable, irascible • unsurpassable

assail \äs-əl\ see OSSAL

assal \as-əl\ see ASSEL[2]

assar \as-ər\ see ASSER

asse[1] \as\ see ASS[3]

asse[2] \äs\ see OS[1]

assed \ast\ see AST[2]

assee \as-ē\ see ASSY

assel[1] \äs-əl\ see OSSAL

assel[2] \as-əl\ Basil, castle, facile, hassle, passel, tassel, vassal, wres-tle • forecastle

asser \as-ər\ crasser, gasser • amasser, harasser • antimacassar

asset \as-ət\ see ACET

assian \ash-ən\ see ASSION

assible \as-ə-bəl\ see ASSABLE

assic \as-ik\ classic • Jurassic, Triassic • neoclassic, semiclassic

assical \as-i-kəl\ classical, fascicle • semiclassical

assid \as-əd\ see ACID

assie[1] \as-ē\ see ASSY

assie[2] \äs-ē\ see OSSY[1]

assim \äs-əm\ see OSSUM

assin \as-³n\ see ASTEN[2]

assion \ash-ən\ ashen, fashion, passion, ration • compassion, high fashion, impassion, refashion • after a fashion

assis \as-ē\ see ASSY

assist \ā-sist\ bassist, racist • con-trabassist, double bassist

assive \as-iv\ massive, passive • impassive

assle \as-əl\ see ASSEL[2]

assness \as-nəs\ see ASTNESS

asso[1] \as-ō\ basso, lasso • El Paso, Picasso, sargasso

asso[2] \äs-ō\ Picasso • Burkina Faso

assock \as-ək\ cassock, hassock

assus \as-əs\ see ASSIS

assy \as-ē\ brassy, chassis, classy, gassy, glassy, grassy, lassie, sassy • Tallahassee • Haile Selassie

ast[1] \əst\ see UST[1]

ast[2] \ast\ blast, cast, caste, fast, hast, last, mast, past, vast • aghast, at last, avast, Belfast, bombast, broadcast, contrast, downcast, forecast, foremast, full blast, gymnast, half-caste, half-mast, mainmast, miscast, news-cast, offcast, outcast, repast,

sandblast, sportscast, steadfast, topmast, typecast, unasked, webcast, windblast • acid-fast, at long last, colorcast, colorfast, counterblast, flabbergast, hard-and-fast, mizzenmast, overcast, plaster cast, simulcast, telecast, weathercast • enthusiast, iconoclast
—*also* -ed *forms of verbs listed at* ASS³

asta \as-tə\ canasta • Mount Shasta

astable \at-ə-bəl\ see ATIBLE

astard \as-tərd\ bastard, dastard, plastered

aste¹ \āst\ see ACED

aste² \ast\ see AST²

asted \as-təd\ blasted, masted
—*also* -ed *forms of verbs listed at* AST²

asteful \āst-fəl\ tasteful, wasteful • distasteful

asten¹ \ās-ᵊn\ see ASON¹

asten² \as-ᵊn\ fasten • assassin, unfasten

aster¹ \ā-stər\ baster, taster • wine taster

aster² \as-tər\ aster, Astor, blaster, caster, castor, faster, master, pastor, plaster • bandmaster, brewmaster, broadcaster, choirmaster, disaster, dockmaster, drillmaster, grand master, headmaster, newscaster, past master, paymaster, postmaster, quizmaster, remaster, ringmaster, sandblaster, schoolmaster, scoutmaster, sportscaster, spymaster, surf caster, taskmaster, toastmaster, webcaster • alabaster, burgomaster, China aster, concertmaster, ghetto blaster, harbormaster, quartermaster, stationmaster, telecaster, wagon master, weathercaster

astered \as-tərd\ see ASTARD

astering \as-tə-riŋ\ plastering • overmastering

—*also* -ing *forms of verbs listed at* ASTER²

astes \as-tēz\ Ecclesiastes
—*also* -s, -'s, *and* -s' *forms of nouns listed at* ASTY²

asthma \az-mə\ see ASMA

astic \as-tik\ drastic, plastic, spastic • bombastic, dynastic, elastic, fantastic, gymnastic, monastic, sarcastic, scholastic • ecclesiastic, enthusiastic, iconoclastic, interscholastic

astics \as-tiks\ gymnastics, slimnastics

astid \as-təd\ see ASTED

astie \as-tē\ see ASTY²

astiness \ā-stē-nəs\ hastiness, tastiness

asting¹ \ā-stiŋ\ basting, wasting
—*also* -ing *forms of verbs listed at* ACED

asting² \as-tiŋ\ casting, lasting • fly casting, linecasting, surf casting, typecasting • central casting, everlasting
—*also* -ing *forms of verbs listed at* AST²

astle \as-əl\ see ASSEL²

astly \ast-lē\ ghastly, lastly, vastly • steadfastly

astness \as-nəs\ crassness • steadfastness • colorfastness

astor \as-tər\ see ASTER²

astoral \as-trəl\ see ASTRAL

astral \as-trəl\ astral, pastoral

astre \as-tər\ see ASTER²

asty¹ \ā-stē\ hasty, pasty, tasty

asty² \as-tē\ nasty • capacity, contrasty • angioplasty, overcapacity

asuble \as-ə-bəl\ see ASSABLE

asure¹ \ā-shər\ glacier • erasure

asure² \ā-zhər\ see AZIER

asy \as-ē\ see ASSY

at¹ \ä\ see A¹

at² \ät\ see OT¹

at³ \ət\ see UT¹

at⁴ \ȯt\ see OUGHT¹

at[5] \at\ bat, brat, cat, chat, drat, fat, flat, frat, gat, gnat, hat, mat, Matt, matte, pat, Pat, phat, plait, plat, rat, sat, scat, slat, spat, splat, stat, that, vat • all that, at bat, at that, bath mat, begat, bobcat, brickbat, brown rat, Cassatt, chitchat, combat, comsat, coon cat, cowpat, cravat, Croat, defat, dingbat, doormat, fat cat, fiat, fly at, format, fruit bat, get at, go at, hard hat, have at, hellcat, high-hat, house cat, keep at, look at, Manx cat, meerkat, milk fat, mole rat, mudflat, muskrat, nonfat, old hat, pack rat, pick at, place mat, polecat, rug rat, salt flat, silk hat, sneeze at, snowcat, stand pat, tomcat, top hat, trans fat, whereat, white hat, wildcat, wombat • acrobat, alley cat, Ararat, arrive at, autocrat, bell the cat, bureaucrat, butterfat, Cheshire cat, chew the fat, copycat, cowboy hat, democrat, diplomat, habitat, hang one's hat, jungle cat, Laundromat, leopard cat, Norway rat, off the bat, Persian cat, photostat, pit-a-pat, plutocrat, poke fun at, pussycat, rat-a-tat, reformat, scaredy-cat, smell a rat, take aim at, technocrat, thermostat, tiger cat, tit for tat, vampire bat, water rat, welcome mat, where it's at • Angora cat, aristocrat, go to the mat, Jehoshaphat, kangaroo rat, Siamese cat, single combat, talk through one's hat, ten-gallon hat, throw money at, under one's hat • proletariat, secretariat

at[6] \a\ see AH[3]

ata[1] \ät-ə\ cantata, Carlotta, pinata, regatta, ricotta, sonata • terracotta • persona non grata, Rio de la Plata

ata[2] \ät-ə\ beta, data, eta, strata, theta, zeta • peseta, potato, substrata, tomato

ata[3] \at-ə\ data • regatta • persona non grata

atable[1] \āt-ə-bəl\ debatable, inflatable, locatable, relatable, rotatable, translatable • cultivatable, untranslatable

atable[2] \at-ə-bəl\ see ATIBLE

atal \āt-ᵊl\ fatal, natal • nonfatal, postnatal, prenatal

atalie \at-ᵊl-ē\ see ATTILY

atally \āt-ᵊl-ē\ fatally, natally • postnatally, prenatally

atalyst \at-ᵊl-əst\ catalyst • philatelist

atan[1] \āt-ən\ see ATEN[1]

atan[2] \at-ᵊn\ see ATIN[2]

atant[1] \āt-ᵊnt\ blatant, latent, patent

atant[2] \at-ᵊnt\ patent • combatant • noncombatant

atar \ät-ər\ see OTTER

atary \ät-ə-rē\ see OTTERY

atch[1] \ech\ see ETCH

atch[2] \äch\ see OTCH

atch[3] \ach\ batch, catch, hatch, latch, match, natch, patch, scratch, snatch, thatch • attach, crosshatch, detach, dispatch, fair catch, from scratch, mismatch, night latch, nuthatch, outmatch, rematch, Sasquatch, unlatch, Wasatch • booby hatch, coffee klatch, escape hatch, safety match, shoulder patch

atcher[1] \äch-ər\ watcher • birdwatcher, clock-watcher, topnotcher

atcher[2] \ach-ər\ batcher, catcher, stature • cowcatcher, dispatcher, dogcatcher, eye-catcher, flycatcher, head-scratcher • body snatcher, train dispatcher

atchet \ach-ət\ hatchet, ratchet • bury the hatchet

atchily \ach-ə-lē\ patchily,
scratchily

atching \ach-iŋ\ catching • back-
scratching, cross-hatching, eye-
catching, head-scratching,
nonmatching
—*also* -ing *forms of verbs listed at*
ATCH³

atchman \ach-mən\ see OTCHMAN

atchment \ach-mənt\ catchment
• attachment, detachment

atchouli \ach-ə-lē\ see ATCHILY

atchy \ach-ē\ catchy, patchy,
scratchy • Apache

ate¹ \āt\ ate, bait, Cate, crate, date,
eight, fate, freight, gait, gate,
grate, great, hate, Kate, late,
mate, pate, plait, plate, rate, sate,
skate, slate, spate, state, straight,
strait, trait, wait, weight • abate,
aerate, age-mate, airfreight, await,
bandmate, baseplate, Bass Strait,
berate, birthrate, blank slate,
blind date, bookplate, breastplate,
cheapskate, checkmate, citrate,
classmate, collate, create, cre-
mate, curate, cut-rate,
deadweight, death rate, debate,
deflate, dictate, dilate, donate,
elate, equate, estate, filtrate, first-
rate, fixate, floodgate, flyweight,
frustrate, gestate, gyrate, help-
mate, home plate, hot plate,
housemate, hydrate, ice-skate,
inflate, ingrate, inmate, innate,
instate, irate, khanate, Kuwait,
lactate, legate, lightweight, locate,
magnate, mandate, messmate,
migrate, misstate, mutate, name-
plate, narrate, negate, nitrate,
notate, of late, orate, ornate,
outwait, placate, playdate, play-
mate, portrait, postdate, predate,
primate, prime rate, probate,
prorate, prostrate, pulsate, rain
date, rebate, relate, restate, room-
mate, rotate, schoolmate, seat-
mate, sedate, shipmate, soul mate,
spectate, stagnate, stalemate,
substrate, tailgate, teammate,
tenth-rate, third-rate, tinplate, to
date, tollgate, translate, tristate,
truncate, update, upstate, V-8,
vacate, vibrate, workmate • abdi-
cate, acclimate, activate, advo-
cate, aggravate, aggregate, agitate,
allocate, alternate, amputate,
animate, annotate, apartheid,
apostate, arbitrate, automate,
bantamweight, Bering Strait,
cabinmate, Cabot Strait, calcu-
late, calibrate, caliphate, candi-
date, captivate, carbonate,
carbon-date, castigate, celebrate,
chief of state, chlorinate, circu-
late, city-state, cogitate, collocate,
compensate, complicate, concen-
trate, condensate, confiscate,
conjugate, consecrate, constipate,
consummate, contemplate, cop-
perplate, correlate, corrugate,
counterweight, culminate, culti-
vate, Davis Strait, decimate, deco-
rate, dedicate, dehydrate,
delegate, demarcate, demonstrate,
denigrate, Denmark Strait, deviate, deprecate, desecrate, desig-
nate, desolate, detonate,
devastate, deviate, dislocate,
dissipate, distillate, dominate,
double date, duplicate, educate,
elevate, elongate, emanate, emi-
grate, emirate, emulate, escalate,
estimate, excavate, exchange rate,
exculpate, explicate, expurgate,
extirpate, extricate, fabricate,
fascinate, fashion plate, feather-
weight, federate, flagellate, fluctu-
ate, formulate, fulminate,
fumigate, generate, germinate,
Golden Gate, graduate, granulate,
gravitate, heavyweight, hesitate,
hibernate, Hudson Strait, hyphen-
ate, illustrate, imitate, immigrate,

immolate, implicate, incarnate, incubate, inculcate, indicate, infiltrate, in-line skate, innovate, instigate, insulate, interstate, intimate, inundate, irrigate, irritate, isolate, iterate, lacerate, laminate, laureate, legislate, levitate, liberate, license plate, liquidate, litigate, lubricate, magistrate, marinate, masticate, mediate, medicate, meditate, middleweight, militate, mitigate, moderate, modulate, mortgage rate, motivate, multistate, mutilate, nation-state, nauseate, navigate, nominate, obfuscate, obligate, obviate, on a plate, operate, orchestrate, oscillate, out-of-date, overstate, overweight, paperweight, penetrate, percolate, perforate, permeate, perpetrate, police state, pollinate, populate, potentate, predicate, profligate, promulgate, propagate, punctuate, radiate, real estate, recreate, re-create, regulate, reinstate, relegate, relocate, renovate, replicate, reprobate, resonate, roller-skate, ruminate, running mate, salivate, saturate, scintillate, second-rate, segregate, self-portrait, separate, ship of state, silver plate, simulate, situate, speculate, stablemate, starting gate, steady state, stimulate, stipulate, subjugate, sublimate, suffocate, sultanate, supplicate, surrogate, syncopate, syndicate, tablemate, tabulate, target date, terminate, tête-à-tête, titillate, tolerate, triplicate, underrate, understate, underweight, vaccinate, vacillate, validate, vegetate, venerate, ventilate, vertebrate, vindicate, violate, vitiate, Watergate, welfare state, welterweight • abbreviate, accel-

erate, accentuate, accommodate, accumulate, adjudicate, adulterate, affiliate, agglomerate, alienate, alleviate, amalgamate, ameliorate, annihilate, anticipate, appreciate, appropriate, approximate, articulate, asphyxiate, assassinate, assimilate, associate, at any rate, attenuate, authenticate, barbiturate, bicarbonate, capitulate, certificate, coagulate, collaborate, commemorate, commiserate, communicate, compassionate, confederate, conglomerate, congratulate, consolidate, contaminate, cooperate, coordinate, corroborate, deactivate, decapitate, decelerate, deescalate, defoliate, degenerate, deliberate, delineate, depopulate, depreciate, desegregate, devaluate, discriminate, disintegrate, disseminate, dissociate, domesticate, elaborate, electroplate, eliminate, elucidate, emaciate, emancipate, emasculate, encapsulate, enumerate, enunciate, equivocate, eradicate, evacuate, evaluate, evaporate, exaggerate, exasperate, exfoliate, exhilarate, exonerate, expropriate, extenuate, exterminate, facilitate, fish or cut bait, gesticulate, hallucinate, humiliate, illuminate, impersonate, inactivate, inaugurate, incarcerate, incinerate, incorporate, incriminate, indoctrinate, inebriate, infatuate, infuriate, ingratiate, initiate, inoculate, insinuate, interpolate, interrelate, interrogate, intimidate, intoxicate, invalidate, investigate, invigorate, irradiate, Italianate, Korea Strait, legitimate, manipulate, necessitate, negotiate, noncandidate, obliterate, officiate, Orange Free State, orientate, originate, oxygenate, participate, perpetuate, pontificate, precipitate, predominate, prefabricate, premeditate, prevaricate, procrastinate, prognosticate, proliferate, proportionate, quadruplicate, quintuplicate, reciprocate, recuperate, redecorate, reduplicate, reeducate, refrigerate, regenerate, regurgitate, reincarnate, reiterate, rejuvenate, repudiate, resuscitate, retaliate, reverberate, Singapore Strait, sophisticate, subordinate, substantiate, vanity plate • adjustable rate, circumnavigate, decontaminate, deteriorate, differentiate, discombobulate, disorientate, disproportionate, excommunicate, expiration date, hyperventilate, incapacitate, intermediate, misappropriate, overcompensate, overeducate, overestimate, overmedicate, overpopulate, overstimulate, recapitulate, rehabilitate, renegotiate, superannuate, underestimate

ate² \at\ see AT⁵
ate³ \ät\ see OT¹
ate⁴ \ät-ē\ see ATI¹
ate⁵ \ət\ see UT¹

ated \āt-əd\ dated, fated, gated, stated • belated, ill-fated, outdated, related, truncated • animated, antiquated, caffeinated, calculated, carbonated, complicated, corrugated, dedicated, educated, elevated, hyphenated, integrated, laminated, liberated, perforated, saturated, simulated, syncopated, understated • affiliated, articulated, coordinated, decaffeinated, domesticated, encapsulated, incorporated, inebriated, interrelated, intoxicated, opinionated, premeditated, sophisticated, uncalculated, uncomplicated, underinflated,

unmitigated, unsaturated • unadulterated, unanticipated, undereducated, underpopulated, unsophisticated • underappreciated
—*also* -ed *forms of verbs listed at* ATE¹

ateful \āt-fəl\ fateful, grateful, hateful • ungrateful
atel¹ \ət-ᵊl\ see OTTLE
atel² \āt-ᵊl\ see ATAL
ateless \āt-ləs\ dateless, weightless
atelist \at-ᵊl-əst\ see ATALYST
ately¹ \āt-lē\ greatly, lately, stately • innately • Johnny-come-lately
ately² \at-ᵊl-ē\ see ATTILY
atem \ät-əm\ see ATUM¹
atement \āt-mənt\ statement • abatement, misstatement, restatement • overstatement, reinstatement, understatement
aten¹ \āt-ᵊn\ Dayton, Satan, straighten
aten² \at-ᵊn\ see ATIN²
aten³ \ät-ᵊn\ see OTTEN
atent¹ \āt-ᵊnt\ see ATANT¹
atent² \at-ᵊnt\ see ATANT²
ater¹ \ȯt-ər\ daughter, slaughter, tauter, water • backwater, bathwater, breakwater, deepwater, dishwater, floodwater, forequarter, freshwater, goddaughter, Goldwater, granddaughter, groundwater, headwater, highwater, hindquarter, hold water, hot water, ice water, jerkwater, manslaughter, meltwater, rainwater, saltwater, seawater, selfslaughter, stepdaughter, still water, tap water, tidewater, tread water, wastewater, white-water • above water, holy water, in deep water, mineral water, overwater, running water, soda water, toilet water, underwater • dead in the water, fish out of water, hell or high water

ater[2] \āt-ər\ see ATOR
atering \ȯt-ə-riŋ\ slaughtering
• mouthwatering • overwatering
atery \ät-ə-rē\ see OTTERY
ates[1] \āts\ Yeats • Gulf States
• Levant States, Papal States,
Trucial States • Persian Gulf
States, United States • house of
delegates
—*also* -s, -'s, *and* -s' *forms of
nouns and* -s *forms of verbs listed
at* ATE[1]
ates[2] \āt-ēz\ Euphrates
—*also* -s, -'s, *and* -s' *forms of
nouns listed at* ATY
atest \āt-əst\ latest • at the latest
—*also* -est *forms of adjectives
listed at* ATE[1]
atey \āt-ē\ see ATY
ath[1] \äth\ see OTH[1]
ath[2] \ȯth\ see OTH[2]
ath[3] \ath\ bath, hath, lath, math,
path, wrath • birdbath, blood-
bath, flight path, footbath, foot-
path, glide path, half bath,
sunbath, towpath, warpath • af-
termath, bridle path, psychopath,
shower bath, take a bath,
telepath, whirlpool bath • so-
ciopath
atha \ät-ə\ see ATA[1]
athe[1] \āth\ bathe, lathe, scathe,
swathe • sunbathe
athe[2] \ath\ see ATH[3]
ather[1] \äth-ər\ bother, father,
rather • forefather, godfather,
grandfather, Our Father, stepfa-
ther • city father, founding father,
Holy Father
ather[2] \əth-ər\ see OTHER[1]
ather[3] \ath-ər\ blather, Cather,
gather, lather, rather, slather
• woolgather
athering \ath-riŋ\ woolgathering
—*also* -ing *forms of verbs listed at*
ATHER[3]
athi \ät-ē\ see ATI[1]

athlon \ath-lən\ decathlon, pentathlon, triathlon
ati[1] \ät-ē\ Dottie, dotty, knotty,
naughty, potty, Scotty, snotty,
spotty • karate, Scarlatti • glit-
terati, Gujarati, literati, manicotti,
Maserati • illuminati
ati[2] \atē\ see ATTY
ati[3] \äts\ see OTS
ati[4] \as\ see ASS[3]
atia \ā-shə\ see ACIA
atial \ā-shəl\ see ACIAL
atian \ā-shən\ see ATION[1]
atians \ā-shənz\ see ATIONS
atible \at-ə-bəl\ compatible, getat-
able • incompatible
atic[1] \ät-ik\ see OTIC
atic[2] \at-ik\ attic, static • aquatic,
asthmatic, chromatic, climatic,
dogmatic, dramatic, ecstatic,
emphatic, erratic, fanatic, lym-
phatic, phlegmatic, pneumatic,
pragmatic, prismatic, quadratic,
rheumatic, schematic, Socratic,
thematic, traumatic • acrobatic,
Adriatic, aerobatic, antistatic,
aromatic, Asiatic, autocratic,
automatic, bureaucratic, charis-
matic, cinematic, democratic,
diplomatic, emblematic, enig-
matic, Hippocratic, nonemphatic,
operatic, photostatic, problem-
atic, programmatic, symptomatic,
systematic, technocratic, thermo-
static, undogmatic, undramatic
• aristocratic, axiomatic, diagram-
matic, electrostatic, idiomatic,
melodramatic, overdramatic,
overemphatic, psychosomatic,
uncinematic, undemocratic,
undiplomatic • semiautomatic
atica \at-i-kə\ hepatica, sciatica,
viatica
atical \at-i-kəl\ fanatical, grammat-
ical, sabbatical • mathematical,
ungrammatical
atics \at-iks\ dramatics • acro-

batics, mathematics
—*also* -s, -'s, *and* -s' *forms of
nouns listed at* ATIC[2]
atie \āt-ē\ see ATY
atiens \ā-shənz\ see ATIONS
atik \at-ik\ see ATIC[2]
atile \at-ᵊl-ē\ see ATTILY
atim \āt-əm\ see ATUM[1]
atin[1] \ät-ᵊn\ see OTTEN
atin[2] \at-ᵊn\ batten, fatten, flatten,
Latin, Patton, satin • Manhattan,
Mountbatten, pig latin, Powhatan
atin[3] \āt-ᵊn\ see ATEN[1]
ating \āt-iŋ\ grating, plating, rating,
skating • bearbaiting, bullbaiting,
call-waiting, frustrating, race-
baiting, self-hating, self-rating,
speed skating • aggravating, cal-
culating, carbon dating, fascinat-
ing, figure skating, in-line skating,
maid-in-waiting, nauseating,
operating, penetrating, suffocat-
ing, titillating • accommodating,
discriminating, humiliating, lady-
in-waiting, self-deprecating, self-
operating, self-regulating,
self-replicating, subordinating,
undeviating, unhesitating • self-
perpetuating
—*also* -ing *forms of verbs listed at*
ATE[1]
atinous \at-nəs\ see ATNESS
ation[1] \ā-shən\ Asian, Haitian,
nation, ration, station, Thracian
• aeration, Alsatian, carnation,
causation, cessation, cetacean,
citation, Claymation, conflation,
C ration, creation, cremation,
Croatian, crustacean, dalmatian,
damnation, deflation, dictation,
dilation, donation, duration,
elation, equation, Eurasian, filtra-
tion, fixation, flirtation, flotation,
formation, foundation, frustra-
tion, gas station, gestation, grada-
tion, gyration, hydration,
inflation, K ration, lactation,

legation, libation, location, migra-
tion, mutation, narration, nega-
tion, notation, oration, ovation,
plantation, privation, probation,
prostration, pulsation, quotation,
relation, rotation, salvation, seda-
tion, sensation, space station,
stagnation, starvation, substation,
summation, taxation, temptation,
translation, truncation, vacation,
vibration, vocation, way station,
workstation • abdication, aberra-
tion, acclamation, accusation,
activation, adaptation, admira-
tion, adoration, adulation, affec-
tation, affirmation, aggravation,
aggregation, agitation, allegation,
allocation, amputation, altera-
tion, altercation, alternation,
Amerasian, animation, annexa-
tion, annotation, Appalachian,
application, approbation, arbitra-
tion, aspiration, attestation, aug-
mentation, automation, aviation,
avocation, calculation, calibra-
tion, cancellation, carbonation,
celebration, chlorination, circula-
tion, coloration, combination,
commendation, commutation,
compensation, compilation,
complication, computation, con-
centration, condemnation,
condensation, confirmation,
confiscation, conflagration, con-
frontation, congregation, conjuga-
tion, connotation, consecration,
conservation, consolation, con-
stellation, consternation,
constipation, consultation, con-
templation, conversation, convo-
cation, coronation, corporation,
correlation, corrugation, crop
rotation, culmination, cultivation,
cumulation, declamation, declara-
tion, decoration, dedication,
defamation, defecation, deforma-
tion, degradation, dehydration,

delegation, demonstration, denigration, deportation, deprivation, derivation, desecration, designation, desolation, desperation, destination, detonation, devastation, deviation, dislocation, dissertation, divination, domination, duplication, education, elevation, emigration, emulation, escalation, estimation, evocation, exaltation, excavation, exclamation, expectation, expiration, explanation, exploitation, exploration, exportation, exultation, fabrication, fascination, federation, fermentation, filling station, fire station, flagellation, fluoridation, fluctuation, forestation, formulation, fragmentation, fumigation, gene mutation, generation, germination, graduation, habitation, heat prostration, hesitation, hibernation, hyphenation, illustration, imitation, immigration, implantation, implication, importation, incantation, incarnation, inclination, incubation, indentation, indication, indignation, infestation, infiltration, inflammation, information, innovation, inspiration, installation, instigation, insulation, integration, intonation, invitation, invocation, irrigation, irritation, isolation, jubilation, laceration, lamentation, legislation, levitation, liberation, limitation, liquidation, litigation, lubrication, medication, meditation, misquotation, mistranslation, moderation, modulation, molestation, motivation, multination, mutilation, navigation, nomination, obfuscation, obligation, observation, occupation, operation, orchestration, ordination, oscillation, ostentation, penetration, percolation, perforation, perspiration, pigmentation, police station, pollination, population, power station, preparation, presentation, preservation, proclamation, procreation, prolongation, propagation, protestation, provocation, publication, punctuation, radiation, recitation, re-creation, recreation, reformation, refutation, registration, regulation, rehydration, relaxation, relocation, renovation, replication, reputation, reservation, resignation, respiration, restoration, retardation, revelation, revocation, ruination, sanitation, saturation, segmentation, segregation, separation, service station, simulation, situation, speculation, stimulation, stipulation, stylization, suffocation, syncopation, syndication, tabulation, termination, T formation, titillation, toleration, transformation, transmigration, transportation, trepidation, tribulation, usurpation, vaccination, valuation, variation, vegetation, veneration, ventilation, vindication, violation, weather station • abbreviation, abomination, acceleration, accommodation, accreditation, accumulation, adjudication, administration, affiliation, alienation, amplification, annihilation, anticipation, appreciation, appropriation, approximation, argumentation, articulation, asphyxiation, assassination, assimilation, association, authentication, authorization, beautification, centralization, certification, civilization, clarification, classification, coeducation, cohabitation, collaboration, colonization, commemoration, communication, confederation, configuration, congratulation, consideration, consolidation, contamination, continuation, cooperation, coordination, cross-pollination, crystallization, de-escalation, deforestation, degeneration, deification, deliberation, demonization, denomination, denunciation, depreciation, deregulation, desegregation, determination, devaluation, digitization, discoloration, discrimination, disinclination, disintegration, dissemination, documentation, dramatization, echolocation, elaboration, elimination, elucidation, emancipation, enumeration, equalization, eradication, evacuation, evaluation, evaporation, exaggeration, examination, exasperation, exhilaration, extermination, falsification, feminization, fertilization, fortification, globalization, glorification, gratification, hallucination, harmonization, humiliation, hyperinflation, illumination, imagination, immunization, impersonation, implementation, improvisation, inauguration, incarceration, incineration, incorporation, incrimination, indoctrination, infatuation, initiation, inoculation, instrumentation, interpretation, interrelation, interrogation, intimidation, intoxication, invalidation, investigation, itemization, justification, legalization, liberalization, magnetization, magnification, manifestation, manipulation, mechanization, memorization, misapplication, miscalculation, misinformation, mobilization, modernization, modification, multiplication, mystification, nationalization, naturalization, negotiation, normalization, notifi-

cation, obliteration, organization, origination, orientation, ornamentation, overinflation, oxygenation, participation, pasteurization, perpetuation, polarization, postgraduation, post-Reformation, precipitation, predestination, preoccupation, prepublication, preregistration, prettification, procrastination, proliferation, pronunciation, purification, qualification, ratification, reaffirmation, realization, recommendation, recuperation, redecoration, rededication, reduplication, reforestation, reformulation, refrigeration, regeneration, regimentation, reincarnation, reiteration, rejuvenation, remuneration, renunciation, representation, retaliation, reverberation, sedimentation, Serbo-Croatian, signification, simplification, socialization, solicitation, sophistication, specialization, specification, stabilization, standardization, sterilization, subordination, supplementation, transfiguration, uglification, unification, unionization, urbanization, verification, victimization, vocalization, vulgarization, westernization, x-radiation • characterization, circumnavigation, commercialization, criminalization, cross-examination, decentralization, decontamination, deterioration, differentiation, disorientation, disorganization, disqualification, diversification, electrification, excommunication, experimentation, generalization, homogenization, hospitalization, hyperventilation, idealization, identification, insubordination, intensification, megacorporation, militarization, miniaturization, misappropriation, miscommuni-

cation, misinterpretation, mispro-
nunciation, misrepresentation,
monopolization, overcompensa-
tion, overpopulation, personifica-
tion, popularization,
reconciliation, reconsideration,
rehabilitation, reorganization,
revitalization, solidification, un-
derestimation, visualization

ation² \ā-zhən\ see ASION

ation³ \ash-ən\ see ASSION

ational¹ \ā-shnəl\ sensational • con-
frontational, congregational,
conversational, educational, gen-
erational, gravitational, inspira-
tional, motivational, recreational
• coeducational, improvisational,
organizational

ational² \ash-nəl\ national, rational
• irrational • international, multi-
national

ationist \ā-shnəst\ conservationist,
isolationist, preservationist, segre-
gationist

ations \ā-shənz\ Galatians, rela-
tions • Lamentations, League of
Nations, Revelations • United
Nations

atious \ā-shəs\ see ACIOUS

atis \at-əs\ see ATUS²

atist \āt-əst\ see ATEST

atitude \at-ə-tüd\ see ATTITUDE

atius \ā-shəs\ see ACIOUS

ative \āt-iv\ dative, native • cre-
ative, nonnative • contemplative,
cumulative, decorative, imitative,
innovative, irritative, legislative,
meditative, operative, penetrative,
qualitative, quantitative, spec-
ulative, vegetative • admin-
istrative, appreciative, au-
thoritative, collaborative, com-
memorative, communicative,
cooperative, degenerative,
deliberative, investigative, post-
operative • uncommunica-
tive

atl \ät-ᵊl\ see OTTLE

atlas \at-ləs\ atlas, Atlas, fatless,
hatless

atless \at-ləs\ see ATLAS

atli \ät-lē\ see OTLY

atling \at-liŋ\ rattling • saber rattling
   —*also* -ing *forms of verbs listed at*
ATTLE

atly \at-lē\ flatly, rattly

atness \at-nəs\ fatness, flatness
• gelatinous

ato¹ \ät-ō\ auto, blotto, grotto,
lotto, motto, Otto • legato, stac-
cato, tomato, vibrato • moderato,
pizzicato

ato² \āt-ō\ Cato, Plato • potato,
tomato • couch potato, hot potato, plum tomato, sweet potato
• cherry tomato

atom \at-əm\ see ATUM²

aton \at-ᵊn\ see ATIN²

ator \āt-ər\ crater, dater, freighter,
gator, grater, hater, later, satyr,
skater, traitor, waiter • creator,
curator, debater, dictator, dona-
tor, dumbwaiter, equator, first-
rater, headwaiter, ice-skater,
locator, Mercator, migrator,
narrator, pond skater, rotator,
spectator, speed skater, tailgater,
theater, third-rater, translator
• abdicator, activator, agitator,
alligator, alternator, animator,
arbitrator, aviator, calculator,
carburetor, circulator, commen-
tator, cultivator, decorator,
demonstrator, educator, elevator,
escalator, estimator, excavator,
figure skater, fumigator, genera-
tor, gladiator, illustrator, imitator,
incubator, indicator, in-line
skater, innovator, inspirator,
instigator, insulator, liberator,
mediator, moderator, motivator,
navigator, numerator, operator,
orchestrator, percolator, perpe-

trator, pollinator, radiator, regulator, renovator, respirator, roller skater, second-rater, separator, simulator, Sunset Crater, terminator, valuator, ventilator, violator • accelerator, administrator, annihilator, collaborator, conciliator, coordinator, denominator, emancipator, enumerator, evaluator, exterminator, facilitator, grain elevator, impersonator, incinerator, interrogator, investigator, negotiator, perambulator, procrastinator, refrigerator, sooner or later
—*also* -er *forms of adjectives listed at* ATE[1]

atre \at\ see AT[5]

atric \a-trik\ Patrick • theatric • geriatric, pediatric, psychiatric

atrick \a-trik\ see ATRIC

atrics \a-triks\ theatrics • pediatrics

atrix \ā-triks\ matrix • Beatrix

atron \ā-trən\ matron, patron

ats[1] \äts\ see OTS

ats[2] \ats\ bats, rats • Bonneville Salt Flats
—*also* -s, -'s, *and* -s' *forms of nouns and* -s *forms of verbs listed at* AT[5]

atsa \ät-sə\ see ATZO[1]

atsch \ach\ see ATCH[3]

atsu \ät-sü\ Matsu • shiatsu

atsy \at-sē\ see AZI[3]

att[1] \at\ see AT[5]

att[2] \ät\ see OT[1]

atta \ät-ə\ see ATA[1]

attage \ät-ij\ see OTTAGE

attan \at-ᵊn\ see ATIN[2]

atte \at\ see AT[5]

attel \at-ᵊl\ see ATTLE

atten \at-ᵊn\ see ATIN[2]

atter \at-ər\ batter, chatter, clatter, fatter, flatter, hatter, latter, matter, patter, platter, satyr, scatter, shatter, spatter, splatter, tatter

• dark matter, gray matter, no matter, standpatter, the matter • antimatter, for that matter, pitter-patter, printed matter, subject matter

attering \at-ə-riŋ\ scattering, smattering • earth-shattering, unflattering
—*also* -ing *forms of verbs listed at* ATTER

attern \at-ərn\ pattern, Saturn, slattern • test pattern • holding pattern

attery \at-ə-rē\ battery, flattery

atti[1] \ät-ē\ see ATI[1]

atti[2] \at-ē\ see ATTY

attic \at-ik\ see ATIC[2]

attica \at-i-kə\ see ATICA

attice[1] \at-əs\ see ATUS[2]

attice[2] \at-ish\ see ATTISH

attie \at-ē\ see ATTY

attily \at-ᵊl-ē\ cattily, chattily, Natalie, nattily, rattly • philately

atting \at-iŋ\ batting, matting, tatting
—*also* -ing *forms of verbs listed at* AT[5]

attish \at-ish\ brattish, fattish, flattish

attitude \at-ə-tüd\ attitude, gratitude, latitude, platitude • beatitude, ingratitude, midlatitude

attle \at-ᵊl\ battle, cattle, prattle, rattle, tattle • beef cattle, death rattle, embattle, pitched battle, Seattle • dairy cattle, tittle-tattle

attling \at-liŋ\ see ATLING

attly[1] \at-ᵊl-ē\ see ATTILY

attly[2] \at-lē\ see ATLY

atto[1] \at-ə\ see ATA[3]

atto[2] \ät-ō\ see ATO[1]

atton \at-ᵊn\ see ATIN[2]

atty \at-ē\ batty, bratty, catty, chatty, fatty, Hattie, natty, patty, Patty, ratty • nonfatty • Cincinnati

atum[1] \ät-əm\ substratum, verbatim • ultimatum

atum[2] \at-əm\ atom • substratum
atur \āt-ər\ see ATOR
ature[1] \ā-chər\ nature • 4-H'er
• force of nature, freak of nature, human nature, Mother Nature, nomenclature, second nature
ature[2] \ach-ər\ see ATCHER[2]
aturn \at-ərn\ see ATTERN
atus[1] \āt-əs\ gratis, status, stratus • hiatus • altostratus, apparatus, cirrostratus, nimbostratus
atus[2] \at-əs\ gratis, lattice, status, stratus • clematis • altostratus, apparatus, cirrostratus, nimbostratus
atute \ach-ət\ see ATCHET
aty \āt-ē\ eighty, Haiti, Katie, Leyte, matey, weighty, yeti • Papeete
atyr \āt-ər\ see ATOR
atz[1] \ats\ see ATS[2]
atz[2] \äts\ see OTS
atzo[1] \ät-sə\ matzo • piazza
atzo[2] \ät-sō\ see AZZO
atzu \ät-sü\ see ATSU
au[1] \ō\ see OW[1]
au[2] \ü\ see EW[1]
au[3] \aù\ see OW[2]
au[4] \ò\ see AW[1]
aub \äb\ see OB[1]
aube \ōb\ see OBE[1]
auber \òb-ər\ Micawber, mud dauber
auble \äb-əl\ see ABBLE[1]
auce \òs\ see OSS[1]
aucer \ò-sər\ see OSSER
auch \äch\ see OTCH
auche \ōsh\ see OCHE[2]
auckland \òk-lənd\ Auckland, Falkland
aucous \ò-kəs\ caucus, raucous
aucus \ò-kəs\ see AUCOUS
aud[1] \òd\ awed, broad, Claude, clawed, flawed, fraud, god, jawed, laud, Maude • abroad, applaud, defraud, maraud • antifraud, wire fraud

—also -ed *forms of verbs listed at* AW[1]
aud[2] \äd\ see OD[1]
audable \òd-ə-bəl\ audible, laudable • applaudable, inaudible
aude[1] \aùd-ē\ see OWDY
aude[2] \òd-ē\ see AWDY
aude[3] \òd\ see AUD[1]
audible \òd-ə-bəl\ see AUDABLE
audit \òd-ət\ audit, plaudit
audy[1] \äd-ē\ see ODY[1]
audy[2] \òd-ē\ see AWDY
auer \aùr\ see OWER[2]
auffeur \ō-fər\ see OFER
auge \āj\ see AGE[3]
auged \ājd\ see AGED
auger[1] \ò-gər\ see OGGER[2]
auger[2] \ā-jər\ see AGER[1]
augh[1] \af\ see APH
augh[2] \ä\ see A[1]
augh[3] \äk\ see ACH[1]
augh[4] \ò\ see AW[1]
aughable \af-ə-bəl\ see AFFABLE
augham \òm\ see AUM[1]
aughn[1] \än\ see ON[1]
aughn[2] \òn\ see ON[3]
aught[1] \ät\ see OT[1]
aught[2] \òt\ see OUGHT[1]
aughter[1] \af-tər\ see AFTER
aughter[2] \òt-ər\ see ATER[1]
aughty[1] \òt-ē\ haughty, naughty • Buonarroti
aughty[2] \ät-ē\ see ATI[1]
augre \òg-ər\ see OGGER[2]
augur \òg-ər\ see OGGER[2]
aui \aù-ē\ see OWIE
auk \òk\ see ALK
aukee \ò-kē\ see ALKIE
aul \òl\ see ALL[1]
aulay \ò-lē\ see AWLY
auld[1] \òl\ see ALL[1]
auld[2] \ō\ see OW[1]
auled \òld\ see ALD[1]
auler \ò-lər\ see ALLER[1]
aulin \ò-lən\ see ALLEN
auling \ò-liŋ\ see ALLING
aulish \ò-lish\ see ALLISH

aulk \ȯk\ see ALK
aulker \ȯ-kər\ see ALKER
aulking \ȯ-kiŋ\ see ALKING
aulle \ȯl\ see ALL[1]
aulm \ȯm\ see AUM[1]
ault[1] \ȯlt\ see ALT
ault[2] \ō\ see OW[1]
aulter \ȯl-tər\ see ALTER
aulting \ȯl-tiŋ\ see ALTING
aultless \ȯlt-ləs\ see ALTLESS
aulty \ȯl-tē\ see ALTY
aum[1] \ȯm\ qualm • meerschaum
aum[2] \äm\ see OM[1]
aun[1] \än\ see ON[1]
aun[2] \ən\ see UN[1]
aun[3] \ȯn\ see ON[3]
aun[4] \aůn\ see OWN[2]
auna[1] \än-ə\ see ANA[1]
auna[2] \ȯn-ə\ see ONNA[1]
aunch[1] \änch\ conch, paunch, stanch
aunch[2] \ȯnch\ haunch, launch, paunch, stanch, staunch
aunchy \ȯn-chē\ paunchy, raunchy
aunder[1] \ȯn-dər\ launder, maunder
aunder[2] \än-dər\ see ONDER[1]
aunish \än-ish\ see ONISH
aunt[1] \ȯnt\ daunt, flaunt, gaunt, haunt, jaunt, taunt, want • avaunt
aunt[2] \ant\ see ANT[5]
aunt[3] \änt\ see ANT[2]
aunted \ȯnt-əd\ see ONTED
aunter[1] \änt-ər\ saunter, taunter
aunter[2] \ȯnt-ər\ haunter, saunter, taunter
aunty[1] \ȯnt-ē\ flaunty, jaunty
aunty[2] \änt-ē\ see ANTI[1]
aunus \än-əs\ see ONUS[1]
aupe \ōp\ see OPE
auphin \ō-fən\ see OFFIN
aur[1] \aůr\ see OWER[2]
aur[2] \ȯr\ see OR[1]
aura[1] \ȯr-ə\ see ORA
aura[2] \är-ə\ see ARA[1]
aural \ȯr-əl\ see ORAL
aure \ȯr\ see OR[1]
aurea \ȯr-ē-ə\ see ORIA

aurean \ȯr-ē-ən\ see ORIAN
aurel \ȯr-əl\ see ORAL
auren[1] \är-ən\ see ARIN
auren[2] \ȯr-ən\ see ORIN[1]
aurence \ȯr-ən(t)s\ see AWRENCE
aureus \ȯr-ē-əs\ see ORIOUS
auri \aůr-ē\ see OWERY
aurian \ȯr-ē-ən\ see ORIAN
auric \ȯr-ik\ see ORIC
aurice[1] \är-əs\ see ORRIS[1]
aurice[2] \ȯr-əs\ see AURUS
auricle \ȯr-i-kəl\ see ORICAL
aurie[1] \ȯr-ē\ see ORY
aurie[2] \är-ē\ see ARI[1]
aurous \ȯr-əs\ see AURUS
aurus \ȯr-əs\ Boris, chorus, Doris, Horace, Maurice, morris, Morris, Norris, porous, Taurus • Centaurus, decorous, Dolores, phosphorous, sonorous, thesaurus • allosaurus, brontosaurus, stegosaurus • apatosaurus, tyrannosaurus
aury \ȯr-ē\ see ORY
aus[1] \aůs\ see OUSE[2]
aus[2] \ȯz\ see AUSE[1]
ausal \ȯ-zəl\ causal • menopausal
ause[1] \ȯz\ cause, 'cause, clause, gauze, pause, yaws • applause, because • grasp at straws, menopause, Santa Claus
— *also -s, -'s, and -s' forms of nouns and -s forms of verbs listed at* AW[1]
ause[2] \əz\ see EUSE[1]
auseous \ȯ-shəs\ see AUTIOUS
auss \aůs\ see OUSE[1]
aussie[1] \äs-ē\ see OSSY[1]
aussie[2] \ȯ-sē\ see OSSY[2]
aust[1] \aůst\ see OUST[1]
aust[2] \ȯst\ see OST[3]
austen \ȯs-tən\ see OSTON
austin \ȯs-tən\ see OSTON
austless \ȯst-ləs\ costless • exhaustless
aut[1] \ō\ see OW[1]
aut[2] \aůt\ see OUT[3]

aut³ \ät\ see OT[1]
aut⁴ \ȯt\ see OUGHT[1]
aute \ȯt\ see OAT
autics \ät-iks\ see OTICS
autious \ȯ-shəs\ cautious, nauseous • incautious • overcautious
auto¹ \ȯt-ō\ auto, Giotto • risotto
auto² \ät-ō\ see ATO[1]
auve \ōv\ see OVE[2]
auze \ȯz\ see AUSE[1]
auzer \au̇-zər\ see OUSER
av¹ \äv\ see OLVE[2]
av² \av\ see ALVE[2]
ava¹ \äv-ə\ fava, guava, java, Java, lava • cassava • balaclava, Bratislava, Costa Brava
ava² \av-ə\ java • balaclava
avage \av-ij\ ravage, savage
avan \ā-vən\ see AVEN[1]
avant \av-ənt\ haven't, savant
avarice \av-rəs\ see AVEROUS
ave¹ \äv-ā\ clave, grave, Jahveh
ave² \āv\ brave, cave, crave, Dave, fave, gave, grave, knave, lave, nave, pave, rave, save, shave, slave, stave, they've, waive, wave, Wave • airwave, behave, brain wave, close shave, cold wave, concave, conclave, deprave, enclave, engrave, enslave, forgave, Great Slave, heat wave, octave, repave, shock wave, shortwave, sine wave, sound wave, wage slave • after-shave, Fingal's Cave, Mammoth Cave, microwave, misbehave, tidal wave • permanent wave, radio wave
ave³ \av\ see ALVE[3]
ave⁴ \äv\ see OLVE[2]
aved \āvd\ waved • depraved, unsaved
—also -ed forms of verbs listed at AVE[2]
avel \av-əl\ cavil, gavel, gravel, ravel, travel • unravel • gavel-to-gavel
aveling \av-liŋ\ traveling

—also -ing forms of verbs listed at AVEL
avement \āv-mənt\ pavement • enslavement
aven¹ \ā-vən\ Avon, craven, graven, haven, maven, raven, shaven • New Haven, night raven • riboflavin, Winter Haven • Stratford-upon-Avon
aven² \av-ən\ see AVIN
aven't \av-ənt\ see AVANT
aver¹ \äv-ər\ slaver • palaver
aver² \ā-vər\ braver, caver, favor, flavor, graver, quaver, raver, savor, shaver, slaver, waiver, waver • disfavor, engraver, facesaver, flag-waver, lifesaver, screen saver, time-saver
aver³ \av-ər\ slaver • cadaver, palaver
avern \av-ərn\ cavern, tavern
averous \av-rəs\ avarice • cadaverous
avery \āv-rē\ Avery, bravery, knavery, quavery, savory, slavery • unsavory, white slavery • antislavery
avey \ā-vē\ see AVY
avia \ā-vē-ə\ Belgravia, Moldavia, Moravia • Scandinavia
avian \ā-vē-ən\ avian • Moravian • Scandinavian
avid \av-əd\ avid, gravid
avie \ā-vē\ see AVY
avil \av-əl\ see AVEL
avin \av-ən\ Avon, raven
aving \ā-viŋ\ caving, craving, paving, raving, saving, shaving • engraving, face-saving, flagwaving, lifesaving, time-saving • laborsaving
—also -ing forms of verbs listed at AVE[2]
avis \ā-vəs\ Davis, Mavis
avish¹ \ā-vish\ knavish, slavish
avish² \av-ish\ lavish, ravish
avity \av-ət-ē\ cavity, gravity • de-

pravity • antigravity, body cavity, zero gravity • center of gravity

avl \äv-əl\ see OVEL[1]

avo \äv-ō\ bravo • centavo • Rio Bravo

avon[1] \ā-vən\ see AVEN[1]

avon[2] \a-vən\ see AVIN

avor \ā-vər\ see AVER[2]

avored \ā-vərd\ favored, flavored • ill-favored
—*also* -ed *forms of verbs listed at* AVER[2]

avory \āv-rē\ see AVERY

avus \ā-vəs\ see AVIS

avvy \av-ē\ navvy, savvy

avy \ā-vē\ Davy, gravy, navy, slavey, wavy

aw[1] \ȯ\ aw, awe, caw, claw, craw, draw, flaw, gnaw, haw, jaw, la, law, maw, pa, paw, pshaw, Ra, rah, raw, saw, shah, slaw, spa, squaw, straw, thaw, yaw • band saw, bedstraw, blue law, bucksaw, buzz saw, bylaw, chain saw, Choctaw, coleslaw, Corn Law, Danelaw, declaw, dewclaw, Esau, forepaw, geegaw, grandma, grandpa, guffaw, hacksaw, handsaw, hee-haw, hurrah, in-law, jackdaw, jigsaw, last straw, leash law, lockjaw, macaw, Moose Jaw, Nassau, outdraw, outlaw, pasha, pawpaw, rickshaw, ripsaw, scofflaw, scrimshaw, seesaw, southpaw, Utah, Warsaw, whipsaw, withdraw • Arkansas, Chickasaw, Chippewa, civil law, common-law, court of law, crosscut saw, foofaraw, higher law, homestead law, in the raw, keyhole saw, Kiowa, lemon law, mackinaw, Murphy's Law, Omaha, Ottawa, oversaw, panama, private law, public law, roman law, Saginaw, son-in-law, tragic flaw, Wichita, williwaw • brother-in-law, circular saw, criminal law, daughter-in-law, father-in-law, mother-in-law, sister-in-law, stick in one's craw, unwritten law

aw[2] \äv\ see OLVE[2]

aw[3] \ȯf\ see OFF[2]

aw[4] \af\ see OFF[1]

awa[1] \ä-wə\ Chihuahua, Tarawa • Okinawa, Tokugawa

awa[2] \ä-və\ see AVA[1]

awar \aů̇r\ see OWER[2]

awber[1] \äb-ər\ see OBBER

awber[2] \ȯb-ər\ see AUBER

awd \ȯd\ see AUD[1]

awddle \äd-ᵊl\ see ODDLE

awdry \ȯ-drē\ Audrey, tawdry

awdy \ȯd-ē\ bawdy, gaudy

awe \ȯ\ see AW[1]

awed \ȯd\ see AUD[1]

aweless \ȯ-ləs\ see AWLESS

awer \ȯr\ see OR[1]

awers \ȯrz\ see OORS

awful \ȯ-fəl\ awful, lawful, offal • unlawful

awfully \ȯf-ə-lē\ awfully, lawfully • unlawfully

awing \ȯiŋ\ cloying, drawing • line drawing
—*also* -ing *forms of verbs listed at* AW[1]

awk \ȯk\ see ALK

awker \ȯ-kər\ see ALKER

awkish \ȯ-kish\ hawkish, mawkish

awky \ȯ-kē\ see ALKIE

awl \ȯl\ see ALL[1]

awler \ȯ-lər\ see ALLER[1]

awless \ȯ-ləs\ flawless, lawless

awling \ȯ-liŋ\ see ALLING

awly \ȯ-lē\ brawly, crawly, dolly, drawly, Raleigh, scrawly, squally • Bengali

awm \ȯm\ see AUM[1]

awn[1] \än\ see ON[1]

awn[2] \ȯn\ see ON[3]

awner[1] \ȯn-ər\ fawner, goner

awner[2] \än-ər\ see ONOR[1]

awney \ȯ-nē\ see AWNY[1]

awning \än-iŋ\ see ONING[1]

awny[1] \ȯ-nē\ brawny, scrawny, tawny • mulligatawny

awny[2] \än-ē\ see ANI[1]

awrence \ȯr-ən(t)s\ Florence, Lawrence, warrants • abhorrence, Saint Lawrence

awry \ȯr-ē\ see ORY

aws \ȯz\ see AUSE[1]

awse \ȯz\ see AUSE[1]

awy \ȯi\ see OY

awyer \ȯ-yər\ lawyer, sawyer • trial lawyer • criminal lawyer

ax[1] \äks\ see OX

ax[2] \aks\ ax, fax, flax, lax, max, Max, sax, tax, wax • Ajax, anthrax, beeswax, borax, broadax, climax, earwax, Fairfax, IMAX, meat-ax, pickax, poll tax, pretax, relax, sales tax, surtax, syntax, thorax • aftertax, ball of wax, battle-ax, Halifax, hidden tax, income tax, overtax, sealing wax, to the max, Turtle Wax • anticlimax
—also -s, -'s, and -s' forms of nouns and -s forms of verbs listed at ACK[2]

axant \ak-sənt\ see ACCENT

axen \ak-sən\ see AXON

axi \ak-sē\ see AXY

axon \ak-sən\ flaxen, Jackson, Saxon, waxen • Anglo-Saxon

axy \ak-sē\ maxi, taxi, waxy • air taxi • water taxi

ay[1] \ā\ a, ae, bay, bray, clay, day, eh, Faye, fey, flay, fray, gay, gray, hay, hey, Hue, j, jay, Jay, k, Kay, lay, lei, may, May, nay, née, neigh, pay, play, pray, prey, quay, Rae, ray, Ray, re, say, slay, sleigh, spay, splay, spray, stay, stray, sway, they, tray, way, weigh, whey, yea • airplay, airway, aisleway, all-day, allay, archway, array, ashtray, assay, astray, at bay, away, aweigh, ballet, base pay, belay, beltway, beret, betray, bikeway, birthday, Biscay, Bizet, blasé, Bombay, bouquet, breezeway, Broadway, buffet, byway, café, Cape May, Cartier, Cathay, causeway, chalet, child's play, cliché, convey, Coos Bay, crawlway, crochet, croquet, DA, daresay, D-day, death ray, decay, deejay, defray, delay, dismay, display, DJ, doomsday, doorway, dossier, downplay, driveway, duvet, Earl Grey, entrée, essay, fair play, fairway, field day, filet, fillet, fishway, Flag Day, flight pay, flyway, foray, forte, foul play, foyer, frappé, freeway, Friday, Galway, gangway, Gaspé, gateway, give way, gourmet, Green Bay, gunplay, hair spray, halfway, hallway, harm's way, hatchway, headway, hearsay, heyday, highway, hold sway, hooray, horseplay, in play, inlay, Jolliet, leeway, Lord's day, maguey, mainstay, make hay, Malay, Manet, Marseilles, match play, May Day, Mayday, melee, midday, midway, Midway, Millay, mislay, misplay, Monday, Monet, moray, noonday, Norway, no way, obey, OK, olé, one-way, osprey, outlay, outplay, outstay, outweigh, PA, parfait, parkway, parlay, parquet, partway, passé, pathway, payday, pearl gray, Pele, per se, Pompeii, portray, prepay, puree, purvey, raceway, Rahway, railway, relay, Rene, Renee, repay, replay, risqué, roadway, Roget, role-play, runway, sachet, saint's day, sashay, sauté, screenplay, seaway, Shark Bay, shar-pei, shipway, sick bay, sick day, sick pay, slideway, soiree, someday, soufflé, speedway, spillway, squeeze play, stairway, Steinway, stingray, straightway, stroke play, subway, Sunday, survey, swordplay, Taipei, tea tray, three-way, thruway, Thursday, today, tollway, touché, toupee, trackway, Tuesday, Twelfth Day, two-way, valet, V-day, veejay, walkway, waylay, Wednesday, weekday, wordplay, workday, X ray • Agnus Dei, A-OK, alleyway, All Fools' Day, All Saints' Day, All Souls' Day, all the way, antigay, anyway, appliqué, Arbor Day, attaché, back away, Baffin Bay, bang away, Bastille Day, beta ray, bird of prey, Biscayne Bay, blow away, Boxing Day, breakaway, break away, Bristol Bay, Buzzards Bay, by the way, cabaret, cableway, Cam Ranh Bay, canapé, Cape Cod Bay, caraway, carriageway, Cartier, castaway, cathode ray, china clay, Chippewa, cog railway, consommé, cosmic ray, croupier, cutaway, day-to-day, déclassé, devotee, Dingle Bay, disarray, disobey, divorcé, divorcée, DNA, dollar day, double play, dress-down day, eagle ray, ember day, émigré, Empire Day, entranceway, entryway, everyday, exposé, expressway, fall away, Faraday, faraway, Fathers Day, feet of clay, fiancé, fiancée, fire away, foldaway, gal Friday, gamma ray, getaway, girl Friday, giveaway, give away, Glacier Bay, Groundhog Day, Guy Fawkes Day, hell to pay, Hemingway, hideaway, hit the hay, holiday, holy day, Hudson Bay, Hugh Capet, Humboldt Bay, in a way, interplay, IRA, Joliet, judgment day, keep-away, Labor Day, layaway, lay away, lingerie, macramé, Mandalay, manta ray, matinee, meet halfway, MIA, Milky Way, Monterrey, Mother's

Day, motorway, multiday, mystery play, negligee, New Year's Day, New York Bay, night and day, off Broadway, Ojibwa, on the way, out of play, overlay, overpay, overplay, overstay, overweigh, Paraguay, passageway, pass away, passion play, pepper spray, photoplay, play-by-play, plug-and-play, power play, present-day, protégé, Prudhoe Bay, pull away, put away, Rabelais, rainy-day, reconvey, repartee, résumé, ricochet, right away, right-of-way, RNA, runaway, run away, salt away, San Jose, Santa Fe, São Tomé, Saturday, severance pay, sock away, square away, stowaway, straightaway, street railway, Table Bay, takeaway, taxiway, thataway, throwaway, throw away, Thunder Bay, triple play, turn away, Turtle Bay, underlay, underpay, underway, Uruguay, vertebra, waterway, Whitsunday, workaday, working day, Zuider Zee • Appian Way, April Fool's Day, Armistice Day, Ascension Day, Australia Day, Bay of Biscay, Botany Bay, carry away, Chesapeake Bay, Columbus Day, communiqué, corps de ballet, Delaware Bay, devil to pay, Dominion Day, Election Day, electric ray, far and away, fiddle away, Frobisher Bay, Giant's Causeway, High Holiday, instant replay, Jamaica Bay, Korea Bay, medley relay, Midsummer Day, miracle play, Montego Bay, Morgan le Fay, off-off-Broadway, out-of-the-way, papier-mâché, Patriots' Day, photo-essay, preholiday, Presidents' Day, Rogation Day, Saginaw Bay, Saint Patrick's Day, superhighway, Thanksgiving Day, Valentine's

Day, Veterans Day • Independence Day, Memorial Day, morality play • cinema verité

ay² \ē\ see EE[1]

ay³ \ī\ see Y[1]

aya¹ \ī-ə\ see IAH[1]

aya² \ä-ə\ see AIA[1]

ayable \ā-ə-bəl\ payable, playable, sayable • displayable, unplayable, unsayable

ayah \ī-ə\ see IAH[1]

ayal \āl\ see AIL

ayan¹ \ä-ən\ crayon • Chilean, Malayan, Pompeian • Galilean, Himalayan

ayan² \ī-ən\ see ION[1]

aybe¹ \ā-bē\ see ABY

aybe² \eb-ē\ see EBBY

ayday \ā-dā\ Mayday, May Day

aye¹ \ā\ see AY[1]

aye² \ī\ see Y[1]

ayed \ād\ see ADE[1]

ayer \ā-ər\ layer, mayor, payer, player, prayer, slayer, sprayer, stayer • ballplayer, betrayer, bricklayer, cardplayer, conveyor, doomsayer, manslayer, naysayer, purveyor, soothsayer, surveyor, taxpayer
—also -er *forms of adjectives listed at* AY[1]

ayered \erd\ see AIRED

ayest \ā-əst\ mayest, sayest • essayist
—also -est *forms of adjectives listed at* AY[1]

ayin¹ \ī-ən\ see ION[1]

ayin² \īn\ see INE[1]

aying \ā-iŋ\ fraying, playing, saying • bricklaying, doomsaying, longplaying, nay-saying, soothsaying, surveying, taxpaying
—also -ing *forms of verbs listed at* AY[1]

ayish \ā-ish\ clayish, grayish

ayist \ā-əst\ see AYEST

ayle \āl\ see AIL

ayless \ā-ləs\ rayless, talus, wayless • aurora australis

ayling \ā-liŋ\ see AILING

aylor \ā-lər\ see AILER

ayman \ā-mən\ see AMEN[1]

ayment \ā-mənt\ claimant, payment, raiment • co-payment, down payment, nonpayment, prepayment, stop payment

ayne \ān\ see ANE[1]

ayness \ā-nəs\ grayness, heinous, Janus • everydayness

ayo¹ \ā-ō\ see EO[1]

ayo² \ī-ō\ see IO[1]

ayon \ā-ən\ see AYAN[1]

ayor \ā-ər\ see AYER

ayou¹ \ī-ə\ see IAH[1]

ayou² \ī-ō\ see IO[1]

ayr \er\ see ARE[4]

ays¹ \ez\ fez, Fez, prez, says • Chávez, Cortés, Inez, Suez, unsays • Mayagüez

ays² \āz\ see AZE[1]

aysia \ā-zhə\ see ASIA

ay-so \ā-sō\ see ESO

ayyid¹ \ī-əd\ see YAD

ayyid² \ēd-ē\ see EEDY

az¹ \az\ see AZZ

az² \äz\ see OISE[1]

az³ \äts\ see OTS

aza¹ \äz-ə\ Gaza, plaza • piazza

aza² \az-ə\ plaza • piazza

aze¹ \āz\ blaze, braise, chaise, craze, days, daze, faze, gaze, glaze, graze, haze, laze, maize, Mays, maze, phase, phrase, praise, raise, raze, vase, ways • ablaze, amaze, appraise, crossways, dog days, edgeways, endways, leastways, lengthways, malaise, pj's, rephrase, Roget's, sideways, slantways, stargaze, weekdays • anyways, holidays, hollandaise, mayonnaise, multiphase, nowadays, out of phase, overgraze, overpraise, paraphrase • parting of the ways

—also -s, -'s, *and* -s' *forms of
nouns and* -s *forms of verbs listed
at* AY[1]

aze² \äz\ see OISE[1]

aze³ \äz-ē\ see AZI[1]

azed \āzd\ unfazed

—also -ed *forms of verbs listed at*
AZE[1]

azen \āz-ᵊn\ see AZON

azer \ā-zər\ blazer, glazer, laser,
razor, Taser • appraiser, fund-
raiser, hair-raiser, hell-raiser,
stargazer, trailblazer • crystal-
gazer, curtain-raiser

azi¹ \äz-ē\ quasi, Swazi • Benghazi
• Anasazi, Ashkenazi, kamikaze

azi² \az-ē\ see AZZY

azi³ \at-sē\ Nazi, patsy, Patsy • neo-
Nazi

azier \ā-zhər\ brazier, Frasier,
leisure, measure, pleasure, treasure

azing \ā-zin\ see AISING

azon \az-ᵊn\ blazon, brazen, raisin
• emblazon

azor \ā-zər\ see AZER

azquez \as-kəs\ see ASCUS

azy \ā-zē\ crazy, daisy, Daisy, hazy,
lazy, mazy • like crazy, stir-crazy
• Shasta daisy

azz \az\ as, has, jazz, razz • free
jazz, Hejaz, La Paz, pizzazz,
topaz, whereas • razzmatazz

azza¹ \az-ə\ see AZA²

azza² \äz-ə\ see AZA¹

azza³ \ät-sə\ see ATZO[1]

azzle \az-əl\ basil, Basil, dazzle,
frazzle • bedazzle, sweet basil
• razzle-dazzle

azzo \ät-sō\ matzo • palazzo • pa-
parazzo

azzy \az-ē\ jazzy, snazzy • pizzazzy
• Ashkenazi

E

e¹ \ā\ see AY[1]

e² \ē\ see EE[1]

é \ā\ see AY[1]

ea¹ \ā\ see AY[1]

ea² \ā-ə\ see AIA[1]

ea³ \ē\ see EE[1]

ea⁴ \ē-ə\ see IA[1]

eabee \ē-bē\ see EBE[1]

eace \ēs\ see IECE

eaceable \ē-sə-bəl\ see EASABLE[1]

each \ēch\ beach, beech, bleach,
breach, each, leach, leech, peach,
preach, reach, screech, speech,
teach • beseech, free speech, im-
peach, Long Beach, outreach, Palm
Beach, unteach • copper beech,
Myrtle Beach, Newport Beach,

overreach, part of speech, practice-
teach • Daytona Beach, figure of
speech, Huntington Beach, Miami
Beach, Omaha Beach, Redondo
Beach, Virginia Beach

eachable \ē-chə-bəl\ bleachable,
reachable, teachable • impeach-
able, unreachable, unteachable
• unimpeachable

eacher \ē-chər\ bleacher, creature,
feature, preacher, reacher,
screecher, teacher • schoolteacher
• double feature, overreacher,
practice teacher, student teacher

eaching \ē-chin\ see EECHING

eachy \ē-chē\ beachy, chichi, Nietz-
sche, peachy, preachy, screechy

eacly \ē-klē\ see EEKLY

eacon \ē-kən\ beacon, deacon, sleeken, weaken • archdeacon, Mohican, subdeacon • Nuyorican, radar beacon • radio beacon

ead[1] \ed\ bed, bled, bread, bred, dead, dread, ed, Ed, fed, fled, Fred, head, Jed, lead, led, med, Ned, pled, read, red, Red, said, shed, shred, sled, sped, spread, stead, Ted, thread, tread, wed • abed, ahead, airhead, baldhead, beachhead, bedspread, bedstead, behead, biped, blackhead, blockhead, bloodred, bloodshed, bobsled, bonehead, brain-dead, break bread, brown bread, bulkhead, bullhead, coed, corn bread, cornfed, cowshed, crossbred, daybed, deadhead, death's-head, deathbed, dogsled, drop-dead, egghead, embed, farmstead, fathead, flatbed, forehead, French bread, fry bread, gearhead, godhead, highbred, hogshead, homebred, homestead, hotbed, hothead, illbred, inbred, instead, jarhead, knock dead, lowbred, lunkhead, masthead, meathead, misled, misread, moped, outsped, outspread, phys ed, pinhead, point spread, premed, purebred, quick bread, redhead, red lead, retread, roadbed, roadstead, saphead, scarehead, screw thread, seabed, seedbed, sheepshead, shortbread, sickbed, skinhead, sorehead, spearhead, spoon bread, streambed, subhead, sweetbread, toolshed, towhead, trailhead, unbred, undead, unread, unsaid, unthread, warhead, well-bred, well-read, white-bread, whitehead, white lead, widespread, wingspread, woodshed • aforesaid, arrowhead, bubblehead, chowderhead, chucklehead, copperhead, Diamond Head, dunderhead, featherbed, featherhead, fiddlehead, figurehead, fountainhead, get ahead, gingerbread, go-ahead, hammerhead, head-tohead, infrared, interbred, knucklehead, letterhead, Lizard Head, loggerhead, Marblehead, metalhead, newlywed, overhead, overspread, pinniped, quadruped, riverbed, Samoyed, scratch one's head, showerhead, sleepyhead, slugabed, soda bread, standardbred, straight-ahead, talking head, thoroughbred, thunderhead, turn one's head, underbred, underfed, watershed • cylinder head, fireengine red, go to one's head, over one's head

ead[2] \ēd\ see EED

ead[3] \əd\ see UD[1]

eadable \ed-ə-bəl\ see EDIBLE

eaded \ed-əd\ bedded, headed • bareheaded, bullheaded, clearheaded, coolheaded, embedded, hardheaded, hotheaded, lightheaded, pigheaded, unleaded, wrongheaded • empty-headed, hydra-headed, levelheaded, muddleheaded
—*also* -ed *forms of verbs listed at* EAD[1]

eaden \ed-ᵊn\ deaden, leaden, redden • Armageddon

eader[1] \ēd-ər\ beader, bleeder, breeder, cedar, feeder, kneader, leader, pleader, reader, seeder, speeder, weeder • bandleader, cheerleader, floor leader, lay reader, lip-reader, loss leader, mind reader, nonreader, proofreader, ringleader, sight reader, stockbreeder • bottom-feeder

eader[2] \ed-ər\ cheddar, header, shredder, sledder, spreader, threader, treader • homesteader • doubleheader, triple-header

eadily \ed-ᵊl-ē\ headily, readily,
steadily • unsteadily

eading[1] \ed-iŋ\ bedding, heading,
Reading, sledding, wedding • bob-
sledding, farmsteading, subhead-
ing • featherbedding
—*also* -ing *forms of verbs listed at*
EAD[1]

eading[2] \ed-ᵊn\ see EADEN

eading[3] \ēd-ᵊn\ see EDON

eading[4] \ēd-iŋ\ see EEDING[1]

eadle[1] \ed-ᵊl\ see EDAL[1]

eadle[2] \ēd-ᵊl\ see EEDLE

eadly \ed-lē\ see EDLEY

eady[1] \ed-ē\ Eddie, eddy, Freddie,
heady, ready, steady, Teddy • al-
ready, go steady, unsteady • at the
ready, rough-and-ready

eady[2] \ēd-ē\ see EEDY

eaf[1] \ef\ see EF[1]

eaf[2] \ēf\ see IEF[1]

eafy \ē-fē\ see EEFY

eag \ēg\ see IGUE

eagan \ā-gən\ see AGIN

eager \ē-gər\ eager, meager • be-
leaguer, big leaguer, bush leaguer,
intriguer • Ivy Leaguer, Little
Leaguer, major leaguer, overeager

eagh \ā\ see AY[1]

eagle \ē-gəl\ see EGAL

eague \ēg\ see IGUE

eaguer \ē-gər\ see EAGER

eah \ē-ə\ see IA[1]

eak[1] \ēk\ beak, bleak, cheek, chic,
clique, creak, creek, Creek, eke,
freak, geek, Greek, leak, leek,
meek, peak, peek, pique, reek,
seek, sheikh, shriek, Sikh, sleek,
sneak, speak, squeak, streak,
teak, tweak, weak, week, wreak
• antique, batik, Belgique, be-
speak, blue streak, boutique,
Cloud Peak, critique, debeak,
Grays Peak, grosbeak, hairstreak,
midweek, misspeak, muzhik,
mystique, nonpeak, oblique, off-
peak, physique, Pikes Peak, pip-
squeak, technique, Tajik, unique,
workweek • Battle Creek, Boundary Peak, Chesapeake, control
freak, doublespeak, ecofreak,
Granite Peak, hide-and-seek, Holy
Week, Lassen Peak, Lenin Peak,
Martinique, Mozambique, Passion
Week, tongue-in-cheek, up the
creek, Wheeler Peak, widow's
peak • microtechnique, quarterback sneak, semi-antique • Communism Peak, opéra comique,
turn the other cheek

eak[2] \āk\ see AKE[1]

eak[3] \ek\ see ECK

eakable \ā-kə-bəl\ see AKABLE

eake \ēk\ see EAK[1]

eaked[1] \ē-kəd\ peaked, streaked

eaked[2] \ēkt\ beaked, freaked,
peaked, streaked
—*also* -ed *forms of verbs listed at*
EAK[1]

eaken \ē-kən\ see EACON

eaker[1] \ē-kər\ beaker, leaker,
phreaker, seeker, sneaker,
speaker, squeaker • loudspeaker,
self-seeker, sunseeker • keynote
speaker
—*also* -er *forms of adjectives listed
at* EAK[1]

eaker[2] \ā-kər\ see AKER[1]

eaking \ē-kiŋ\ freaking, phreaking,
sneaking, speaking, streaking
• heat-seeking, self-seeking • public speaking
—*also* -ing *forms of verbs listed at*
EAK[1]

eakish \ē-kish\ cliquish, freakish,
weakish

eakly \ē-klē\ see EEKLY

eaky \ē-kē\ cheeky, cliquey,
creaky, freaky, geeky, leaky,
sneaky, squeaky, streaky, tiki
• boutiquey, dashiki

eal[1] \ē-əl\ laryngeal, marmoreal,
pharyngeal

eal[2] \ēl\ creel, deal, eel, feel, heal,

heel, he'll, keel, kneel, meal, Neil, peal, peel, real, reel, seal, she'll, spiel, squeal, steal, steel, teal, veal, we'll, wheel, zeal • all-wheel, anneal, appeal, Bastille, big deal, big wheel, bonemeal, Camille, cam wheel, Castile, cartwheel, Cecile, chenille, cogwheel, conceal, congeal, cornmeal, done deal, eared seal, fifth wheel, fish meal, flywheel, for real, four-wheel, freewheel, fur seal, genteel, get real, good deal, great seal, handwheel, harp seal, ideal, Lucille, mill wheel, misdeal, mobile, Mobile, monk seal, mouthfeel, New Deal, newsreel, nosewheel, oatmeal, ordeal, piecemeal, pinwheel, prayer wheel, raw deal, repeal, reveal, schlemiel, spike heel, surreal, Tar Heel, unreal, unreel, unseal • bearded seal, bloodmobile, bookmobile, carbon steel, chamomile, cockatiel, color wheel, commonweal, conger eel, cut a deal, dishabille, down-at-heel, Ferris wheel, glockenspiel, goldenseal, Guayaquil, harbor seal, lamprey eel, leopard seal, megadeal, mercantile, moray eel, orange peel, package deal, paddle wheel, pedal steel, potter's wheel, reel-to-reel, skimobile, snob appeal, snowmobile, spinning reel, stainless steel, thunderpeal, waterwheel • automobile, electric eel, elephant seal, Solomon's seal, stiletto heel

eal³ \āl\ see AIL

eal⁴ \il\ see ILL

ealable \ē-lə-bəl\ peelable, reelable, stealable • appealable, concealable, resealable

ealand \ē-lənd\ see ELAND

eald \ēld\ see IELD

ealed \ēld\ see IELD

ealer \ē-lər\ dealer, feeler, healer, peeler, sealer • concealer, faith healer, four-wheeler, freewheeler, New Dealer, newsdealer, scene-stealer, side-wheeler, stern-wheeler, three-wheeler, two-wheeler, ward heeler • double-dealer, eighteen-wheeler, 18-wheeler, paddle wheeler, snowmobiler, wheeler-dealer

ealie \ē-lē\ see EELY

ealing \ē-liŋ\ see EELING

eally¹ \il-ē\ see ILLY

eally² \ē-lē\ see EELY

ealm \elm\ see ELM

ealot \el-ət\ see ELLATE

ealotry \el-ə-trē\ see ELOTRY

ealous \el-əs\ Ellis, jealous, trellis, zealous • Marcellus

ealousy \el-ə-sē\ see ELACY

ealth \elth\ health, stealth, wealth • bill of health, commonwealth, public health

ealthy \el-thē\ healthy, stealthy, wealthy • heart-healthy, unhealthy

ealty \ēl-tē\ fealty, realty

eam¹ \ēm\ beam, cream, crèeme, deem, dream, gleam, meme, Nîmes, ream, scheme, scream, seam, seem, steam, stream, team, teem, theme • agleam, airstream, bireme, blaspheme, bloodstream, centime, coal seam, cold cream, crossbeam, daydream, downstream, dream team, esteem, extreme, Gulf Stream, high beam, hornbeam, I beam, ice cream, inseam, jet stream, low beam, mainstream, midstream, millstream, moonbeam, pipe dream, redeem, regime, rhyme scheme, slipstream, sour cream, sunbeam, supreme, tag team, trireme, upstream • academe, balance beam, blow off steam, double-team, head of steam, heavy cream, on the beam, Ponzi scheme, self-

esteem • ancien régime, in the
extreme, vanishing cream • Amer-
ican dream, Bavarian cream

eam² \im\ see IM¹

eaman \ē-mən\ see EMON¹

eamed¹ \emt\ see EMPT

eamed² \emd\ steamed
—*also* -ed *forms of verbs listed at*
EAM¹

eamer \ē-mər\ creamer, dreamer,
femur, lemur, reamer, screamer,
steamer, streamer • blasphemer,
daydreamer, redeemer

eaming \ē-miŋ\ see EEMING

eamish \ē-mish\ beamish, squeam-
ish

eamless \ēm-ləs\ dreamless, seam-
less

eamon \ē-mən\ see EMON¹

eamster \ēm-stər\ seamster, team-
ster

eamy \ē-mē\ creamy, dreamy,
gleamy, preemie, seamy, steamy

ean¹ \ē-ən\ eon, Ian, Leon, paean,
peon • Aegean, Chilean, Crimean,
Fijian, Judaean, Korean, plebeian
• Caribbean, cyclopean,
empyrean, European, Galilean,
Herculean, Jacobean,
Manichaean, Sisyphean, Ten-
nessean • epicurean, Ponce de
Leon, Pythagorean, un-European
• Indo-European

ean² \ēn\ see INE³

ean³ \ȯn\ see ON³

ean⁴ \ā-ən\ see AYAN¹

eane \ēn\ see INE³

eaner \ē-nər\ cleaner, gleaner,
screener, wiener • demeanor, dry
cleaner, pipe cleaner • misde-
meanor, submariner, trampoliner,
vacuum cleaner
—*also* -er *forms of adjectives listed
at* INE³

eanery \ēn-rē\ beanery, greenery,
scenery • machinery

eanie \ē-nē\ see INI¹

eaning \ē-niŋ\ leaning, meaning,
screening • dry cleaning, house-
cleaning, spring-cleaning, well-
meaning • overweening
—*also* -ing *forms of verbs listed at*
INE³

eanist \ē-nəst\ see INIST²

eanliness \en-lē-nəs\ see ENDLINESS

eanly¹ \ēn-lē\ cleanly, keenly,
meanly, queenly • routinely

eanly² \en-lē\ see ENDLY

eanne \ēn\ see INE³

eanness \ēn-nəs\ cleanness, green-
ness, keenness, meanness • un-
cleanness

eannie \ē-nē\ see INI¹

eano \ē-nō\ see INO²

eanor \ē-nər\ see EANER

eanse \enz\ see ENS¹

eant \ent\ see ENT¹

eany \ē-nē\ see INI¹

eap \ēp\ see EEP

eapen \ē-pən\ see EEPEN

eaper \ē-pər\ see EEPER

eapie \ē-pē\ see EEPY

eapo \ē-pō\ see EPOT

ear¹ \er\ see ARE⁴

ear² \ir\ see EER²

earable¹ \er-ə-bəl\ bearable, shareable, spareable, tearable, terrible,
wearable • unbearable, unwear-
able

earable² \ar-ə-bəl\ see ARABLE

earage \ir-ij\ see EERAGE

earance¹ \ir-əns\ see ERENCE¹

earance² \er-əns\ see ARENCE¹

earch \ərch\ see URCH

eard¹ \ird\ beard, eared, tiered,
weird • bat-eared, crop-eared,
dog-eared, graybeard, jug-eared,
lop-eared, spade beard, white-
beard • chandeliered, engineered,
multitiered • pre-engineered
—*also* -ed *forms of verbs listed at*
EER²

eard² \ərd\ see IRD

eare \ir\ see EER²

earean \ir-ē-ən\ see ERIAN[1]
eared[1] \erd\ see AIRED
eared[2] \ird\ see EARD[1]
earer[1] \er-ər\ bearer, error, sharer, terror, wearer • cupbearer, pallbearer, seafarer, talebearer, torchbearer, wayfarer
• standard-bearer, stretcher-bearer
—*also* -er *forms of adjectives listed at* ARE[4]
earer[2] \ir-ər\ mirror • sheepshearer
• rearview mirror
—*also* -er *forms of adjectives listed at* EER[2]
earful \ir-fəl\ cheerful, earful, fearful, tearful
earies \ir-ēz\ see ERIES
earing[1] \ir-iŋ\ clearing, earring, gearing, searing • God-fearing, sheepshearing • engineering, hard-of-hearing, mountaineering, power steering • orienteering
• bioengineering, social engineering
—*also* -ing *forms of verbs listed at* EER[2]
earing[2] \er-iŋ\ see ARING[1]
earish \er-ish\ see ARISH[1]
earl \ərl\ see IRL
earler \ər-lər\ see IRLER
earless \ir-ləs\ cheerless, fearless, peerless, tearless
earling \ər-lən\ see ERLIN
early[1] \ir-lē\ clearly, dearly, merely, nearly, queerly, sheerly, yearly • austerely, biyearly, severely, sincerely • cavalierly, insincerely, semiyearly
early[2] \ər-lē\ see URLY
earn \ərn\ see URN
earned \ərnd\ see URNED
earner \ər-nər\ see URNER
earnist \ər-nəst\ see ERNIST
earnt \ərnt\ burnt, learnt, weren't
earring \ir-iŋ\ see EARING[1]
earsal \ər-səl\ see ERSAL

earse \ərs\ see ERSE
earst \ərst\ see URST
eart \ärt\ see ART[1]
earted \ärt-əd\ parted • bighearted, coldhearted, departed, downhearted, fainthearted, goodhearted, greathearted, halfhearted, hard-hearted, kindhearted, largehearted, lighthearted, softhearted, stouthearted, truehearted, uncharted, warmhearted, wholehearted
• brokenhearted, chickenhearted, openhearted, tenderhearted
—*also* -ed *forms of verbs listed at* ART[1]
earth[1] \ärth\ see ARTH
earth[2] \ərth\ see IRTH
eartha \ər-thə\ see ERTHA
earthy \ər-<u>th</u>ē\ see ORTHY
eartily \ärt-ᵊl-ē\ see ARTILY
eartless \ärt-ləs\ see ARTLESS
earty \ärt-ē\ see ARTY[1]
eary \ir-ē\ aerie, beery, bleary, cheery, dreary, eerie, Erie, leery, Peary, query, teary, veery, weary
• Fort Erie, Kashmiri, Lake Erie, Valkyrie, world-weary • hara-kiri
eas \ē-əs\ see EUS[1]
easable[1] \ē-sə-bəl\ leasable, peaceable
easable[2] \ē-zə-bəl\ see EASIBLE
easand \iz-ᵊn\ see ISON[2]
ease[1] \ēs\ see IECE
ease[2] \ēz\ see EZE
eased[1] \ēzd\ diseased, self-pleased
—*also* -ed *forms of verbs listed at* EZE
eased[2] \ēst\ see EAST[1]
easel \ē-zəl\ bezel, diesel, easel, teasel, weasel
easeless \ē-sləs\ ceaseless, creaseless, greaseless
easelly \ē-zlē\ see EASLY
easer[1] \ē-sər\ greaser, piecer
easer[2] \ē-zər\ Caesar, freezer, geezer, greaser, pleaser, squeezer,

teaser, tweezer • appeaser, brain-
teaser, crowd-pleaser

eash \ēsh\ see ICHE[2]

easible \ē-zə-bəl\ feasible, squeez-
able

easil \ē-zəl\ see EASEL

easily \ēz-lē\ see EASLY

easing[1] \ē-siŋ\ leasing • unceasing
—*also* -*ing forms of verbs listed at*
IECE

easing[2] \ē-ziŋ\ freezing, pleasing
• subfreezing
—*also* -*ing forms of verbs listed at*
EZE

easingly \ē-siŋ-lē\ decreasingly,
increasingly, unceasingly

easle \ē-zəl\ see EASEL

easly \ēz-ə-lē\ easily, measly,
weaselly

eason \ēz-ᵊn\ reason, season, treason • high treason, in season, off-
season, postseason, preseason,
with reason • age of reason,
diocesan, open season, out of
season, rhyme or reason, silly
season, within reason

easonable \ēz-nə-bəl\ reasonable,
seasonable, treasonable • unrea-
sonable, unseasonable

easoning \ēz-niŋ\ reasoning, sea-
soning • unreasoning

easor \ē-zər\ see EASER[2]

east[1] \ēst\ beast, east, East, feast,
fleeced, least, priest, yeast • arch-
priest, artiste, at least, batiste,
deceased, Far East, Near East,
northeast, southeast • baker's
yeast, hartebeest, Middle East,
north-northeast, pointillist, wilde-
beest
—*also* -*ed forms of verbs listed at*
IECE

east[2] \est\ see EST

easted \es-təd\ see ESTED

easter \ē-stər\ Easter, feaster,
keister • northeaster

eastly \ēst-lē\ beastly, priestly

easurable \ezh-rə-bəl\ pleasurable,
treasurable • immeasurable

easure[1] \ezh-ər\ leisure, measure,
pleasure, treasure • displeasure,
dry measure, square measure,
tape measure • countermeasure,
cubic measure, for good measure,
liquid measure

easure[2] \ā-zhər\ see AZIER

easurer \ezh-ər-ər\ measurer,
treasurer

easy[1] \ē-zē\ breezy, cheesy, easy,
greasy, queasy, sleazy, sneezy,
wheezy • breathe easy, go easy,
Parcheesi, speakeasy, uneasy,
Zambezi • free and easy, over
easy

easy[2] \ē-sē\ see EECY

eat[1] \ēt\ beat, beet, bleat, cheat,
cleat, Crete, deet, eat, feat, fleet,
greet, heat, meat, meet, mete,
neat, peat, Pete, pleat, seat, sheet,
skeet, sleet, street, suite, sweet,
teat, treat, tweet, wheat • aes-
thete, athlete, backbeat, backseat,
backstreet, bedsheet, box seat,
browbeat, buckwheat, car seat,
cheat sheet, cold feet, compete,
complete, conceit, concrete,
crabmeat, crib sheet, deadbeat,
dead heat, dead meat, deceit,
defeat, delete, deplete, discreet,
discrete, downbeat, drumbeat,
dutch treat, effete, elite, entreat,
esthete, excrete, gamete, ground-
sheet, hard wheat, heartbeat,
helpmeet, hoofbeat, hot seat, ice
sheet, ill-treat, jump seat, love
seat, Main Street, maltreat,
mesquite, mincemeat, mistreat,
offbeat, petite, preheat, rap sheet,
receipt, red heat, red meat, re-
heat, repeat, replete, retreat,
secrete, side street, soft wheat,
spreadsheet, swap meet, through
street, unseat, upbeat, Wall Street,
white heat • balance sheet, bitter-

sweet, booster seat, bucket seat,
cellulite, cookie sheet, county
seat, decathlete, drag one's feet,
driver's seat, durum wheat, easy
street, incomplete, indiscreet,
lorikeet, make ends meet, Mar-
guerite, meet and greet, miss a
beat, nonathlete, obsolete, on
one's feet, overeat, overheat,
Paraclete, parakeet, pentathlete,
prickly heat, rumble seat, saddle
seat, scandal sheet, semisweet,
shredded wheat, spirochete, to
one's feet, triathlete, trick or
treat, two-way street, window seat
• beat a retreat, ejection seat, man
in the street, radiant heat, take a
back seat, vote with one's feet

eat² \āt\ see ATE[1]

eat³ \et\ see ET[1]

eat⁴ \it\ see IT[1]

eatable \ēt-ə-bəl\ beatable, eatable,
heatable, treatable • defeatable,
repeatable, unbeatable

eated¹ \ēt-əd\ heated, pleated
• conceited, deep-seated, repeated
• overheated, superheated
—*also* -ed *forms of verbs listed at*
EAT[1]

eated² \et-əd\ see ETID

eated³ \it-əd\ see ITTED

eaten¹ \ēt-ᵊn\ eaten, beaten, Cre-
tan, cretin, Eton, neaten, sweeten,
wheaten • browbeaten, Grand
Teton, moth-eaten, unbeaten,
worm-eaten • overeaten, weather-
beaten

eaten² \āt-ᵊn\ see ATEN[1]

eater¹ \ēt-ər\ beater, cheater, eater,
greeter, heater, liter, meter, Peter,
teeter, tweeter • ammeter,
anteater, beefeater, Demeter,
eggbeater, fire-eater, flowmeter,
light meter, man-eater, ohmme-
ter, repeater, space heater, volt-
meter, Wall Streeter, wattmeter,
world-beater • altimeter, cen-

tiliter, centimeter, deciliter,
decimeter, dekaliter, dekameter,
hectoliter, lotus-eater, milliliter,
millimeter, overeater, parking
meter, postage meter, taximeter,
trick-or-treater, water heater,
water meter
—*also* -er *forms of adjectives listed
at* EAT[1]

eater² \et-ər\ see ETTER

eath¹ \ēth\ heath, Keith, sheath,
wreath • beneath, bequeath • un-
derneath

eath² \ēth\ see EATHE

eathe \ēth\ breathe, seethe,
sheathe, teethe, wreathe • bequeath, unsheathe

eather¹ \eth-ər\ see ETHER[1]

eather² \ē-thər\ see EITHER

eathery \eth-rē\ feathery, leathery

eathing \ē-thiŋ\ breathing, sheath-
ing, teething • air-breathing, fire-
breathing
—*also* -ing *forms of verbs listed at*
EATHE

eathless \eth-ləs\ breathless, death-
less

eating \ēt-iŋ\ beating, eating, fleet-
ing, greeting, meeting, seating,
sheeting • breast-beating, camp
meeting, drumbeating, fire-eating,
man-eating, prayer meeting, space
heating, town meeting
—*also* -ing *forms of verbs listed at*
EAT[1]

eatise \ēt-əs\ see ETUS

eatly¹ \āt-lē\ see ATELY[1]

eatly² \et-lē\ see EETLY

eaton \ēt-ᵊn\ see EATEN[1]

eats¹ \ēts\ Keats
—*also* -s, -'s, *and* -s' *forms of nouns
and* -s *forms of verbs listed at* EAT[1]

eats² \āts\ see ATES[1]

eature \ē-chər\ see EACHER

eaty \ēt-ē\ meaty, peaty, sleety,
sweetie, treaty, ziti • entreaty,
graffiti, Tahiti • spermaceti

eau \ō\ see OW[1]

eaucracy \äk-rə-sē\ see OCRACY

eauteous \üt-ē-əs\ see UTEOUS

eautiful \üt-i-fəl\ see UTIFUL

eauty \üt-ē\ see OOTY[1]

eaux \ō\ see OW[1]

eavable \ē-və-bəl\ see EIVABLE

eaval \ē-vəl\ see IEVAL

eave[1] \ēv\ eve, Eve, grieve, heave, leave, peeve, sheave, sleeve, Steve, thieve, weave, we've • achieve, aggrieve, believe, bereave, conceive, deceive, frost heave, Maldive, motive, naive, perceive, pet peeve, receive, relieve, reprieve, retrieve, shirtsleeve, shore leave, sick leave, unweave • basket weave, disbelieve, Genevieve, interleave, interweave, makebelieve, misconceive, on one's sleeve, preconceive, Tel Aviv, up one's sleeve • overachieve, Saint Agnes' Eve, underachieve • absent without leave

eave[2] \iv\ see IVE[2]

eaved \ēvd\ leaved, sleeved • aggrieved, bereaved, broad-leaved, relieved
  —also -ed forms of verbs listed at EAVE[1]

eavement \ēv-mənt\ see EVEMENT

eaven \ev-ən\ Devon, Evan, heaven, Kevin, leaven, seven • eleven, hog heaven • seventh heaven

eaver \ē-vər\ see IEVER

eaward \ē-wərd\ see EEWARD

eaze[1] \ēz\ see EZE

eaze[2] \āz\ see AZE[1]

eazo \ē-zō\ see IZO

eazy \ē-zē\ see EASY[1]

eb \eb\ deb, ebb, reb, web • celeb, cobweb, Horeb, subdeb, Zagreb • cause célèbre, Johnny Reb, spiderweb, World Wide Web

eba \ē-bə\ Reba, Sheba • amoeba, Beersheba

ebate \ab-ət\ see ABIT

ebb \eb\ see EB

ebbie \eb-ē\ see EBBY

ebble \eb-əl\ pebble, rebel, treble

ebby \eb-ē\ Debbie, webby • cobwebby

ebe[1] \ē-bē\ BB, freebie, Phoebe, Seabee

ebe[2] \ēb\ plebe • sahib

ebel \eb-əl\ see EBBLE

eber \ā-bər\ see ABOR

ebes \ēbz\ Thebes
  —also -s, -'s, and -s' forms of nouns listed at EBE[2]

eble \eb-əl\ see EBBLE

ebo \ē-bō\ see IBO

ebral \ē-brəl\ cerebral, vertebral

ebs \eps\ see EPS

ebt \et\ see ET[1]

ebted \et-əd\ see ETID

ebtor \et-ər\ see ETTER

ec[1] \ek\ see ECK

ec[2] \ets\ see ETS

eca \ē-kə\ see IKA[1]

ecan \ek-ən\ see ECKON

ecca \ek-ə\ Decca, mecca, Mecca • Rebecca

eccable \ek-ə-bəl\ see ECKABLE

eccan \ek-ən\ see ECKON

ecce \ek-ē\ see ECKY

ecco \ek-ō\ see ECHO

ecency \ēs-ᵊn-sē\ decency, recency • indecency

ecent \ēs-ᵊnt\ decent, recent • indecent

ech[1] \ek\ see ECK

ech[2] \ək\ see UCK[1]

ech[3] \esh\ see ESH[1]

eche[1] \āsh\ crèche • Andhra Pradesh, Madhya Pradesh, Uttar Pradesh

eche[2] \esh\ see ESH[1]

eche[3] \ē-chē\ see EACHY

êche \esh\ see ESH[1]

èche \esh\ see ESH[1]

eched \echt\ see ETCHED

echie \ek-ē\ see ECKY

echin \ek-ən\ see ECKON

echo \ek-ō\ echo, gecko • art deco, El Greco, reecho

echt \ekt\ see ECT

ecia \ē-shə\ see ESIA[1]

ecially \esh-lē\ see ESHLY

ecian \ē-shən\ see ETION[1]

ecibel \es-ə-bəl\ see ESSIBLE

ecie[1] \ē-sē\ see EECY

ecie[2] \ē-shē\ see ISHI

ecies \ē-sēz\ species, theses • prostheses, subspecies

ecil[1] \ē-səl\ Cecil, diesel

ecil[2] \es-əl\ see ESTLE[1]

ecile \es-əl\ see ESTLE[1]

eciman \es-mən\ see ESSMAN

ecious \ē-shəs\ specious • capricious, facetious, Lucretius

eck \ek\ beck, check, Czech, deck, dreck, fleck, heck, Lech, neck, pec, peck, sec, spec, speck, trek, wreak, wreck • Aztec, bed check, bedeck, Bishkek, blank check, breakneck, bull neck, crew neck, cross-check, exec, fact-check, flight deck, flyspeck, gooseneck, gut check, hatcheck, henpeck, high tech, in check, kopeck, low-tech, Lubeck, on deck, OPEC, parsec, paycheck, poop deck, Quebec, rain check, roughneck, shipwreck, spell-check, spot-check, Steinbeck, sundeck, tape deck, Toltec, Uzbek, V-neck, vo-tech • biotech, bottleneck, cashier's check, Chiang Kai-shek, countercheck, discotheque, double-check, double-deck, hunt-and-peck, leatherneck, neck and neck, quarterdeck, rubber check, rubberneck, turtleneck, weather deck, Yucatec, Zapotec • breathe down one's neck, cinematheque, Melchizedek, mock turtleneck, promenade deck, Toulouse-Lautrec, traveler's check • reality check

eckable \ek-ə-bəl\ checkable • impeccable

ecked \ekt\ see ECT

ecker \ek-ər\ checker, decker, pecker, trekker, wrecker • fact-checker, Quebecer, spell-checker, three-decker, woodpecker • double-decker, rubbernecker, triple-decker

ecking \ek-iŋ\ necking

—*also* -ing *forms of verbs listed at* ECK

ecklace \ek-ləs\ see ECKLESS

eckle \ek-əl\ freckle, heckle, shekel, speckle

eckless \ek-ləs\ feckless, necklace, reckless

ecko \ek-ō\ see ECHO

eckon \ek-ən\ beckon, reckon • Aztecan, misreckon, Toltecan • Yucatecan

ecks, eks see EX

ecky \ek-ē\ Becky, techie

econ \ek-ən\ see ECKON

econd \ek-ənd\ see ECUND

ecque \ek\ see ECK

ecs \eks\ see EX

ect \ekt\ Brecht, necked, sect, specked • abject, affect, aspect, bisect, bullnecked, collect, connect, correct, cowl-necked, defect, deflect, deject, detect, direct, dissect, Dordrecht, effect, eject, elect, erect, expect, goosenecked, infect, inflect, inject, insect, inspect, neglect, object, perfect, project, prospect, protect, reflect, reject, respect, roll-necked, select, stiff-necked, subject, suspect, transect, trisect, Utrecht, V-necked • architect, birth defect, circumspect, deselect, dialect, disconnect, disinfect, disrespect, double-decked, genuflect, incorrect, indirect, in effect, intellect, interject, intersect, misdirect, preselect, recollect, reconnect,

redirect, reelect, resurrect, retrospect, self-respect, side effect, turtlenecked • aftereffect, Doppler effect, idiolect, interconnect, ripple effect • domino effect, landscape architect, placebo effect • politically correct
—also -ed *forms of verbs listed at* ECK

ectable \ek-tə-bəl\ collectible, connectable, correctable, delectable, detectable, electable, expectable, injectable, perfectible, respectable, selectable • undetectable

ectacle \ek-ti-kəl\ see ECTICAL

ectal \ek-tᵊl\ see ECTILE

ectant \ek-tənt\ expectant • disinfectant

ectar \ek-tər\ see ECTOR

ected \ek-təd\ affected, collected, connected, dejected, directed, dissected • disaffected, disconnected, fuel-injected, self-selected, unaffected, undirected, unexpected, unprotected, unselected • inner-directed, interconnected, other-directed
—also -ed *forms of verbs listed at* ECT

ecter \ek-tər\ see ECTOR

ectible \ek-tə-bəl\ see ECTABLE

ectic \ek-tik\ hectic • eclectic • anorectic, apoplectic, dialectic

ectical \ek-ti-kəl\ spectacle • dialectical

ectile \ek-tᵊl\ projectile • dialectal

ecting \ek-tiŋ\ affecting, respecting • self-correcting, self-respecting
—also -ing *forms of verbs listed at* ECT

ection \ek-shən\ flexion, section • affection, collection, complexion, confection, connection, convection, correction, cross section, C-section, defection, deflection, dejection, detection, direction, ejection, election, infection, inflection, injection, inspection, midsection, objection, perfection, projection, protection, reflection, rejection, selection, subjection, subsection, trisection • circumspection, conic section, disaffection, disinfection, fuel injection, golden section, imperfection, indirection, insurrection, interjection, intersection, introspection, misdirection, predilection, recollection, reconnection, redirection, reelection, reinfection, resurrection, self-direction, self-protection, self-selection, stage direction, vivisection • equal protection, general election, house of correction, interconnection • cesarean section

ectional \ek-shnəl\ sectional • correctional, cross-sectional, directional • omnidirectional, unidirectional

ectionist \ek-shə-nəst\ perfectionist, projectionist, protectionist • insurrectionist

ective \ek-tiv\ affective, collective, connective, corrective, defective, detective, directive, effective, elective, invective, objective, perspective, prospective, protective, reflective, respective, selective, subjective • cost-effective, house detective, ineffective, introspective, nonobjective, retrospective, self-reflective • private detective

ectless \ek-ləs\ see ECKLESS

ectly \ekt-lē\ abjectly, correctly, directly, erectly • circumspectly, incorrectly, indirectly

ectomy \ek-tə-mē\ mastectomy, vasectomy • appendectomy, hysterectomy, laryngectomy, tonsillectomy

ector \ek-tər\ hector, Hector, lector, nectar, rector, sector, specter, vector • collector, connector, defector, detector, director, ejector, elector, erector, injector, inspector, objector, projector, prospector, protector, reflector, selector, subsector • lie detector, smoke detector, stage director • casting director, funeral director, program director, solar collector

ectoral \ek-trəl\ pectoral, spectral • electoral

ectorate \ek-tə-rət\ directorate, electorate, protectorate

ectory \ek-tə-rē\ rectory • directory, trajectory

ectral \ek-trəl\ see ECTORAL

ectrum \ek-trəm\ plectrum, spectrum • broad-spectrum

ectual \ek-chə-wəl\ effectual • ineffectual, intellectual • anti-intellectual

ectually \ek-chə-lē\ effectually • ineffectually, intellectually

ectural[1] \ek-chə-rəl\ conjectural • architectural

ectural[2] \ek-shrəl\ conjectural • architectural

ecture \ek-chər\ lecture • conjecture • architecture

ecular \ek-yə-lər\ secular • molecular

ecund \ek-ənd\ fecund, second • split-second • microsecond, millisecond, nanosecond
—also -ed *forms of verbs listed at* ECKON

ed \ed\ see EAD[1]

e'd \ēd\ see EED

eda[1] \ēd-ə\ Frieda, Leda • Alameda

eda[2] \äd-ə\ see ADA[2]

edal[1] \ed-ªl\ medal, meddle, pedal, peddle • Air Medal, backpedal, soft-pedal • service medal

edal[2] \ēd-ªl\ see EEDLE

edance \ēd-ªns\ see EDENCE

edar[1] \ed-ər\ see EADER[2]

edar[2] \ēd-ər\ see EADER[1]

edator \ed-ət-ər\ see EDITOR

edd \ed\ see EAD[1]

eddar \ed-ər\ see EADER[2]

edded \ed-əd\ see EADED

edden \ed-ªn\ see EADEN

edder \ed-ər\ see EADER[2]

eddie \ed-ē\ see EADY[1]

edding \ed-iŋ\ see EADING[1]

eddle \ed-ªl\ see EDAL[1]

eddler \ed-lər\ meddler, peddler • intermeddler

eddon \ed-ªn\ see EADEN

eddy \ed-ē\ see EADY[1]

ede[1] \ād\ see ADE[1]

ede[2] \ēd\ see EED

ede[3] \ā-dā\ see AYDAY

edel \ād-əl\ see ADLE

eden \ēd-ªn\ Eden, Sweden • Garden of Eden

edence \ēd-ªns\ credence • impedance, precedence

edent \ēd-ªnt\ needn't • decedent, precedent • antecedent

eder[1] \ād-ər\ see ADER

eder[2] \ēd-ər\ see EADER[1]

edge \ej\ dredge, edge, fledge, hedge, ledge, pledge, sedge, sledge, veg, wedge • allege, gilt-edge, knife-edge, on edge, straightedge • cutting edge, flying wedge, leading edge, trailing edge

edged \ejd\ edged, wedged • alleged, full-fledged, gilt-edged, hard-edged, rough-edged, unfledged • double-edged
—also -ed *forms of verbs listed at* EDGE

edger \ej-ər\ dredger, hedger, ledger, pledger

edgie \ej-ē\ see EDGY

edgy \ej-ē\ edgy, Reggie, veggie, wedgie

edi \äd-ē\ see ADY

edia \ēd-ē-ə\ media • mixed media • multimedia • encyclopedia

edian \ēd-ē-ən\ median • comedian, tragedian

ediant \ēd-ē-ənt\ see EDIENT

edible \ed-ə-bəl\ credible, edible, spreadable • incredible, inedible

edic \ēd-ik\ comedic • orthopedic • encyclopedic

edience \ēd-ē-əns\ expedience, obedience • disobedience
—also -s, -'s, and -s' forms of nouns listed at EDIENT

edient \ēd-ē-ənt\ expedient, ingredient, obedient • disobedient, inexpedient

ediment \ed-ə-mənt\ pediment, sediment • impediment

edin \ēd-ᵊn\ see EDEN

eding \ēd-iŋ\ see EEDING¹

edious \ē-jəs\ see EGIS

edit \ed-ət\ credit, edit • accredit, discredit • copyedit, line of credit

editor \ed-ət-ər\ creditor, editor, predator • chief editor, coeditor • city editor, copy editor

edium \ēd-ē-əm\ medium, tedium • mass medium

edlar \ed-lər\ see EDDLER

edley \ed-lē\ deadly, medley

edly \ed-lē\ see EDLEY

edo¹ \ēd-ō\ credo, speedo • aikido, libido, Toledo, torpedo, tuxedo

edo² \ad-ō\ see ADO²

edo³ \ēd-ə\ see EDA¹

edo⁴ \e-dō\ Edo, meadow

edom \ēd-əm\ see EDUM

edon \ēd-ᵊn\ Eden • cotyledon

edouin \ed-wən\ see EDWIN

edulous \ej-ə-ləs\ credulous, sedulous • incredulous

edum \ēd-əm\ Edam, freedom • Medal of Freedom

edure \ē-jər\ besieger, procedure

edwin \ed-wən\ Edwin • bedouin

ee¹ \ē\ b, be, bee, Brie, c, cay, cee, Cree, d, Dee, e, fee, flea, flee, free, g, gee, glee, he, key, knee, lea, lee, Lee, Leigh, me, mi, p, pea, pee, plea, quay, re, sea, see, she, si, ski, spree, t, tea, tee, the, thee, three, ti, tree, v, vee, we, wee, whee, ye, z, zee • agree, at sea, bailee, banshee, bee tree, Belgae, big tree, Black Sea, bootee, break free, bungee, Capri, carefree, CB, CD, Chablis, chickpea, chili, cowpea, curie, Curie, Dead Sea, debris, decree, deepsea, degree, draftee, Dundee, emcee, ennui, esprit, flame tree, foresee, for free, germfree, goatee, grandee, grand prix, grantee, greens fee, green tea, he/she, high tea, home free, hot key, Humvee, IV, Jaycee, jayvee, KP, latchkey, look-see, low-key, LP, lychee, Marie, marquee, MC, métis, ming tree, must-see, Nancy, North Sea, OD, off-key, Parsi, passkey, Pawnee, payee, PC, peewee, pewee, PG, puree, qt, rani, Red Sea, Ross Sea, rupee, RV, scot-free, settee, shade tree, Shawnee, s/he, shift key, shoe tree, sightsee, signee, sirree, smoke tree, snap pea, snow pea, spondee, squeegee, standee, state tree, strophe, suttee, TB, tepee, testee, 3-D, to-be, toll-free, to sea, trainee, trochee, trustee, turnkey, tutee, Tutsi, TV, White Sea, whoopee, would-be, Yangtze • abductee, absentee, addressee, adoptee, advisee, amputee, apogee, appointee, Aral Sea, assignee, attendee, awardee, Beaufort Sea, Bering Sea, bourgeoisie, bumblebee, camphor tree, Cherokee, chickadee, chimpanzee, China Sea, Christmas tree, coati, conferee, cop a plea, Coral Sea, counselee, cruelty-free, DDT, Debussy, deportee, detainee, devotee, disagree, divorcé, divorcée, dungaree, duty-free, employee, enlistee, enrollee, escapee, ESP, evictee, family tree, fancy-free, fantasy, filigree, franchisee, fricassee, function key, Galilee, Gemini, Greenland Sea, guarantee, Hawaii, HIV, Holy See, honeybee, honoree, housemaid's knee, inductee, Inland Sea, invitee, Irish Sea, jamboree, Java Sea, Joshua tree, jubilee, Judas tree, killer bee, LCD, LED, licensee, LSD, maître d', Malay Sea, master key, Medici, Model T, nominee, oversea, oversee, parolee, pedigree, peppertree, pharisee, planer tree, potpourri, referee, refugee, repartee, retiree, Rosemarie, rubber tree, Sadducee, Salton Sea, selectee, shivaree, spelling bee, Tappan Zee, Tennessee, third degree, TNT, to a tee, transferee, tulip tree, undersea, user fee, VIP, vis-à-vis, wannabe, warrantee, Wounded Knee • advanced degree, Aegean Sea, Amundsen Sea, carpenter bee, Caspian Sea, Celebes Sea, East China Sea, evacuee, fortunately, Galilei, interviewee, Labrador Sea, omega-3, Sargasso Sea, Sault Sainte Marie, Simon Legree, skeleton key, South China Sea, to a degree, umbrella tree • Adriatic Sea, Africanized bee, Arabian Sea, bark up the wrong tree, Caribbean Sea, Ionian Sea, Sea of Galilee • Tweedledum and Tweedledee

ee² \ā\ see AY¹

ée \ā\ see AY¹

eeable \ē-ə-bəl\ seeable, skiable • agreeable, foreseeable • disagreeable, unforeseeable

eebie \ē-bē\ see EBE¹

eece \ēs\ see IECE

eeced \ēst\ see EAST¹

eech \ēch\ see EACH

eecher \ē-chər\ see EACHER

eeches \ich-əz\ see ITCHES

eeching \ē-chiŋ\ screeching, teaching • far-reaching • practice teaching, student teaching
—*also* -ing *forms of verbs listed at* EACH

eechy \ē-chē\ see EACHY

eecy \ē-sē\ fleecy, greasy • Tbilisi, AC/DC

eed \ēd\ bead, bleed, breed, cede, creed, deed, feed, greed, he'd, heed, keyed, knead, kneed, lead, mead, need, plead, read, reed, Reed, Reid, screed, seed, she'd, speed, steed, Swede, treed, tweed, Tweed, we'd, weed • accede, airspeed, bindweed, birdseed, blueweed, breast-feed, cheerlead, chickweed, concede, crossbreed, duckweed, exceed, fireweed, flaxseed, force-feed, Godspeed, ground speed, gulfweed, halfbreed, hand-feed, hawkweed, hayseed, high-speed, horseweed, impede, inbreed, indeed, ironweed, knapweed, knotweed, Lake Mead, linseed, lip-read, milkweed, misdeed, mislead, misread, moonseed, nosebleed, oilseed, pigweed, pinweed, pokeweed, pondweed, precede, proceed, proofread, ragweed, rapeseed, recede, reseed, rockweed, seaweed, secede, Siegfried, sight-read, smartweed, sneezeweed, speed-read, spoonfeed, stall-feed, stampede, stinkweed, succeed, ten-speed, warp speed, weak-kneed, witchweed, wormseed • aniseed, beggarweed, bottle-feed, bugleweed, centipede, chicken feed, cottonseed, crazyweed, double reed, Ganymede, go to seed, interbreed, intercede, jewelweed, jimsonweed, locoweed, millipede, Nicene Creed, overfeed, pedi-

greed, poppy seed, Port Said,
pumpkinseed, Runnymede, super-
sede, thimbleweed, title deed,
tumbleweed, underfeed, up to
speed, waterweed • Apostles'
Creed, canary seed, caraway seed
—*also* -ed *forms of verbs listed at*
EE[1]

eedal \ēd-°l\ see EEDLE
eeder \ēd-ər\ see EADER[1]
eedful \ēd-fəl\ heedful, needful
eeding[1] \ēd-iŋ\ bleeding, breeding,
leading, reading • inbreeding,
lipreading, preceding, proceeding
• care and feeding
—*also* -ing *forms of verbs listed at*
EED
eeding[2] \ēd-°n\ see EDON
eedle \ēd-°l\ needle, wheedle
• darning needle
eedless \ēd-ləs\ heedless, needless,
seedless
eedn't \ēd-°nt\ see EDENT
eedo \ēd-ō\ see EDO[1]
eedom \ēd-əm\ see EDUM
eeds \ēdz\ Leeds, needs • love
beads, prayer beads, proceeds
• special needs, worry beads
—*also* -s, -'s, *and* -s' *forms of nouns
and* -s *forms of verbs listed at* EED
eedy \ēd-ē\ beady, greedy, needy,
reedy, seedy, speedy, tweedy,
weedy
eef \ēf\ see IEF[1]
eefe \ēf\ see IEF[1]
eefy \ē-fē\ beefy, leafy
eegee \ē-jē\ see IJI
eeing \ē-iŋ\ being, seeing, skiing
• farseeing, sightseeing, well-being
• waterskiing
—*also* -ing *forms of verbs listed at*
EE[1]
eek[1] \ik\ see ICK
eek[2] \ēk\ see EAK[1]
eeked \ēkt\ see EAKED[2]
eeken \ē-kən\ see EACON
eeker \ē-kər\ see EAKER[1]

eekie \ē-kē\ see EAKY
eeking \ē-kiŋ\ see EAKING
eekly \ē-klē\ bleakly, meekly,
sleekly, weakly, weekly, treacly
• biweekly, midweekly,
newsweekly
eeky \ē-kē\ see EAKY
eel \ēl\ see EAL[2]
eelable \ē-lə-bəl\ see EALABLE
eele \ēl\ see EAL[2]
eeled \ēld\ see IELD
eeler \ē-lər\ see EALER
eeley \ē-lē\ see EELY
eelie \ē-lē\ see EELY
eeling \ē-liŋ\ ceiling, dealing, feel-
ing, peeling • appealing, Darjeel-
ing, faith healing, freewheeling,
glass ceiling, revealing, self-seal-
ing, unfeeling • double-dealing,
hit the ceiling, snowmobiling,
unappealing
—*also* -ing *forms of verbs listed at*
EAL[2]
eely \ē-lē\ eely, freely, mealy,
really, steelie, steely, stele,
wheelie • Swahili • Isle of Ely,
touchy-feely
eem \ēm\ see EAM[1]
eeman \ē-mən\ see EMON[1]
eemer \ē-mər\ see EAMER
eemie \ē-mē\ see EAMY
eeming \ē-miŋ\ scheming, scream-
ing, seeming, streaming
—*also* -ing *forms of verbs listed at*
EAM[1]
eemly \ēm-lē\ seemly • extremely,
supremely, unseemly
een[1] \in\ see IN[1]
een[2] \ēn\ see INE[3]
e'en \ēn\ see INE[3]
eena \ē-nə\ see INA[2]
eene \ēn\ see INE[3]
eener \ē-nər\ see EANER
eenery \ēn-rē\ see EANERY
eening \ē-niŋ\ see EANING
eenly \ēn-lē\ see EANLY[1]
eenness \ēn-nəs\ see EANNESS

eens \ēnz\ Queens, teens • by all means, by no means, Grenadines, New Orleans, Philippines, refried beans, smithereens, ways and means

eenwich \in-ich\ see INACH

eeny \ē-nē\ see INI[1]

eep \ēp\ beep, bleep, cheap, cheep, creep, deep, heap, Jeep, keep, leap, peep, reap, seep, sheep, sleep, steep, sweep, veep, weep • asleep, barkeep, black sheep, bopeep, dirt cheap, housekeep, knee-deep, scrap heap, skin-deep, upkeep, upsweep • bighorn sheep, chimney sweep, mountain sheep, on the cheap, overleap, oversleep, quantum leap • Louis Philippe

eepage \ē-pij\ creepage, seepage

eepen \ē-pən\ cheapen, deepen, steepen

eepence \əp-əns\ see UPPANCE

eeper \ē-pər\ beeper, creeper, Dnieper, keeper, leaper, peeper, reaper, sleeper, sweeper, weeper • barkeeper, beekeeper, bookkeeper, doorkeeper, gamekeeper, gatekeeper, goalkeeper, grim reaper, groundskeeper, housekeeper, innkeeper, minesweeper, peacekeeper, scorekeeper, shopkeeper, spring peeper, storekeeper, timekeeper, zookeeper • chimney sweeper
—*also* -er *forms of adjectives listed at* EEP

eepie \ē-pē\ see EEPY

eeping \ē-piŋ\ creeping, keeping, weeping • beekeeping, bookkeeping, gatekeeping, housekeeping, minesweeping, peacekeeping, safekeeping, timekeeping
—*also* -ing *forms of verbs listed at* EEP

eeple \ē-pəl\ see EOPLE

eepy \ē-pē\ cheapie, creepy, seepy, sleepy, tepee, weepy

eer[1] \ē-ər\ seer, skier, we're • sightseer • overseer, water-skier

eer[2] \ir\ beer, bier, blear, cheer, clear, dear, deer, ear, fear, gear, hear, here, jeer, Lear, leer, mere, near, peer, pier, Pierre, queer, rear, sear, seer, shear, sheer, smear, sneer, spear, sphere, steer, tear, tier, veer, weir, we're, year • adhere, all clear, ampere, appear, austere, besmear, brassiere, Bronx cheer, by ear, Cape Fear, career, cashier, cashmere, Cheshire, clavier, cohere, dog-ear, endear, footgear, frontier, headgear, inhere, Kashmir, killdeer, leap year, light-year, man-year, midyear, mishear, monsieur, mule deer, musk deer, nadir, New Year, off year, premier, premiere, red deer, rehear, reindeer, revere, Revere, roe deer, root beer, severe, Shakespeare, Shropshire, sincere, steer clear, Tangier, tapir, tin ear, veneer, Vermeer, vizier, wind shear, worm gear, Yorkshire, Zaire • atmosphere, auctioneer, balladeer, bandolier, belvedere, biosphere, black-tailed deer, bombardier, boutonniere, brigadier, buccaneer, budgeteer, cannoneer, canyoneer, cavalier, chandelier, chanticleer, chocolatier, commandeer, crystal clear, disappear, domineer, ecosphere, engineer, fallow deer, financier, fiscal year, gadgeteer, gazetteer, ginger beer, Gloucestershire, gondolier, grenadier, Guinevere, hemisphere, Herefordshire, Hertfordshire, Holy Year, inner ear, insincere, interfere, in the clear, Lancashire, landing gear, marketeer, middle ear, mountaineer, Mount Rainier, muleteer, multiyear, musketeer, mutineer, outer ear, overhear, overseer, Oxford-

shire, pamphleteer, persevere,
pioneer, privateer, profiteer,
puppeteer, racketeer, rocketeer,
sloganeer, sonneteer, souvenir,
Staffordshire, steering gear, strat-
osphere, summiteer, swimmer's
ear, troposphere, vintage year,
Vladimir, volunteer, Warwick-
shire, white-tailed deer, Worcestershire, yesteryear • black
marketeer, charioteer, conven-
tioneer, electioneer, ionosphere,
Nottinghamshire, orienteer • academic year, bioengineer, cauliflower ear, civil engineer, Jammu
and Kashmir
e'er \er\ see ARE⁴

eerage \ir-ij\ peerage, steerage

eered \ird\ see EARD¹

eerer \ir-ər\ see EARER²

eeress \ir-əs\ see EROUS

eerful \ir-fəl\ see EARFUL

eerie \ir-ē\ see EARY

eering \ir-iŋ\ see EARING¹

eerist \ir-əst\ see ERIST¹

eerless \ir-ləs\ see EARLESS

eerly \ir-lē\ see EARLY¹

eersman \irz-mən\ steersman
• frontiersman

eerut \ir-ət\ see IRIT

eery \ir-ē\ see EARY

ees \ēz\ see EZE

eese \ēz\ see EZE

eesh \ēsh\ see ICHE²

eesi \ē-zē\ see EASY¹

eesia \ē-zhə\ see ESIA²

eest¹ \āst\ see ACED

eest² \ēst\ see EAST¹

eesy \ē-zē\ see EASY¹

eet \ēt\ see EAT¹

eetah \ēt-ə\ see ITA

eete \āt-ē\ see ATY

eeten \ēt-ᵊn\ see EATEN¹

eeter \ēt-ər\ see EATER¹

eethe \ēth\ see EATHE

eether \ē-thər\ see EITHER

eething \ē-thiŋ\ see EATHING

eetie \ēt-ē\ see EATY

eeting \ēt-iŋ\ see EATING

eetle \ēt-ᵊl\ see ETAL¹

eetly \ēt-lē\ fleetly, neatly, sweetly
• completely, concretely, dis-
creetly • bittersweetly, incom-
pletely, indiscreetly

eety \ēt-ē\ see EATY

ee-um \ē-əm\ see EUM¹

eeve \ēv\ see EAVE¹

eeved \ēvd\ see EAVED

eevil \ē-vəl\ see IEVAL

eevish \ē-vish\ peevish, thievish

eeward \ē-wərd\ leeward, seaward

eewee \ē-wē\ kiwi, peewee, pewee

eewit \ü-ət\ see UET

eez \ēz\ see EZE

eezable \ē-zə-bəl\ see EASIBLE

eeze \ēz\ see EZE

eezer \ē-zər\ see EASER²

eezing \ē-ziŋ\ see EASING²

eezy \ē-zē\ see EASY¹

ef¹ \ef\ chef, clef, deaf, ef, f, ref
• bass clef, Brezhnev, C clef, Kiev,
stone-deaf, tone-deaf • emf, Gorbachev, treble clef, UNICEF
• Prokofiev

ef² \ā\ see AY¹

ef³ \ēf\ see IEF¹

efanie \ef-ə-nē\ see EPHONY

efany \ef-ə-nē\ see EPHONY

eferable \ef-rə-bəl\ preferable,
referable

eference \ef-rəns\ deference, pref-
erence, reference • cross-refer-
ence • frame of reference

eferent \ef-rənt\ deferent, referent

eff \ef\ see EF¹

effer \ef-ər\ see EPHOR

eficence \ef-ə-səns\ beneficence,
maleficence

eft \eft\ cleft, deft, eft, heft, left,
theft • bereft, grand theft, stage
left • identity theft

efty \ef-tē\ hefty, lefty

eg¹ \āg\ Craig, plague, vague • The
Hague • bubonic plague

eg[2] \eg\ beg, Craig, egg, Greg, keg, leg, peg, reg • bootleg, bowleg, foreleg, JPEG, MPEG, nutmeg, peg leg, renege • break a leg, powder keg, pull one's leg, Winnipeg • mumblety-peg

eg[3] \ej\ see EDGE

ega[1] \eg-ə\ mega • omega • Lake Onega, rutabaga

ega[2] \ä-gə\ see AGA[2]

ega[3] \ē-gə\ see IGA

egal \ē-gəl\ beagle, eagle, legal, regal • bald eagle, illegal, sea eagle, spread-eagle • golden eagle

egan \ē-gən\ Megan, vegan • Mohegan, Monhegan, Waukegan

ege[1] \ezh\ cortege, Liège

ege[2] \eg\ see EG[2]

ege[3] \ej\ see EDGE

ege[4] \ēg\ see IGUE

ege[5] \ig\ see IG

eged \ejd\ see EDGED

egel \āgəl\ see AGEL

eger \ej-ər\ see EDGER

egg \eg\ see EG[2]

eggar \eg-ər\ see EGGER

eggary \eg-ə-rē\ beggary, Gregory

egger \eg-ər\ beggar • bootlegger • thousand-legger, Winnipegger

eggie \ej-ē\ see EDGY

eggs \egz\ see EGS

eggy \eg-ē\ leggy, Peggy, plaguey • Carnegie

egia \ē-jə\ Ouija • paraplegia, quadriplegia

egian \ē-jən\ see EGION

egic \ē-jik\ strategic • paraplegic, quadriplegic

egie \eg-ē\ see EGGY

egion \ē-jən\ legion, region • collegian, Norwegian, subregion

egious \ē-jəs\ see EGIS

egis \ē-jəs\ aegis, Regis, tedious • egregious

egm \em\ see EM[1]

egn \ān\ see ANE[1]

egnant \eg-nənt\ pregnant, regnant

egnly \ān-lē\ see AINLY

ego[1] \ē-gō\ ego • amigo • alter ego, impetigo

ego[2] \ä-gō\ see AGO[2]

egory \eg-ə-rē\ see EGGARY

egs \egz\ yellowlegs • daddy longlegs
—*also* -s, -'s, *and* -s' *forms of nouns and* -s *forms of verbs listed at* EG[2]

eh[1] \ā\ see AY[1]

eh[2] \a\ see AH[3]

ehen \ān\ see ANE[1]

ehner \ā-nər\ see AINER

ei[1] \ā\ see AY[1]

ei[2] \ī\ see Y[1]

eia[1] \ē-ə\ see IA[1]

eia[2] \ī-ə\ see IAH[1]

eial \ē-əl\ see EAL[1]

eian[1] \ē-ən\ see EAN[1]

eian[2] \ā-ən\ see AYAN[1]

eiche \āsh\ see ECHE[1]

eickel \ī-kəl\ see YCLE[1]

eid[1] \āt\ see ATE[1]

eid[2] \īt\ see ITE[1]

eid[3] \ēd\ see EED

eidel[1] \ād-əl\ see ADLE

eidel[2] \īd-ᵊl\ see IDAL

eidi \īd-ē\ see IDAY

eidon \īd-ᵊn\ see IDEN

eier \īr\ see IRE[1]

eifer \ef-ər\ see EPHOR

eige \āzh\ beige • Mount Neige

eiger \ī-gər\ see IGER

eigh[1] \ā\ see AY[1]

eigh[2] \ē\ see EE[1]

eighbor \ā-bər\ see ABOR

eight[1] \āt\ see ATE[1]

eight[2] \īt\ see ITE[1]

eighter \āt-ər\ see ATOR

eightless \āt-ləs\ see ATELESS

eights \īts\ see IGHTS

eighty \āt-ē\ see ATY

eign \ān\ see ANE[1]

eigner \ā-nər\ see AINER

eii \ā\ see AY[1]

eiian \ā-ən\ see AYAN[1]

eiji \ā-jē\ see AGY

eik \ēk\ see EAK[1]

eikh \ēk\ see EAK[1]

eil[1] \āl\ see AIL

eil[2] \el\ see EL[1]

eil[3] \ēl\ see EAL[2]

eil[4] \īl\ see ILE[1]

eila \ē-lə\ see ELA[1]

eiled \āld\ see AILED

eiler \ī-lər\ see ILAR

eiling[1] \ā-liŋ\ see AILING

eiling[2] \ē-liŋ\ see EELING

eill \ēl\ see EAL[2]

eilles[1] \ā\ see AY[1]

eilles[2] \ālz\ see ALES[1]

eilly \ā-lē\ see AILY

eim[1] \ām\ see AME[1]

eim[2] \īm\ see IME[1]

eimer \ī-mər\ see IMER[1]

eims[1] \änˢ\ see ANCE[1]

eims[2] \ēmz\ Rheims
—also -s, -'s, and -s' forms of
nouns and -s forms of verbs listed
at EAM[1]

ein[1] \ān\ see ANE[1]

ein[2] \ē-ən\ see EAN[1]

ein[3] \ēn\ see INE[3]

ein[4] \īn\ see INE[1]

eine[1] \ān\ see ANE[1]

eine[2] \ēn\ see INE[3]

eine[3] \ī-nə\ see INA[1]

eine[4] \en\ see EN[1]

eined \ānd\ see AINED

einer[1] \ā-nər\ see AINER

einer[2] \ē-nər\ see EANER

eing \ē-iŋ\ see EEING

einie \ī-nē\ see INY[1]

eining \ā-niŋ\ see AINING

einous \ā-nəs\ see AYNESS

eins \ānz\ see AINS

eint \ānt\ see AINT

einte \ant\ see ANT[5]

einy \ā-nē\ see AINY

eipt \ēt\ see EAT[1]

eir \er\ see ARE[4]

eira \ir-ə\ see ERA[2]

eird \ird\ see EARD[1]

eiress \ar-əs\ see ARIS[2]

eiric \ī-rik\ see YRIC

eiro \er-ō\ see ERO[2]

eirs \erz\ see AIRS

eis[1] \ās\ see ACE[1]

eis[2] \ē-əs\ see EUS[1]

eis[3] \īs\ see ICE[1]

eisant \ēs-ᵊnt\ see ECENT

eise \ēz\ see EZE

eisel \ī-zəl\ see ISAL[2]

eisen \īz-ᵊn\ see IZEN[1]

eiser \ī-zər\ see IZER

eisha[1] \ā-shə\ see ACIA

eisha[2] \ē-shə\ see ESIA[1]

eisin \ēz-ᵊn\ see EASON

eiss \īs\ see ICE[1]

eissen \īs-ᵊn\ see ISON[1]

eist[1] \ā-əst\ see AYEST

eist[2] \īst\ see IST[1]

eister[1] \ī-stər\ keister, shyster
• spinmeister • concertmeister

eister[2] \ē-stər\ see EASTER

eisure \ē-zhər\ see EIZURE

eit[1] \ē-ət\ fiat • albeit

eit[2] \it\ see IT[1]

eit[3] \ēt\ see EAT[1]

eit[4] \īt\ see ITE[1]

eited \ēt-əd\ see EATED[1]

eiter[1] \it-ər\ see ITTER

eiter[2] \ī-tər\ see ITER[1]

eith \ēth\ see EATH[1]

either \ē-thər\ breather, either,
neither • fire-breather

eitus \īt-əs\ see ITIS

eity \ē-ət-ē\ deity • spontaneity
• homogeneity, simultaneity

eivable \ē-və-bəl\ achievable, be-
lievable, conceivable, perceivable,
receivable, retrievable • incon-
ceivable, irretrievable, unbeliev-
able

eive \ēv\ see EAVE[1]

eiver \ē-vər\ see IEVER

eix \āsh\ see ECHE[1]

eize[1] \āz\ see AZE[1]

eize[2] \ēz\ see EZE

eizure \ē-zhər\ leisure, seizure

eji \ej-ē\ see EDGY
ejo \ā-ō\ see EO[1]
ek \ek\ see ECK
eka[1] \ek-ə\ see ECCA
eka[2] \ē-kə\ see IKA[1]
ekah \ek-ə\ see ECCA
eke \ēk\ see EAK[1]
ekel \ek-əl\ see ECKLE
ekh \ek\ see ECK
eki \ek-ē\ see ECKY
ekker \ek-ər\ see ECKER
ekoe \ē-kō\ see ICOT
el[1] \el\ bell, Bell, belle, cell, dell,
dwell, el, Elle, fell, gel, hell, jell,
knell, l, quell, sell, shell, smell,
spell, swell, tell, they'll, well, yell
• Adele, band shell, barbell, be-
fell, bluebell, bombshell, Boswell,
cartel, Chanel, clamshell, com-
pel, Cornell, corral, cowbell,
Cromwell, Danielle, dispel, door-
bell, dry cell, dumbbell, eggshell,
Estelle, excel, expel, farewell, fat
cell, foretell, fuel cell, gazelle,
germ cell, Giselle, groundswell,
half shell, handbell, hard sell,
hotel, impel, inkwell, lapel,
Maxwell, Michelle, misspell,
Moselle, motel, nerve cell, Nobel,
noel, nutshell, oil well, Orwell,
outsell, pastel, pell-mell, pixel,
propel, rappel, Ravel, rebel, repel,
respell, retell, Roswell, scalpel,
seashell, sequel, Seychelles, sleigh
bell, soft sell, soft-shell, stairwell,
star shell, stem cell, tooth shell,
unwell, wind-bell • Annabelle,
Appenzell, asphodel, bagatelle,
Cape Farewell, caramel, caravel,
carousel, chanterelle, chaparral,
citadel, clientele, cockleshell,
Cozumel, decibel, diving bell,
fare-thee-well, Isabel, Jezebel,
killer cell, kiss-and-tell, ne'er-do-
well, New Rochelle, nonpareil,
oversell, parallel, personnel,
Philomel, pimpernel, Raphael,

rebel yell, red blood cell, Sanctus
bell, San Rafael, São Miguel,
show-and-tell, sickle cell, solar
cell, tortoiseshell, undersell, white
blood cell, William Tell, zinfandel
• Aix-la-Chapelle, artesian well,
au naturel, crème caramel, made-
moiselle, maître d'hôtel, matériel,
Mont-Saint-Michel • antiperson-
nel • AWOL
el[2] \äl\ see AIL
ela[1] \ē-lə\ chela, Leila, Sheila
• tequila • Philomela
ela[2] \ā-lə\ see ALA[3]
ela[3] \el-ə\ see ELLA
elable \el-ə-bəl\ see ELLABLE
elacy \el-ə-sē\ jealousy, prelacy
elagh \ā-lē\ see AILY
elah \ē-lə\ see ELA[1]
eland \ē-lənd\ eland, Zeeland
• New Zealand
elanie \el-ə-nē\ see ELONY
elar \ē-lər\ see EALER
elate \el-ət\ see ELLATE
elatin \el-ət-ᵊn\ see ELETON
elba \el-bə\ Elba, Elbe, Melba
elbe \el-bə\ see ELBA
elbert \el-bərt\ Delbert, Elbert
• Mount Elbert
elch \elch\ belch, squelch, welch
eld[1] \eld\ geld, held, meld, shelled,
weld • beheld, handheld, hard-
shelled, upheld, withheld • jet-
propelled, self-propelled
• unparalleled
—*also* -ed *forms of verbs listed at*
EL[1]
eld[2] \elt\ see ELT
elder \el-dər\ elder, welder
eldt \elt\ see ELT
ele[1] \ā-lē\ see AILY
ele[2] \el\ see EL[1]
ele[3] \el-ē\ see ELLY
ele[4] \ē-lē\ see EELY
eled[1] \eld\ see ELD[1]
eled[2] \ēld\ see IELD
elen \el-ən\ see ELON

eleon \ēl-yən\ see ELIAN[2]

eleton \el-ət-ᵊn\ gelatin, skeleton

eleus \ē-lē-əs\ see ELIOUS

elf \elf\ elf, pelf, self, shelf • bookshelf, herself, himself, itself, myself, oneself, ourself, top-shelf, thyself, yourself • mantelshelf, off-the-shelf, Ross Ice Shelf • do-it-yourself • continental shelf

elfish \el-fish\ elfish, selfish • unselfish

elhi \el-ē\ see ELLY

eli \el-ē\ see ELLY

elia[1] \ēl-yə\ Delia, Lelia, Sheila • Amelia, camellia, Camellia, Cecilia, Cornelia, Karelia, lobelia, Ophelia • psychedelia

elia[2] \il-ē-ə\ see ILIA[1]

elian[1] \ē-lē-ən\ Pelion • Mendelian

elian[2] \ēl-yən\ Aurelian, chameleon, Mendelian, parhelion • perihelion • Aristotelian, Mephistophelian

elian[3] \el-ē-ən\ see ELLIAN

elible \el-ə-bəl\ see ELLABLE

elic \el-ik\ relic • angelic, smart aleck • archangelic, philatelic, psychedelic

elion[1] \el-ē-ən\ see ELLIAN

elion[2] \ēl-yən\ see ELIAN[2]

elion[3] \ēl-ē-ən\ see ELIAN[1]

elios \ē-lē-əs\ see ELIOUS

elious \ē-lē-əs\ Helios • Cornelius

elish \el-ish\ see ELLISH

elist \el-əst\ cellist, trellised • Nobelist, pastelist

elius \ē-lē-əs\ see ELIOUS

elix \ē-liks\ Felix, helix • double helix

elk[1] \elk\ elk, whelk

elk[2] \ilk\ see ILK

ell \el\ see EL[1]

e'll \ēl\ see EAL[2]

ella \el-ə\ Della, Ella, fella, fellah, Stella • Estella, Gisela, Luella, Marcella, Mandela, novella, patella, rubella, umbrella, vanilla • a cappella, Cinderella, citronella, Isabella, mozzarella, salmonella, sarsaparilla, tarantella

ellable \el-ə-bəl\ sellable • compellable, indelible

ellah \el-ə\ see ELLA

ellan \el-ən\ see ELON

ellant \el-ənt\ appellant, flagellant, propellant, repellent • water-repellent

ellar \el-ər\ see ELLER

ellas \el-əs\ see EALOUS

ellate \el-ət\ pellet, prelate, zealot • appellate

elle[1] \el\ see EL[1]

elle[2] \el-ə\ see ELLA

ellean \el-ē-ən\ see ELLIAN

elled \eld\ see ELD[1]

ellen \el-ən\ see ELON

ellent \el-ənt\ see ELLANT

eller \el-ər\ cellar, dweller, seller, sheller, speller, stellar, teller, yeller • best seller, bookseller, foreteller, propeller, tale-teller • fortune-teller, interstellar, Rockefeller, storyteller

elles[1] \el\ see EL[1]

elles[2] \elz\ see ELLS

ellet \el-ət\ see ELLATE

elley \el-ē\ see ELLY

elli \el-ē\ see ELLY

ellia \ēl-yə\ see ELIA[1]

ellian \el-ē-ən\ Orwellian • Machiavellian

ellie \el-ē\ see ELLY

elline \el-ən\ see ELON

elling \el-iŋ\ dwelling, selling, spelling, swelling, telling • best-selling, bookselling, cliff-dwelling, compelling, lake dwelling, misspelling, tale-telling, upwelling • fortune-telling, self-propelling, storytelling
—*also* -ing *forms of verbs listed at* EL[1]

ellington \el-iŋ-tən\ Ellington, Wellington • beef Wellington

ellion \el-yən\ hellion • rebellion
ellis \el-əs\ see EALOUS
ellised \el-əst\ see ELIST
ellish \el-ish\ hellish, relish • embellish
ellist \el-əst\ see ELIST
ello \el-ō\ bellow, cello, fellow, Jell-O, mellow, yellow • bedfellow, bordello, Longfellow, marshmallow, Odd Fellow, Othello, playfellow, schoolfellow • Pirandello • Robin Goodfellow, violoncello
ell-o \el-ō\ see ELLO
ellous \el-əs\ see EALOUS
ellow[1] \el-ə\ see ELLA
ellow[2] \el-ō\ see ELLO
ells \elz\ Seychelles • Dardanelles —*also* -s, -'s, *and* -s' *forms of nouns and* -s *forms of verbs listed at* EL[1]
ellum \el-əm\ vellum • clitellum, flagellum, postbellum • antebellum, cerebellum
ellus \el-əs\ see EALOUS
elly \el-ē\ belly, Delhi, deli, jelly, Kelly, Nellie, Shelley, smelly, telly • New Delhi, pork belly, potbelly, sowbelly • Botticelli, Delhi belly, nervous Nellie, royal jelly, underbelly, vermicelli • Machiavelli
ellyn \el-ən\ see ELON
elm \elm\ elm, helm, realm • overwhelm
elma \el-mə\ Selma, Velma
elmar \el-mər\ see ELMER
elmer \el-mər\ Delmar, Elmer
elmet \el-mət\ helmet, Helmut • crash helmet, pith helmet
elmut \el-mət\ see ELMET
elo \ē-lō\ see ILO[2]
elon \el-ən\ Ellen, felon, Helen, melon • Magellan, muskmelon • watermelon • Strait of Magellan
elony \el-ə-nē\ felony, Melanie
elop \el-əp\ develop, envelop • overdevelop

elos \ā-ləs\ see AYLESS
elot \el-ət\ see ELLATE
elotry \el-ə-trē\ helotry, zealotry
elp \elp\ help, kelp, whelp, yelp • self-help
elsea \el-sē\ see ELSIE
elsie \el-sē\ Chelsea, Elsie
elt \elt\ belt, Celt, dealt, dwelt, felt, melt, pelt, smelt, spelt, svelte, veld, welt • black belt, Frostbelt, greenbelt, heartfelt, lap belt, rust belt, seat belt, snowbelt, snowmelt, Sunbelt, web belt • Bible Belt, cartridge belt, Roosevelt, safety belt, shoulder belt • asteroid belt, below the belt
elte \elt\ see ELT
elted \el-təd\ belted, melted, pelted
elter \el-tər\ shelter, smelter, swelter, welter • tax shelter • helterskelter
eltered \el-tərd\ tax-sheltered —*also* -ed *forms of verbs listed at* ELTER
elting \el-tiŋ\ belting, felting, melting —*also* -ing *forms of verbs listed at* ELT
elve \elv\ delve, shelve, twelve
elves \elvz\ elves • ourselves, themselves, yourselves —*also* -s, -'s, *and* -s' *forms of nouns and* -s *forms of verbs listed at* ELVE
elvin \el-vən\ Elvin, Kelvin, Melvin
elvyn \el-vən\ see ELVIN
ely \ē-lē\ see EELY
em[1] \em\ Clem, crème, em, gem, hem, m, phlegm, REM, stem, them • ahem, AM, brain stem, condemn, FM, item, mayhem, modem, poem, problem, pro tem • ABM, Bethlehem, diadem, stratagem • ad hominem, cable modem, carpe diem, crème de la crème, ICBM • collector's item, post meridiem

em² \əm\ see UM¹

ema \ē-mə\ Lima • eczema, edema • emphysema, Hiroshima, Iwo Jima

emacist \em-ə-səst\ see EMICIST

eman¹ \em-ən\ see EMON²

eman² \ē-mən\ see EMON¹

emane \em-ə-nē\ see EMONY

ember \em-bər\ ember, member • December, dismember, nonmember, November, remember, September • charter member

emble \em-bəl\ tremble • assemble, dissemble, resemble • disassemble

embler \em-blər\ temblor • assembler, dissembler

emblor \em-blər\ see EMBLER

embly \em-blē\ trembly • assembly • disassembly, subassembly

eme¹ \em\ see EM¹

eme² \ēm\ see EAM¹

emely \ēm-lē\ see EEMLY

emen¹ \ē-mən\ see EMON¹

emen² \em-ən\ see EMON²

emen³ \ā-mən\ see AMEN¹

emer \ē-mər\ see EAMER

emery \em-rē\ emery, Emory, memory

emi \em-ē\ see EMMY

emia \ē-mē-ə\ anemia, bohemia, Bohemia, leukemia, toxemia, uremia • academia

emic¹ \ē-mik\ anemic, uremic • emphysemic

emic² \em-ik\ endemic, pandemic, polemic, systemic, totemic • academic, epidemic

emical \em-i-kəl\ chemical • alchemical, polemical • biochemical, petrochemical

emicist \em-ə-səst\ polemicist, supremacist • white supremacist

eming \em-iŋ\ Fleming, lemming —also -ing forms of verbs listed at EM¹

eminge \em-iŋ\ see EMING

emini \em-ə-nē\ see EMONY

eminy \em-ə-nē\ see EMONY

emis \ē-məs\ see EMUS

emish \em-ish\ blemish, Flemish

emlin \em-lən\ gremlin, Kremlin

emma \em-ə\ Emma • dilemma

emme \em\ see EM¹

emmer \em-ər\ hemmer, tremor

emming \em-iŋ\ see EMING

emmy \em-ē\ Emmy, phlegmy, semi, stemmy

emn \em\ see EM¹

emner \em-ər\ see EMMER

emnity \em-nət-ē\ indemnity, solemnity

emo \em-ō\ demo, memo

emon¹ \ē-mən\ demon, freeman, seaman • Lake Leman, Philemon

emon² \em-ən\ Bremen, lemon, Yemen

emone \em-ə-nē\ see EMONY

emony \em-ə-nē\ Gemini, lemony • anemone, Gethsemane, hegemony

emor \em-ər\ see EMMER

emory \em-rē\ see EMERY

emous \ē-məs\ see EMUS

emp \emp\ hemp, temp

emplar \em-plər\ exemplar, Knight Templar

emps \äⁿ\ see ANT¹

empt \emt\ dreamt, tempt • attempt, contempt, exempt, preempt, undreamed, unkempt • tax-exempt

emption \em-shən\ exemption, preemption, redemption

emptive \em-tiv\ preemptive, redemptive

emur \ē-mər\ see EAMER

emus \ē-məs\ Remus • in extremis, Polyphemus

emy \ē-mē\ see EAMY

en¹ \en\ Ben, den, en, glen, Glen, Gwen, hen, Ken, Len, men, n, pen, Penn, Seine, Sten, ten, then, when, wren, yen, Zen • again, amen, Ardennes, Big Ben, bull pen, Cayenne, Cheyenne, Estienne, game hen, hang ten, light pen, marsh hen, moorhen, peahen, pigpen, Phnom Penh, playpen, RN • Adrienne, bornagain, cactus wren, five-and-ten, fountain pen, guinea hen, lion's den, LPN, mother hen, Sun Yatsen, water hen • carcinogen, comedienne, equestrienne, time and again • again and again

en² \ēn\ see INE³

en³ \aⁿ\ see IN⁴

en⁴ \ən\ see UN¹

en⁵ \äⁿ\ see ANT¹

ena¹ \ā-nə\ see ANA²

ena² \ē-nə\ see INA²

enable \en-ə-bəl\ tenable • amenable, untenable

enace \en-əs\ see ENIS

enae \e-nē\ see INI¹

enal \ēn-ᵊl\ penal, renal, venal • adrenal, vaccinal

enant \en-ənt\ pennant, tenant • lieutenant, subtenant • sublieutenant

enary \en-ə-rē\ hennery, plenary • centenary, millenary • bicentenary

enas \ē-nəs\ see ENUS¹

enate \en-ət\ see ENNET

enator \en-ət-ər\ see ENITOR

ençal \en-səl\ see ENCIL

ence¹ \ens\ see ENSE

ence² \äⁿs\ see ANCE¹

ence³ \äns\ see ANCE²

encel \en-səl\ see ENCIL

enceless \en-sləs\ see ENSELESS

encer \en-sər\ see ENSOR

ench \ench\ bench, clench, drench, French, mensch, quench, stench, trench, wench, wrench • entrench, pipe wrench, retrench, unclench, workbench • Allen wrench, monkey wrench, socket wrench • Mariana Trench

enchant \en-chənt\ see ENTIENT

encher \en-chər\ see ENTURE

enchman \ench-mən\ Frenchman, henchman

encia \en-chə\ see ENTIA

encil \en-səl\ pencil, stencil, tensile • grease pencil, lead pencil, prehensile, utensil • eyebrow pencil

end \end\ bend, blend, end, fend, friend, lend, mend, rend, send, spend, tend, trend, vend, wend • amend, append, ascend, attend, bartend, befriend, Big Bend, bookend, boyfriend, commend, contend, dead end, dead-end, defend, depend, descend, distend, downtrend, emend, expend, extend, front-end, girlfriend, godsend, high-end, impend, intend, Land's End, loose end, low-end, misspend, no end, offend, on end, outspend, portend, pretend, rearend, resend, South Bend, split end, stipend, suspend, tag end, tail end, tight end, transcend, unbend, upend, uptrend, weekend, year-end • apprehend, bitter end, business end, comprehend, condescend, dividend, in the end, on the mend, overspend, recommend • at one's wit's end, hyperextend, misapprehend, overextend, stock dividend, superintend • go off the deep end —*also* -ed *forms of verbs listed at* EN¹

enda \en-də\ Brenda, Glenda • agenda • hacienda • hidden agenda

endable \en-də-bəl\ lendable, mendable, spendable • commendable, defendable, dependable, expendable, extendable, unbendable • recommendable, undependable

endal \en-dᵊl\ Grendel, Kendall, Mendel, Wendell

endall \en-dᵊl\ see ENDAL

endance \en-dəns\ see ENDENCE
endancy \en-dən-sē\ see ENDENCY
endant \en-dənt\ see ENDENT
ende[1] \end\ see END
ende[2] \en-dē\ see ENDI
ended \en-dəd\ ended, splendid
• extended, intended, pretended,
unfriended • open-ended
—*also* -ed *forms of verbs listed at*
END
endel \en-dᵊl\ see ENDAL
endell \en-dᵊl\ see ENDAL
endence \en-dəns\ ascendance,
attendance, dependence, tran-
scendence • independence, Independence
—*also* -s, -'s, *and* -s' *forms of*
nouns listed at ENDENT
endency \en-dən-sē\ tendency
• ascendancy, dependency • code-
pendency
endent \en-dənt\ pendant • ascen-
dant, attendant, defendant, de-
pendent, descendant, intendant,
transcendent • codependent,
independent • overdependent,
superintendent
ender \en-dər\ bender, blender,
fender, gender, lender, render,
sender, slender, spender, splen-
dor, tender, vendor • bartender,
commender, contender, defender,
engender, extender, fork-tender,
goaltender, hellbender, offender,
pretender, surrender, suspender,
transgender, weekender • money-
lender
endi \en-dē\ trendy, Wendy
• modus vivendi
endible \en-də-bəl\ see ENDABLE
endid \en-dəd\ see ENDED
ending \en-diŋ\ ending, pending,
sending • ascending, attending,
fence-mending, goaltending,
heartrending, mind-bending,
nerve ending, unbending, unend-
ing • condescending, gender-

bending • uncomprehending
—*also* -ing *forms of verbs listed at*
END
endless \end-ləs\ endless, friend-
less
endliness \en-lē-nəs\ cleanliness,
friendliness • uncleanliness, un-
friendliness
endly \en-lē\ friendly • uncleanly,
unfriendly • user-friendly
endo \en-dō\ kendo • crescendo
• innuendo
endor \en-dər\ see ENDER
endous \en-dəs\ horrendous, stu-
pendous, tremendous
ends \enz\ see ENS[1]
endum \en-dəm\ addendum • ref-
erendum
endy \en-dē\ see ENDI
ene[1] \en\ see EN[1]
ene[2] \en-ē\ see ENNY
ene[3] \ē-nē\ see INI[1]
ene[4] \ēn\ see INE[3]
ene[5] \ān\ see ANE[1]
enel \en-ᵊl\ see ENNEL
ener \ē-nər\ see EANER
enery[1] \en-ə-rē\ see ENARY
enery[2] \ēn-rē\ see EANERY
enet \en-ət\ see ENNET
eng[1] \aŋ\ see ANG[2]
eng[2] \əŋ\ see UNG[1]
enge \enj\ avenge, revenge, Stone-
henge
ength[1] \eŋth\ length, strength
• arm's-length, at length, floor-
length, full-length, half-length,
wavelength • industrial-strength
ength[2] \enth\ see ENTH
engthen \eŋ-thən\ lengthen,
strengthen
enh \en\ see EN[1]
enia[1] \ē-nē-ə\ Armenia, Slovenia
• schizophrenia
enia[2] \ē-nyə\ Armenia, Eugenia,
gardenia
enial \ē-nē-əl\ genial, menial, ve-
nial • congenial

enian \ē-nē-ən\ Armenian, Athenian, Cyrenian, Slovenian, Turkmenian

enic[1] \ēn-ik\ scenic • hygienic

enic[2] \en-ik\ arsenic, Edenic, Hellenic, hygienic • allergenic, calisthenic, cryogenic, hygienic, photogenic, schizophrenic, telegenic • carcinogenic • hallucinogenic, hypoallergenic

enice \en-əs\ see ENIS

enics \en-iks\ calisthenics, cryogenics
—also -s, -'s, and -s' forms of nouns listed at ENIC[2]

enie[1] \en-ē\ see ENNY

enie[2] \ē-nē\ see INI[1]

enience \ē-nyəns\ lenience • convenience • inconvenience

enient \ēn-yənt\ lenient • convenient • inconvenient

enim \en-əm\ see ENOM

enin \en-ən\ see ENNON

enis \en-əs\ Dennis, genus, menace, tennis, Venice • lawn tennis • table tennis

enison[1] \en-ə-sən\ Tennyson, venison

enison[2] \en-ə-zən\ denizen, venison

enitor \en-ət-ər\ senator • progenitor

enity \en-ət-ē\ see ENTITY

enizen \en-ə-zən\ see ENISON[2]

enn \en\ see EN[1]

enna \en-ə\ Glenna, henna • antenna, sienna, Vienna • whip antenna

ennae \en-ē\ see ENNY

ennant \en-ənt\ see ENANT

enne[1] \en\ see EN[1]

enne[2] \en-ē\ see ENNY

enne[3] \an\ see AN[5]

ennec \en-ik\ see ENIC[2]

enned \end\ see END

ennel \en-ᵊl\ fennel, kennel

ennery \en-ə-rē\ see ENARY

ennes \en\ see EN[1]

ennet \en-ət\ senate, tenet

ennett \en-ət\ see ENNET

enney \en-ē\ see ENNY

enni \en-ē\ see ENNY

ennial \en-ē-əl\ biennial, centennial, decennial, millennial, perennial, quadrennial, triennial • bicentennial

ennig \en-ik\ see ENIC[2]

ennin \en-ən\ see ENNON

ennis \en-əs\ see ENIS

ennit \en-ət\ see ENNET

ennium \en-ē-əm\ biennium, millennium

ennon \en-ən\ Lenin, Lennon • antivenin

enny \en-ē\ any, benny, Benny, Denny, genie, Jenny, Kenny, many, penny, Penny • antennae, halfpenny, sixpenny, so many, tenpenny, threepenny, twopenny • spinning jenny

ennyson \en-ə-sən\ see ENISON[1]

eno \ā-nō\ see ANO[2]

enom \en-əm\ denim, venom

enon \en-ən\ see ENNON

enous \ē-nəs\ see ENUS[1]

ens[1] \enz\ cleanse, lens • amends, hand lens, weekends, zoom lens • odds and ends • Homo sapiens
—also -s, -'s, and -s' forms of nouns and -s forms of verbs listed at EN[1]

ens[2] \ens\ see ENSE

ensable \en-sə-bəl\ see ENSIBLE

ensal \en-səl\ see ENCIL

ensary \ens-rē\ see ENSORY

ensch \ench\ see ENCH

ense \ens\ dense, fence, hence, pence, sense, tense, thence, whence • commence, condense, defense, dispense, expense, horse sense, immense, incense, intense, nonsense, offense, past tense, pretense, sequence, sixpence, sixth sense, suspense, twopence • common sense, confidence,

consequence, diffidence, evidence, frankincense, no-nonsense, present tense, providence, Providence, recompense, residence, self-defense, zone defense • coincidence, inconsequence, nonresidence, self-confidence
—*also* -s, -'s, *and* -s' *forms of nouns listed at* ENT[1]

enseful \ens-fəl\ senseful • suspenseful

enseless \en-sləs\ fenceless, senseless • defenseless, offenseless

enser \en-sər\ see ENSOR

ensian \en-chən\ see ENSION

ensible \en-sə-bəl\ sensible • defensible, dispensable, extensible, insensible, ostensible • commonsensible, comprehensible, indefensible, indispensable, reprehensible • incomprehensible

ensil \en-səl\ see ENCIL

ensile \en-səl\ see ENCIL

ension \en-shən\ mention, pension, tension • abstention, ascension, attention, contention, convention, declension, detention, dimension, dissension, extension, high-tension, indention, intention, invention, pretension, prevention, retention, suspension • apprehension, circumvention, comprehension, condescension, contravention, fourth dimension, hypertension, hypotension, inattention, reinvention, third dimension • hyperextension, incomprehension, misapprehension, nonintervention, overextension • Geneva convention, honorable mention

ensional \ench-nəl\ conventional, dimensional, intentional • four-dimensional, one-dimensional, three-dimensional, two-dimensional, unconventional, unintentional

ensis \en-səs\ see ENSUS

ensity \en-sət-ē\ density • immensity, intensity, propensity

ensive \en-siv\ pensive • defensive, expensive, extensive, intensive, offensive • apprehensive, comprehensive, inexpensive, inoffensive • counteroffensive, labor-intensive

ensor \en-sər\ censor, fencer, sensor, Spencer, tensor • condenser, dispenser, extensor, sequencer
—*also* -er *forms of adjectives listed at* ENSE

ensory \ens-rē\ sensory • dispensary • extrasensory, multisensory

ensual[1] \en-chəl\ see ENTIAL

ensual[2] \ench-wəl\ see ENTUAL[1]

ensure \en-chər\ see ENTURE

ensus \en-səs\ census • consensus • amanuensis

ent[1] \ent\ bent, Brent, cent, dent, gent, Ghent, Kent, lent, Lent, meant, pent, rent, scent, sent, spent, tent, Trent, vent, went • absent, accent, Advent, ascent, assent, augment, cement, comment, consent, content, convent, descent, dissent, event, extent, ferment, foment, fragment, frequent, hell-bent, indent, intent, invent, lament, low-rent, outspent, percent, pigment, portent, present, prevent, pup tent, relent, repent, resent, segment, Tashkent, torment, well-meant • accident, argument, circumvent, compartment, complement, compliment, confident, diffident, discontent, document, evident, heaven-sent, implement, incident, instrument, malcontent, nonevent, ornament, orient, president, provident, regiment, reinvent, represent, resident, sediment, Stoke-on-Trent, subsequent, supplement, underwent • age of consent, disorient, experiment, glove compartment, misrepresent, nonresident, oxygen tent, portland cement, rubber cement, self-confident, self-evident, vice president • in any event, media event

ent² \änt\ see ANT²

ent³ \äⁿ\ see ANT¹

enta \ent-ə\ magenta, placenta, polenta

entable \ent-ə-bəl\ rentable • lamentable, presentable, preventable • documentable, representable

entacle \ent-i-kəl\ see ENTICAL

entage \ent-ij\ tentage • percentage

ental \ent-ᵊl\ dental, gentle, lentil, mental, rental • judgmental, parental • accidental, apartmental, compartmental, continental, departmental, detrimental, elemental, fundamental, governmental, grandparental, incidental, incremental, instrumental, monumental, nonjudgmental, occidental, oriental, ornamental, regimental, sacramental, sentimental, supplemental, temperamental, transcendental • coincidental, developmental, environmental, experimental, transcontinental • intercontinental, interdepartmental

entalist \ent-ᵊl-əst\ fundamentalist, instrumentalist, orientalist, sentimentalist, transcendentalist • environmentalist

entance \ent-ᵊns\ see ENTENCE

entary \en-trē\ entry, gentry, sentry • reentry, subentry • alimentary, complementary, complimentary, documentary, elementary, mockumentary, parliamentary, port of entry, sedimentary, supplementary • uncomplimentary

entative \ent-ət-iv\ tentative • preventative • argumentative, representative

ente¹ \ent-ē\ see ENTY

ente² \änt\ see ANT²

ented \ent-əd\ contented, demented, lamented, segmented • discontented, malcontented, oriented, self-contented • unprecedented • overrepresented, underrepresented
—*also* -ed *forms of verbs listed at* ENT¹

enten \ent-ᵊn\ dentin, Lenten, Quentin, Trenton

entence \ent-ᵊns\ sentence • death sentence, repentance

enter \ent-ər\ center, enter, mentor, renter • dissenter, frequenter, inventor, nerve center, presenter, reenter, tormentor • epicenter, front and center, shopping center, trauma center • experimenter

entered \en-tərd\ centered • self-centered
—*also* -ed *forms of verbs listed at* ENTER

enterie \en-trē\ see ENTARY

entful \ent-fəl\ eventful, resentful • uneventful

enth \enth\ nth, strength, tenth • crème de menthe • industrial-strength

enthe \enth\ see ENTH

enti \ent-ē\ see ENTY

entia \en-shə\ dementia, Valencia • in absentia

ential \en-shəl\ consensual, credential, essential, eventual, potential, prudential, sequential, tangential, torrential • confidential, consequential, deferential, differential, existential, exponential, inessential, influential, nonessential, penitential, pestilential, preferential, presidential, providential, quintessential, residential, reverential, unessential • inconsequential, vice presidential

entian \en-shən\ see ENSION

entiary \ensh-rē\ century • penitentiary • plenipotentiary

entical \ent-i-kəl\ tentacle • identi-
cal

entice \ent-əs\ see ENTOUS

enticle \ent-i-kəl\ see ENTICAL

entient \en-chənt\ penchant, sen-
tient, trenchant

entil \ent-ᵊl\ see ENTAL

entin \ent-ᵊn\ see ENTEN

enting \ent-iŋ\ dissenting • unre-
lenting
—*also* -ing *forms of verbs listed at*
ENT[1]

ention \en-shən\ see ENSION

entional \ensh- nəl\ see ENSIONAL

entioned \en-shənd\ mentioned
• aforementioned, well-inten-
tioned

entious \en-chəs\ contentious,
licentious, pretentious, senten-
tious, tendentious • conscientious,
unpretentious

entis \ent-əs\ see ENTOUS

entity \en-ət-ē\ entity • amenity,
identity, nonentity, obscenity,
serenity

entive \ent-iv\ attentive, incentive,
inventive, preventive, retentive
• inattentive

entle \ent-ᵊl\ see ENTAL

entment \ent-mənt\ contentment,
resentment • discontentment

ento \en-tō\ lento • memento,
pimiento, Sorrento • Sacramento
• divertimento, risorgimento
• pronunciamento

enton \ent-ᵊn\ see ENTEN

entor \ent-ər\ see ENTER

entous \ent-əs\ apprentice, mo-
mentous, portentous • compos
mentis • non compos mentis

entry \en-trē\ see ENTARY

ents \ents\ two cents • at all events,
dollars-and-cents
—*also* -s, -'s, *and* -s' *forms of nouns
and* -s *forms of verbs listed at* ENT[1]

entual[1] \en-shə-wəl\ sensual • ac-
centual, consensual, eventual

entual[2] \en-chəl\ see ENTIAL

enture \en-chər\ censure, denture,
quencher, venture • adventure,
backbencher, debenture, inden-
ture • misadventure

entury \ench-rē\ see ENTIARY

enty \ent-ē\ plenty, twenty
• aplenty • horn of plenty, twenty-
twenty

enuis \en-yə-wəs\ see ENUOUS

enum \en-əm\ see ENOM

enuous \en-yə-wəs\ strenuous,
tenuous • ingenuous • disingenu-
ous

enus[1] \ē-nəs\ genus, venous, Venus
• Maecenas • intravenous

enus[2] \en-əs\ see ENIS

eny \ā-nē\ see AINY

enys \en-əs\ see ENIS

enza \en-zə\ cadenza, credenza
• influenza

eo[1] \ā-ō\ kayo, mayo • cacao,
rodeo • Galileo, San Mateo
• Montevideo

eo[2] \ē-ō\ see IO[2]

eoff[1] \ef\ see EF[1]

eoff[2] \ēf\ see IEF[1]

eoffor \ef-ər\ see EPHOR

eoman \ō-mən\ see OMAN

eon[1] \ē-ən\ see EAN[1]

eon[2] \ē-än\ eon, Freon, neon, prion

eopard \ep-ərd\ leopard, peppered,
shepherd • snow leopard • German shepherd

eopardess \ep-ərd-əs\ leopardess,
shepherdess

eople \ē-pəl\ people, steeple
• craftspeople, laypeople, sales-
people, townspeople, tradespeople
• businesspeople, little people
• beautiful people

eorem \ir-əm\ see ERUM

eorge \órj\ see ORGE

eorist \ir-əst\ see ERIST[1]

eoul \ōl\ see OLE[1]

eous \ē-əs\ see EUS[1]

ep \ep\ pep, prep, rep, schlepp, step, steppe, strep, yep • doorstep, footstep, goose-step, half step, instep, in step, lockstep, misstep, sidestep, twelve-step, whole step • in lockstep, out of step, overstep, step-by-step

eparable \ep-rə-bəl\ reparable, separable • inseparable, irreparable

epard \ep-ərd\ see EOPARD

epe \āp\ see APE[1]

epee \ē-pē\ see EEPY

eper \ep-ər\ see EPPER

eperous \ep-rəs\ leprous • obstreperous

eph \ef\ see EF[1]

ephen \ē-vən\ see EVEN

epherd \ep-ərd\ see EOPARD

epherdess \ep-ərd-əs\ see EOPARDESS

ephone \ef-ə-nē\ see EPHONY

ephony \ef-ə-nē\ Stephanie • Persephone, telephony

ephor \ef-ər\ heifer, zephyr

epht \eft\ see EFT

ephyr \ef-ər\ see EPHOR

epid \ep-əd\ tepid • intrepid

epo \ēp-ō\ see EPOT

epot \ēp-ō\ depot • el cheapo

epp \ep\ see EP

eppe \ep\ see EP

epped \ept\ see EPT

epper \ep-ər\ leper, pepper • bell pepper, green pepper, hot pepper, red pepper, sidestepper, sweet pepper • chili pepper

eppy \ep-ē\ peppy, preppy

eprous \ep-rəs\ see EPEROUS

eps \eps\ biceps, forceps, triceps • quadriceps
—*also* -s, -'s, *and* -s' *forms of nouns and* -s *forms of verbs listed at* EP

ept \ept\ crept, kept, slept, stepped, swept, wept • accept, adept, backswept, concept, except, inept, precept, upswept, windswept • intercept, overslept
—*also* -ed *forms of verbs listed at* EP

eptable \ep-tə-bəl\ see EPTIBLE

eptacle \ep-ti-kəl\ skeptical • receptacle

eptible \ep-tə-bəl\ acceptable, perceptible, susceptible • imperceptible, unacceptable

eptic \ep-tik\ peptic, septic, skeptic • dyspeptic • antiseptic, epileptic, narcoleptic

eptical \ep-ti-kəl\ see EPTACLE

eption \ep-shən\ conception, deception, exception, inception, perception, reception • interception, misconception, preconception, take exception

epy \ep-ē\ see EPPY

epys \ēps\ for keeps
—*also* -s, -'s, *and* -s' *forms of nouns and* -s *forms of verbs listed at* EEP

equal \ē-kwəl\ equal, sequel • coequal, unequal

eque \ek\ see ECK

equel \ē-kwəl\ see EQUAL

equer \ek-ər\ see ECKER

er[1] \ā\ see AY[1]

er[2] \er\ see ARE[4]

er[3] \ər\ see EUR[1]

er[4] \ir\ see EER[2]

era[1] \er-ə\ Berra, era, Hera, Sarah • mascara, Rivera, Sahara, sierra, tiara • aloe vera, Common Era, habanera, riviera, Riviera, Santa Clara • Islamic Era, Spanish Sahara, Western Sahara

era[2] \ir-ə\ era, Hera, lira, Vera • chimera, Madeira, mbira • Common Era • Islamic Era

erah \ir-ə\ see ERA[2]

eral[1] \ir-əl\ Cyril, feral, virile

eral[2] \er-əl\ see ERIL

eral[3] \ər-əl\ see ERRAL

erald \er-əld\ Gerald, Harold, herald

eraph \er-əf\ see ERIF

eratin \er-ət-ᵊn\ keratin, Sheraton • Samaritan

erative \er-ət-iv\ see ARATIVE¹

eraton \er-ət-ᵊn\ see ERATIN

erb \ərb\ blurb, curb, herb, Serb, verb • adverb, disturb, exurb, perturb, proverb, reverb, suburb, superb

erbal \ər-bəl\ burble, gerbil, herbal, verbal • nonverbal

erbally \ər-bə-lē\ verbally • hyperbole, nonverbally

erber \ər-bər\ see URBER

erbia \ər-bē-ə\ see URBIA

erbil \ər-bəl\ see ERBAL

erbole \ər-bə-lē\ see ERBALLY

erby \ər-bē\ derby, herby, Kirby • Roller Derby • demolition derby

erce \ərs\ see ERSE

ercery \ərs-rē\ see URSARY

erch \ərch\ see URCH

ercial \ər-shəl\ Herschel • commercial • controversial, infomercial, uncommercial

ercian \ər-shən\ see ERTIAN

ercible \ər-sə-bəl\ see ERSIBLE

ercion \ər-zhən\ see ERSION¹

ercive \ər-siv\ see ERSIVE

ercular \ər-kyə-lər\ see IRCULAR

ercy \ər-sē\ Circe, mercy, Percy • controversy

erd \ərd\ see IRD

erde¹ \erd\ see AIRED

erde² \ərd\ see IRD

erde³ \ərd-ē\ see URDY

erder \ərd-ər\ birder, girder, herder, murder • sheepherder

erdi \ər-dē\ see URDY

erding \ərd-iŋ\ wording • sheepherding
—*also* -ing *forms of verbs listed at* IRD

erdure \ər-jər\ see ERGER

ere¹ \er\ see ARE⁴

ere² \er-ē\ see ARY¹

ere³ \ir\ see EER²

ere⁴ \ir-ē\ see EARY

ere⁵ \ər\ see EUR¹

e're \ē-ər\ see EER¹

ère \er\ see ARE⁴

ereal \ir-ē-əl\ see ERIAL

ereid \ir-ē-əd\ see ERIOD

erek \erik\ see ERIC¹

erely \ir-lē\ see EARLY¹

erence¹ \ir-əns\ clearance • adherence, appearance, coherence • disappearance, incoherence, interference, perseverance • run interference

erence² \ər-əns\ see URRENCE

erence³ \er-əns\ see ARENCE¹

erent \er-ənt\ see ARENT¹

eren't¹ \ərnt\ see EARNT

eren't² \ər-ənt\ see URRENT

ereo \er-ē-ō\ see ARIO

ereous \ir-ē-əs\ see ERIOUS

erer \ir-ər\ see EARER²

eres¹ \erz\ see AIRS

eres² \ir-ēz\ see ERIES

eres³ \ərs\ see ERS¹

ereth \er-ət\ see ERIT

ereus \ir-ē-əs\ see ERIOUS

erf \ərf\ see URF

erge \ərj\ see URGE

ergence \ər-jəns\ convergence, divergence, emergence, resurgence
—*also* -s, -'s, *and* -s' *forms of nouns listed at* URGENT

ergency \ər-jən-sē\ urgency • emergency, insurgency • counterinsurgency

ergent \ər-jənt\ see URGENT

ergeon \ər-jin\ see URGEON

erger \ər-jər\ merger, perjure, verdure

ergic \ər-jik\ allergic • dramaturgic

ergne¹ \ərn\ see URN

ergne² \ern\ see ERN¹

ergy \ər-jē\ see URGY

eri¹ \er-ē\ see ARY¹

eri² \ir-ē\ see EARY

eria¹ \ir-ē-ə\ Syria • Algeria, Assyria, bacteria, criteria, diphtheria, Elyria, Iberia, Illyria, Liberia, Nigeria, Siberia, wisteria • cafeteria

eria² \er-ē-ə\ see ARIA

erial \ir-ē-əl\ aerial, cereal, serial • arterial, bacterial, ethereal, funereal, imperial, material, venereal • immaterial, magisterial, managerial, ministerial, raw material • antibacterial

erian¹ \ir-ē-ən\ Algerian, Assyrian, Chaucerian, criterion, Faulknerian, Hitlerian, Iberian, Liberian, Nigerian, Shakespearean, Siberian, Sumerian, valerian, Wagnerian • Presbyterian

erian² \er-ē-ən\ see ARIAN¹

eric¹ \er-ik\ cleric, Derek, derrick, Eric • generic, Homeric, numeric • atmospheric, esoteric, hemispheric, stratospheric • alphanumeric, ionospheric

eric² \ir-ik\ lyric, Pyrrhic, spheric • satiric, vampiric • atmospheric, hemispheric, panegyric, stratospheric

erica \er-i-kə\ Erica • America • North America, South America • Central America, Latin America, Middle America

erical¹ \er-i-kəl\ clerical, spherical • hysterical, numerical • anticlerical

erical² \ir-i-kəl\ lyrical, miracle, spherical • empirical • hemispherical

erich \erik\ see ERIC¹

erics \er-iks\ hysterics
—also -s, -'s, and -s' forms of nouns listed at ERIC¹

eried \ir-ē-əd\ see ERIOD

eries \ir-ēz\ Ceres, queries, series • in series, World Series • miniseries

—also -s, -'s, and -s' forms of nouns listed at EARY

erif \er-əf\ seraph, sheriff

eriff \er-əf\ see ERIF

erik \erik\ see ERIC¹

erika \er-i-kə\ see ERICA

eril \er-əl\ beryl, Beryl, Cheryl, Errol, feral, peril, Sheryl, sterile • imperil

erile \er-əl\ see ERIL

erilous \er-ə-ləs\ perilous, querulous

erin \er-ən\ see ARON¹

ering \ar-iŋ\ see ARING¹

eriod \ir-ē-əd\ myriad, period • grace period

erion \ir-ē-ən\ see ERIAN¹

erior \ir-ē-ər\ anterior, exterior, inferior, interior, posterior, superior, ulterior • Lake Superior
—also -er forms of adjectives listed at EARY

eriot \er-ē-ət\ see ARIAT¹

erious \ir-ē-əs\ serious, Sirius • delirious, imperious, mysterious, Tiberius • deleterious

eris¹ \ir-əs\ see EROUS

eris² \er-əs\ see ERROUS

erist¹ \ir-əst\ theorist
—also -est forms of adjectives listed at EER²

erist² \er-əst\ see ARIST

erit \er-ət\ ferret, merit • demerit, inherit • disinherit

eritable \er-ət-ə-bəl\ veritable • inheritable

eritor \er-ət-ər\ ferreter • inheritor

erity \er-ət-ē\ rarity, verity • asperity, austerity, dexterity, posterity, prosperity, severity, sincerity, temerity • insincerity

erium \ir-ē-əm\ Miriam • bacterium, delirium

erius¹ \er-ē-əs\ see ARIOUS

erius² \ir-ē-əs\ see ERIOUS

erjure \ər-jər\ see ERGER

erjury \ərj-rē\ perjury, surgery

• tree surgery • microsurgery, neurosurgery, plastic surgery, psychosurgery

erk \ərk\ see ORK[1]

erker \ər-kər\ see ORKER[1]

erkin \ər-kən\ see IRKIN

erking \ər-kiŋ\ see ORKING

erky \ər-kē\ jerky, murky, perky, smirky, turkey, Turkey • talk turkey • Albuquerque, herky-jerky

erle \ərl\ see IRL

erlie \er-lē\ see AIRLY

erlin \ər-lən\ merlin, Merlin, yearling

erling \ər-liŋ\ see URLING

erlon \ər-lən\ see ERLIN

erlyn \ər-lən\ see ERLIN

erm \ərm\ see ORM[1]

erma \ər-mə\ dharma, Irma • terra firma

ermal \ər-məl\ dermal, thermal • epidermal

erman \ər-mən\ ermine, German, Herman, merman, sermon, Sherman, vermin • determine, Mount Hermon • predetermine

ermanent \ərm-nənt\ permanent • determinant, impermanent • semipermanent

ermann \ər-mən\ see ERMAN

erment \ər-mənt\ deferment, interment, preferment • disinterment

ermi \ər-mē\ see ERMY

ermic \ər-mik\ karmic • geothermic, hypodermic, taxidermic

ermin \ər-mən\ see ERMAN

erminal \ərm-nəl\ germinal, terminal

erminant \ərm-nənt\ see ERMANENT

ermine \ər-mən\ see ERMAN

ermined \ər-mənd\ ermined • determined • self-determined • overdetermined

erminous \ər-mə-nəs\ terminus, verminous

erminus \ər-mə-nəs\ see ERMINOUS

ermis \ər-məs\ dermis, thermos • epidermis

ermit \ər-mət\ hermit, Kermit

ermon \ər-mən\ see ERMAN

ermos \ər-məs\ see ERMIS

ermy \ər-mē\ germy, squirmy, wormy • taxidermy

ern[1] \ern\ bairn, cairn

ern[2] \ərn\ see URN

erna \ər-nə\ Myrna, Verna

ernal \ərn-³l\ colonel, journal, kernel, vernal • eternal, external, fraternal, infernal, internal, maternal, nocturnal, paternal

erne[1] \ern\ see ERN[1]

erne[2] \ərn\ see URN

erned \ərnd\ see URNED

ernel \ərn-³l\ see ERNAL

erner \ər-nər\ see URNER

ernes[1] \ern\ see ERN[1]

ernes[2] \ərn\ see URN

ernest \ər-nəst\ see ERNIST

ernia \ər-ne-ə\ hernia • Hibernia

ernian \ər-nē-ən\ Hibernian, Saturnian

ernible \ər-nə-bəl\ see URNABLE

ernie \ər-nē\ see OURNEY[1]

ernion \ər-nē-ən\ see ERNIAN

ernist \ər-nəst\ earnest, Ernest • internist

ernity \ər-nət-ē\ eternity, fraternity, maternity, modernity, paternity

ernment \ərn-mənt\ adjournment, discernment, internment

erny \ər-nē\ see OURNEY[1]

ero[1] \ē-rō\ gyro, hero, Nero, zero • ground zero, subzero • superhero

ero[2] \er-ō\ pharaoh, taro, tarot • bolero, sombrero, torero, vaquero • caballero, pistolero • Rio de Janeiro

ero[3] \ir-ō\ gyro, hero, zero • ground zero, subzero

erold \er-əld\ see ERALD

eron \er-ən\ see ARON[1]

erous \ir-əs\ cirrus, Eris, peeress, Pyrrhus, seeress

erp \ərp\ see URP

erpe \ər-pē\ see IRPY

erque \ər-kē\ see ERKY

err[1] \er\ see ARE[4]

err[2] \ər\ see EUR[1]

erra \er-ə\ see ERA[1]

errace \er-əs\ see ERROUS

erral \ər-əl\ squirrel • conferral, deferral, referral, transferal

errance \er-əns\ see ARENCE[1]

errand \er-ənd\ errand, gerund

errant \er-ənt\ see ARENT[1]

erre \er\ see ARE[4]

errell \er-əl\ see ERIL

errence[1] \ər-əns\ see URRENCE

errence[2] \er-əns\ see ARENCE[1]

erret \er-ət\ see ERIT

erreter \er-ət-ər\ see ERITOR

erria \er-ē-ə\ see ARIA

errible \er-ə-bəl\ see EARABLE[1]

erric \er-ik\ see ERIC[1]

errick \er-ik\ see ERIC[1]

errie \er-ē\ see ARY[1]

erried \er-ēd\ berried, serried, varied
—also -ed *forms of verbs listed at* ARY[1]

errier \er-ē-ər\ terrier • bull terrier, fox terrier, Welsh terrier
—also -er *forms of adjectives listed at* ARY[1]

errill \er-əl\ see ERIL

errily \er-ə-lē\ see ARILY

erring[1] \ar-iŋ\ see ARING[1]

erring[2] \ər-iŋ\ see URRING

erris \er-əs\ see ERROUS

errol \er-əl\ see ERIL

errold \er-əld\ see ERALD

erron \er-ən\ see ARON[1]

error \er-ər\ see EARER[1]

errous \er-əs\ Eris, terrace • millionairess

errule \er-əl\ see ERIL

erry \er-ē\ see ARY[1]

ers[1] \ərz\ hers • somewheres
—also -s, -'s, *and* -s' *forms of nouns and* -s *forms of verbs listed at* EUR[1]

ers[2] \ā\ see AY[1]

ersable \ər-sə-bəl\ see ERSIBLE

ersal \ər-səl\ dispersal, rehearsal, reversal, traversal • dress rehearsal, universal

ersary \ərs-rē\ see URSARY

erse \ərs\ curse, hearse, nurse, purse, terse, verse, worse • adverse, averse, coerce, commerce, converse, Converse, disburse, disperse, diverse, free verse, immerse, inverse, Nez Percé, obverse, perverse, rehearse, reverse, scrub nurse, submerse, transverse, traverse, wet nurse • e-commerce, in reverse, intersperse, nonsense verse, reimburse, universe • chapter and verse, practical nurse, registered nurse, visiting nurse • chamber of commerce

ersed \ərst\ see URST

ersey \ər-zē\ jersey, Jersey, Mersey • New Jersey

erschel \ər-shəl\ see ERCIAL

ershel \ər-shəl\ see ERCIAL

ersial \ər-shəl\ see ERCIAL

ersian \ər-zhən\ see ERSION[1]

ersible \ər-sə-bəl\ conversable, immersible, reversible, submersible • irreversible

ersion[1] \ər-zhən\ Persian, version • aversion, coercion, conversion, dispersion, diversion, excursion, immersion, incursion, inversion, perversion, reversion, submersion, subversion • extroversion, introversion, King James Version, reconversion

ersion[2] \ər-shən\ see ERTIAN

ersive \ər-siv\ cursive • coercive, discursive, subversive

erson \ərs-ᵊn\ person, worsen

• chairperson, craftsperson, first person, in person, layperson, MacPherson, newsperson, salesperson, spokesperson, third person • anchorperson, businessperson, second person, weatherperson

erst \ərst\ see URST

ersy \ər-sē\ see ERCY

ert¹ \ərt\ Bert, blurt, curt, Curt, dirt, flirt, hurt, pert, shirt, skirt, spurt, squirt • advert, alert, assert, avert, concert, convert, covert, desert, dessert, divert, dress shirt, exert, expert, frankfurt, hair shirt, hoopskirt, inert, insert, invert, nightshirt, overt, pay dirt, pervert, revert, Schubert, seagirt, sea squirt, stuffed shirt, subvert, sweatshirt, T-shirt • disconcert, extrovert, in concert, inexpert, introvert, miniskirt, overskirt, polo shirt, reconvert, red alert, undershirt, underskirt • Hawaiian shirt

ert² \er\ see ARE⁴

ert³ \at\ see AT⁵

erta \ərt-ə\ Gerta • Alberta, Roberta

ertain \ərt-ᵊn\ Burton, certain, curtain • for certain, uncertain

erted \ərt-əd\ concerted, perverted, T-shirted • extroverted, miniskirted, undershirted
—*also* -ed *forms of verbs listed at* ERT¹

erter \ərt-ər\ curter, squirter • converter, deserter, frankfurter, Frankfurter

erth \ərth\ see IRTH

ertha \ər-thə\ Bertha, Eartha

ertial \ər-shəl\ see ERCIAL

ertian \ər-shən\ assertion, Cistercian, desertion, exertion, insertion • self-assertion

ertile \ərt-ᵊl\ fertile, hurtle, myrtle, Myrtle, turtle • crape myrtle,
infertile, sea turtle, turn turtle, wax myrtle • snapping turtle

erting \ərt-iŋ\ shirting, skirting • disconcerting
—*also* -ing *forms of verbs listed at* ERT¹

ertion \ər-shən\ see ERTIAN

ertive \ərt-iv\ furtive • assertive • self-assertive, unassertive

erton \ərt-n\ see ERTAIN

ertor \ərt-ər\ see ERTER

erts \ərts\ hertz • gigahertz, kilohertz, megahertz
—*also* -s, -'s, *and* -s' *forms of nouns and* -s *forms of verbs listed at* ERT¹

erty \ər-tē\ see IRTY

ertz \ərts\ see ERTS

erule \er-əl\ see ERIL

erulous \er-ə-ləs\ see ERILOUS

erum \ir-əm\ theorem, serum • blood serum, truth serum

erund \er-ənd\ see ERRAND

erunt \er-ənt\ see ARENT¹

erval \ər-vəl\ see ERVIL

ervancy \ər-vən-sē\ see ERVENCY

ervant \ər-vənt\ fervent, servant • bond servant, maidservant, manservant, observant • civil servant, inobservant, public servant

ervative \ər-vət-iv\ conservative, preservative • ultraconservative

erve \ərv\ curve, MIRV, nerve, serve, swerve, verve • conserve, deserve, hors d'oeuvre, observe, preserve, reserve, self-serve, sine curve, unnerve • facial nerve, in reserve, learning curve, optic nerve, spinal nerve, vagus nerve • cranial nerve, sciatic nerve

erved \ərvd\ nerved • deserved, reserved • unreserved
—*also* -ed *forms of verbs listed at* ERVE

ervency \ər-vən-sē\ fervency • conservancy

ervent \ər-vənt\ see ERVANT

erver \ər-vər\ fervor, server • conserver, observer, timeserver • altar server, life preserver

ervice \ər-vəs\ nervous, service • curb service, disservice, fullservice, lip service, room service, self-service, wire service • civil service, divine service, foreign service, public service, secret service, social service

ervil \ər-vəl\ chervil, servile

ervile \ər-vəl\ see ERVIL

erving \ər-viŋ\ Erving, Irving, serving • deserving, self-serving, timeserving, unswerving
—*also* -ing *forms of verbs listed at* ERVE

ervor \ər-vər\ see ERVER

ervous \ər-vəs\ see ERVICE

ervy \ər-vē\ see URVY

erwick \er-ik\ see ERIC[1]

erwin \ər-wən\ Irwin, Sherwin

ery[1] \er-ē\ see ARY[1]

ery[2] \ir-ē\ see EARY

eryl \er-əl\ see ERIL

es[1] \ā\ see AY[1]

es[2] \ās\ see ACE[1]

es[3] \āz\ see AZE[1]

es[4] \es\ see ESS

es[5] \ēz\ see EZE

e's \ēz\ see EZE

esa \ā-sə\ mesa • Theresa

esage \es-ij\ see ESSAGE

esan[1] \āz-ᵊn\ see AZON

esan[2] \ēz-ᵊn\ see EASON

esant \ez-ᵊnt\ peasant, pheasant, pleasant, present • at present, unpleasant, omnipresent

esce \es\ see ESS

escence \es-ᵊns\ essence • excrescence, florescence, fluorescence, pubescence, quintessence, senescence • acquiescence, adolescence, convalescence, effervescence, efflorescence, evanescence, incandescence,

iridescence, luminescence, obsolescence, phosphorescence
—*also* -s, -'s, *and* -s' *forms of nouns listed at* ESCENT

escent \es-ᵊnt\ crescent • depressant, fluorescent, incessant, pubescent, quiescent, senescent, suppressant • acquiescent, adolescent, convalescent, effervescent, efflorescent, evanescent, Fertile Crescent, incandescent, iridescent, luminescent, obsolescent, phosphorescent • antidepressant, preadolescent

escible \es-ə-bəl\ see ESSIBLE

escive \es-iv\ see ESSIVE

esco \es-kō\ fresco • alfresco, UNESCO • Ionesco

escue \es-kyü\ fescue, rescue

ese[1] \ēs\ see IECE

ese[2] \ēz\ see EZE

ese[3] \ā-sē\ see ACY

eseus \ē-sē-əs\ Theseus • Tiresias

esh[1] \esh\ crèche, flesh, fresh, mesh, thresh • afresh, enmesh, gooseflesh, refresh • Bangladesh, Gilgamesh, intermesh, in the flesh, Marrakech, press the flesh • Uttar Pradesh

esh[2] \āsh\ see ECHE[1]

esh[3] \ash\ see ASH[3]

eshed \esht\ fleshed, meshed
—*also* -ed *forms of verbs listed at* ESH[1]

eshen \esh-ən\ see ESSION

esher \esh-ər\ see ESSURE

eshly \esh-lē\ fleshly, freshly, specially • especially

esi[1] \ā-zē\ see AZY

esi[2] \ā-sē\ see ACY

esia[1] \ē-shə\ Letitia, Lucretia, Phoenicia

esia[2] \ē-zhə\ amnesia, Rhodesia, Silesia, Tunisia • analgesia, anesthesia, Indonesia, kinesthesia, Melanesia, Micronesia, Polynesia, synesthesia • milk of magnesia

esian[1] \ē-zhən\ lesion • adhesion, Cartesian, cohesion, Rhodesian • Indonesian, Melanesian, Micronesian, Polynesian • Peloponnesian

esian[2] \ē-shən\ see ETION[1]

esias \ē-sē-əs\ see ESEUS

esidency \ez-əd-ən-sē\ presidency, residency • vice presidency

esident \ez-əd-ənt\ president, resident • nonresident, vice president

esion \ē-zhən\ see ESIAN[1]

esis \ē-səs\ Croesus, thesis • prosthesis • Dionysus, exegesis • Peloponnesus, telekinesis • amniocentesis

esium \ē-zē-əm\ see EZIUM

esk \esk\ see ESQUE

esley \es-lē\ see ESSLY

eslie \es-lē\ see ESSLY

esne \ēn\ see INE[3]

eso \ā-sō\ peso, say-so

espite \es-pət\ see ESPOT

espot \es-pət\ despot, respite

esque \esk\ desk • burlesque, grotesque • arabesque, copydesk, gigantesque, picaresque, picturesque, statuesque

ess \es\ bless, chess, dress, ess, fess, guess, less, mess, press, s, stress, tress, yes • abscess, access, address, assess, bench-press, caress, clothespress, compress, confess, cross-dress, depress, destress, digress, distress, drill press, duress, excess, express, finesse, full-dress, headdress, housedress, impress, largess, Loch Ness, much less, nightdress, no less, obsess, oppress, outguess, possess, princess, process, profess, progress, recess, regress, repress, shirtdress, SS, success, sundress, suppress, transgress, undress, unless, winepress • ABS, acquiesce, baroness, bitter cress, coa-

lesce, convalesce, crown princess, decompress, deliquesce, dispossess, effervesce, evanesce, fullcourt press, granny dress, in-process, less and less, letterpress, minidress, more or less, nonetheless, overdress, politesse, repossess, reprocess, retrogress, second-guess, SOS, underdress, watercress, word process • keynote address, nevertheless, random-access • limited-access

essa \es-ə\ see ESSE[3]

essable \es-ə-bəl\ see ESSIBLE

essage \es-ij\ message, presage

essamine \es-mən\ see ESSMAN

essan \es-ᵊn\ see ESSEN

essant \es-ᵊnt\ see ESCENT

esse[1] \es\ see ESS

esse[2] \es-ē\ see ESSY

esse[3] \es-ə\ Hesse • Odessa, Vanessa

essed \est\ see EST

essedly \es-əd-lē\ blessedly • confessedly, professedly

essel \es-əl\ see ESTLE[1]

essen \es-ᵊn\ Essen, lessen, lesson • object lesson • delicatessen

essence \es-ᵊns\ see ESCENCE

esser \es-ər\ see ESSOR

essex \es-iks\ Essex, Wessex

essful \es-fəl\ stressful • distressful, successful • unsuccessful

essian \esh-ən\ see ESSION

essible \es-ə-bəl\ decibel, guessable • accessible, assessable, compressible, expressible • inaccessible, inexpressible, irrepressible

essie \es-ē\ see ESSY

essile \es-əl\ see ESTLE[1]

ession \esh-ən\ freshen, session • accession, aggression, bull session, compression, concession, confession, depression, digression, discretion, expression, impression, jam session, obsession, oppression, possession, procession, profession, progression, recession, regression, repression, secession, skull session, succession, suppression, transgression • decompression, indiscretion, intercession, misimpression, nonaggression, repossession, self-confession, self-expression

essional \esh-nəl\ congressional, obsessional, processional, professional, recessional • unprofessional

essionist \esh-nəst\ expressionist, impressionist, secessionist

essity \es-tē\ see ESTY

essive \es-iv\ aggressive, depressive, digressive, excessive, expressive, impressive, obsessive, oppressive, possessive, progressive, successive, transgressive • inexpressive, unexpressive • manic-depressive, passive-aggressive

essly \es-lē\ Leslie, Wesley • expressly

essman \es-mən\ chessman, pressman • specimen

essment \es-mənt\ see ESTMENT

esson \es-ᵊn\ see ESSEN

essor \es-ər\ dresser, lesser, stressor • addresser, aggressor, assessor, compressor, confessor, cross-dresser, hairdresser, oppressor, processor, professor, successor, transgressor • food processor, predecessor, word processor

essure \esh-ər\ fresher, pressure • blood pressure, high-pressure, low-pressure, refresher • acupressure

essy \es-ē\ Bessie, dressy, Jesse, Jessie, messy

est \est\ best, breast, Brest, chest, crest, guest, jest, lest, nest, pest, quest, rest, test, vest, west, West, wrest, zest • abreast, abscessed,

armrest, arrest, at best, at rest, attest, backrest, bed rest, behest, bequest, blood test, Celeste, compressed, conquest, contest, crow's nest, depressed, detest, digest, distressed, divest, field-test, flight-test, footrest, gabfest, hard-pressed, headrest, high-test, hope chest, houseguest, incest, infest, ingest, inquest, interest, invest, Key West, lovefest, love nest, low-test, Midwest, molest, northwest, pretest, professed, protest, repressed, request, road test, scratch test, screen test, sea chest, skin test, slugfest, southwest, stress test, suggest, unblessed, undressed, unrest, unstressed, war chest, Wild West • acid test, anapest, Bucharest, Budapest, decongest, disinvest, empty-nest, false arrest, hornet's nest, house arrest, manifest, north-northwest, placement test, predigest, reinvest, second-best, self-addressed, self-confessed, self-interest, self-possessed, sweatervest, true-false test, vision quest • aptitude test, beauty contest, compound interest, feather one's nest, robin redbreast, simple interest, under arrest, vested interest • citizen's arrest

—*also* -ed *forms of verbs listed at* ESS

esta \es-tə\ Vesta • celesta, fiesta, siesta

estable \es-tə-bəl\ see ESTIBLE

estae \es-tē\ see ESTY

estan \es-tən\ see ESTINE

estant \es-tənt\ contestant, protestant • decongestant

este \est\ see EST

ested \es-təd\ crested, tested, vested • time-tested • barrel-chested, double-breasted, hairy-chested, single-breasted

—also -ed *forms of verbs listed at* EST

ester \es-tər\ Chester, Esther, fester, Hester, jester, Leicester, Lester, nester, pester, quester, tester • ancestor, arrester, investor, Manchester, molester, northwester, Rochester, semester, sequester, southwester, sou'wester, Sylvester, trimester, Winchester • empty nester, polyester

esti \es-tē\ see ESTY

estible \es-tə-bəl\ testable • comestible, detestable, digestible, suggestible • incontestable, indigestible

estic \es-tik\ domestic, majestic • anapestic

estimate \es-tə-mət\ estimate, guesstimate • underestimate

estine \es-tən\ destine • clandestine, intestine, predestine • large intestine, small intestine

esting \es-tiŋ\ resting • arresting • interesting

—also -ing *forms of verbs listed at* EST

estion \es-chən\ question • congestion, cross-question, digestion, ingestion, self-question, suggestion • call in question, decongestion, essay question, indigestion, pop the question • autosuggestion

estive \es-tiv\ festive, restive • congestive, digestive, suggestive • decongestive

estle¹ \es-əl\ Cecil, nestle, pestle, trestle, vessel, wrestle • blood vessel • Indian-wrestle

estle² \as-əl\ see ASSEL²

estle³ \əs-əl\ see USTLE

estment \es-mənt\ vestment • assessment, divestment, investment • reinvestment

esto \es-tō\ pesto, presto • Modesto • manifesto

eston \es-tən\ see ESTINE

estor \es-tər\ see ESTER

estra \es-trə\ orchestra • Clytemnestra

estral \es-trəl\ kestrel • ancestral, orchestral

estrel \es-trəl\ see ESTRAL

estrian \es-trē-ən\ equestrian, pedestrian

estry \es-trē\ vestry • ancestry

esty \es-tē\ chesty, pesty, testy, zesty • necessity

esus \ē-səs\ see ESIS

et¹ \et\ bet, Bret, Chet, debt, fête, fret, get, jet, let, Lett, met, net, pet, set, sweat, Tet, threat, vet, wet, whet, yet • abet, all wet, Annette, asset, Babette, baguette, banquette, barrette, beget, beset, briquette, brochette, brunet, cadet, cassette, Claudette, Colette, coquette, cornet, corvette, croquette, dinette, dip net, diskette, dragnet, duet, egret, fan-jet, fishnet, forget, gazette, Georgette, Gillette, gillnet, gill net, handset, headset, ink-jet, inlet, inset, Jeanette, jet set, Juliet, kismet, layette, life net, Lynette, Marquette, mind-set, moonset, motet, Nanette, nerve net, nonet, octet, offset, onset, outlet, outset, pipette, preset, quartet, quintet, ramjet, regret, reset, rocket, rosette, roulette, septet, sestet, sextet, soubrette, spinet, sublet, subset, sunset, tea set, thickset, Tibet, toilette, typeset, upset, vignette, well-set, Yvette • alphabet, Antoinette, avocet, bassinet, bayonet, Bernadette, calumet, castanet, cigarette, clarinet, coronet, crepe suzette, epaulet, epithet, Ethernet, etiquette, featurette, flannelette, heavyset, Joliet, Juliet, kitchenette, Lafayette, launderette, leatherette, luncheonette, majorette, marmoset, martinet, minaret, minuet, netiquette, novelette, Olivet, parapet, pirouette, safety net, silhouette, sobriquet, soviet, space cadet, statuette, suffragette, superjet, teacher's pet, towelette, triple threat, usherette, vinaigrette • bachelorette, drum majorette, marionette, microcassette, mosquito net, Russian roulette, snowy egret • audiocassette, Marie Antoinette, videocassette

et² \ā\ see AY¹

et³ \āt\ see ATE¹

et⁴ \es\ see ESS

eta¹ \ät-ə\ see ATA²

eta² \et-ə\ see ETTA

eta³ \ēt-ə\ see ITA

etable¹ \et-ə-bəl\ see ETTABLE

etable² \ēt-ə-bəl\ see EATABLE

etal¹ \ēt-ᵊl\ beetle, fetal

etal² \et-ᵊl\ see ETTLE

etan¹ \et-ᵊn\ Breton, threaten • Cape Breton, Tibetan

etan² \ēt-ᵊn\ see EATEN¹

etch \ech\ catch, etch, fetch, ketch, kvetch, retch, sketch, stretch, vetch, wretch • backstretch, homestretch, outstretch

etched \echt\ teched • far-fetched
—*also* -ed *forms of verbs listed at* ETCH

etcher \ech-ər\ etcher, catcher, fetcher, Fletcher, lecher, sketcher, stretcher • cowcatcher, dogcatcher, dream catcher, eyecatcher, flycatcher

etching \ech-iŋ\ etching, fetching
—*also* -ing *forms of verbs listed at* ETCH

etchy \ech-ē\ sketchy, stretchy, tetchy

ete¹ \āt\ see ATE¹

ete² \et\ see ET¹

ete³ \ēt\ see EAT¹

ete⁴ \āt-ē\ see ATY

ête \āt\ see ATE¹

eted \ād\ see ADE¹

etel \ēt-ᵊl\ see ETAL¹

etely \ēt-lē\ see EETLY

eteor \ēt-ē-ər\ meteor
—*also* -er *forms of adjectives listed at* EATY

eter \ēt-ər\ see EATER¹

etera \e-trə\ see ETRA

etes \ēt-əs\ see ETUS

eth¹ \eth\ Beth, breath, breadth, death, saith, Seth • black death, brain death, crib death, handbreadth, hairbreadth, Macbeth • baby's breath, hold one's breath, in one breath, kiss of death, life-and-death, living death, morning breath, out of breath, shibboleth, sudden death, waste one's breath • Elizabeth, under one's breath

eth² \ās\ see ACE¹

eth³ \āt\ see ATE¹

eth⁴ \et\ see ET¹

etha \ē-thə\ Aretha, Ibiza

ethane \e-thān\ ethane, methane

ether¹ \eth-ər\ feather, heather, Heather, leather, nether, tether, weather, whether • bellwether, buff leather, fair-weather, glove leather, kid leather, pinfeather, shoe-leather, together, untether • altogether, get-together, hang together, hell-for-leather, knock together, patent leather, pull together, put together, saddle leather, tar and feather, throw together • under the weather

ether² \əth-ər\ see OTHER¹

ethyl \eth-əl\ Bethel, Ethel, ethyl, methyl

eti¹ \ēt-ē\ see EATY

eti² \āt-ē\ see ATY

etia \ē-shə\ see ESIA¹

etian \ē-shən\ see ETION¹

etic \et-ik\ aesthetic, ascetic, athletic, balletic, bathetic, cosmetic,

eidetic, frenetic, gametic, genetic,
hermetic, kinetic, magnetic,
pathetic, phonetic, poetic,
prophetic, prosthetic, synthetic
• alphabetic, anesthetic, apathetic,
arithmetic, copacetic, cybernetic,
diabetic, dietetic, diuretic, empa-
thetic, energetic, sympathetic,
synesthetic • apologetic, geomag-
netic, hyperkinetic, peripatetic,
telekinetic, unsympathetic • elec-
tromagnetic, general anesthetic,
unapologetic • onomatopoetic

etical \et-i-kəl\ heretical, poeti-
cal • antithetical, arithmetical,
hypothetical, parenthetical, theo-
retical

etics \et-iks\ aesthetics, athletics,
genetics, kinetics, phonetics,
poetics, prosthetics • cybernetics,
dietetics
—*also* -s, -'s, *and* -s' *forms of
nouns listed at* ETIC

etid \et-əd\ fetid, fretted, sweated
• indebted
—*also* -ed *forms of verbs listed at*
ET[1]

etin \ēt-ᵊn\ *see* EATEN[1]

etion[1] \ē-shən\ Grecian • accretion,
completion, deletion, depletion,
excretion, Helvetian, Phoenician,
secretion, Tahitian, Venetian
• Diocletian, Melanesian, Polynesian

etion[2] \esh-ən\ *see* ESSION

etious \ē-shəs\ *see* ECIOUS

etis \ēt-əs\ *see* ETUS

etist \et-əst\ cornetist, librettist
• clarinetist

etius \ē-shəs\ *see* ECIOUS

etl[1] \ät-ᵊl\ *see* ATAL

etl[2] \et-ᵊl\ *see* ETTLE

etland \et-lənd\ Shetland, wetland

eto[1] \ät-ō\ *see* ATO[2]

eto[2] \ēt-ō\ *see* ITO[1]

eton \ēt-ᵊn\ *see* EATEN[1]

etor[1] \et-ər\ *see* ETTER

etor[2] \ēt-ər\ *see* EATER[1]

etous \ēt-əs\ *see* ETUS

etra \e-trə\ Petra, tetra • etcetera

etric \e-trik\ metric • obstetric,
symmetric • asymmetric, baro-
metric, diametric, geometric,
isometric

etrical \e-tri-kəl\ metrical • obstet-
rical, symmetrical • asymmetrical,
diametrical, geometrical, unsym-
metrical

etrics \e-triks\ metrics, obstetrics
• isometrics

ets \ets\ let's
—*also* -s, -'s, *and* -s' *forms of nouns
and* -s *forms of verbs listed at* ET[1]

ett \et\ *see* ET[1]

etta \et-ə\ Etta, feta, Greta
• biretta, bruschetta, Loretta,
poinsettia, Rosetta, vendetta
• Henrietta, Marietta, operetta

ettable \et-ə-bəl\ forgettable, re-
grettable • unforgettable

ette \et\ *see* ET[1]

etter \et-ər\ better, bettor, debtor,
fetter, letter, setter, sweater
• abettor, air letter, bed wetter,
begetter, block letter, bonesetter,
chain letter, dead letter, fan letter, four-letter, go-getter, jet-
setter, Ledbetter, newsletter,
pacesetter, pinsetter, red-letter,
trendsetter, typesetter, unfetter
• English setter, go one better,
Irish setter, open letter, scarlet
letter

ettered \et-ərd\ lettered • unfet-
tered, unlettered

ettes \ets\ *see* ETS

ettia \et-ə\ *see* ETTA

ettie \et-ē\ *see* ETTY[1]

ettier \it-ē-ər\ *see* ITTIER

ettiness \it-ē-nəs\ *see* ITTINESS

etting \et-iŋ\ netting, setting • bed-
wetting, bloodletting, jet-setting,
pacesetting, place setting, trend-
setting, typesetting

—*also* -ing *forms of verbs listed at*
ET[1]

ettish \et-ish\ fetish, Lettish, pet-
tish, wettish • coquettish

ettle \et-ᵊl\ fettle, kettle, metal,
mettle, nettle, petal, settle, shtetl
• bimetal, nonmetal, teakettle,
unsettle • Popocatépetl

etto \et-ō\ ghetto • falsetto, palmetto, stiletto • saw palmetto,
Tintoretto

etty[1] \et-ē\ Betty, Getty, jetty,
Nettie, netty, petty, sweaty, yeti
• brown Betty, confetti, machete,
Rossetti, spaghetti • Donizetti,
Serengeti, spermaceti

etty[2] \it-ē\ see ITTY

etus \ēt-əs\ fetus, Thetis, treatise
• diabetes

etzsche \ē-chē\ see EACHY

euben \ü-bən\ Cuban, Reuben,
Steuben

euce \üs\ see USE[1]

eucey \ü-sē\ see UICY

euch \ük\ see UKE

eud[1] \üd\ see UDE[1]

eud[2] \óid\ see OID[1]

eudal \üd-ᵊl\ see OODLE

eudist \üd-əst\ see UDIST[1]

eudo \üd-ō\ see UDO

eue \ü\ see EW[1]

euer \ü-ər\ see EWER[1]

euil \āl\ see AIL

euille \ē\ see EE[1]

euk \ük\ see UKE

eul[1] \əl\ see ULL[1]

eul[2] \ərl\ see IRL

eulah \ü-lə\ see ULA

eulean \ü-lē-ən\ see ULEAN

eum[1] \ē-əm\ lyceum, museum, no-
see-um, per diem • coliseum,
colosseum, mausoleum, wax
museum

eum[2] \ä-əm\ see AHUM

eum[3] \üm\ see OOM[1]

euma \ü-mə\ see UMA

eume \üm\ see OOM[1]

eumon \ü-mən\ see UMAN

eumy \ü-mē\ see OOMY

eunice \ü-nəs\ see EWNESS

eunuch \ü-nik\ see UNIC

eur[1] \ər\ blur, burr, Burr, cur, err,
fir, for, fur, her, myrrh, per, purr,
sir, slur, spur, stir, 'twere, were,
whir, your, you're • as per, astir,
aver, bestir, Big Sur, chauffeur,
coiffeur, concur, confer, danseur,
defer, demur, deter, hauteur,
him/her, his/her, incur, infer,
inter, jongleur, larkspur, liqueur,
masseur, occur, Pasteur, poseur,
prefer, recur, refer, sandbur,
sandspur, transfer, voyeur, white
fir • amateur, balsam fir, cockle-
bur, connoisseur, curvature, de
rigueur, disinter, Douglas fir,
Fraser fir, monseigneur, ra-
conteur, saboteur, underfur,
voyageur • carillonneur, entrepreneur, provocateur, restaurateur

eur[2] \ùr\ see URE[1]

eure \ər\ see EUR[1]

eurish \ər-ish\ see OURISH

eurs \ərz\ see ERS[1]

eury \ùr-ē\ see URY[1]

eus[1] \ē-əs\ Aeneas, Linnaeus • Judas Maccabaeus

eus[2] \üs\ see USE[1]

euse[1] \əz\ buzz, 'cause, does, fuzz,
'twas, was • abuzz, because, out-
does, undoes

euse[2] \üs\ see USE[1]

euse[3] \üz\ see USE[2]

eut \üt\ see UTE

euter \üt-ər\ see UTER

euth \üth\ see OOTH[2]

eutian \ü-shən\ see UTION

eutical \üt-i-kəl\ see UTICAL

eutist \üt-əst\ see UTIST

euton \üt-ᵊn\ see UTAN

euve \əv\ see OVE[1]

euver \ü-vər\ see OVER[3]

eux \ü\ see EW[1]

ev[1] \ef\ see EF[1]

ev² \ȯf\ see OFF²
eva \ē-və\ see IVA²
eval \ē-vəl\ see IEVAL
evalent \ev-ə-lənt\ see EVOLENT
evan¹ \ē-vən\ see EVEN
evan² \ev-ən\ see EAVEN
eve¹ \ev\ rev • Kiev, Negev
eve² \ēv\ see EAVE¹
evel \ev-əl\ bevel, devil, level, Neville, revel • bedevil, daredevil, dishevel, dust devil, high-level, low-level, sea level, split-level • entry-level, on the level, water level
eveler \ev-lər\ leveler, reveler
evelly \ev-ə-lē\ heavily, reveille
evement \ēv-mənt\ achievement, bereavement • underachievement
even \ē-vən\ even, Stephen • break even, Genevan, get even, uneven
eventh \ev-ənth\ seventh • eleventh
ever¹ \ev-ər\ clever, ever, lever, never, sever, Trevor • endeavor, forever, however, whatever, whenever, wherever, whichever, whoever, whomever • whatsoever, whomsoever, whosoever
ever² \ē-vər\ see IEVER
everage \ev-rij\ beverage, leverage
everence \ev-rəns\ reverence, severance • irreverence
every \ev-rē\ every, reverie
evice \ev-əs\ crevice • Ben Nevis
evil \ē-vəl\ see IEVAL
eville \ev-əl\ see EVEL
evilry \ev-əl-rē\ devilry, revelry • daredevilry
evin \ev-ən\ see EAVEN
evious \ē-vē-əs\ devious, previous
evis¹ \ev-əs\ see EVICE
evis² \ē-vəs\ see EVUS
evity \ev-ət-ē\ brevity, levity • longevity
evocable \ev-ə-kə-bəl\ evocable, revocable • irrevocable
evolence \ev-ə-ləns\ prevalence • benevolence, malevolence

evolent \ev-ə-lənt\ prevalent • benevolent, malevolent
evor \ev-ər\ see EVER¹
evous \ē-vəs\ grievous • Saint Kitts-Nevis
evus \ē-vəs\ see EVOUS
evy \ev-ē\ bevy, heavy, levee, levy • top-heavy
ew¹ \ü\ blue, boo, brew, chew, clue, coo, coup, crew, cue, dew, do, Drew, due, ewe, few, flew, flu, flue, glue, gnu, goo, hew, hue, Hugh, Jew, knew, lieu, loo, Lou, mew, moo, new, ooh, pew, phew, pooh, q, queue, rue, screw, shoe, shoo, shrew, Sioux, skew, slew, slough, slue, spew, stew, strew, sue, Sue, threw, through, to, too, true, two, u, view, whew, who, woo, Wu, yew, you, zoo • accrue, achoo, adieu, ado, aircrew, anew, Anjou, askew, au jus, Baku, bamboo, bayou, bijou, boo-boo, brand-new, breakthrough, can-do, canoe, Cebu, construe, Corfu, corkscrew, coypu, cuckoo, curfew, debut, doo-doo, ensue, eschew, fondue, ground crew, gumshoe, guru, hairdo, hereto, Hindu, home brew, Honshu, horseshoe, how-to, HQ, Hutu, igloo, IQ, K2, kazoo, Khufu, kung fu, lean-to, long view, make-do, Matthew, me-too, mildew, milieu, miscue, muumuu, Nehru, one-two, on view, outdo, outgrew, Peru, preview, pursue, purview, ragout, redo, renew, review, revue, run-through, see-through, set-to, shampoo, sinew, skiddoo, snafu, snowshoe, subdue, taboo, tattoo, thank-you, thereto, thumbscrew, to-do, tree shrew, undo, undue, unglue, unscrew, untrue, venue, voodoo, wahoo, walk-through, whereto, who's who, withdrew, worldview, ya-

hoo, yoo-hoo • avenue, baby
blue, ballyhoo, barbecue, bird's-
eye view, black-and-blue,
Brunswick stew, buckaroo, buga-
boo, caribou, cobalt blue, cocka-
too, counterview, curlicue,
derring-do, follow-through, hith-
erto, honeydew, Iguaçu, ingenue,
interview, IOU, Irish stew,
Jiangsu, kangaroo, Kathmandu,
kinkajou, manitou, marabou,
microbrew, midnight blue, Mon-
tague, Montesquieu, Mountain
View, ormolu, overdo, overdue,
overflew, overgrew, overshoe,
overthrew, overview, parvenu,
pay-per-view, PDQ, peacock blue,
peekaboo, petting zoo, point of
view, rendezvous, residue, ret-
inue, revenue, Richelieu, Ryukyu,
seppuku, sneak preview,
switcheroo, talking-to, teleview,
thitherto, Timbuktu, w, waterloo,
well-to-do, what have you,
whoop-de-do, Xanadu • bolt from
the blue, Brian Boru, cardinal
virtue, cornflower blue, didgeri-
doo, downy mildew, hullabaloo,
in deep doo-doo, Kalamazoo,
mulligan stew, Ouagadougou, out
of the blue, Seattle Slew, Vanu-
atu, Wandering Jew
ew² \ō\ see OW¹
ewable¹ \ō-ə-bəl\ see OWABLE¹
ewable² \ü-ə-bəl\ see UABLE
ewal \ü-əl\ see UEL¹
ewar \ü-ər\ see EWER¹
eward¹ \urd\ see URED¹
eward² \ü-ərd\ Seward, steward
• shop steward
ewd \üd\ see UDE¹
ewdness \üd-nəs\ see UDINOUS
ewe¹ \ō\ see OW¹
ewe² \ü\ see EW¹
ewed \üd\ see UDE¹
ewee \ē-wē\ see EEWEE
ewel \ü-əl\ see UEL¹

eweled \üld\ see OOLED
ewell \ü-əl\ see UEL¹
ewer¹ \ü-ər\ brewer, chewer, doer,
ewer, fewer, sewer, skewer,
viewer, you're • me-tooer, mis-
doer, reviewer, snowshoer,
wrongdoer • barbecuer, evildoer,
interviewer, microbrewer
—*also* -er *forms of adjectives listed
at* EW¹
ewer² \ur\ see URE¹
ewer³ \ō-ər\ see OER⁴
ewerage \ur-ij\ see OORAGE¹
ewery \ur-ē\ see URY¹
ewey \ü-ē\ see EWY
ewie \ü-ē\ see EWY
ewing¹ \ō-iŋ\ see OING¹
ewing² \ü-iŋ\ see OING²
ewish \ü-ish\ bluish, Jewish,
newish, shrewish
ewl \ül\ see OOL¹
ewless \ü-ləs\ clueless, crewless,
dewless, shoeless, viewless
ewly \ü-lē\ see ULY
ewman \ü-mən\ see UMAN
ewn \ün\ see OON¹
ewness \ü-nəs\ blueness, Eunice,
newness, Tunis
ewpie \ü-pē\ see OOPY
ews \üz\ see USE²
ewsman \üz-mən\ bluesman, newsman
ewsy \ü-zē\ see OOZY
ewt \üt\ see UTE
ewter \üt-ər\ see UTER
ewton \üt-°n\ see UTAN
ewy \ü-ē\ bluey, buoy, chewy,
Dewey, dewy, gluey, gooey,
hooey, Louie, Louis, newie,
phooey, screwy • bell buoy, chop
suey, life buoy, mildewy • rata-
touille
ex \eks\ ex, flex, hex, sex, specs,
vex, x • annex, apex, codex, complex, convex, cortex, duplex,
funplex, ibex, index, Kleenex,
latex, narthex, perplex, Pyrex,

reflex, Rx, spandex, telex, Tex-
Mex, triplex, unsex, vertex, vor-
tex • belowdecks, circumflex,
cross-index, gentle sex, haruspex,
intersex, Malcolm X, megaplex,
Middlesex, multiplex, Rolodex,
thumb index, unisex • cerebral
cortex, Oedipus complex
—*also* -s, -'s, *and* -s' *forms of
nouns and* -s *forms of verbs listed
at* ECK

exas \ek-səs\ see EXUS
exed \ekst\ see EXT
exia \ek-sē-ə\ dyslexia • anorexia
exion \ek-shən\ see ECTION
exis \ek-səs\ see EXUS
exity \ek-sət-ē\ complexity, con-
vexity, perplexity
ext \ekst\ next, sexed, text, vexed
• context, perplexed, pretext
• hypertext
—*also* -ed *forms of verbs listed at*
EX
extant \ek-stənt\ extant, sextant
exural \ek-shrəl\ see ECTURAL²
exus \ek-səs\ nexus, Texas • Alexis
• solar plexus
exy \ek-sē\ sexy • apoplexy
ey¹ \ā\ see AY¹
ey² \ē\ see EE¹
ey³ \ī\ see Y¹
eya¹ \ā-ə\ see AIA¹
eya² \ē-ə\ see IA¹
eyance \ā-əns\ abeyance, con-
veyance, surveillance
ey'd \ād\ see ADE¹
eye \ī\ see Y¹
eyed¹ \ēd\ see EED
eyed² \īd\ see IDE¹
eyeless \ī-ləs\ see ILUS
eyelet \ī-lət\ see ILOT
eyen \īn\ see INE¹
eyer \īr\ see IRE¹
eyes \īz\ see IZE¹
eying \ā-iŋ\ see AYING
ey'll¹ \āl\ see AIL
ey'll² \el\ see EL¹

eyn \in\ see IN¹
eynes \ānz\ see AINS
eyness \ā-nəs\ see AYNESS
eyor \ā-ər\ see AYER
eyre \er\ see ARE⁴
ey're \er\ see ARE⁴
eyrie \īr-ē\ see IRY
eys \ēz\ see EZE
eyser \ī-zər\ see IZER
eyte \ā-tē\ see ATY
ey've \āv\ see AVE²
ez¹ \ez\ see AYS¹
ez² \ā\ see AY¹
ez³ \ās\ see ACE¹
eza \ē-zə\ Giza, Lisa, Pisa, visa, Visa
eze \ēz\ breeze, cheese, ease,
freeze, frieze, he's, jeez, please,
seize, she's, sleaze, sneeze,
squeeze, tease, tweeze, wheeze
• Andes, appease, Aries, at ease,
Belize, big cheese, blue cheese,
Burmese, chemise, Chinese, deep-
freeze, Denise, disease, displease,
d.t.'s, Elise, Ganges, Hermes, jack
cheese, Kirghiz, Louise, Maltese,
marquise, Pisces, quick-freeze,
Ramses, reprise, sea breeze,
striptease, strong breeze, Swiss
cheese, Tabriz, trapeze, unease,
unfreeze, Xerxes • antifreeze,
Balinese, Bengalese, Bhutanese,
Brooklynese, Cantonese, Cervantes, Ceylonese, cheddar
cheese, Congolese, cottage cheese,
Damocles, diocese, Eloise, expertise, Hebrides, Heracles, Hercules,
ill at ease, Japanese, Javanese,
journalese, Lake Louise, legalese,
overseas, Pekingese, Pericles,
Pyrenees, shoot the breeze,
Siamese, Socrates, Sophocles, to
one's knees • antipodes, archdiocese, bona fides, computerese,
Diogenes, Dodecanese, Dutch elm
disease, eminence grise, Euripi-
des, Florida Keys, Great Pyrenees, Hippocrates, Indo-Chinese,

mad cow disease, Thucydides, Vietnamese • Aristophanes, foot-and-mouth disease, Legionnaires' disease, Lou Gehrig's disease, Mephistopheles, Parkinson's disease, sword of Damocles • Pillars of Hercules

—also -s, -'s, *and* -s' *forms of nouns and* -s *forms of verbs listed at* EE[1]
ezel \ē-zəl\ see EASEL
ezi \ē-zē\ see EASY[1]
ezium \ē-zē-əm\ cesium • magnesium, trapezium

I

i[1] \ē\ see EE[1]
i[2] \ī\ see Y[1]
i[3] \ā\ see AY[1]
ia[1] \ē-ə\ Gaea, Leah, Mia, rhea, Rhea, via • Crimea, idea, Judaea, Korea, mantilla, Maria, Medea, Nicaea, rupiah, sangria, Sophia, tortilla • bougainvillea, diarrhea, Eritrea, fantasia, Galatea, gonorrhea, Hialeah, Kampuchea, Nicosia, panacea, pizzeria, pyorrhea, Santeria, Tanzania • Andalusia, Ave Maria, Cassiopeia, Sacagawea • onomatopoeia
ia[2] \ī-ə\ see IAH[1]
ia[3] \ä\ see A[1]
iable[1] \ī-ə-bəl\ dryable, dyeable, flyable, friable, liable, pliable, viable • deniable, reliable • certifiable, classifiable, falsifiable, justifiable, quantifiable, undeniable, verifiable • identifiable
iable[2] \ē-ə-bəl\ see EEABLE
iacal \ī-ə-kəl\ maniacal, zodiacal • egomaniacal
iad \ī-əd\ see YAD
iah[1] \ī-ə\ Maya, via • Mariah, messiah, papaya, pariah, Thalia • Hezekiah, jambalaya, Jeremiah, Nehemiah, Obadiah, Zechariah, Zephaniah • Iphigenia
iah[2] \ē-ə\ see IA[1]

ial \īl\ see ILE[1]
ialer \ī-lər\ see ILAR
ially \ē-ə-lē\ see EALLY[1]
iam \ī-əm\ Priam • per diem • carpe diem
ian[1] \ē-ən\ see EAN[1]
ian[2] \ī-ən\ see ION[1]
iance \ī-əns\ science • alliance, appliance, compliance, defiance, nonscience, reliance • misalliance, noncompliance, self-reliance
—also -s, -'s, *and* -s' *forms of nouns listed at* IANT
iant \ī-ənt\ Bryant, client, giant, pliant • compliant, defiant, reliant • self-reliant, sleeping giant, supergiant
iao \aů\ see OW[2]
iaour \aůr\ see OWER[2]
iaper \ī-pər\ see IPER
iar \īr\ see IRE[1]
iary[1] \ī-ə-rē\ diary, fiery, friary, priory
iary[2] \īr-ē\ see IRY
ias[1] \ī-əs\ bias, dais, pious, Pius • Elias, Tobias
ias[2] \ē-əs\ see EUS[1]
ias[3] \äsh\ see ASH[1]
iasis \ī-ə-səs\ diocese • archdiocese, psoriasis • elephantiasis, schistosomiasis
iat[1] \ē-ət\ see EIT[1]

iat² \ī-ət\ see IET
iate \ī-ət\ see IET
iath¹ \ī-əth\ Wyeth • Goliath
iath² \ē-ə\ see IA¹
iatry \ī-ə-trē\ podiatry, psychiatry
iaus \aús\ see OUSE²
ib¹ \ib\ bib, crib, fib, glib, jib, nib, rib, sib, squib • ad-lib, corncrib, false rib, sahib • floating rib
ib² \ēb\ see EBE²
ib³ \ēv\ see EAVE¹
iba \ē-bə\ see EBA
ibable \ī-bə-bəl\ bribable • indescribable
ibal \ī-bəl\ bible, Bible, libel, scribal, tribal • family Bible
ibb \ib\ see IB¹
ibband \ib-ən\ see IBBON
ibbed \ibd\ rock-ribbed
—also -ed forms of verbs listed at IB¹
ibber \ib-ər\ cribber, fibber, gibber, ribber
ibbet \ib-ət\ exhibit, inhibit, prohibit • flibbertigibbet
ibble \ib-əl\ dribble, kibble, nibble, quibble, scribble, sibyl, Sibyl • double dribble
ibbler \ib-lər\ dribbler, nibbler, quibbler, scribbler
ibbon \ib-ən\ gibbon, ribbon • blue ribbon
ibby \ib-ē\ Libby, ribby
ibe¹ \īb\ bribe, jibe, scribe, tribe, vibe • ascribe, describe, imbibe, inscribe, prescribe, proscribe, subscribe, transcribe • circumscribe, diatribe • oversubscribe
ibe² \ē-bē\ see EBE¹
ibel \ī-bəl\ see IBAL
iber \ī-bər\ briber, fiber, Khyber, Tiber • subscriber
ibi \ē-bē\ see EBE¹
ibia \i-bē-ə\ Libya, tibia • Namibia
ibin \ib-ən\ see IBBON
ibit \ib-ət\ see IBBET
ibitor \ib-ət-ər\ exhibitor, inhibitor

ible \ī-bəl\ see IBAL
iblet \ib-lət\ driblet, giblet
ibo \ē-bō\ gazebo, placebo
ibs \ibz\ dibs • short ribs, spareribs
—also -s, -'s, and -s' forms of nouns and -s forms of verbs listed at IB¹
ibute¹ \ib-yət\ tribute • attribute, contribute, distribute • redistribute
ibute² \ib-ət\ see IBBET
ibutive \ib-yət-iv\ attributive, contributive, distributive
ibutor \ib-ət-ər\ see IBITOR
ibyl \ib-əl\ see IBBLE
ic¹ \ik\ see ICK
ic² \ēk\ see EAK¹
ica¹ \ī-kə\ mica, Micah, pica • Formica • balalaika
ica² \ē-kə\ see IKA¹
icable \ik-ə-bəl\ despicable, explicable, extricable • inexplicable, inextricable
icah \ī-kə\ see ICA¹
ical \ik-əl\ see ICKLE
ican \ē-kən\ see EACON
icar \ik-ər\ see ICKER¹
icative \ik-ət-iv\ applicative, indicative
iccative \ik-ət-iv\ see ICATIVE
ice¹ \īs\ Bryce, dice, ice, lice, mice, nice, price, rice, slice, spice, splice, thrice, twice, vice, vise • advice, allspice, black ice, brown rice, concise, deice, device, dry ice, entice, excise, fried rice, list price, make nice, no dice, on ice, pack ice, precise, shelf ice, suffice, white rice, wild rice • asking price, break the ice, comma splice, imprecise, merchandise, on thin ice, overprice, paradise, roll the dice, sacrifice, Spanish rice, sticker price • basmati rice, self-sacrifice
ice² \ē-chä\ see ICHE¹
ice³ \ēs\ see IECE
ice⁴ \ī-sē\ see ICY

ice⁵ \īz\ see IZE¹
iceless \ī-sləs\ iceless, priceless, spiceless
icely \is-lē\ see ISTLY
iceous \ish-əs\ see ICIOUS¹
icey \ī-sē\ see ICY
ich¹ \ich\ see ITCH
ich² \ik\ see ICK
ichael \ī-kəl\ see YCLE¹
iche¹ \ēsh\ leash, niche, quiche, sheesh • pastiche, unleash • nouveau riche
iche² \ish\ see ISH¹
iche³ \ich\ see ITCH
iche⁴ \ē-chē\ see EACHY
icher \ich-ər\ see ITCHER
iches \ich-əz\ see ITCHES
ichi¹ \ē-chē\ see EACHY
ichi² \ē-shē\ see ISHI
ichment \ich-mənt\ see ITCHMENT
ichore \ik-rē\ see ICKERY
ichu \ish-ü\ see ISSUE¹
icia¹ \ish-ə\ see ITIA¹
icia² \ēsh-ə\ see ESIA¹
icial \ish-əl\ initial, judicial, official • artificial, beneficial, prejudicial, sacrificial, superficial, unofficial
ician \ē-shən\ see ETION¹
icient \ish-ənt\ deficient, efficient, omniscient, proficient, sufficient • coefficient, cost-efficient, inefficient, insufficient, self-sufficient
icing¹ \ī-siŋ\ icing • gene-splicing • self-sacrificing
—*also* -ing *forms of verbs listed at* ICE¹
icing² \ī-ziŋ\ see IZING
icious¹ \ish-əs\ vicious • ambitious, auspicious, capricious, delicious, fictitious, judicious, malicious, Mauritius, nutritious, officious, pernicious, propitious, seditious, suspicious • avaricious, expeditious, inauspicious, injudicious, meretricious, Red Delicious, repetitious, superstitious, surreptitious
icious² \ē-shəs\ see ECIOUS

icipal \is-ə-bəl\ see ISSIBLE
icit \is-ət\ complicit, elicit, explicit, illicit, implicit, solicit
icitor \is-tər\ see ISTER
icitous \is-ət-əs\ duplicitous, felicitous, solicitous • infelicitous
icity¹ \is-ət-ē\ centricity, complicity, duplicity, ethnicity, felicity, publicity, simplicity, toxicity, triplicity • authenticity, domesticity, eccentricity, elasticity, electricity, infelicity, multiplicity, specificity • ethnocentricity, inauthenticity, inelasticity, periodicity
icity² \is-tē\ Christie, misty, twisty, wristy • Corpus Christi
ick \ik\ brick, chick, click, crick, creek, Dick, flick, hick, kick, lick, nick, Nick, pic, pick, prick, quick, rick, sic, sick, slick, stick, thick, tic, tick, trick, wick • airsick, broomstick, carsick, Chap Stick, chick flick, chopstick, cowlick, deer tick, dipstick, dog tick, drop-kick, drumstick, ear pick, firebrick, fish stick, free kick, frog kick, goal kick, handpick, hat trick, hayrick, heartsick, homesick, ice pick, joystick, lipstick, lovesick, matchstick, nightstick, nitpick, nonstick, nutpick, oil slick, peacenik, pinprick, placekick, rubric, salt lick, seasick, self-stick, sidekick, slapstick, toothpick, unstick, uptick, wood tick, yardstick • bailiwick, biopic, Bolshevik, bone to pick, call in sick, candlestick, cattle tick, cherry-pick, corner kick, Dominic, do the trick, double-quick, flutter kick, heretic, lunatic, meterstick, pogo stick, point-and-click, politic, Reykjavik, rhythm stick, scissors kick, walking stick • arithmetic, carrot-and-stick, impolitic, penalty kick

icka \ē-kə\ see IKA[1]
icked \ikt\ see ICT[1]
ickel \ik-əl\ see ICKLE
icken \ik-ən\ chicken, quicken, sicken, stricken, thicken • awestricken, spring chicken • panic-stricken, prairie chicken, rubber-chicken • poverty-stricken
ickens \ik-ənz\ dickens, Dickens, pickings
—*also* -s, -'s, *and* -s' *forms of nouns and* -s *forms of verbs listed at* ICKEN
icker[1] \ik-ər\ bicker, clicker, dicker, flicker, kicker, liquor, nicker, picker, pricker, slicker, snicker, sticker, ticker, vicar, wicker • dropkicker, nitpicker, placekicker, ragpicker • bumper sticker, cherry picker, city slicker, politicker
—*also* -er *forms of adjectives listed at* ICK
icker[2] \ek-ər\ see ECKER
ickery \ik-rē\ chicory, flickery, hickory, trickery • Terpsichore
icket \ik-ət\ cricket, picket, spigot, thicket, ticket, wicket • big-ticket, hot ticket, meal ticket • season ticket
ickett \ik-ət\ see ICKET
ickety \ik-ət-ē\ rickety, thickety • persnickety
ickey \ik-ē\ see ICKY
icki \ik-ē\ see ICKY
ickie \ik-ē\ see ICKY
icking \ik-iŋ\ flat-picking, high-sticking, nit-picking, rollicking • cotton-picking, fingerpicking
—*also* -ing *forms of verbs listed at* ICK
ickings \ik-ənz\ see ICKENS
ickish \ik-ish\ sickish, thickish
ickit \ik-ət\ see ICKET
ickle \ik-əl\ fickle, nickel, pickle, prickle, sickle, tickle, trickle • bicycle, dill pickle, icicle, obsta-

cle, Popsicle, tricycle • pumpernickel • hammer and sickle
ickler \ik-lər\ stickler, tickler • bicycler, particular
ickly \ik-lē\ prickly, quickly, sickly, slickly, thickly
ickness \ik-nəs\ quickness, sickness, slickness, thickness • airsickness, car sickness, homesickness, lovesickness, seasickness • motion sickness, mountain sickness, sleeping sickness
icksy \ik-sē\ see IXIE
icky \ik-ē\ dickey, hickey, icky, Mickey, picky, quickie, sickie, sticky, tricky, Vicky • doohickey, slapsticky
icle \ik-əl\ see ICKLE
icly[1] \ik-lē\ see ICKLY
icly[2] \ē-klē\ see EEKLY
ico \ē-kō\ see ICOT
icory \ik-rē\ see ICKERY
icot \ē-kō\ tricot • Puerto Rico
ics \iks\ see IX[1]
ict[1] \ikt\ strict, ticked • addict, afflict, conflict, constrict, convict, depict, district, edict, evict, inflict, lipsticked, predict, restrict, verdict • Benedict, contradict, derelict, interdict, Lake District • eggs Benedict
—*also* -ed *forms of verbs listed at* ICK
ict[2] \īt\ see ITE[1]
ictable \īt-ə-bəl\ see ITABLE[1]
icted \ik-təd\ conflicted, restricted
—*also* -ed *forms of verbs listed at* ICT[1]
icter \ik-tər\ see ICTOR
ictim \ik-təm\ see ICTUM
iction \ik-shən\ diction, fiction, friction • addiction, affliction, constriction, conviction, depiction, eviction, infliction, nonfiction, prediction, restriction • benediction, contradiction, crucifixion, dereliction, interdiction, jurisdiction, science fiction

ictional \ik-shnəl\ fictional • non-fictional • jurisdictional

ictive \ik-tiv\ fictive • addictive, afflictive, constrictive, predictive, restrictive, vindictive • nonrestrictive

ictment \īt-mənt\ see ITEMENT

ictor \ik-tər\ victor • constrictor, depicter, inflicter • boa constrictor

ictory \ik-tə-rē\ victory • contradictory, valedictory

ictual \it-ᵊl\ see ITTLE

ictum \ik-təm\ dictum, victim

icture \ik-chər\ picture, stricture • big picture • motion picture

icular[1] \ik-yə-lər\ curricular, funicular, particular, vehicular • in particular, perpendicular • extracurricular

icular[2] \ik-lər\ see ICKLER

iculate \ik-yə-lət\ articulate, particulate • inarticulate

iculous \ik-yə-ləs\ meticulous, ridiculous

icy \ī-sē\ dicey, icy, pricey, spicy

id[1] \id\ bid, did, grid, hid, id, kid, Kidd, lid, mid, quid, rid, skid, slid, squid • amid, backslid, El Cid, eyelid, forbid, grandkid, Madrid, nonskid, outdid, schoolkid, undid • arachnid, giant squid, katydid, pyramid, underbid • Valladolid

id[2] \ēd\ see EED

l'd \id\ see IDE[1]

ida[1] \ēd-ə\ see EDA[1]

ida[2] \ī-də\ Haida, Ida • Oneida

idal \īd-ᵊl\ bridal, bridle, idle, idol, idyll, sidle, tidal • fratricidal, fungicidal, genocidal, germicidal, herbicidal, homicidal, pesticidal, suicidal

idance \īd-ᵊns\ guidance • misguidance

iday \īd-ē\ Friday, Heidi, tidy • girl Friday, Good Friday, man Friday, untidy • bona fide

idd \id\ see ID[1]

idden \id-ᵊn\ bidden, hidden, ridden • bedridden, forbidden • overridden

idder \id-ər\ bidder, kidder • consider • reconsider

iddie \id-ē\ see IDDY

iddish \id-ish\ kiddish, Yiddish

iddity \id-ət-ē\ see IDITY

iddle \id-ᵊl\ fiddle, griddle, middle, piddle, riddle, twiddle • bass fiddle • play second fiddle

iddling \id-liŋ\ fiddling, middling, piddling

iddly \id-le\ diddly, piddly, Ridley

iddock \id-ik\ see IDIC

iddur \id-ər\ see IDDER

iddy \id-ē\ biddy, giddy, kiddie

ide[1] \īd\ bide, bride, chide, Clyde, eyed, fried, glide, guide, hide, I'd, pied, plied, pride, ride, side, slide, snide, stride, tide, tried, wide • abide, allied, applied, aside, astride, backside, backslide, beachside, bedside, beside, bestride, betide, blue-eyed, broadside, bromide, bug-eyed, clear-eyed, cockeyed, cold-eyed, collide, confide, courtside, cowhide, cross-eyed, curbside, decide, deride, divide, dockside, downside, downslide, dry-eyed, ebb tide, elide, field guide, fireside, flip side, flood tide, fluoride, four-eyed, free ride, freeze-dried, Girl Guide, graveside, hang glide, hawkeyed, hayride, high tide, hillside, horsehide, inside, in stride, joyride, lakeside, landslide, low tide, lynx-eyed, misguide, noontide, offside, onside, outride, outside, poolside, pop-eyed, preside, provide, rawhide, red tide, reside, ringside, riptide, roadside, seaside, sharp-eyed, shipside, snowslide, springtide, squint-eyed, stateside, statewide, storewide,

streamside, subside, tongue-tied,
topside, untried, upside, vat-dyed,
walleyed, wayside, wide-eyed,
wild-eyed, worldwide, yuletide
• alongside, bleary-eyed, bona
fide, chicken-fried, Christmastide,
citified, citywide, classified, coin-
cide, countrified, countryside,
countrywide, cut-and-dried,
cyanide, dignified, dioxide, dou-
ble-wide, eagle-eyed, Eastertide,
eventide, far and wide, fratricide,
fungicide, genocide, germicide,
goggle-eyed, googly-eyed, harbor-
side, herbicide, homicide, misty-
eyed, monoxide, mountainside,
nationwide, Naugahyde, on the
side, open-eyed, override, Pas-
siontide, pesticide, planetwide,
qualified, rarefied, riverside, side
by side, sissified, subdivide, sui-
cide, underside, waterside, winter-
tide • by the wayside, dissatisfied,
fit to be tied, formaldehyde, in-
fanticide, insecticide, Jekyll and
Hyde, preoccupied, self-satisfied
• carbon dioxide, carbon monoxide, overqualified
—also -ed *forms of verbs listed at*
Y[1]

ide[2] \ēd\ see EED
idean \id-ē-ən\ see IDIAN
ided \īd-əd\ sided • divided, lop-
sided; misguided, one-sided
• many-sided
—also -ed *forms of verbs listed at*
IDE[1]

iden \īd-ᵊn\ guidon, Haydn, Lei-
den, Sidon, widen • Poseidon
idence \īd-ᵊns\ see IDANCE
ident \īd-ᵊnt\ strident, trident
ideon \id-ē-ən\ see IDIAN
ideous \id-ē-əs\ see IDIOUS
ider[1] \īd-ər\ cider, glider, rider,
snider, spider, wider • backslider,
decider, divider, hang glider,
insider, joyrider, lowrider, mis-

guider, outrider, outsider,
provider, sea spider, Top-Sider,
wolf spider • paraglider, water-
strider
ider[2] \id-ər\ see IDDER
ides \īdz\ ides • besides
—also -s, -'s, *and* -s' *forms of*
nouns and -s *forms of verbs listed*
at IDE[1]

idge \ij\ bridge, fridge, midge,
ridge • abridge, Blue Ridge, draw-
bridge, footbridge, Oak Ridge,
truss bridge • biting midge, contract bridge, covered bridge • suspension bridge
idged \ijd\ unabridged
—also -ed *forms of verbs listed at*
IDGE
idgen \ij-ən\ see YGIAN
idget \ij-ət\ Brigitte, digit, fidget,
midget, widget • double-digit
idgin \ij-ən\ see YGIAN
idi \id-ē\ see IDDY
idia \i-dē-ə\ Lydia • Numidia
idian \id-ē-ən\ Gideon, Lydian,
Midian • Floridian, meridian,
obsidian, quotidian • prime
meridian
idic \id-ik\ acidic, druidic, Hasidic
idical \id-i-kəl\ druidical, juridical
• pyramidical
idiem \id-ē-əm\ idiom • iridium
• post meridiem • ante meridiem
iding \īd-iŋ\ riding, siding, tiding
• abiding, confiding, deciding,
hang gliding, joyriding • law-
abiding, paragliding
—also -ing *forms of verbs listed at*
IDE[1]
idiom \id-ē-əm\ see IDIEM
idious \id-ē-əs\ hideous • fastidious,
insidious, invidious, perfidious
idity \id-ət-ē\ acidity, aridity, avid-
ity, cupidity, fluidity, frigidity,
humidity, liquidity, lucidity,
morbidity, rapidity, rigidity, solid-
ity, stupidity, timidity, validity

idium \id-ē-əm\ see IDIEM
idle \īd-ᵊl\ see IDAL
idley \id-lē\ see IDDLY
idney \id-nē\ kidney, Sidney, Sydney
ido¹ \īd-ō\ Dido, fido • Hokkaido
ido² \ēd-ō\ see EDO¹
idol \īd-ᵊl\ see IDAL
ids¹ \idz\ rapids • Grand Rapids
—*also* -s, -'s, *and* -s' *forms of nouns and* -s *forms of verbs listed at* ID¹
ids² \ēdz\ see EEDS
idst \idst\ didst, midst • amidst
idual¹ \ij-wəl\ residual • individual
idual² \ij-əl\ see IGIL
idy \īd-ē\ see IDAY
idyll \īd-ᵊl\ see IDAL
ie¹ \ā\ see AY¹
ie² \ē\ see EE¹
ie³ \ī\ see Y¹
iece \ēs\ cease, crease, fleece, grease, Greece, lease, Nice, niece, peace, piece • apiece, at peace, Bernice, Burmese, caprice, chemise, Chinese, Clarice, Cochise, crosspiece, decease, decrease, Denise, Dumfries, earpiece, Elise, eyepiece, Felice, grandniece, hairpiece, headpiece, increase, Maltese, Matisse, Maurice, mouthpiece, nosepiece, obese, one-piece, police, release, showpiece, sublease, Therese, timepiece, three-piece, two-piece, valise • altarpiece, Balinese, Bengalese, Brooklynese, Cantonese, centerpiece, Ceylonese, chimneypiece, Congolese, diocese, expertise, frontispiece, Gabonese, Golden Fleece, Guyanese, hold one's peace, Japanese, Javanese, journalese, kiss of peace, Lebanese, legalese, manganese, mantelpiece, masterpiece, Nepalese, of a piece, Pekingese, Portuguese, predecease, rerelease,

Siamese, timed-release, Viennese • archdiocese, bureaucratese, computerese, Indo-Chinese, officialese, Peloponnese, secret police, Vietnamese • conversation piece, justice of the peace
iecer \ē-sər\ see EASER¹
ied¹ \ēd\ see EED
ied² \ēt\ see EAT¹
ied³ \īd\ see IDE¹
ieda \ēd-ə\ see EDA¹
ief¹ \ēf\ beef, brief, chief, fief, grief, leaf, reef, sheaf, thief • bay leaf, belief, chipped beef, crew chief, debrief, fig leaf, fire chief, gold leaf, in brief, kerchief, loose-leaf, motif, relief, sneak thief, Tallchief • bas-relief, cloverleaf, come to grief, disbelief, handkerchief, misbelief, neckerchief, unbelief • barrier reef, comic relief • commander in chief, editor in chief, Great Barrier Reef
ief² \ēv\ see EAVE¹
iefly \ē-flē\ briefly, chiefly
ieg¹ \ēg\ see IGUE
ieg² \ig\ see IG
iege¹ \ēj\ siege • besiege, prestige
iege² \ēzh\ see IGE¹
ieger \ē-jər\ see EDURE
iek \ēk\ see EAK¹
iel \ēl\ see EAL²
iela \el-ə\ see ELLA
ield \ēld\ field, shield, wheeled, wield, yield • afield, airfield, coalfield, cornfield, force field, four-wheeled, Garfield, goldfield, heat shield, ice field, infield, left field, midfield, minefield, oil field, outfield, right field, snowfield, Springfield, unsealed, well-heeled, windshield • Bakersfield, battlefield, center field, landing field, Mount Mansfield, playing field, track-and-field
—*also* -ed *forms of verbs listed at* EAL²

ielder \ēl-dər\ fielder, shielder
• infielder, left fielder, midfielder,
outfielder, right fielder • center
fielder

ields \ēldz\ elysian fields
—*also* -s, -'s, *and* -s' *forms of
nouns and* -s *forms of verbs listed
at* IELD

ieler \ē-lər\ see EALER

ieless \ī-ləs\ see ILUS

ieling \ē-liŋ\ see EELING

iem¹ \ē-əm\ see EUM¹

iem² \ī-əm\ see IAM

ien \ēn\ see INE³

ience \ī-əns\ see IANCE

iend \end\ see END

iendless \en-ləs\ see ENDLESS

iendliness \en-lē-nəs\ see ENDLINESS

iendly \en-lē\ see ENDLY

iene \ēn\ see INE³

iener¹ \ē-nər\ see EANER

iener² \ē-nē\ see INI¹

ienic \en-ik\ see ENIC²

ienics \en-iks\ see ENICS

ienie \ē-nē\ see INI¹

ienist \ē-nəst\ see INIST²

iennes \en\ see EN¹

ient \ī-ənt\ see IANT

ieper \ē-pər\ see EEPER

ier¹ \ir\ see EER²

ier² \ē-ər\ see EER¹

ier³ \īr\ see IRE¹

ierate \ir-ət\ see IRIT

ierce \irs\ fierce, pierce

iere¹ \er\ see ARE⁴

iere² \ir\ see EER²

iered \ird\ see EARD¹

ieria \ir-ē-ə\ see ERIA¹

ierial \ir-ē-əl\ see ERIAL

ierian \ir-ē-ən\ see ERIAN¹

ierly \ir-lē\ see EARLY¹

ierre¹ \ir\ see EER²

ierre² \er\ see ARE⁴

iers \irz\ Sears • Algiers
—*also* -s, -'s, *and* -s' *forms of
nouns and* -s *forms of verbs listed
at* EER²

iersman \irz-mən\ see EERSMAN

iery \ī-ə-rē\ see IARY¹

ies¹ \ēz\ see EZE

ies² \ē\ see EE¹

ies³ \ēs\ see IECE

iesel¹ \ē-zəl\ see EASEL

iesel² \ē-səl\ see ECIL¹

iesian \ē-zhən\ see ESIAN¹

iesis \ī-ə-səs\ see IASIS

iest \ēst\ see EAST¹

iester \ē-stər\ see EASTER

iestley \ēst-lē\ see EASTLY

iestly \ēst-lē\ see EASTLY

iet \ī-ət\ diet, fiat, quiet, riot • dis-
quiet, race riot, run riot, unquiet

ietal \ī-ət-ᵊl\ parietal, societal,
varietal

ieter \ī-ət-ər\ dieter, rioter • propri-
etor

ietor \ī-ət-ər\ see IETER

iety \ī-ət-ē\ piety • anxiety, impiety,
propriety, sobriety, society, variety • impropriety, notoriety • garden variety, honor society, secret
society

ietzsche \ē-chē\ see EACHY

ieu \ü\ see EW²

ieur \ir\ see EER²

iev \ef\ see EF¹

ievable \ē-və-bəl\ see EIVABLE

ieval \ē-vəl\ evil, weevil • boll
weevil, coeval, medieval,
primeval, retrieval, upheaval

ieve¹ \iv\ see IVE²

ieve² \ēv\ see EAVE¹

ieved \ēvd\ see EAVED

ievement \ēv-mənt\ see EVEMENT

iever \ē-vər\ beaver, cleaver, fever,
weaver • achiever, believer, con-
ceiver, deceiver, orb weaver,
receiver, reliever, retriever, trans-
ceiver • cantilever, disbeliever,
eager beaver, true believer, unbe-
liever, wide receiver • golden
retriever, overachiever, under-
achiever

ievish \ē-vish\ see EEVISH

ievous \ē-vəs\ see EVOUS
ieze \ēz\ see EZE
if¹ \if\ see IFF
if² \ēf\ see IEF¹
ife¹ \īf\ fife, Fife, knife, life, rife,
strife, wife • good life, half-life,
housewife, jackknife, lowlife,
midlife, nightlife, penknife, real-
life, shelf life, steak knife, still
life, true-life, wildlife • afterlife,
bowie knife, Duncan Phyfe, fact
of life, get a life, nurse-midwife,
palette knife, paring knife, pock-
etknife, putty knife, Yellowknife
• utility knife
ife² \ēf\ see IEF¹
ifeless \ī-fləs\ lifeless, strifeless,
wifeless
ifer \ī-fər\ see IPHER
iferous \if-ər-əs\ coniferous, pestif-
erous, splendiferous, vociferous
• odoriferous
iff \if\ biff, cliff, diff, glyph, if, jiff,
miff, riff, skiff, sniff, stiff, tiff,
whiff • midriff, what-if • hiero-
glyph
iffany \if-ə-nē\ see IPHONY
iffe \if\ see IFF
iffed \ift\ see IFT
iffey \if-ē\ see IFFY
iffish \if-ish\ sniffish, stiffish
iffle \if-əl\ riffle, sniffle, Wiffle
iffness \if-nəs\ stiffness, swiftness
iffy \if-ē\ iffy, jiffy, Liffey, sniffy,
spiffy
ific \if-ik\ horrific, pacific, Pacific,
prolific, specific, terrific • be-
atific, hieroglyphic, honorific,
scientific, soporific, South Pacific
ifle \ī-fəl\ rifle, stifle, trifle • air
rifle, a trifle, squirrel rifle • assault rifle, Enfield rifle, M1 rifle,
Springfield rifle
ifling \ī-fliŋ\ rifling, stifling, trifling
ift \ift\ drift, gift, lift, rift, shift,
shrift, sift, swift, Swift, thrift
• adrift, airlift, chairlift, down-
shift, face-lift, forklift, gearshift,
makeshift, shape-shift, shoplift,
ski lift, snowdrift, spendthrift,
spindrift, split shift, stick shift,
swing shift, uplift, upshift • chimney swift, graveyard shift • continental drift
—*also* -ed *forms of verbs listed at*
IFF
ifter \if-tər\ drifter, sifter • scene-
shifter, shape-shifter, shoplifter,
weight lifter
ifth \ith\ see ITH²
iftness \if-nəs\ see IFFNESS
ifty \if-tē\ drifty, fifty, nifty, shifty,
thrifty • fifty-fifty, LD₅₀
ig \ig\ big, brig, cig, dig, fig, gig,
Grieg, jig, pig, prig, rig, sprig,
swig, twig, Whig, wig, zig • big-
wig, Danzig, earwig, Leipzig,
renege, shindig • guinea pig,
hit it big, jury-rig, whirligig,
WYSIWYG • potbellied pig,
thingamajig
iga \ē-gə\ Antigua, omega
igamous \ig-ə-məs\ bigamous
• polygamous
igamy \ig-ə-mē\ bigamy
• polygamy
igate \ig-ət\ see IGOT¹
ige¹ \ēzh\ siege • prestige
ige² \ēj\ see IEGE¹
igel \ij-əl\ see IGIL
igenous \ij-ə-nəs\ see IGINOUS
igeon \ij-ən\ see YGIAN
iger \ī-gər\ tiger • Bengal tiger,
paper tiger • saber-toothed tiger
• Siberian tiger, Tasmanian tiger
igerent \ij-rənt\ belligerent, refrig-
erant
iggard \ig-ərd\ triggered
—*also* -ed *forms of verbs listed at*
IGGER
igged \igd\ twigged • jerry-rigged
—*also* -ed *forms of verbs listed at* IG
igger \ig-ər\ chigger, jigger, rigor,
snigger, trigger, vigor • ditchdig-

ger, gold digger, hair trigger, outrigger • pull the trigger

iggered \ig-ərd\ see IGGARD

iggie \ig-ē\ see IGGY

iggish \ig-ish\ biggish, piggish, priggish

iggle \ig-əl\ giggle, jiggle, squiggle, wiggle, wriggle

iggler \ig-lər\ giggler, wiggler, wriggler

iggy \ig-ē\ biggie, piggy, twiggy

igh \ī\ see Y[1]

ighed \īd\ see IDE[1]

ighland \ī-lənd\ highland, island, Thailand • Long Island, Rhode Island, Wake Island • Christmas Island, Coney Island, Devil's Island, Easter Island, Ellis Island, Staten Island • Prince Edward Island, Vancouver Island

ighlander \ī-lən-dər\ highlander, islander

ighlands \ī-lənz\ Highlands • Aran Islands, Cayman Islands, Channel Islands, Falkland Islands, Gilbert Islands, Leeward Islands, Marshall Islands, Thousand Islands, Virgin Islands, Windward Islands • Aegean Islands, Aleutian Islands, Canary Islands, Hawaiian Islands, Philippine Islands
—*also* -s, -'s, *and* -s' *forms of nouns listed at* IGHLAND

ighly \ī-lē\ see YLY

ighness \ī-nəs\ see INUS[1]

ight \īt\ see ITE[1]

ightable \īt-ə-bəl\ see ITABLE[1]

ighted \īt-əd\ blighted, sighted • benighted, clear-sighted, far-sighted, foresighted, nearsighted, shortsighted, united
—*also* -ed *forms of verbs listed at* ITE[1]

ighten \īt-ᵊn\ brighten, chitin, frighten, heighten, lighten, tighten, titan, Titan, triton, whiten • enlighten

ightener \īt-nər\ brightener, lightener, tightener, whitener

ightening \īt-niŋ\ see IGHTNING

ighter \īt-ər\ see ITER[1]

ightful \īt-fəl\ frightful, rightful, spiteful • delightful, insightful

ightie \īt-ē\ see ITE[2]

ighting \īt-iŋ\ see ITING

ightless \īt-ləs\ flightless, lightless, nightless, sightless

ightly \īt-lē\ brightly, knightly, lightly, nightly, rightly, slightly, sprightly, tightly • contritely, finitely, forthrightly, politely, unsightly, uprightly • impolitely

ightment \īt-mənt\ see ITEMENT

ightning \īt-niŋ\ lightning, tightening • ball lightning, belt-tightening, heat lightning, sheet lightning
—*also* -ing *forms of verbs listed at* IGHTEN

ighton \īt-ən\ see IGHTEN

ights \īts\ lights, nights, tights • by rights, footlights, houselights, last rites, states' rights, weeknights • bill of rights, civil rights, Golan Heights, human rights, northern lights, Shaker Heights, southern lights • animal rights
—*also* -s, -'s, *and* -s' *forms of nouns and* -s *forms of verbs listed at* ITE[1]

ighty \īt-ē\ see ITE[2]

igian \ij-ən\ see YGIAN

igid \ij-əd\ Brigid, frigid, rigid

igil \ij-əl\ vigil • residual

iginous \ij-ə-nəs\ indigenous, vertiginous

igion \ij-ən\ see YGIAN

igious \ij-əs\ litigious, prestigious, prodigious, religious • irreligious

igit \ij-ət\ see IDGET

igitte \ij-ət\ see IDGET

igm[1] \im\ see IM[1]

igm[2] \īm\ see IME[1]

igma \ig-mə\ sigma, stigma • enigma

igment \ig-mənt\ figment, pigment
ign \īn\ see INE[1]
ignant \ig-nənt\ indignant, malignant
igned \īnd\ see IND[1]
igner \ī-nər\ see INER[1]
igning \ī-niŋ\ see INING
ignity \ig-nət-ē\ dignity • indignity
ignly \īn-lē\ see INELY[1]
ignment \īn-mənt\ alignment, assignment, confinement, refinement • realignment
ignon \in-yən\ see INION
igo \ē-gō\ see EGO[1]
igoe \ē-gō\ see EGO[1]
igor \ig-ər\ see IGGER
igorous \ig-rəs\ rigorous, vigorous
igot[1] \ig-ət\ bigot, frigate, spigot
igot[2] \ik-ət\ see ICKET
igour \ig-ər\ see IGGER
igue \ēg\ Grieg, league • big-league, blitzkrieg, bush-league, colleague, fatigue, intrigue • Ivy League, Little League, major-league, minor-league • battle fatigue, combat fatigue
iguer \ē-gər\ see EAGER
iguous \ig-yə-wəs\ ambiguous, contiguous • unambiguous
igured \ig-ərd\ see IGGARD
ii \ī\ see Y[1]
iing \ē-iŋ\ see EEING
ija \ē-jə\ see EGIA
iji \ē-jē\ Fiji, squeegee
ijia \ē-jə\ see EGIA
ijl \īl\ see ILE[1]
ijn \īn\ see INE[1]
ik[1] \ik\ see ICK
ik[2] \ēk\ see EAK[1]
ika[1] \ē-kə\ paprika, Topeka • Costa Rica, Dominica, Frederica, Tanganyika
ika[2] \ī-kə\ see ICA[1]
ike[1] \ī-kē\ crikey, Nike, Psyche, spiky
ike[2] \īk\ bike, dike, hike, like, mike, Mike, pike, psych, shrike, spike, strike, trike, tyke • alike, boatlike, childlike, Christlike, dirt bike, dislike, dreamlike, feel like, fishlike, flu-like, godlike, grasslike, hitchhike, Klondike, lifelike, rocklike, springlike, suchlike, trail bike, trancelike, turnpike, unlike, vicelike, warlike, wavelike, winglike • and the like, businesslike, down the pike, hunger strike, ladylike, leatherlike, look-alike, machinelike, minibike, motorbike, mountain bike, northern pike, open mike, soundalike, sportsmanlike, statesmanlike, take a hike, workmanlike • exercise bike, sympathy strike, unsportsmanlike
iked \īkt\ spiked
—*also* -ed *forms of verbs listed at* IKE[2]
iker \ī-kər\ biker, hiker, striker • hitchhiker • hunger striker, minibiker, mountain biker
ikey \ī-kē\ see IKE[1]
ikh \ēk\ see EAK[1]
iki[1] \ik-ē\ see ICKY
iki[2] \ē-kē\ see EAKY
iking \ī-kiŋ\ liking, striking, Viking
—*also* -ing *forms of verbs listed at* IKE[2]
ikker \ik-ər\ see ICKER[1]
iky \ī-kē\ see IKE[1]
il[1] \il\ see ILL
il[2] \ēl\ see EAL[2]
ila[1] \il-ə\ see ILLA[2]
ila[2] \ē-lə\ see ELA[1]
ilae \ī-lē\ see YLY
ilage \ī-lij\ mileage, silage
ilar \ī-lər\ dialer, filer, miler, smiler, styler, tiler, Tyler • compiler, rottweiler, stockpiler
ilate \ī-lət\ see ILOT
ilbert \il-bərt\ filbert, Gilbert
ilch[1] \ilk\ see ILK
ilch[2] \ilch\ filch, zilch
ild[1] \īld\ child, mild, piled, wild,

Wilde • brainchild, godchild, grandchild, hog-wild, Rothschild, schoolchild, self-styled, stepchild, with child • flower child, latchkey child, poster child, self-exiled
—*also* -ed *forms of verbs listed at* ILE[1]

ild² \il\ see ILL

ild³ \ilt\ see ILT

ild⁴ \ild\ see ILLED

ilde \īld\ see ILD[1]

ilder¹ \il-dər\ builder • bewilder, boatbuilder, Mound Builder, shipbuilder • bodybuilder

ilder² \īl-dər\ Wilder
—*also* -er *forms of adjectives listed at* ILD[1]

ilding \il-diŋ\ building, gilding • boatbuilding, outbuilding, shipbuilding • bodybuilding
—*also* -ing *forms of verbs listed at* ILLED

ildish \īl-dish\ childish, wildish

ildly \īld-lē\ mildly, wildly

ile¹ \īl\ aisle, bile, dial, file, guile, I'll, isle, Kyle, Lyle, mile, Nile, pile, rile, smile, style, tile, trial, vial, vile, viol, while • agile, air mile, argyle, awhile, bass viol, beguile, Blue Nile, compile, defile, denial, docile, erstwhile, exile, febrile, field trial, fragile, freestyle, futile, gentile, hairstyle, high style, hostile, lifestyle, meanwhile, mistrial, mobile, nail file, nubile, on file, profile, puerile, quartile, redial, reptile, retrial, revile, sandpile, senile, servile, stockpile, sundial, tactile, tensile, textile, time trial, turnstile, unpile, virile, woodpile, worthwhile • chamomile, crocodile, domicile, family style, in denial, infantile, insectile, juvenile, low-profile, mercantile, percentile, prehensile, projectile, rank and file, reconcile, self-denial, single file, statute

mile, versatile • audiophile, circular file, Indian file, once in a while • cafeteria-style

ile² \il\ see ILL

ile³ \ē-lē\ see EELY

ile⁴ \ēl\ see EAL²

ile⁵ \il-ē\ see ILLY

ilead \il-ē-əd\ see ILIAD

ileage \ī-lij\ see ILAGE

ileal \il-ē-əl\ see ILIAL

iler¹ \ē-lər\ see EALER

iler² \ī-lər\ see ILAR

iles \īlz\ Giles, Miles • British Isles, Western Isles
—*also* -s, -'s, *and* -s' *forms of nouns and* -s *forms of verbs listed at* ILE[1]

iley \ī-lē\ see YLY

ili¹ \il-ē\ see ILLY

ili² \ē-lē\ see EELY

ilia¹ \il-ē-ə\ Celia, cilia • Cecilia • hemophilia • memorabilia

ilia² \il-yə\ Brasília • bougainvillea • memorabilia

ilia³ \ēl-yə\ see ELIA[1]

iliad \il-ē-əd\ Gilead, Iliad • balm of Gilead

ilial \il-ē-əl\ filial • familial

ilian¹ \il-ē-ən\ Gillian, Ilian, Lillian • reptilian • crocodilian

ilian² \il-yən\ see ILLION

ilias \il-ē-əs\ see ILIOUS[1]

ilic \il-ik\ acrylic, Cyrillic, dactylic, idyllic

ilience \il-yəns\ see ILLIANCE

iliency \il-yən-sē\ see ILLIANCY

ilient \il-yənt\ brilliant • resilient

iling¹ \ī-liŋ\ filing, piling, styling, tiling • hairstyling
—*also* -ing *forms of verbs listed at* ILE[1]

iling² \ē-liŋ\ see EELING

ilion¹ \il-yən\ see ILLION

ilion² \il-ē-ən\ see ILIAN[1]

ilious¹ \il-ē-əs\ punctilious • supercilious

ilious² \il-yəs\ bilious • supercilious

ility \il-ət-ē\ ability, agility, civility, debility, docility, facility, fertility, fragility, futility, gentility, hostility, humility, mobility, nobility, senility, stability, sterility, tranquility, utility, virility • affability, capability, countability, credibility, culpability, disability, durability, fallibility, feasibility, flexibility, gullibility, imbecility, immobility, inability, incivility, infertility, instability, legibility, liability, likability, livability, plausibility, portability, possibility, probability, readability, sensibility, sociability, suitability, tunability, usability, versatility, viability, visibility, volatility • acceptability, accessibility, accountability, adaptability, advisability, affordability, applicability, attainability, availability, believability, compatibility, deniability, dependability, desirability, electability, eligibility, excitability, illegibility, impossibility, improbability, incapability, infallibility, inflexibility, invisibility, manageability, marketability, measurability, navigability, predictability, profitability, public utility, reliability, respectability, responsibility, susceptibility, sustainability, upward mobility, variability, vulnerability

ilk \ilk\ bilk, ilk, milk, silk • corn silk, ice milk, skim milk • buttermilk, condensed milk, malted milk • cry over spilled milk

ilky \il-kē\ milky, silky

ill \il\ bill, Bill, chill, dill, drill, fill, frill, gill, grill, grille, hill, ill, Jill, kill, krill, mill, nil, Phil, pill, quill, rill, shrill, sill, skill, spill, still, swill, thrill, til, till, trill, twill, will, Will • anthill, at will, backfill, bluegill, Brazil, Catskill, Churchill, crossbill, de Mille, distill, doorsill, downhill, duckbill, dullsville, dunghill, fire drill, foothill, freewill, free will, fulfill, goodwill, gristmill, handbill, hornbill, Huntsville, ill will, instill, Knoxville, landfill, Melville, mixed grill, molehill, Nashville, pep pill, playbill, refill, roadkill, sawmill, Schuylkill, Seville, spoonbill, standstill, stock-still, storksbill, treadmill, true bill, twin bill, twist drill, unreal, until, uphill, vaudeville, waxbill, windchill, windmill • Brazzaville, Bunker Hill, Chapel Hill, chlorophyll, daffodil, de Tocqueville, double bill, espadrille, Evansville, fiberfill, fill the bill, fit to kill, if you will, Jacksonville, living will, Louisville, overfill, overkill, pepper mill, poison pill, puppy mill, rototill, San Juan Hill, sleeping pill, sugar pill, windowsill, whippoor-will • Buffalo Bill, Capitol Hill, over-the-hill, run-of-the-mill

I'll \īl\ see ILE[1]

illa[1] \ē-yə\ mantilla, tortilla • quesadilla

illa[2] \il-ə\ villa, Willa • Anguilla, Attila, Camilla, cedilla, chinchilla, flotilla, gorilla, guerrilla, manila, mantilla, Priscilla, scintilla, vanilla • sarsaparilla

illa[3] \ē-ə\ see IA[1]

illa[4] \ēl-yə\ see ELIA[1]

illa[5] \ē-lə\ see ELA[1]

illable \il-ə-bəl\ billable, drillable, fillable, spillable, syllable, tillable • refillable, trisyllable • monosyllable, polysyllable

illage \il-ij\ pillage, spillage, tillage, village • global village, Greenwich Village • Potemkin village

illah \il-ə\ see ILLA[2]

illain \il-ən\ see ILLON

illar \il-ər\ see ILLER

illate \il-ət\ see ILLET
ille¹ \il\ see ILL
ille² \ē\ see EE¹
ille³ \ēl\ see EAL²
illea \il-yə\ see ILIA²
illed \ild\ build, gild, gilled, guild, skilled, willed • gold-filled, re-build, tendriled, unskilled • over-build, semiskilled
  —*also* -ed *forms of verbs listed at* ILL
illedness \il-nəs\ see ILLNESS
illein \il-ən\ see ILLON
iller \il-ər\ chiller, filler, killer, miller, pillar, thriller, tiller • dis-tiller, painkiller, time killer • caterpillar, lady-killer, Rototiller, techno-thriller
  —*also* -er *forms of adjectives listed at* ILL
illery \il-rē\ pillory • artillery, dis-tillery • field artillery
illes \il-ēz\ see ILLIES
illet \il-ət\ millet, skillet • distillate
illful \il-fəl\ skillful, willful • un-skillful
illi¹ \il-ē\ see ILLY
illi² \ē-lē\ see EELY
illian¹ \il-ē-ən\ see ILIAN¹
illian² \il-yən\ see ILLION
illiance \il-yəns\ brilliance • re-silience
illiancy \il-yən-sē\ brilliancy • re-siliency
illiant \il-yənt\ see ILIENT
illick \il-ik\ see ILIC
illie \il-ē\ see ILLY
illies \il-ēz\ willies • Achilles, An-tilles • Greater Antilles, Lesser Antilles
  —*also* -s, -'s, *and* -s' *forms of nouns listed at* ILLY
illin \il-ən\ see ILLON
illing \il-iŋ\ billing, drilling, filling, killing, milling, shilling, willing • bone-chilling, fulfilling, painkilling, spine-chilling, top

billing, unwilling • mercy killing, self-fulfilling
  —*also* -ing *forms of verbs listed at* ILL
illion \il-yən\ billion, Lillian, mil-lion, trillion, zillion • Brazilian, Castilian, civilian, cotillion, gazil-lion, pavilion, quadrillion, rep-tilian, Sicilian, vaudevillian, vermilion • crocodilian, Maxi-milian
illis \il-əs\ see ILLUS
illness \il-nəs\ illness, shrillness, stillness
illo¹ \il-ō\ billow, pillow, willow • Amarillo, armadillo, cigarillo, peccadillo
illo² \ē-ō\ see IO²
illon \il-ən\ Dylan, villain • peni-cillin
illory \il-rē\ see ILLERY
illous \il-əs\ see ILLUS
illow¹ \il-ə\ see ILLA²
illow² \il-ō\ see ILLO¹
illowy \il-ə-wē\ billowy, pillowy, willowy
ills \ilz\ Black Hills, no-frills • Al-ban Hills, Berkshire Hills, Chiltern Hills, Cotswold Hills, Malvern Hills, Naga Hills • Bev-erly Hills, Cheviot Hills, Grampian Hills
  —*also* -s, -'s, *and* -s' *forms of nouns and* -s *forms of verbs listed at* ILL
illus \il-əs\ Phyllis, Willis • bacillus • amaryllis
illy \il-ē\ Billie, billy, Chile, chili, chilly, dilly, filly, frilly, hilly, Lillie, lily, Lily, Millie, really, shrilly, silly, Tilly, Willie • daylily, hillbilly • rockabilly, willy-nilly
iln¹ \il\ see ILL
iln² \iln\ kiln, Milne
ilne \iln\ see ILN²
ilo¹ \ī-lō\ Milo, phyllo, silo
ilo² \ē-lō\ kilo, phyllo

ilom \ī-ləm\ see ILUM
iloquist \il-ə-kwəst\ soliloquist, ventriloquist
iloquy \il-ə-kwē\ soliloquy, ventriloquy
ilot \ī-lət\ eyelet, islet, Pilate, pilot • bush pilot, copilot, test pilot • autopilot, Pontius Pilate • automatic pilot
ilt \ilt\ built, gilt, guilt, hilt, jilt, kilt, lilt, quilt, silt, stilt, tilt, wilt • atilt, Brunhild, full tilt, homebuilt, rebuilt, unbuilt • crazy-quilt, custom-built, jerry-built, patchwork quilt, to the hilt, Vanderbilt
ilter \il-tər\ filter, kilter, quilter • off-kilter • color filter
ilth \ilth\ filth, tilth
iltie \il-tē\ see ILTY
ilton \ilt-ᵊn\ Hilton, Milton
ilty \il-tē\ guilty, silty
ilum \ī-ləm\ phylum, xylem • asylum, subphylum
ilus \ī-ləs\ eyeless, stylus, tieless
ily[1] \ī-lē\ see YLY
ily[2] \il-ē\ see ILLY
im[1] \im\ brim, dim, grim, Grimm, gym, him, hymn, Jim, Kim, limb, prim, rim, scrim, skim, slim, swim, Tim, trim, vim, whim • forelimb, prelim, Purim, Sikkim • acronym, antonym, pseudonym, seraphim, synonym • Pacific Rim
im[2] \ēm\ see EAM[1]
I'm \īm\ see IME[1]
ima \ē-mə\ see EMA
image \im-ij\ image, scrimmage • self-image • father image, graven image, mirror image, spitting image, line of scrimmage
iman \ē-mən\ see EMON[1]
imate \ī-mət\ climate, primate • acclimate
imb[1] \im\ see IM[1]
imb[2] \īm\ see IME[1]
imbal \im-bəl\ see IMBLE
imbale \im-bəl\ see IMBLE

imbed \imd\ brimmed, limbed, rimmed
—*also* -ed *forms of verbs listed at* IM[1]
imber[1] \im-bər\ limber, timber
imber[2] \ī-mər\ see IMER[1]
imble \im-bəl\ cymbal, nimble, symbol, thimble • peace symbol
imbo \im-bō\ bimbo, limbo • akimbo
imbre \am-bər\ see AMBAR[2]
ime[1] \īm\ chime, climb, clime, crime, dime, grime, I'm, lime, mime, prime, rhyme, slime, thyme, time • all-time, bedtime, big time, big-time, buy time, call time, daytime, downtime, enzyme, full-time, halftime, hate crime, in time, key lime, lead time, lifetime, longtime, lunchtime, make time, Mannheim, mark time, mealtime, meantime, nighttime, noontime, old-time, onetime, on time, part-time, pastime, peacetime, playtime, prime time, quicklime, quick time, ragtime, real time, rock climb, schooltime, seedtime, showtime, small-time, sometime, Sondheim, space-time, springtime, sublime, teatime, two-time, war crime, wartime, wind chime • Anaheim, anytime, borrowed time, central time, Christmastime, dinnertime, double-time, eastern time, Father Time, harvesttime, local time, maritime, mountain time, nursery rhyme, on a dime, overtime, pantomime, paradigm, running time, standard time, summertime, take one's time, wintertime • Alaska time, Atlantic time, at the same time, from time to time, Greenwich mean time, Pacific time, nickel-and-dime • daylight saving time, geologic time

ime² \ēm\ see EAM¹
imeless \īm-ləs\ crimeless, timeless
imely \īm-lē\ timely • sublimely, untimely
imen \ī-mən\ hymen, Hymen, Simon
imeon \im-ē-ən\ see IMIAN
imer¹ \ī-mər\ climber, primer, rhymer, timer • big-timer, egg timer, full-timer, old-timer, part-timer, small-timer • Oppenheimer, wisenheimer
imer² \im-ər\ see IMMER
imes \ēm\ see EAM¹
imeter \im-ət-ər\ scimitar • altimeter, perimeter
imian \im-ē-ən\ Simeon, simian • Endymion
imic \im-ik\ see YMIC
imicry \im-i-krē\ gimmickry, mimicry
imile \im-ə-lē\ simile, swimmily • facsimile
iminal \im-ən-ᵊl\ criminal • subliminal, war criminal
imitable \im-ət-ə-bəl\ illimitable, inimitable
imitar \im-ət-ər\ see IMETER
imiter \im-ət-ər\ see IMETER
imits \im-its\ Nimitz • off-limits
imity \im-ət-ē\ proximity, sublimity • anonymity, equanimity, magnanimity, unanimity
imitz \im-its\ see IMITS
imm \im\ see IM¹
immage \im-ij\ see IMAGE
imme \i-mē\ see IMMY
immed \imd\ see IMBED
immer \im-ər\ dimmer, glimmer, grimmer, primer, shimmer, simmer, skimmer, slimmer, swimmer
immick \im-ik\ see YMIC
immickry \im-i-krē\ see IMICRY
immily \im-ə-lē\ see IMILE
immy \im-ē\ gimme, jimmy, shimmy
imn \im\ see IM¹

imner \im-ər\ see IMMER
imon \ī-mən\ see IMEN
imp \imp\ blimp, chimp, crimp, imp, limp, primp, scrimp, shrimp, skimp, wimp • brine shrimp, rock shrimp • Colonel Blimp, fairy shrimp, tiger shrimp
impe \imp\ see IMP
imper \im-pər\ shrimper, simper, whimper
imple \im-pəl\ dimple, pimple, simple
imply \im-plē\ limply, pimply, simply
impy \im-pē\ shrimpy, skimpy, wimpy
imsy \im-zē\ flimsy, whimsy
imy \ī-mē\ grimy, limey, limy, slimy, stymie • old-timey
in¹ \in\ been, bin, chin, din, fin, Finn, gin, grin, Gwyn, in, inn, kin, Lynn, pin, shin, sin, skin, spin, thin, tin, twin, win, yin • again, akin, backspin, bearskin, begin, Benin, Berlin, blow in, Boleyn, break-in, bring in, buckskin, build in, built-in, butt in, calfskin, call in, call-in, cash in, cave-in, chagrin, check in, check-in, chime in, chip in, close in, clothespin, come in, coonskin, Corinne, crankpin, cut in, deerskin, dig in, doeskin, do in, drive-in, drop in, fade-in, fall in, fill in, fill-in, give in, goatskin, go in, hairpin, hang in, has-been, herein, horn in, kick in, kidskin, kingpin, lambskin, lay in, lead-in, linchpin, live-in, lived-in, log in, love-in, moleskin, move in, munchkin, ninepin, no-win, oilskin, phone-in, pigskin, pitch in, plug-in, plugged-in, pull in, pushpin, put in, rub in, ruin, sealskin, send in, set in, sharkskin, sheepskin, shoo-in, shut-in, sign in, sit-in, sleep in, sleep-in, sloe gin, snakeskin, sock

in, stand in, stand-in, step in, stickpin, suck in, swear in, swim fin, tail fin, tailspin, take in, tenpin, therein, throw in, tie-in, tiepin, tip-in, Tonkin, topspin, trade in, trade-in, tune in, tuned-in, Turin, turn in, unpin, walk-in, wear thin, weigh in, wherein, wineskin, win-win, within, work in, write-in, Yeltsin • bobby pin, born-again, candlepin, come again, cotter pin, cotton gin, deadly sin, firing pin, Ho Chi Minh, listen in, listener-in, Lohengrin, loony bin, mandolin, mortal sin, motor inn, next of kin, onionskin, paper-thin, pelvic fin, rolling pin, safety pin, set foot in, thick and thin, violin • Gulf of Tonkin, Holiday Inn, original sin, pectoral fin, rub one's nose in, Siamese twin, under one's skin • again and again • on-again off-again

in² \ēn\ see INE³

in³ \an\ see AN⁵

in⁴ \aⁿ\ Chopin, dauphin, Gauguin, Louvain, Rodin • Claude Lorrain, Saint-Germain

in⁵ \ən\ see UN¹

ina¹ \ī-nə\ china, China, Dinah, Ina, mynah • angina, bone china, Regina, stone china • Carolina, Indochina, kamaaina • North Carolina, South Carolina

ina² \ē-nə\ Lena, Nina, Tina • arena, Athena, Christina, czarina, Edwina, farina, Georgina, hyena, Kristina, marina, Marina, Medina, Messina, novena, patina, Regina, Rowena, subpoena • Angelina, Argentina, ballerina, Carolina, Catalina, concertina, Filipina, Katerina, ocarina, Pasadena, semolina, signorina, Wilhelmina • Herzegovina, Pallas Athena, Strait of Messina

inach \in-ich\ Greenwich, spinach

inah¹ \ē-nə\ see INA²

inah² \ī-nə\ see INA¹

inal¹ \īn-ᵊl\ final, spinal, vinyl • doctrinal • quarterfinal, semifinal

inal² \ēn-ᵊl\ see ENAL

inally \īn-ᵊl-ē\ finally, spinally

inas¹ \ī-nəs\ see INUS¹

inas² \ē-nəs\ see ENUS¹

inative \in-ət-iv\ see INITIVE

inc \iŋk\ see INK

inca \iŋ-kə\ Dinka, Inca

incal \iŋ-kəl\ see INKLE

incan \iŋ-kən\ Incan, Lincoln

ince¹ \ins\ blintz, chintz, mince, prince, quince, rinse, since, wince • convince, crown prince, evince, shin splints • Port-au-Prince
—*also* -s, -'s, *and* -s' *forms of nouns and* -s *forms of verbs listed at* INT

ince² \ans\ see ANCE³

incely \in-slē\ princely, tinselly

incer \in-chər\ see INCHER

inch \inch\ cinch, clinch, finch, flinch, grinch, inch, lynch, pinch, winch • bullfinch, chaffinch, goldfinch • every inch, inch by inch, purple finch

incher \in-chər\ clincher, pincer • penny-pincher • Doberman pinscher

inching \in-chiŋ\ unflinching • penny-pinching
—*also* -ing *forms of verbs listed at* INCH

incible \in-sə-bəl\ principal, principle • invincible

incing \in-siŋ\ ginseng • convincing • unconvincing
—*also* -ing *forms of verbs listed at* INCE¹

incipal \in-sə-bəl\ see INCIBLE

inciple \in-sə-bəl\ see INCIBLE

inck \iŋk\ see INK

incky \iŋ-kē\ see INKY

incoln \iŋ-kən\ see INCAN

inct \iŋt\ linked • distinct, extinct, instinct, precinct, succinct • indistinct • killer instinct

inction \iŋ-shən\ distinction, extinction • contradistinction

ind[1] \īnd\ bind, blind, find, grind, hind, kind, mind, rind, spined, wind • behind, confined, fly blind, inclined, mankind, refined, remind, rewind, sand-blind, snow-blind, spellbind, streamlined, unbind, unkind, unwind • ax to grind, bear in mind, blow one's mind, bring to mind, color-blind, fall behind, frame of mind, humankind, in a bind, mastermind, never mind, nonaligned, put in mind, unaligned, undersigned, well-defined, womankind • back of one's mind, piece of one's mind, presence of mind, venetian blind
—*also* -ed *forms of verbs listed at* INE[1]

ind[2] \ind\ finned, skinned, wind • crosswind, downwind, headwind, rescind, tailwind, thick-skinned, thin-skinned, upwind, whirlwind, woodwind • in the wind, solar wind, spiny-finned • twist in the wind
—*also* -ed *forms of verbs listed at* IN[1]

ind[3] \int\ see INT

inda \in-də\ Linda • Lucinda, Melinda

indar \in-dər\ see INDER[2]

inded[1] \īn-dəd\ minded • broad-minded, fair-minded, high-minded, like-minded, small-minded, snow-blinded, strong-minded, tough-minded, weak-minded • absentminded, bloody-minded, civic-minded, evil-minded, feebleminded, narrow-minded, open-minded, simpleminded, single-minded

—*also* -ed *forms of verbs listed at* IND[1]

inded[2] \in-dəd\ long-winded, short-winded
—*also* -ed *forms of verbs listed at* IND[2]

inder[1] \īn-dər\ binder, finder, grinder • bookbinder, fact finder, faultfinder, pathfinder, range finder, reminder, ring binder, sidewinder, spellbinder, stem-winder, viewfinder, organ-grinder
—*also* -er *forms of adjectives listed at* IND[1]

inder[2] \in-dər\ cinder, hinder, Pindar, tinder

indhi \in-dē\ see INDY

indi \in-dē\ see INDY

indie \in-dē\ see INDY

inding \īn-diŋ\ binding, finding, winding • bookbinding, fact-finding, faultfinding, self-winding, spellbinding
—*also* -ing *forms of verbs listed at* IND[1]

indlass \in-ləs\ see INLESS

indle \in-dᵊl\ dwindle, kindle, spindle, swindle

indless \īn-ləs\ mindless, spineless

indling \ind-liŋ\ dwindling, kindling

indly[1] \in-lē\ see INLY

indly[2] \īn-lē\ see INELY[1]

indness \īn-nəs\ blindness, fineness, kindness • night blindness, snow blindness, unkindness • color blindness, loving-kindness

indowed \in-dəd\ see INDED[2]

indy \in-dē\ Cindy, Hindi, indie, windy

ine[1] \īn\ brine, dine, fine, kine, line, mine, nine, pine, Rhine, rind, shine, shrine, sign, spine, stein, swine, thine, tine, twine, vine, whine, wine • A-line, airline, align, alpine, assign, at sign, baseline, beeline, benign, Bernstein, bloodline, blush wine, bovine, bowline, breadline, bustline, byline, call sign, canine, carbine, chow line, clothesline, cloud nine, coastline, combine, condign, confine, consign, cosign, cosine, dateline, deadline, decline, define, design, divine, earthshine, Einstein, enshrine, ensign, entwine, equine, feline, foul line, fräulein, frontline, front line, goal line, gold mine, grapevine, guideline, hairline, hard-line, hard pine, headline, hemline, high sign, Holstein, hotline, incline, in-line, Irvine, jawline, landline, land mine, lifeline, main line, malign, midline, moonshine, neckline, offline, old-line, online, opine, outline, outshine, Pauline, peace sign, pipeline, pitch pine, plumb line, plus sign, porcine, pound sign, punch line, quinine, recline, red pine, refine, resign, Rhine wine, ridgeline, roofline, saline, Scotch pine, scrub pine, shoreline, sideline, skyline, snow line, straight-line, streamline, strip mine, strychnine, sunshine, supine, time-line, times sign, towline, trapline, tree line, truckline, trunk line, turbine, untwine, ursine, V sign, waistline, white pine, white wine, woodbine, yard line • alkaline, Angeline, Apennine, aquiline, asinine, auld lang syne, balloon vine, battle line, borderline, bottom-line, Byzantine, calamine, Calvin Klein, Caroline, centerline, claymore mine, columbine, concubine, conga line, Constantine, contour line, coralline, countermine, countersign, credit line, crystalline, disincline, draw the line, equal sign, finish line, firing line, Florentine, Frankenstein, gas

turbine, genuine, intertwine, iodine, knotty pine, leonine, Levantine, Liechtenstein, lodgepole pine, longleaf pine, minus sign, monkeyshine, mugho pine, on deadline, on the line, Palestine, party line, picket line, porcupine, realign, redefine, redesign, riverine, Rubenstein, saturnine, second-line, serpentine, shortleaf pine, sibylline, subalpine, sparkling wine, steam turbine, story line, table wine, timberline, toe the line, turpentine, underline, undermine, valentine, waterline, wind turbine, worry line • assembly line, elephantine, Evangeline, fall into line, Frankfurt am Main, graphic design, labyrinthine, lateral line, loblolly pine, Maginot Line, poverty line, production line, receiving line, Rembrandt van Rijn, ship of the line, sweetheart neckline, top-of-the-line • Mason-Dixon line

ine² \ēn\ bean, clean, dean, e'en, gene, Gene, glean, green, jean, Jean, Jeanne, keen, lean, lien, mean, mien, preen, queen, scene, screen, seen, sheen, spleen, teen, tween, wean • Aileen, Arlene, baleen, Benin, benzene, benzine, Bernstein, between, black bean, bovine, broad bean, caffeine, canteen, carbine, careen, Carlene, Cathleen, Charlene, chlorine, chorine, Christine, Claudine, codeine, colleen, Colleen, convene, Coreen, cuisine, Darlene, demean, dentine, Doreen, dryclean, eighteen, Eileen, Eugene, e-zine, fanzine, fifteen, fluorine, fourteen, Francine, gamine, gangrene, glassine, Helene, Hellene, Hermine, Holstein, houseclean, hygiene, Ilene, Irene, Jacqueline, Jeannine, Jolene, Justine, Kath-

leen, Kristine, lateen, latrine,
Lorene, Lublin, machine, marine,
Marlene, Maureen, Maxine, mor-
phine, mung bean, Nadine,
Nicene, nineteen, Noreen, ob-
scene, offscreen, on-screen,
Pauline, praline, preteen, pristine,
protein, Racine, ravine, red bean,
routine, saline, saltine, sardine,
sateen, serene, Sharlene, siren,
Sistine, sixteen, Slovene, snap
bean, soybean, string bean,
strychnine, subteen, sunscreen,
thirteen, Tolkien, tureen,
umpteen, unclean, unseen, vac-
cine, wax bean, white bean, wind-
screen • Aberdeen, almandine,
amandine, Angeline, Argentine,
Augustine, Balanchine, barken-
tine, Bernadine, brigantine, bril-
liantine, Byzantine, carotene,
clandestine, columbine, Constantine, contravene, crystalline,
Dramamine, drum machine,
endocrine, Ernestine, evergreen,
fava bean, figurine, Florentine,
gabardine, gasoline, Geraldine,
go-between, golden mean, guillo-
tine, Halloween, Imogene, in-
between, intervene, jelly bean,
Josephine, jumping bean,
kerosene, kidney bean, lethal
gene, Levantine, libertine, lima
bean, limousine, M16, magazine,
make the scene, mezzanine, navy
bean, Nazarene, nectarine, nico-
tine, overseen, Philistine, pinto
bean, riverine, quarantine, sac-
charine, San Joaquin, San Martín,
serpentine, seventeen, slot machine, submarine, subroutine,
tambourine, tangerine, time machine, trampoline, Vaseline, vel-
veteen, wintergreen, wolverine
• acetylene, amphetamine, aqua-
marine, Benedictine, elephantine,
Evangeline, flying machine, gar-

banzo bean, heart-lung machine,
internecine, labyrinthine, mer-
chant marine, milling machine,
mujahideen, nouvelle cuisine,
pinball machine, rowing machine,
simple machine, threshing machine, ultramarine, vanilla bean,
vending machine, voting machine,
washing machine • answering
machine, antihistamine, arithmetic mean, Mary Magdalene,
NC-17 • oleomargarine

ine³ \in-ē\ see INNY

ine⁴ \ē-nē\ see INI¹

ine⁵ \ən\ see UN¹

inea \in-ē\ see INNY

ined \īnd\ see IND¹

inee \ī-nē\ see INY¹

ineless \īn-ləs\ see INDLESS

inely¹ \īn-lē\ blindly, finely, kindly
• divinely, unkindly

inely² \ēn-lē\ see EANLY¹

inement \īn-mənt\ see IGNMENT

ineness \īn-nəs\ see INDNESS

iner¹ \ī-nər\ diner, finer, liner,
miner, minor, shiner, Shriner,
signer, whiner • airliner, cosigner,
designer, eyeliner, hard-liner,
headliner, jetliner, moonshiner,
one-liner, recliner, refiner • Asia
Minor, forty-niner • graphic
designer

iner² \ē-nər\ see EANER

inery¹ \īn-rē\ finery, vinery, winery
• refinery

inery² \ēn-rē\ see EANERY

ines¹ \ēn\ see INE³

ines² \ēnz\ see EENS

ines³ \īnz\ Apennines • between
the lines
—also -s, -'s, and -s' forms of
nouns and -s forms of verbs listed
at INE¹

inest \ī-nəst\ see INIST¹

inet \in-ət\ see INNET

inew \in-yü\ see INUE

ing \iŋ\ bring, cling, ding, fling,

king, King, Ming, ping, ring, sing, sling, spring, sting, string, swing, thing, wing, wring, zing • backswing, bedspring, Beijing, bitewing, bowstring, bullring, downswing, drawstring, earring, first-string, growth ring, hamstring, handspring, heartstring, hot spring, lacewing, latchstring, left-wing, mainspring, Nanjing, offspring, plaything, redwing, right-wing, shoestring, unstring, upswing, waxwing, wellspring, wingding • à la king, anything, apron string, ding-a-ling, everything, fairy ring, Highland fling, innerspring, on the wing, secondstring, signet ring, teething ring, underwing • buffalo wing, cedar waxwing, if anything, under one's wing

inge \inj\ binge, cringe, fringe, hinge, singe, tinge, twinge • butt hinge, impinge, infringe, syringe, unhinge • lunatic fringe

inged \ind\ pinged, ringed, stringed, winged

ingement \inj-mənt\ impingement, infringement

ingency \in-jən-sē\ stringency • contingency

ingent \in-jənt\ stringent • astringent, contingent

inger[1] \in-ər\ bringer, ringer, singer, stinger, stringer, swinger, wringer, zinger • Beijinger, firststringer, folksinger, gunslinger, humdinger, left-winger, mudslinger, right-winger, torch singer

inger[2] \in-gər\ finger, linger • forefinger, ring finger • index finger, ladyfinger, little finger, middle finger

inger[3] \in-jər\ ginger, Ginger, injure, singer, swinger • infringer

ingery \inj-rē\ gingery, injury

inghy \in-ē\ see INGY[1]

inging \in-in\ ringing, springing, stringing, swinging • folksinging, free-swinging, gunslinging, handwringing, mudslinging, upbringing

—*also* -ing *forms of verbs listed at* ING

ingit \in-kət\ see INKET

ingle \in-gəl\ jingle, mingle, shingle, single, tingle • Kriss Kringle • intermingle

ingli \in-glē\ see INGLY

ingly \in-glē\ jingly, singly, tingly, Zwingli

ingo \in-gō\ bingo, dingo, gringo, jingo, lingo • flamingo, Mandingo • Santo Domingo

ings \inz\ Hot Springs, Palm Springs, pull strings, purse strings, see things • Coral Springs, in the wings • Colorado Springs, Saratoga Springs

—*also* -s, -'s, *and* -s' *forms of nouns and* -s *forms of verbs listed at* ING

ingue \an\ see ANG[2]

ingy[1] \in-ē\ clingy, dinghy, springy, stringy, zingy

ingy[2] \in-jē\ dingy, mingy, stingy

inh \in\ see IN[1]

ini[1] \ē-nē\ beanie, genie, greeny, Jeannie, meanie, sheeny, teeny, weenie, weeny, wienie • Bernini, bikini, Bikini, Cyrene, Eugenie, Houdini, linguine, Mancini, martini, Mycenae, Puccini, Rossini, tahini, tankini, zucchini • fettuccine, Mussolini, Paganini, scaloppine, spaghettini, string bikini, teeny-weeny, tetrazzini, tortellini, Toscanini

ini[2] \in-ē\ see INNY

inia \in-ē-ə\ zinnia • gloxinia, Lavinia, Sardinia, Virginia • Abyssinia, West Virginia

inian[1] \in-ē-ən\ Darwinian, Sardinian, Virginian • Abyssinian, Argentinian, Augustinian, Carolinian, Carthaginian, Palestinian

inian[2] \in-yən\ see INION

inic \in-ik\ clinic, cynic • rabbinic

inical \in-i-kəl\ clinical, cynical, pinnacle

ining \ī-niŋ\ lining, mining, shining • declining, designing, inclining • interlining, silver lining —*also* -ing *forms of verbs listed at* INE[1]

inion \in-yən\ minion, pinion, piñon • dominion, Justinian, opinion, Sardinian • Abyssinian

inis \ī-nəs\ see INUS[1]

inish \in-ish\ finish, Finnish, thinnish • diminish, refinish • photo finish

inist[1] \ī-nəst\ dynast, finest

inist[2] \ē-nəst\ hygienist, machinist • trampolinist • dental hygienist

initive \in-ət-iv\ definitive, infinitive • split infinitive

inity \in-ət-ē\ trinity, Trinity • affinity, divinity, infinity, salinity, sanguinity, vicinity, virginity • femininity, masculinity

inium \in-ē-əm\ delphinium • condominium

injure \in-jər\ see INGER[3]

injury \inj-rē\ see INGERY

ink \iŋk\ blink, brink, chink, clink, dink, drink, fink, gink, ink, kink, link, mink, pink, plink, rink, shrink, sink, skink, slink, stink, sync, think, wink, zinc • cuff link, eyeblink, groupthink, hoodwink, hot link, lip-synch, outthink, preshrink, rat fink, red ink, rethink, soft drink, uplink • bobolink, countersink, doublethink, hyperlink, interlink, in the pink, kitchen-sink, missing link, on the blink, rinky-dink, salmon pink, shocking pink

inka \iŋ-kə\ see INCA

inkable \iŋ-kə-bəl\ drinkable, shrinkable, sinkable, thinkable • undrinkable, unsinkable, unthinkable

inkage \iŋ-kij\ linkage, shrinkage

inke \iŋ-kē\ see INKY

inked \iŋt\ see INCT

inker \iŋ-kər\ clinker, drinker, sinker, stinker, thinker, tinker • freethinker, headshrinker, hoodwinker, nondrinker • hook line and sinker

inket \iŋ-kət\ Tlingit, trinket

inkey \iŋ-kē\ see INKY

inkgo \iŋ-kō\ see INKO

inki \iŋ-kē\ see INKY

inkie \iŋ-kē\ see INKY

inking \iŋ-kiŋ\ freethinking, unblinking, unthinking • wishful thinking —*also* -ing *forms of verbs listed at* INK

inkle \iŋ-kəl\ crinkle, sprinkle, tinkle, twinkle, wrinkle • periwinkle, Rip van Winkle

inkling \iŋ-kliŋ\ inkling, sprinkling, twinkling —*also* -ing *forms of verbs listed at* INKLE

inkly \iŋ-klē\ crinkly, tinkly, twinkly, wrinkly

inko \iŋ-kō\ ginkgo, pinko

inks \iŋs\ see INX

inky \iŋ-kē\ dinky, inky, kinky, pinkie, pinky, slinky, stinky • Helsinki

inland \in-lənd\ Finland, inland

inless \in-ləs\ chinless, sinless, skinless

inley \in-lē\ see INLY

inly \in-lē\ spindly, thinly • McKinley • Mount McKinley

inn \in\ see IN[1]

innacle \in-i-kəl\ see INICAL

inned \ind\ see IND[2]

inner \in-ər\ dinner, inner, pinner, sinner, skinner, spinner, thinner, winner • beginner, blood thinner, breadwinner, prizewinner • TV dinner

innet \in-ət\ linnet, minute, spinet

inney \in-ē\ see INNY

inni \ē-nē\ see INI[1]

innia \in-ē-ə\ see INIA

innic \in-ik\ see INIC

innie \in-ē\ see INNY

inning \in-iŋ\ inning, spinning, winning • beginning, bloodthinning, breadwinning, prizewinning • underpinning
—also -ing forms of verbs listed at IN[1]

innish \in-ish\ see INISH

innity \in-ət-ē\ see INITY

innow \in-ō\ minnow, winnow

inny \in-ē\ finny, Guinea, mini, Minnie, ninny, Pliny, shinny, skinny, tinny, whinny, Winnie • New Guinea • Papua New Guinea

ino[1] \ī-nō\ dino, rhino, wino • albino

ino[2] \ē-nō\ beano, chino, vino • bambino, casino, Latino, merino, neutrino • cappuccino, concertino, Filipino, maraschino, palomino, San Marino • San Bernardino

ino[3] \ē-nə\ see INA[2]

iñon \in-yən\ see INION

inor[1] \in-ər\ see INNER

inor[2] \ī-nər\ see INER[1]

inot \ē-nō\ see INO[2]

inous \ī-nəs\ see INUS[1]

inscher \in-chər\ see INCHER

inse \ins\ see INCE[1]

inselly \in-slē\ see INCELY

inseng \in-siŋ\ see INCING

insk \insk\ Minsk, Pinsk

insky \in-skē\ Nijinsky, Stravinsky

inster \in-stər\ minster, spinster • Westminster

int \int\ Clint, dint, flint, Flint, glint, hint, lint, mint, print, quint, splint, sprint, squint, stint, tint

• blueprint, footprint, handprint, hoofprint, imprint, in-print, largeprint, newsprint, reprint, skinflint, spearmint, thumbprint, voiceprint, wind sprint • aquatint, fingerprint, peppermint, wunderkind

intage \int-ij\ mintage, vintage • nonvintage

intain \int-ᵊn\ see INTON

inter \int-ər\ hinter, Pinter, printer, splinter, sprinter, winter • imprinter, line printer, midwinter • impact printer, laser printer, overwinter, teleprinter

inth \inth\ plinth, synth • hyacinth, labyrinth

inting \int-iŋ\ printing • imprinting, unstinting
—also -ing forms of verbs listed at INT

into[1] \in-tō\ pinto, Shinto

into[2] \in-tü\ back into, break into, bump into, buy into, check into, come into, get into, go into, look into, plug into, rip into, run into, tap into, tear into • enter into, marry into

inton \int-ᵊn\ Clinton • badminton

ints \ins\ see INCE[1]

inty \int-ē\ flinty, linty, minty, squinty • peppperminty

intz \ins\ see INCE[1]

inue \in-yü\ sinew • continue • discontinue

inuous \in-yə-wəs\ sinuous • continuous • discontinuous

inus[1] \ī-nəs\ dryness, highness, Minos, minus, shyness, sinus, slyness • Longinus • Antoninus, plus or minus

inus[2] \ē-nəs\ see ENUS[1]

inute \in-ət\ see INNET

inx \iŋs\ Brink's, jinx, links, lynx, minx, sphinx • hijinks, methinks • tiddledywinks
—also -s, -'s, and -s' forms of

nouns and -s forms of verbs listed at INK

iny[1] \ī-nē\ briny, heinie, piny, shiny, spiny, tiny, viny, whiny, winy • sunshiny

iny[2] \in-ē\ see INNY

inya \ē-nyə\ see ENIA[2]

inyan \in-yən\ see INION

inyl \īn-ᵊl\ see INAL[1]

io[1] \ī-ō\ bayou, bio, Clio, Io • Ohio • Cinco de Mayo

io[2] \ē-ō\ brio, Clio, Leo, Rio, trio • Trujillo

iocese \ī-ə-səs\ see IASIS

ion[1] \ī-ən\ Brian, Bryan, ion, lion, Mayan, Ryan, scion, Zion • Orion • dandelion, Paraguayan, Uruguayan

ion[2] \ē-ən\ see EAN[1]

ion[3] \ē-än\ see EON[2]

ior \īr\ see IRE[1]

iory \ī-ə-rē\ see IARY[1]

iot \ī-ət\ see IET

ioter \ī-ət-ər\ see IETER

iouan \ü-ən\ see UAN

ious \ī-əs\ see IAS[1]

ioux \ü\ see EW[1]

ip \ip\ blip, chip, clip, dip, drip, flip, grip, grippe, gyp, hip, lip, nip, pip, quip, rip, scrip, ship, sip, skip, slip, snip, strip, tip, trip, whip, yip, zip • airship, airstrip, backflip, blue-chip, bullwhip, catnip, cleft lip, clerkship, corn chip, courtship, death grip, drag strip, ear clip, equip, felt-tip, field trip, filmstrip, flagship, foul tip, friendship, frostnip, guilt-trip, gunship, half-slip, handgrip, hardship, harelip, horsewhip, judgeship, jump ship, kinship, let rip, longship, lordship, nonslip, palship, pink slip, road trip, rose hip, round-trip, sales slip, sideslip, spaceship, starship, steamship, tall ship, township, transship, troopship, unzip, V-chip, warship • au-thorship, battleship, brinkmanship, censorship, chairmanship, comic strip, crack the whip, dealership, draftsmanship, ego trip, ego-trip, fellowship, filter tip, fingertip, gamesmanship, Gaza Strip, horsemanship, internship, ladyship, landing strip, leadership, marksmanship, membership, microchip, mother ship, motor ship, ownership, paper clip, partnership, penmanship, pistol grip, pistol-whip, power strip, readership, rocket ship, scholarship, seamanship, showmanship, skinny-dip, sponsorship, sportsmanship, statesmanship, stewardship, swordsmanship, underlip, viewership, weather strip, workmanship • apprenticeship, championship, citizenship, companionship, containership, dictatorship, factory ship, Freudian slip, good-fellowship, guardianship, median strip, Möbius strip, musicianship, one-upmanship, partisanship, postnasal drip, potato chip, receivership, rejection slip, relationship, run a tight ship, shoot from the hip, stiff upper lip • bipartisanship, nonpartisanship

ipal \ē-pəl\ see EOPLE

ipari \ip-rē\ see IPPERY

ipatus \ip-ət-əs\ see IPITOUS

ipe \īp\ gripe, hype, pipe, ripe, snipe, stripe, swipe, tripe, type, wipe • bagpipe, blood type, blowpipe, drainpipe, half-pipe, hornpipe, pitch pipe, panpipe, pinstripe, sideswipe, stovepipe, tailpipe, touch-type, unripe, windpipe • archetype, corncob pipe, guttersnipe, overripe, prototype, Teletype • daguerreotype, stereotype

iped \īpt\ striped • pin-striped

—*also* -ed *forms of verbs listed at*
IPE

ipend \ī-pənd\ ripened, stipend

iper \ī-pər\ diaper, griper, hyper,
piper, riper, sniper, viper, wiper
• bagpiper, pied piper, pit viper,
sandpiper • candy striper, pay the
piper • stereotyper

ipety \ip-ət-ē\ snippety • serendip-
ity

iph \if\ see IFF

iphany \if-ə-nē\ see IPHONY

ipher \ī-fər\ cipher, lifer • decipher,
pro-lifer • right-to-lifer

iphon \ī-fən\ see YPHEN

iphony \if-ə-nē\ Tiffany
• epiphany, polyphony

ipi \ē-pē\ see EEPY

ipid \ip-əd\ lipid • insipid

iping \ī-piŋ\ piping, striping
• blood-typing
—*also* -ing *forms of verbs listed at*
IPE

ipit \ip-ət\ see IPPET

ipitous \ip-ət-əs\ precipitous
• serendipitous

ipity \ip-ət-ē\ see IPETY

iple[1] \ip-əl\ see IPPLE

iple[2] \ī-pəl\ see YPAL

ipless \ip-ləs\ dripless, lipless,
zipless

ipling \ip-liŋ\ Kipling, stripling
—*also* -ing *forms of verbs listed at*
IPPLE

ipment \ip-mənt\ shipment • equip-
ment, transshipment

ipo \ēp-ō\ see EPOT

ipoli \ip-ə-lē\ see IPPILY

ippe[1] \ip\ see IP

ippe[2] \ip-ē\ see IPPY

ippe[3] \ēp\ see EEP

ipped \ipt\ see IPT

ippee \ip-ē\ see IPPY

ipper \ip-ər\ chipper, clipper, flip-
per, gripper, kipper, nipper, rip-
per, shipper, skipper, slipper,
tipper, zipper • Big Dipper, day-
tripper, horsewhipper, Yom Kippur • double-dipper, ego-tripper,
lady's slipper, Little Dipper,
skinny-dipper

ippery \ip-rē\ frippery, slippery

ippet \ip-ət\ snippet, whippet

ippety \ip-ət-ē\ see IPETY

ippi \ip-ē\ see IPPY

ippie \ip-ē\ see IPPY

ippily \ip-ə-lē\ Tripoli • Gallipoli

ipping \ip-iŋ\ clipping, ripping,
shipping, whipping • double-
dipping, skinny-dipping
—*also* -ing *forms of verbs listed at*
IP

ipple \ip-əl\ cripple, ripple, stipple,
tipple, triple • participle

ippur \ip-ər\ see IPPER

ippy \ip-ē\ dippy, drippy, hippie,
hippy, lippy, nippy, Skippy,
snippy, tippy, yippee, zippy
• Xanthippe • Mississippi

ips \ips\ snips • eclipse, ellipse,
midships • amidships, fish-and-
chips • apocalypse, lunar eclipse,
solar eclipse, total eclipse
—*also* -s, -'s, *and* -s' *forms of
nouns and* -s *forms of verbs listed
at* IP

ipse \ips\ see IPS

ipster \ip-stər\ hipster, tipster

ipsy \ip-sē\ see YPSY

ipt \ipt\ crypt, hipped, ripped,
script • conscript, harelipped,
postscript, tight-lipped, transcript,
typescript • manuscript, nonde-
script, shooting script
—*also* -ed *forms of verbs listed at*
IP

iptic \ip-tik\ see YPTIC

iption \ip-shən\ conniption, de-
scription, Egyptian, encryption,
inscription, prescription, sub-
scription, transcription • nonpre-
scription

iptych \ip-tik\ see YPTIC

ique \ēk\ see EAK[1]

iquey \ē-kē\ see EAKY

iquish \ē-kish\ see EAKISH

iquitous \ik-wət-əs\ iniquitous, ubiquitous

iquity \ik-wət-ē\ antiquity, iniquity, ubiquity

iquor \ik-ər\ see ICKER[1]

ir[1] \ir\ see EER[2]

ir[2] \ər\ see EUR[1]

ira[1] \ir-ə\ see ERA[2]

ira[2] \ī-rə\ see YRA

iracle \ir-i-kəl\ see ERICAL[2]

irae \ir-ē\ see IRY

iral \ī-rəl\ spiral, viral

irant \ī-rənt\ tyrant • aspirant

irate \ir-ət\ see IRIT

irby \ər-bē\ see ERBY

irca \ər-kə\ see URKA

irce \ər-sē\ see ERCY

irch \ərch\ see URCH

irchen \ər-kən\ see IRKIN

ircon \ər-kən\ see IRKIN

ircular \ər-kyə-lər\ circular • tubercular • semicircular

ird \ərd\ bird, curd, furred, gird, heard, herd, nerd, third, word • absurd, bean curd, bellbird, blackbird, bluebird, buzzword, byword, Cape Verde, catbird, catchword, cowbird, cowherd, crossword, cussword, game bird, goatherd, good word, guide word, headword, jailbird, jaybird, kingbird, last word, lovebird, lyrebird, password, rainbird, redbird, reword, ricebird, seabird, Sigurd, shorebird, snakebird, snowbird, songbird, state bird, sunbird, surfbird, swearword, swineherd, textured, unheard, watchword, yardbird • afterword, bowerbird, butcher-bird, cedarbird, dickey bird, dirty word, early bird, fighting word, frigate bird, hummingbird, in a word, ladybird, mockingbird, ovenbird, overheard, tailorbird, thunderbird,

undergird, wading bird, weaverbird, whirlybird, word for word
—*also* -ed *forms of verbs listed at* EUR[1]

irder \ərd-ər\ see ERDER

irdie \ərd-ē\ see URDY

irdle \ərd-əl\ see URDLE

ire[1] \īr\ briar, choir, dire, drier, fire, flier, friar, fryer, hire, ire, liar, lyre, mire, prior, pyre, shire, sire, spire, squire, tire, Tyre, wire • acquire, admire, afire, aspire, attire, backfire, barbed wire, barbwire, blow-dryer, bonfire, brushfire, bushfire, campfire, catbrier, catch fire, cease-fire, conspire, cross fire, denier, desire, empire, Empire, entire, esquire, expire, for hire, fox fire, grandsire, greenbrier, gunfire, haywire, hellfire, high-wire, hot-wire, inquire, inspire, live wire, misfire, on fire, perspire, prior, quagmire, require, respire, retire, sapphire, satire, Shropshire, snow tire, spitfire, surefire, suspire, sweetbriar, tightwire, town crier, transpire, trip wire, umpire, vampire, wildfire • amplifier, ball of fire, balloon tire, beautifier, chicken wire, like wildfire, multiplier, pacifier, play with fire, qualifier, rapid-fire, razor wire, retrofire, signifier, simplifier, star sapphire, under fire • British Empire, down-to-the-wire, identifier, intensifier, under the wire, water saffire • concertina wire, iron in the fire • Holy Roman Empire
—*also* -er *forms of adjectives listed at* Y[1]

ire[2] \ir\ see EER[2]

ire[3] \īr-ē\ see IRY

ire[4] \ər\ see EUR[1]

ired \īrd\ fired, spired, tired, wired • hardwired, inspired, retired
—*also* -ed *forms of verbs listed at* IRE[1]

ireless \īr-ləs\ tireless, wireless

ireman \īr-mən\ fireman, wireman

irement \īr-mənt\ acquirement, environment, requirement, retirement

iren \ī-rən\ Byron, Myron, siren • environ

irge \ərj\ see URGE

irgin \ər-jən\ see URGEON

iri \ir-ē\ see EARY

iriam \ir-ē-əm\ see ERIUM

iric \ir-ik\ see ERIC[2]

irile \ir-əl\ see ERAL[1]

irin \ī-rən\ see IREN

irine \ī-rən\ see IREN

iring \īr-iŋ\ firing, wiring • inspiring, retiring
—*also* -ing *forms of verbs listed at* IRE[1]

irious \ir-ē-əs\ see ERIOUS

iris \ī-rəs\ see IRUS

irish \īr-ish\ Irish • vampirish

irit \ir-ət\ spirit • dispirit, free spirit • Holy Spirit

irium \ir-ē-əm\ see ERIUM

irius \ir-ē-əs\ see ERIOUS

irk \ərk\ see ORK[1]

irker \ər-kər\ see ORKER[1]

irkie \ər-kē\ see ERKY

irkin \ər-kən\ firkin, gherkin, jerkin, zircon

irky \ər-kē\ see ERKY

irl \ərl\ churl, curl, earl, Earl, furl, girl, hurl, Merle, pearl, Pearl, purl, squirrel, swirl, twirl, whirl • awhirl, ball girl, bat girl, cowgirl, home girl, pin curl, playgirl, salesgirl, schoolgirl, shopgirl, showgirl, spit curl, uncurl, unfurl • Camp Fire girl, chorus girl, cover girl, flower girl, pinup girl, poster girl, Valley girl • mother-of-pearl

irler \ər-lər\ curler, twirler

irley \ər-lē\ see URLY

irlie \ər-lē\ see URLY

irling \ər-liŋ\ see URLING

irlish \ər-lish\ see URLISH

irly \ər-lē\ see URLY

irm \ərm\ see ORM[1]

irma \ər-mə\ see ERMA

irmess \ər-məs\ see ERMIS

irmy \ər-mē\ see ERMY

irn \ərn\ see URN

iro[1] \ir-ō\ see ERO[3]

iro[2] \ē-rō\ see ERO[1]

iro[3] \ī-rō\ see YRO[1]

iron[1] \īrn\ iron • andiron, cast-iron, environ, flatiron, gridiron, pig iron, pump iron, steam iron, wrought iron • climbing iron, curling iron, shooting iron, waffle iron • soldering iron

iron[2] \ī-rən\ see IREN

ironment \īr-mənt\ see IREMENT

irp \ərp\ see URP

irpy \ər-pē\ chirpy • Euterpe

irque \ərk\ see ORK[1]

irr[1] \ir\ see EER[2]

irr[2] \ər\ see EUR[1]

irra \ir-ə\ see ERA[2]

irrah \ir-ə\ see ERA[2]

irrel[1] \ərl\ see IRL

irrel[2] \ər-əl\ see ERRAL

irrely \ər-lē\ see URLY

irrhous \ir-əs\ see EROUS

irring \ər-iŋ\ see URRING

irror \ir-ər\ see EARER[2]

irrup \ər-əp\ chirrup, stirrup, syrup • corn syrup, cough syrup • maple syrup

irrupy \ər-ə-pē\ chirrupy, syrupy

irrus \ir-əs\ see EROUS

irry \ər-ē\ see URRY

irs \irz\ see IERS

irse[1] \irs\ see IERCE

irse[2] \ərs\ see ERSE

irst \ərst\ see URST

irt \ərt\ see ERT[1]

irted \ərt-əd\ see ERTED

irter \ərt-ər\ see ERTER

irth \ərth\ berth, birth, dearth, earth, firth, girth, mirth, Perth, worth • childbirth, Farnsworth,

Fort Worth, give birth, on earth, rebirth, scorched-earth, self-worth, stillbirth, unearth, Woolworth, Wordsworth • down-to-earth, pennyworth, Solway Firth, two cents' worth, virgin birth

irthless \ərth-ləs\ mirthless, worthless

irting \ərt-iŋ\ see ERTING

irtle \ərt-ᵊl\ see ERTILE

irtually \ərch-lē\ see URCHLY

irty \ərt-ē\ dirty, flirty, QWERTY, thirty

irus \ī-rəs\ Cyrus, iris, Iris, Skyros, virus • desirous, Osiris, papyrus • bearded iris, rhinovirus, rotavirus, West Nile virus

irv \ərv\ see ERVE

irving \ər-viŋ\ see ERVING

irwin \ər-wən\ see ERWIN

iry \īr-ē\ diary, eyrie, friary, miry, wiry • expiry, inquiry

is¹ \is\ see ISS

is² \iz\ see IZ¹

is³ \ē\ see EE

is⁴ \ēs\ see IECE

is⁵ \ish\ see ISH¹

i's \īz\ see IZE¹

isa \ē-zə\ see EZA

isable \ī-zə-bəl\ see IZABLE

isal¹ \ī-səl\ sisal • paradisal

isal² \ī-zəl\ Geisel, sisal • reprisal, revisal, surprisal • paradisal

isan \is-ᵊn\ see ISTEN

isbane \iz-bən\ see ISBON

isbon \iz-bən\ Brisbane, Lisbon

isc \isk\ see ISK

iscate \is-kət\ see ISKET

isce \is\ see ISS

iscean¹ \ī-sē-ən\ Piscean • Dionysian

iscean² \is-ē-ən\ see YSIAN¹

ische \ēsh\ see ICHE²

iscia \ish-ə\ see ITIA¹

iscible \is-ə-bəl\ see ISSIBLE

iscient \ish-ənt\ see ICIENT

isco \is-kō\ disco • Francisco • San Francisco

iscous \is-kəs\ see ISCUS

iscuit \is-kət\ see ISKET

iscus \is-kəs\ discus, viscous • hibiscus

ise¹ \ēs\ see IECE

ise² \ēz\ see EZE

ise³ \īs\ see ICE¹

ise⁴ \īz\ see IZE¹

ised¹ \īst\ see IST¹

ised² \īzd\ see IZED

isel \iz-əl\ see IZZLE

iseled \iz-əld\ see IZZLED

iseler \iz-lər\ see IZZLER

isement \īz-mənt\ chastisement, disguisement • advertisement, enfranchisement

iser \ī-zər\ see IZER

ish¹ \ish\ dish, fish, squish, swish, whish, wish • blindfish, blowfish, bluefish, bonefish, catfish, clownfish, codfish, cold fish, crawfish, crayfish, death wish, deep-dish, dogfish, finfish, flatfish, fly-fish, game fish, garfish, goldfish, goosefish, hagfish, hogfish, jewfish, kingfish, knish, lungfish, monkfish, moonfish, panfish, pipefish, redfish, rockfish, sailfish, sawfish, shellfish, side dish, spearfish, sport fish, starfish, sunfish, swordfish, toadfish, trash fish, whitefish • angelfish, anglerfish, bony fish, chafing dish, cuttlefish, flying fish, jellyfish, John Bullish, lionfish, needlefish, overfish, petri dish, pilot fish, puffer fish, silverfish • gefilte fish, kettle of fish, satellite dish, tropical fish, walking catfish

ish² \ēsh\ see ICHE²

isha \ish-ə\ see ITIA¹

isher \ish-ər\ fisher, fissure • kingfisher, well-wisher

ishi \ē-shē\ chichi • maharishi

ishing \ish-iŋ\ fly-fishing, sportfish-

ing, well-wishing
—*also* -ing *forms of verbs listed at*
ISH[1]
ishioner \ish-nər\ see ITIONER
ishna \ish-nə\ Krishna, Mishnah
ishnah \ish-nə\ see ISHNA
ishu \ish-ü\ see ISSUE[1]
ishy \ish-ē\ fishy, squishy, swishy
isi[1] \ē-zē\ see EASY[1]
isi[2] \ē-sē\ see EECY
isia \ē-zhə\ see ESIA[2]
isian[1] \izh-ən\ see ISION
isian[2] \ē-zhən\ see ESIAN[1]
isible \iz-ə-bəl\ risible, visible
 • divisible, invisible • indivisible
isin \i-zən\ see ISON[2]
ising \ī-ziŋ\ see IZING
ision \izh-ən\ fission, vision • collision, concision, decision, derision,
division, elision, elysian, envision,
incision, Parisian, precision, pro-
vision, revision, Tunisian • cell
division, circumcision, Dionysian,
double vision, field of vision,
imprecision, indecision, long
division, short division, split
decision, subdivision, supervision,
television, tunnel vision
isional \izh-nəl\ divisional, provi-
sional
isis \ī-səs\ crisis, Isis • Dionysus,
midlife crisis
isit \iz-ət\ visit • exquisite, revisit
isite \iz-ət\ see ISIT
isitor \iz-ət-ər\ visitor • inquisitor
isive \ī-siv\ decisive, derisive, divi-
sive, incisive • indecisive
isk \isk\ bisque, brisk, disk, frisk,
risk, whisk • fly whisk, hard disk,
slipped disk • asterisk, basilisk,
compact disc, floppy disk, laser
disc, obelisk, optic disk • optical
disk, videodisc
isket \is-kət\ biscuit, brisket
iskey \is-kē\ see ISKY
iskie \is-kē\ see ISKY
isky \is-kē\ frisky, risky, whiskey

island \ī-lənd\ see IGHLAND
islander \ī-lən-dər\ see IGHLANDER
islands \ī-lənz\ see IGHLANDS
isle \īl\ see ILE[1]
isles \īlz\ see ILES
islet \ī-lət\ see ILOT
isling \iz-liŋ\ brisling, quisling
isly \iz-lē\ see IZZLY
ism \iz-əm\ ism, prism, schism
 • abysm, ageism, autism, baptism,
bossism, Buddhism, charism,
cubism, czarism, dwarfism, fas-
cism, Maoism, Marxism, Nazism,
nudism, racism, sadism, sexism,
snobbism, Taoism, theism,
tourism, truism • activism,
alarmism, altruism, anarchism,
aneurysm, animism, aphorism,
archaism, atheism, barbarism,
botulism, Briticism, Calvinism,
careerism, Castroism, cataclysm,
catechism, chauvinism, classi-
cism, communism, criticism,
cynicism, Darwinism, defeatism,
despotism, dogmatism, dualism,
dynamism, egoism, egotism, elit-
ism, escapism, euphemism, exor-
cism, extremism, fatalism,
feminism, feudalism, fogyism,
formalism, futurism, globalism,
gnosticism, gradualism,
heathenism, Hebraism, hedonism,
Hellenism, heroism, Hinduism,
Hitlerism, humanism, hypnotism,
idealism, Islamism, jingoism,
journalism, John Bullism, Ju-
daism, legalism, Leninism, lyri-
cism, magnetism, mannerism,
masochism, mechanism, method-
ism, me-tooism, modernism,
monarchism, moralism, Mor-
monism, mysticism, narcissism,
nationalism, nepotism, nihilism,
NIMBYism, nomadism,
occultism, optimism, organism,
ostracism, pacifism, paganism,
pantheism, paroxysm, pessimism,

plagiarism, pointillism, populism, pragmatism, Quakerism, realism, rheumatism, satanism, Semitism, Shakerism, Shamanism, Shinto-ism, skepticism, socialism, sole-cism, solipsism, Southernism, spiritism, Stalinism, stoicism, syllogism, symbolism, terrorism, tribalism, unionism, urbanism, vandalism, veganism, vocalism, vulgarism, warlordism, witticism, Zionism • absenteeism, abso-lutism, Africanism, alcoholism, anachronism, Anglicanism, antag-onism, astigmatism, athleticism, behaviorism, Big Brotherism, bilingualism, cannibalism, capital-ism, Catholicism, commercialism, Confucianism, conservatism, consumerism, creationism, eco-tourism, empiricism, ethnocen-trism, evangelism, exoticism, expressionism, factionalism, fanaticism, favoritism, federalism, hooliganism, impressionism, infantilism, Keynesianism, liberal-ism, Lutheranism, McCarthyism, mercantilism, metabolism, mili-tarism, minimalism, monasticism, monotheism, negativism, neo-Nazism, opportunism, pacificism, parallelism, paternalism, patriot-ism, perfectionism, photo-realism, postmodernism, primitivism, progressivism, protectionism, Protestantism, provincialism, puritanism, radicalism, rational-ism, regionalism, revisionism, revivalism, romanticism, scholas-ticism, sectionalism, secularism, somnambulism, surrealism, ven-triloquism • abolitionism, anti-Semitism, colloquialism, colonialism, hyperrealism, imperi-alism, isolationism, materialism, neoclassicism, orientalism, photo-journalism, Postimpressionism,

professionalism, sensationalism, spiritualism, traditionalism, tran-scendentalism, universalism

ismal \iz-məl\ see YSMAL

isme[1] \īm\ see IME[1]

isme[2] \iz³m\ see ISM

isom \iz-əm\ see ISM

ison[1] \īs-³n\ bison, Meissen, Tyson • streptomycin

ison[2] \iz-³n\ prison, risen • arisen, imprison

isor \ī-zər\ see IZER

isory \īz-rē\ advisory • supervisory

isp \isp\ crisp, lisp, wisp • will-o-the-wisp

isper \is-pər\ crisper, lisper, whis-per • stage whisper

ispy \is-pē\ crispy, wispy

isque \isk\ see ISK

iss \is\ bliss, Chris, dis, Dis, hiss, kiss, miss, sis, Swiss, this • abyss, amiss, can't-miss, dismiss, French kiss, near miss, remiss • amber-gris, hit-and-miss, hit-or-miss, junior miss, reminisce

issa \is-ə\ abscissa, Larissa, Melissa

issable \is-ə-bəl\ see ISSIBLE

issal \is-əl\ see ISTLE

isse[1] \is\ see ISS

isse[2] \ēs\ see IECE

issed \ist\ see IST[2]

issel \is-əl\ see ISTLE

issible \is-ə-bəl\ kissable, miscible • admissible, municipal, omissi-ble, permissible, transmissible • impermissible, inadmissible

issile \is-əl\ see ISTLE

ission[1] \ish-ən\ see ITION

ission[2] \izh-ən\ see ISION

issioner \ish-nər\ see ITIONER

issive \is-iv\ missive • derisive, dismissive, permissive, submis-sive, transmissive

issor \iz-ər\ scissor, whizzer

issue[1] \ish-ü\ issue, tissue • nonis-sue, reissue, scar tissue, take issue • Mogadishu

issue[2] \ish-ə\ see ITIA[1]

issure \ish-ər\ see ISHER

issus \is-əs\ missus, Mrs. • narcissus, Narcissus

issy \is-ē\ missy, prissy, sissy

ist[1] \īst\ Christ, heist • zeitgeist • Antichrist, poltergeist
—also -ed *forms of verbs listed at* ICE[1]

ist[2] \ist\ cyst, fist, gist, grist, list, Liszt, mist, schist, tryst, twist, whist, wrist • A-list, assist, blacklist, checklist, consist, desist, enlist, exist, hit list, insist, persist, playlist, resist, short list, subsist, untwist, wish list • coexist, exorcist • love-in-a-mist
—also -ed *forms of verbs listed at* ISS

ist[3] \ēst\ see EAST[1]

ista \ē-stə\ barista • fashionista, Sandinista • hasta la vista

istaed \is-təd\ see ISTED

istal \is-tᵊl\ Bristol, crystal, Crystal, pistil, pistol

istan \is-tən\ see ISTON

istance \is-təns\ see ISTENCE

istant \is-tənt\ see ISTENT

iste[1] \is-tē\ see ICITY[2]

iste[2] \ēst\ see EAST[1]

isted \is-təd\ closefisted, enlisted, hardfisted, limp-wristed, tightfisted, two-fisted, unlisted • ironfisted, unassisted
—also -ed *forms of verbs listed at* IST[2]

istel \is-tᵊl\ see IST[2]

isten \is-ᵊn\ christen, glisten, listen

istence \is-təns\ distance • assistance, existence, insistence, long-distance, outdistance, persistence, resistance, subsistence • coexistence, go the distance, keep one's distance, nonexistence, shouting distance, striking distance • passive resistance, public assistance

istent \is-tənt\ distant • assistant,

consistent, insistent, persistent, resistant • equidistant, inconsistent, nonexistent

ister \is-tər\ blister, glister, lister, Lister, mister, sister, twister • half sister, resister, resistor, solicitor, stepsister, tongue twister, transistor • water blister

istery \is-trē\ see ISTORY

isthmus \is-məs\ see ISTMAS

isti \is-tē\ see ICITY[2]

istic \is-tik\ mystic • artistic, autistic, ballistic, fascistic, holistic, linguistic, logistic, sadistic, simplistic, sophistic, statistic, stylistic • altruistic, anarchistic, animistic, aphoristic, atavistic, atheistic, egoistic, egotistic, euphemistic, fatalistic, futuristic, hedonistic, humanistic, idealistic, inartistic, jingoistic, journalistic, legalistic, masochistic, modernistic, moralistic, narcissistic, nationalistic, nihilistic, optimistic, pessimistic, realistic, unrealistic • anachronistic, antagonistic, cannibalistic, capitalistic, characteristic, impressionistic, militaristic, opportunistic, paternalistic, propagandistic • imperialistic, materialistic

istical \is-ti-kəl\ mystical • logistical, statistical • egotistical

istich \is-tik\ see ISTIC

istics \is-tiks\ ballistics, linguistics, statistics • vital statistics
—also -s, -'s, *and* -s' *forms of nouns listed at* ISTIC

istie \is-tē\ see ICITY[2]

istil \is-tᵊl\ see ISTAL

istin \is-tən\ see ISTON

istine \is-tən\ see ISTON

istle \is-əl\ bristle, gristle, missal, missile, thistle, whistle • bull thistle, cruise missile, dismissal, epistle, globe thistle, wolf whistle • blow the whistle, guided missile, wet one's whistle • ballistic missile

istler \is-lər\ whistler, Whistler

istly \is-lē\ bristly, gristly, thistly
• sweet cicely

istmas \is-məs\ Christmas, isthmus

isto \is-tō\ Christo • Callisto

istol \is-t³l\ see ISTAL

iston \is-tən\ Kristin, piston, Tristan

istor \is-tər\ see ISTER

istory \is-trē\ history, mystery • life history, prehistory • ancient history, natural history, oral history

isty \is-tē\ see ICITY²

isus \ī-səs\ see ISIS

iszt \ist\ see IST²

it¹ \it\ bit, Brit, chit, fit, flit, git, grit, hit, it, kit, knit, lit, mitt, nit, pit, quit, sit, skit, slit, snit, spit, split, twit, whit, wit, writ, zit • a bit, acquit, admit, armpit, base hit, befit, bowsprit, Brigitte, catch it, close-knit, cockpit, commit, cool it, culprit, cut it, dimwit, dog it, emit, firelit, gaslit, get it, gill slit, half-wit, hard-hit, house-sit, legit, make it, mess kit, misfit, moonlit, mosh pit, nitwit, no-hit, obit, omit, outfit, outwit, owe it, permit, pinch-hit, press kit, pulpit, refit, remit, rough it, sandpit, Sanskrit, starlit, submit, sunlit, switch-hit, tar pit, tidbit, tightknit, to wit, transmit, twilit, twobit, unfit, watch it, well-knit, with-it • babysit, benefit, bit-by-bit, cable-knit, candlelit, come off it, counterfeit, double knit, get with it, hissy fit, holy writ, hypocrite, infield hit, megahit, out of it, put to it, recommit, retrofit, step on it • banana split, bully pulpit, extra-base hit, fringe benefit, lickety-split, overcommit, sacrifice hit • jack-in-the-pulpit

it² \ē\ see EE¹

it³ \ēt\ see EAT¹

ita \ēt-ə\ cheetah, Nita, pita, Rita • Anita, Bonita, bonito, fajita, gordita, Granita, Juanita, Lolita • senhorita, señorita • Bhagavad Gita

itable¹ \īt-ə-bəl\ citable, writable • excitable, ignitable, indictable • copyrightable, extraditable

itable² \it-ə-bəl\ see ITTABLE

itae \īt-ē\ see ITE²

itain \it-n\ see ITTEN

ital¹ \īt-³l\ title, vital • entitle, recital, requital, subtitle

ital² \it-³l\ see ITTLE

italist \īt-³l-əst\ titlist • recitalist

itan \īt-³n\ see IGHTEN

itany \it-³n-ē\ Brittany, litany

itch \ich\ ditch, glitch, hitch, itch, kitsch, niche, pitch, rich, snitch, stitch, such, switch, twitch, which, witch • backstitch, bewitch, Bowditch, chain stitch, clove hitch, cross-stitch, enrich, fast-pitch, half hitch, jock itch, last-ditch, purl stitch, slow-pitch, topstitch, unhitch, whipstitch, wild pitch • bait and switch, czarevitch, featherstitch, fever pitch, perfect pitch, timber hitch, toggle switch • absolute pitch

itcher \ich-ər\ pitcher, richer, snitcher, stitcher, switcher

itchery \ich-ə-rē\ witchery • obituary

itches \ich-əz\ britches, riches • in stitches • Dutchman's-breeches —*also* -s, -'s, *and* -s' *forms of nouns and* -s *forms of verbs listed at* ITCH

itchman \ich-mən\ pitchman, switchman

itchment \ich-mənt\ bewitchment, enrichment • self-enrichment

itchy \ich-ē\ glitchy, itchy, pitchy, twitchy, witchy

it'd \it-əd\ see ITTED

ite¹ \īt\ bight, bite, blight, bright, byte, cite, Dwight, fight, flight, fright, height, kite, knight, light, lite, might, mite, night, plight, quite, right, rite, sight, site, sleight, slight, smite, spite, sprite, Sprite, tight, trite, white, Wright, write • affright, airtight, Albright, alight, all right, all-night, aright, backbite, backlight, bauxite, birthright, black light, bobwhite, bombsight, box kite, bullfight, calcite, campsite, catfight, cockfight, contrite, cordite, daylight, delight, despite, dogfight, downright, dust mite, earthlight, excite, eyesight, fanlight, finite, firefight, firelight, first night, fistfight, flashlight, fleabite, floodlight, foresight, forthright, fortnight, frostbite, gall mite, gaslight, ghostwrite, graphite, green light, gunfight, Gunite, half-light, handwrite, headlight, highlight, hindsight, Hittite, homesite, hoplite, ignite, in-flight, incite, indict, insight, in sight, invite, klieg light, lamplight, Levite, lignite, limelight, Lucite, Luddite, midnight, moonlight, night-light, off-site, off-white, on sight, on-site, outright, penlight, playwright, polite, preflight, prizefight, pyrite, quartzite, recite, red light, requite, rewrite, searchlight, Semite, Shiite, shipwright, sidelight, sit tight, skintight, skylight, skywrite, snakebite, snow-white, sound bite, spaceflight, spotlight, stage fright, starlight, stoplight, streetlight, sunlight, Sunnite, taillight, termite, tonight, top-flight, torchlight, Twelfth Night, twilight, twinight, typewrite, unite, upright, uptight, Web site, weeknight, wheelwright, zinc white • acolyte, Ammonite, anchorite, anthracite, antiwhite, apartheid, appetite, Bakelite, bedlamite, bipartite, black-and-white, bring to light, Brooklynite, Canaanite, candlelight, Carmelite, cellulite, chestnut blight, Chinese white, copyright, disunite, divine right, dolomite, dynamite, erudite, expedite, extradite, Fahrenheit, featherlight, fight-or-flight, fly-by-night, gesundheit, gigabyte, Hashemite, Hitlerite, Houstonite, impolite, inner light, Isle of Wight, Israelite, Jacobite, Jerseyite, kilobyte, leading light, Leninite, leukocyte, lily-white, line of sight, lymphocyte, magnetite, malachite, Masonite, megabyte, Mennonite, Mr. Right, Muscovite, neophyte, out-of-sight, overbite, overflight, overnight, oversight, parasite, patent right, pilot light, plebiscite, recondite, reunite, running light, satellite, second sight, see the light, serve one right, socialite, speed of light, stalactite, stalagmite, Sydneyite, traffic light, transvestite, tripartite, troglodyte, ultralight, underwrite, urbanite, water sprite, watertight • anti-Semite, cosmopolite, electrolyte, exurbanite, go fly a kite, hermaphrodite, meteorite, Michiganite, multipartite, New Hampshirite, New Jerseyite, potato blight, property right, suburbanite, sweetness and light, Turkish delight, Wyomingite • Great Australian Bight, Pre-Raphaelite

ite² \īt-ē\ flighty, mighty, nightie • almighty, Almighty • Aphrodite, arborvitae, high and mighty

ite³ \it\ see IT¹

ite⁴ \ēt\ see EAT¹

ited \īt-əd\ see IGHTED

iteful \īt-fəl\ see IGHTFUL

itely \īt-lē\ see IGHTLY

item \īt-əm\ item • line-item • ad
infinitum, collector's item
itement \īt-mənt\ excitement,
incitement, indictment
iten \īt-³n\ see IGHTEN
itener \īt-nər\ see IGHTENER
iteor \ēt-ē-ər\ see ETEOR
iter[1] \īt-ər\ biter, fighter, lighter,
miter, writer • all-nighter, back-
biter, bullfighter, dogfighter,
firefighter, ghostwriter,
gunfighter, highlighter, igniter,
inciter, lamplighter, moonlighter,
nail-biter, prizefighter, rewriter,
screenwriter, scriptwriter, sky-
writer, songwriter, speechwriter,
sportswriter, street fighter, type-
writer • candlelighter, copywriter,
fly-by-nighter, freedom fighter,
underwriter
—*also* -er *forms of adjectives listed
at* ITE[1]
iter[2] \it-ər\ see ITTER
iter[3] \ēt-ər\ see EATER[1]
iterally \it-ər-lē\ see ITTERLY
ites \īts\ see IGHTS
itey \īt-ē\ see ITE[2]
ith[1] \ith\ fifth, kith, myth, pith,
smith, Smith, with • bear with,
blacksmith, do with, forthwith,
goldsmith, Goldsmith, go with,
gunsmith, herewith, hold with,
live with, locksmith, run with,
tinsmith • be friends with, come
out with, come up with, complete
with, coppersmith, dispense with,
fall in with, Granny Smith, have
done with, make off with, mega-
lith, monolith, put up with,
reckon with, run off with, silver-
smith, take up with, walk off with
• come to grips with, do away
with, get away with, get even
with, have to do with, make away
with, run away with, wipe the
floor with
ith[2] \ēt\ see EAT[1]

ith[3] \ēth\ see EATH[1]
ithe[1] \īth\ blithe, lithe, scythe,
tithe, writhe
ithe[2] \ith\ see ITH[2]
ithe[3] \ith\ see ITH[1]
ither \ith-ər\ dither, hither, slither,
thither, whither, wither, zither
• come-hither
ithy \ith-ē\ pithy, smithy
iti \ēt-ē\ see EATY
itia[1] \ish-ə\ Alicia, Letitia, militia,
Patricia, Phoenicia • Dionysia
itia[2] \ē-shə\ see ESIA[1]
itial \ish-əl\ see ICIAL
itian[1] \ish-ən\ see ITION
itian[2] \ē-shən\ see ETION[1]
itiate \ish-ət\ initiate, novitiate
itic \it-ik\ critic • arthritic, granitic,
Semitic • analytic, catalytic, dyna-
mitic, paralytic, parasitic,
sybaritic • anti-Semitic, hermaph-
roditic
itical \it-i-kəl\ critical • political,
uncritical • analytical • geopoliti-
cal
itid \it-əd\ see ITTED
itimati \is-məs\ see ISTMAS
itin \īt-³n\ see IGHTEN
iting \īt-iŋ\ biting, lighting, writing
• backbiting, bullfighting, cock-
fighting, exciting, handwriting,
infighting, inviting, nail-biting,
newswriting, playwriting, prize-
fighting, skywriting, songwriting,
typewriting
—*also* -ing *forms of verbs listed at*
ITE[1]
ition \ish-ən\ fission, mission, Ti-
tian • addition, admission, ambi-
tion, attrition, audition,
beautician, clinician, cognition,
commission, condition, contri-
tion, dentition, edition, emission,
fruition, ignition, logician, magi-
cian, mortician, munition, musi-
cian, nutrition, omission,
optician, partition, patrician,

perdition, permission, petition, Phoenician, physician, position, remission, rendition, sedition, submission, suspicion, tactician, technician, tradition, transition, transmission, tuition, volition • abolition, acoustician, acquisition, admonition, air-condition, ammunition, apparition, coalition, competition, composition, decommission, definition, demolition, deposition, dietitian, Dionysian, disposition, disquisition, electrician, erudition, exhibition, expedition, exposition, extradition, imposition, in addition, inhibition, inquisition, intermission, intuition, malnutrition, mathematician, obstetrician, on commission, opposition, politician, precondition, premonition, preposition, prohibition, proposition, recognition, recondition, repetition, requisition, rescue mission, rhetorician, statistician, superstition, supposition, transposition • decomposition, dental technician, family physician, fetal position, general admission, high-definition, indisposition, juxtaposition, lotus position, open admission, out of commission, pediatrician, pocket edition, redefinition, theoretician

itional \ish-nəl\ additional, conditional, nutritional, traditional, transitional • definitional, prepositional, unconditional

itioner \i-shə-nər\ commissioner, conditioner, parishioner, petitioner, practitioner • air conditioner, nurse-practitioner • family practitioner, general practitioner

itionist \i-shə-nəst\ nutritionist • abolitionist, demolitionist, exhibitionist, prohibitionist

itious \ish-əs\ see ICIOUS[1]

itis \īt-əs\ Titus • arthritis, bronchitis, bursitis, colitis, detritus, gastritis, mastitis, nephritis, neuritis, phlebitis, tinnitus • cellulitis, dermatitis, gingivitis, hepatitis, laryngitis, meningitis, sinusitis, tonsillitis, tendinitis • appendicitis, conjunctivitis, encephalitis, endocarditis, peritonitis

itish \it-ish\ British, skittish

itius \ish-əs\ see ICIOUS[1]

itle \īt-ᵊl\ see ITAL[1]

it'll \it-ᵊl\ see ITTLE

itness \it-nəs\ fitness, witness • eyewitness, unfitness • character witness, Jehovah's Witness

itney \it-nē\ jitney, Whitney • Mount Whitney

ito[1] \ēt-ō\ Quito, Tito, veto • bandito, bonito, burrito, graffito, mosquito • Akihito, Hirohito, incognito, pocket veto • line-item veto

ito[2] \ēt-ə\ see ITA

iton[1] \it-ᵊn\ see ITTEN

iton[2] \īt-ᵊn\ see IGHTEN

its \its\ blitz, ditz, fritz, Fritz, glitz, grits, its, it's, quits, Ritz, spitz • Auschwitz, Berlitz, kibitz, Saint Kitts • Clausewitz, Horowitz, Saint Moritz • hominy grits —*also* -s, -'s, *and* -s' *forms of nouns and* -s *forms of verbs listed at* IT[1]

it's \its\ see ITS

itsch \ich\ see ITCH

itschy \ich-ē\ see ITCHY

itsy \it-sē\ see ITZY

itt \it\ see IT[1]

ittable \it-ə-bəl\ habitable, hospitable, transmittable • inhospitable

ittal \it-ᵊl\ see ITTLE

ittance \it-ᵊns\ pittance • admittance, remittance

ittany \it-ᵊn-ē\ see ITANY

itte \it\ see IT[1]

itted \it-əd\ fitted, it'd, pitted
• committed, dim-witted, half-witted, quick-witted, sharp-witted, slow-witted, thick-witted, unfitted • uncommitted
—*also* -ed *forms of verbs listed at* IT[1]

ittee \it-ē\ see ITTY

itten \it-ᵊn\ bitten, Britain, Briton, kitten, Lytton, mitten, smitten, written • flea-bitten, Great Britain, hard-bitten, rewritten, unwritten

ittence \it-ᵊns\ see ITTANCE

itter \it-ər\ bitter, critter, fitter, flitter, fritter, glitter, hitter, litter, quitter, sitter, skitter, titter, twitter • aglitter, atwitter, embitter, emitter, fence-sitter, hairsplitter, house sitter, no-hitter, outfitter, pinch hitter, pipe fitter, railsplitter, switch-hitter, transmitter • babysitter, counterfeiter, heavy hitter • neurotransmitter

itterer \it-ər-ər\ fritterer, litterer

itterly \it-ər-lē\ bitterly, literally

ittery \it-ə-rē\ glittery, jittery, skittery, twittery

ittie \it-ē\ see ITTY

ittier \it-ē-ər\ Whittier
—*also*-er *forms of adjectives listed at* ITTY

ittiness \it-ē-nəs\ grittiness, prettiness, wittiness

itting[1] \it-iŋ\ fitting, knitting, pitting, sitting, splitting, witting • befitting, earsplitting, fencesitting, formfitting, hairsplitting, hard-hitting, house-sitting, pipe fitting, sidesplitting, unfitting, unwitting • unremitting
—*also* -ing *forms of verbs listed at* IT[1]

itting[2] \it-ᵊn\ see ITTEN

ittish \it-ish\ see ITISH

ittle \it-ᵊl\ brittle, it'll, little, spittle, victual, whittle • acquittal, a little, belittle, committal, hospital, lickspittle, transmittal • Chicken Little, noncommittal • little by little

ittol \it-ᵊl\ see ITTLE

ittor \it-ər\ see ITTER

itts \its\ see ITS

itty \it-ē\ bitty, city, ditty, gritty, kitty, Kitty, pity, pretty, witty • committee, Dodge City, self-pity, Sioux City • Carson City, central city, Hello Kitty, holy city, itty-bitty, Kansas City, megacity, New York City, nitty-gritty, Quezon City, Rapid City, Salt Lake City, subcommittee • Atlantic City, Ho Chi Minh City, Long Island City, Mexico City, Panama City, Vatican City

itual \ich-ə-wəl\ ritual • habitual

ituary \ich-ə-rē\ see ITCHERY

itum \it-əm\ see ITEM

itus \īt-əs\ see ITIS

ity[1] \it-ē\ see ITTY

ity[2] \īt-ē\ see ITE[2]

itz \its\ see ITS

itzi \it-sē\ see ITZY

itzy \it-sē\ bitsy, ditzy, glitzy, Mitzi, ritzy

iu \ü\ see EW[1]

ius[1] \ē-əs\ see EUS[1]

ius[2] \ī-əs\ see IAS[1]

iv[1] \iv\ see IVE[2]

iv[2] \ēf\ see IEF[1]

iv[3] \if\ see IFF

iv[4] \ēv\ see EAVE[1]

iva[1] \ī-və\ Godiva, saliva

iva[2] \ē-və\ diva, Eva, kiva, Neva, Shiva, viva • Geneva, yeshiva

ivable[1] \ī-və-bəl\ drivable • derivable, survivable

ivable[2] \iv-ə-bəl\ livable • forgivable

ival \ī-vəl\ rival • archival, archrival, arrival, revival, survival • adjectival

ivalent \iv-ə-lənt\ ambivalent, equivalent

ivan \iv-ən\ see IVEN
ivance \ī-vəns\ connivance, contrivance
ive[1] \īv\ chive, Clive, dive, drive, five, hive, I've, jive, live, strive, thrive • alive, archive, arrive, beehive, connive, contrive, crash-dive, deprive, derive, disk drive, endive, hard drive, high five, high-five, line drive, nosedive, revive, skin-dive, skydive, survive, swan dive, take five, test-drive • eat alive, forty-five, four-wheel drive, hyperdrive, overdrive, power-dive, scuba dive
ive[2] \iv\ give, live, sieve • forgive, outlive, relive
ive[3] \ēv\ see EAVE[1]
ivel \iv-əl\ civil, drivel, shrivel, snivel, swivel • uncivil
iven \iv-ən\ driven, given, riven, striven • forgiven
iver[1] \ī-vər\ diver, driver, fiver, striver • cabdriver, pile driver, screwdriver, skin diver, skydiver, slave driver, survivor
iver[2] \iv-ər\ flivver, giver, liver, quiver, river, shiver, sliver • almsgiver, caregiver, chopped liver, deliver, downriver, East River, Fall River, lawgiver, upriver • up the river • Indian River, sell down the river
ivers \ī-vərz\ divers
—also -s, -'s, and -s' forms of nouns listed at IVER[1]
ivery \iv-rē\ livery, shivery • delivery • general delivery, special delivery
ives \īvz\ fives, hives, Ives
—also -s, -'s, and -s' forms of nouns and -s forms of verbs listed at IVE[1]
ivet \iv-ət\ civet, divot, pivot, privet, rivet, trivet
ivi \iv-ē\ see IVVY
ivia \iv-ē-ə\ trivia • Bolivia, Olivia

ivial \iv-ē-əl\ trivial • convivial
ivid \iv-əd\ livid, vivid
ivil \iv-əl\ see IVEL
iving \iv-iŋ\ giving, living • almsgiving, caregiving, forgiving, free-living, life-giving, misgiving, thanksgiving • cost of living, unforgiving • assisted living, standard of living
—also -ing forms of verbs listed at IVE[2]
ivion \iv-ē-ən\ Vivian • Bolivian, oblivion
ivious \iv-ē-əs\ lascivious, oblivious
ivir \iv-ər\ see IVER[2]
ivity \iv-ət-ē\ activity, captivity, festivity, nativity, passivity, proclivity • conductivity, connectivity, creativity, inactivity, inclusivity, negativity, objectivity, productivity, relativity, selectivity, sensitivity, subjectivity • hyperactivity, insensitivity, overactivity • radioactivity
ivol \iv-əl\ see IVEL
ivor \ī-vər\ see IVER[1]
ivorous \iv-rəs\ carnivorous, herbivorous, omnivorous • insectivorous
ivot \iv-ət\ see IVET
ivus \ē-vəs\ see EVOUS
ivver \iv-ər\ see IVER[2]
ivvy \iv-ē\ chivy, divvy, Livy, privy, skivvy
ivy \iv-ē\ see IVVY
iwi \ē-wē\ see EEWEE
ix[1] \iks\ fix, mix, nix, six, Styx • affix, deep-six, prefix, premix, prix fixe, prolix, suffix, trail mix, transfix • cicatrix, crucifix, intermix, politics • geopolitics
—also -s, -'s, and -s' forms of nouns and -s forms of verbs listed at ICK
ix[2] \ē\ see EE[1]
ixe[1] \iks\ see IX[1]
ixe[2] \ēsh\ see ICHE[2]

ixed \ikst\ fixed, mixed, twixt
• betwixt, well-fixed
—*also* -ed *forms of verbs listed at*
IX[1]
ixen \ik-sən\ Nixon • Mason-Dixon
ixer \ik-sər\ fixer, mixer • elixir
ixie \ik-sē\ Dixie, pixie, tricksy
ixion \ik-shən\ see ICTION
ixir \ik-sər\ see IXER
ixon \ik-sən\ see IXEN
ixt \ikst\ see IXED
ixture \iks-chər\ fixture, mixture
• intermixture
iya \ē-ə\ see IA[1]
iyeh \ē-ə\ see IA[1]
iz[1] \iz\ biz, fizz, frizz, his, is, Ms.,
quiz, 'tis, whiz, wiz • gee-whiz,
pop quiz, show biz
iz[2] \ēz\ see EZE
iza[1] \ē-zə\ see EZA
iza[2] \ē-thə\ see ETHA
izable \ī-zə-bəl\ sizable • advisable
• analyzable, inadvisable, localiz-
able, recognizable
izar \ī-zər\ see IZER
izard \iz-ərd\ blizzard, gizzard,
lizard, wizard
ize[1] \īz\ guise, prize, rise, size, wise
• advise, apprise, arise, baptize,
bite-size, capsize, chastise, clock-
wise, comprise, crabwise, cross-
wise, demise, despise, devise,
disguise, door prize, downsize,
edgewise, endwise, excise, fran-
chise, full-size, high-rise, incise,
king-size, leastwise, lengthwise,
life-size, likewise, low-rise, man-
size, mid-rise, midsize, moonrise,
outsize, pint-size, queen-size,
revise, slantwise, streetwise, styl-
ize, suffice, sunrise, surmise,
surprise, twin-size, unwise • ad-
vertise, aggrandize, agonize,
amortize, analyze, atomize, au-
thorize, balkanize, booby prize,
bowdlerize, brutalize, burglarize,
canonize, capsulize, caramelize,

catalyze, catechize, cauterize,
centralize, Christianize, circum-
cise, civilize, colonize, colorize,
compromise, concertize, criticize,
crystalize, customize, demonize,
deputize, digitize, dramatize,
empathize, emphasize, energize,
enterprise, equalize, eulogize,
exercise, exorcise, fantasize,
feminize, fertilize, finalize, for-
malize, galvanize, ghettoize, glam-
orize, globalize, harmonize,
humanize, hypnotize, idolize,
immunize, improvise, itemize,
jeopardize, legalize, lionize, liq-
uidize, localize, magnetize, maxi-
mize, mechanize, memorize, mini-
mize, mobilize, modernize, mois-
turize, monetize, moralize,
motorize, neutralize, Nobel Prize,
normalize, notarize, novelize,
optimize, organize, ostracize,
otherwise, oversize, oxidize, paradise, paralyze, pasteurize, patron-
ize, penalize, penny-wise,
personalize, plagiarize, pluralize,
pocket-size, polarize, pressurize,
privatize, publicize, pulverize,
rationalize, realize, recognize,
rhapsodize, robotize, sanitize,
satirize, scandalize, scrutinize,
sensitize, sermonize, slenderize,
socialize, solemnize, specialize,
stabilize, standardize, sterilize,
stigmatize, strategize, subsidize,
summarize, supervise, symbolize,
sympathize, synchronize, synthe-
size, systemize, tantalize, televise,
tenderize, terrorize, theorize,
tranquilize, traumatize, tyrannize,
unionize, urbanize, utilize, van-
dalize, vaporize, verbalize, victim-
ize, vocalize, vulcanize, vulgarize,
weather-wise, weatherize, west-
ernize, winterize, worldly-wise
• accessorize, acclimatize,

Africanize, alphabetize, anesthetize, antagonize, anticlockwise, apologize, cannibalize, capitalize, categorize, characterize, computerize, contrariwise, counterclockwise, criminalize, cut down to size, decentralize, de-emphasize, deglamorize, dehumanize, demagnetize, democratize, demoralize, deodorize, depressurize, desensitize, disenfranchise, economize, epitomize, evangelize, familiarize, fictionalize, floor exercise, free enterprise, generalize, homogenize, hospitalize, hypothesize, idealize, immobilize, immortalize, infantilize, internalize, italicize, legitimize, liberalize, marginalize, metabolize, metastasize, militarize, monopolize, nationalize, naturalize, philosophize, politicize, popularize, prioritize, proselytize, Pulitzer prize, regularize, reorganize, revitalize, romanticize, systematize, trivialize, visualize • Americanize, compartmentalize, consolation prize, decriminalize, departmentalize, individualize, industrialize, internationalize, legitimatize, materialize, memorialize, miniaturize, private enterprise, professionalize, psychoanalyze, revolutionize, sensationalize, underutilize, universalize • editorialize, intellectualize
—*also* -s, -'s, *and* -s' *forms of nouns and* -s *forms of verbs listed at* Y^1

ize[2] \ēz\ see EZE

ized \īzd\ sized • advised, kingsized, outsized, pearlized, queensized • ill-advised, organized,

Sanforized, unadvised, undersized, well-advised • elasticized
—*also* -ed *forms of verbs listed at* IZE^1

izen[1] \īz-ᵊn\ bison • horizon
izen[2] \iz-ᵊn\ see ISON[2]
izer \ī-zər\ Dreiser, geyser, kaiser, miser, riser, visor • adviser, divisor, incisor • advertiser, appetizer, atomizer, compromiser, energizer, equalizer, exerciser, fertilizer, improviser, modernizer, moisturizer, moralizer, organizer, pollenizer, pressurizer, stabilizer, sterilizer, supervisor, sympathizer, synthesizer, tenderizer, tranquilizer, vaporizer • popularizer, proselytizer
izing \ī-ziŋ\ rising, sizing • uprising • advertising, agonizing, appetizing, enterprising, merchandising, unsurprising • self-sacrificing, unappetizing, uncompromising
—*also* -ing *forms of verbs listed at* IZE^1
izo \ē-zō\ sleazo • mestizo
izon \īz-ᵊn\ see IZEN[1]
izy \it-sē\ see ITZY
izz \iz\ see IZ[1]
izzard \iz-ərd\ see IZARD
izzen \iz-ᵊn\ see ISON[2]
izzer \iz-ər\ see ISSOR
izzical \iz-i-kəl\ see YSICAL
izzie \i-zē\ see IZZY
izzle \iz-əl\ chisel, drizzle, fizzle, grizzle, sizzle • cold chisel
izzled \iz-əld\ chiseled, grizzled
—*also* -ed *forms of verbs listed at* IZZLE
izzler \iz-lər\ chiseler, sizzler
izzly \iz-lē\ drizzly, grisly, grizzly
izzy \iz-ē\ busy, dizzy, fizzy, frizzy, tizzy • tin lizzie

O

o¹ \ü\ see EW¹

o² \ō\ see OW¹

oa¹ \ō-ə\ boa, Goa, Noah, Shoah • aloha, Balboa, Samoa • Krakatoa, Mauna Loa, Mount Gilboa, Shenandoah

oa² \ō\ see OW¹

oable \ü-ə-bəl\ see UABLE

oach \ōch\ broach, brooch, coach, poach, roach • approach, cockroach, encroach, reproach, stagecoach

oachable \ō-chə-bəl\ coachable • approachable • irreproachable, unapproachable

oacher \ō-chər\ cloture, poacher

oad¹ \ōd\ see ODE

oad² \od\ see AUD¹

oader \ōd-ər\ see ODER

oadie \ōd-ē\ see ODY²

oady \ōd-ē\ see ODY²

oaf \ōf\ loaf, oaf • meat loaf • sugarloaf

oafer \ō-fər\ see OFER

oagie \ō-gē\ see OGIE

oah \ō-ə\ see OA¹

oak \ōk\ see OKE¹

oaken \ō-kən\ see OKEN

oaker \ō-kər\ see OKER

oaky \ō-kē\ see OKY

oal \ōl\ see OLE¹

oalie \ō-lē\ see OLY¹

oam \ōm\ see OME¹

oamer \ō-mər\ see OMER¹

oaming \ō-miŋ\ gloaming • Wyoming
—also -ing forms of verbs listed at OME¹

oamy \ō-mē\ foamy, homey, loamy, show-me • Naomi, Salome

oan¹ \ō-ən\ Owen, roan • Minoan, Samoan • Idahoan, protozoan • strawberry roan

oan² \ōn\ see ONE¹

oaner \ō-nər\ see ONER¹

oaning \ō-niŋ\ see ONING²

oap \ōp\ see OPE

oaper \ō-pər\ see OPER

oapy \ō-pē\ see OPI

oar \or\ see OR¹

oard \ord\ board, bored, chord, cord, floored, ford, Ford, gourd, hoard, horde, lord, Lord, oared, sword, toward, ward, Ward • aboard, accord, afford, award, backboard, baseboard, billboard, blackboard, breadboard, broadsword, cardboard, chalkboard, chessboard, clapboard, clipboard, concord, dart board, dashboard, discord, draft board, fjord, floorboard, headboard, inboard, keyboard, kickboard, landlord, lapboard, nerve cord, onboard, on board, outboard, pasteboard, Peg-Board, rearward, record, reward, scoreboard, shipboard, signboard, skateboard, slumlord, snowboard, soundboard, splashboard, springboard, surfboard, switchboard, untoward, wallboard, warlord, washboard, whiteboard, whipcord • aboveboard, bottle gourd, bungee cord, centerboard, checkerboard, circuit board, clavichord, cutting board, diving board, drawing board, emery board, fiberboard, fingerboard, harpsichord, mortarboard, motherboard, overboard, overlord, paddleboard, plasterboard, room and board, sandwich board, shuf-fleboard, smorgasbord, sounding board, spinal cord, tape-record, teeterboard, untoward • across-the-board, bulletin board, exten-sion cord, go by the board, ironing board, off-the-record, on-the-record, out of one's gourd, particleboard • Federal Reserve Board, platinum record • Acad-emy Award

—*also* -ed *forms of verbs listed at* OR[1]

oarder \ȯrd-ər\ see ORDER

oarding \ȯrd-iŋ\ see ORDING[1]

oared \ȯrd\ see OARD

oarer \ȯr-ər\ see ORER

oaring \ȯr-iŋ\ see ORING

oarious \ȯr-ē-əs\ see ORIOUS

oarse \ȯrs\ see ORSE[1]

oarsman \ȯrz-mən\ oarsman • out-doorsman

oart \ȯrt\ see ORT[1]

oary \ȯr-ē\ see ORY

oast \ōst\ see OST[2]

oastal \ōs-tᵊl\ see OSTAL[1]

oaster \ō-stər\ coaster, poster, roaster, toaster • four-poster • roller-coaster, roller coaster

oat \ōt\ bloat, boat, coat, dote, float, gloat, goat, moat, mote, note, oat, quote, rote, smote, throat, tote, vote, wrote • afloat, airboat, banknote, catboat, C-note, compote, connote, coy-ote, cutthroat, demote, denote, devote, dovecote, dreamboat, eighth note, emote, fireboat, flatboat, footnote, frock coat, grace note, greatcoat, gunboat, half note, houseboat, housecoat, iceboat, keynote, lab coat, lifeboat, longboat, promote, rain-coat, redcoat, remote, rewrote, rowboat, sailboat, sauceboat, scapegoat, seed coat, sheepcote, showboat, sore throat, speedboat,

steamboat, straw vote, strep throat, Sukkoth, surfboat, top-coat, towboat, trench coat, tug-boat, turncoat, U-boat, unquote, wainscot, whaleboat, whole note • anecdote, antidote, assault boat, billy goat, cashmere goat, cre-osote, dead man's float, ferryboat, flying boat, jolly boat, miss the boat, motorboat, mountain goat, nanny goat, overcoat, paddleboat, petticoat, polo coat, powerboat, PT boat, quarter note, riverboat, rock the boat, sixteenth note, sticky note, sugarcoat, Terre Haute, undercoat, yellowthroat • Angorä goat, in the same boat, lump in one's throat, torpedo boat, treasury note

oate \ō-ət\ see OET

oated \ōt-əd\ bloated, coated, noted, throated • devoted

—*also* -ed *forms of verbs listed at* OAT

oaten \ōt-ᵊn\ see OTON

oater \ōt-ər\ boater, motor, rotor, voter • keynoter, promoter, show-boater • outboard motor

oath \ōth\ see OWTH

oathe \ōth\ see OTHE

oathing \ō-thiŋ\ see OTHING

oating \ōt-iŋ\ coating, floating • free-floating, iceboating, sail-boating, speedboating, wain-scoting • motorboating, powerboating, undercoating,

—*also* -ing *forms of verbs listed at* OAT

oaty \ōt-ē\ see OTE[1]

oax \ōks\ coax, hoax

—*also* -s, -'s, *and* -s' *forms of nouns and* -s *forms of verbs listed at* OKE[1]

ob[1] \äb\ blob, bob, Bob, cob, daub, fob, glob, gob, job, knob, lob, mob, nob, rob, Saab, slob, snob, sob, squab, swab, throb • corn-

cob, day job, doorknob, heart-
throb, hobnob, kebab, macabre,
Punjab, snow job • shish kebab
• thingamabob
ob² \ŏb\ see OBE¹
oba \ō-bə\ jojoba • Manitoba
• Lake Manitoba
obably \äb-lē\ see OBBLY
obal \ō-bəl\ see OBLE
obar \ō-bər\ see OBER
obber \äb-ər\ bobber, clobber,
robber, slobber • hobnobber
obbery \äb-rē\ robbery, slobbery,
snobbery • highway robbery
obbie \äb-ē\ see OBBY
obbin \äb-ən\ see OBIN
obble \äb-əl\ see ABBLE¹
obbler \äb-lər\ cobbler, gobbler
obbly \äb-lē\ probably, wobbly
obby \äb-ē\ Bobbie, Bobby,
globby, hobby, knobby, lobby,
slobby, snobby • kohlrabi, Pun-
jabi • Abu Dhabi, Hammurabi
obe¹ \ōb\ globe, Job, lobe, probe,
robe, strobe • bathrobe, disrobe,
earlobe, enrobe, lap robe, mi-
crobe, wardrobe • claustrophobe,
frontal lobe, optic lobe, techno-
phobe, xenophobe • computer-
phobe, election probe, temporal
lobe • occipital lobe
obe² \ō-bē\ see OBY
obeah \ō-bē-ə\ see OBIA
obee \ō-bē\ see OBY
ober \ō-bər\ sober • October
obi \ō-bē\ see OBY
obia \ō-bē-ə\ phobia • Zenobia
• acrophobia, agoraphobia, claus-
trophobia, hydrophobia, techno-
phobia, xenophobia
• arachnophobia, computerpho-
bia
obic \ō-bik\ phobic • aerobic
• acrophobic, anaerobic, claustro-
phobic, hydrophobic, technopho-
bic, xenophobic • agoraphobic,
arachnophobic, computerphobic

obile \ō-bəl\ see OBLE
obin \äb-ən\ bobbin, dobbin, robin,
Robin • round-robin, sea robin
obit \ō-bət\ obit, Tobit
oble \ō-bəl\ global, mobile, noble
• ennoble, Grenoble, ignoble,
immobile • upwardly mobile
obo \ō-bō\ hobo, oboe • bonobo
oboe \ō-bō\ see OBO
obol \äb-əl\ see ABBLE¹
oboree \äb-ə-rē\ see OBBERY
obot \ō-bət\ see OBIT
obster \äb-stər\ lobster, mobster
• spiny lobster
oby \ō-bē\ Gobi, Kobe, Obie, Toby
• adobe, Nairobi • Okeechobee
obyn \äb-ən\ see OBIN
oc¹ \ōk\ see OKE¹
oc² \äk\ see OCK¹
oc³ \ók\ see ALK
oca \ō-kə\ coca, mocha • tapioca
ocal \ō-kəl\ focal, local, vocal,
yokel • bifocal
ocally \ō-kə-lē\ locally, vocally
occa \äk-ə\ see AKA¹
occer \äk-ər\ see OCKER
occie \äch-ē\ see OTCHY
occhi \ò-kē\ see ALKIE
occo \äk-ō\ socko, taco • morocco,
Morocco, sirocco
oce \ō-chē\ see OCHE¹
ocean \ō-shən\ see OTION
ocess \äs-əs\ process • colossus,
due process, proboscis, word
process
och¹ \äk\ see OCK¹
och² \òsh\ see ASH²
och³ \ók\ see ALK
ocha \ō-kə\ see OCA
ochal \äk-əl\ see OCKLE
oche¹ \ō-kē\ see OKY
oche² \ōch\ see OACH
oche³ \òsh\ see ASH²
ochee \ō-kē\ see OKY
ocher \ō-kər\ see OKER
ochi \ō-chē\ see OCHE¹
ochle \ək-əl\ see UCKLE

ochs \äks\ see OX
ociable \ō-shə-bəl\ sociable • negotiable, unsociable • renegotiable
ocile \äs-əl\ see OSSAL
ocious \ō-shəs\ atrocious, ferocious, precocious
ock[1] \äk\ Bach, bloc, block, clock, cock, crock, doc, dock, flock, frock, hock, Jacque, Jacques, jock, knock, loch, lock, moc, mock, pock, roc, rock, schlock, shock, smock, sock, Spock, stock, wok • ad hoc, air lock, amok, armlock, Bangkok, baroque, bedrock, burdock, crew sock, deadlock, debacle, defrock, dreadlock, dry dock, epoch, flintlock, forelock, foreshock, gridlock, Hancock, hard rock, haycock, headlock, hemlock, in stock, Iraq, jazz-rock, Kazakh, kapok, kneesock, Ladakh, livestock, o'clock, oarlock, padlock, peacock, picklock, punk rock, rimrock, roadblock, rootstock, rowlock, seed stock, shamrock, Sheetrock, shell shock, sherlock, shock jock, Sirach, slickrock, Slovak, soft rock, springbok, stopcock, sunblock, ticktock, time clock, time lock, unblock, uncock, van Gogh, warlock, wedlock, windsock, woodcock • acid rock, aftershock, alarm clock, antiknock, antilock, Antioch, Arawak, banjo clock, building block, butcher-block, chockablock, chopping block, cinder block, common stock, country rock, cuckoo clock, culture shock, hammerlock, hollyhock, interlock, John Hancock, laughingstock, Little Rock, manioc, mantlerock, Offenbach, on the block, out of stock, Plymouth Rock, poppycock, preferred stock, rolling stock, septic

shock, starting block, shuttlecock, sticker shock, stumbling block, water clock, weathercock, writer's block • against the clock, around-the-clock, atomic clock, Czechoslovak, electroshock, grandfather clock, insulin shock, Mount Monadnock, out of wedlock, poison hemlock, run out the clock, turn back the clock, Vladivostok • chip off the old block
ock[2] \ȯk\ see ALK
ocke \äk\ see OCK[1]
ocked \äkt\ concoct, dreadlocked, half-cocked, landlocked, shellshocked
—*also* -ed *forms of verbs listed at* OCK[1]
ocker \äk-ər\ blocker, knocker, locker, mocker, rocker, shocker, soccer • alt-rocker, art-rocker, footlocker, punk rocker • knickerbocker • Davy Jones's locker
ockery \äk-rē\ crockery, mockery
ocket \äk-ət\ Crockett, docket, locket, pocket, rocket, socket, sprocket • air pocket, patch pocket, pickpocket, skyrocket, vest-pocket • cargo pocket, retrorocket
ockett \äk-ət\ see OCKET
ockey \äk-ē\ see OCKY
ockian \äk-ē-ən\ Hitchcockian, Slovakian • Czechoslovakian
ocking \äk-iŋ\ flocking, shocking, stocking • body stocking
—*also* -ing *forms of verbs listed at* OCK[1]
ockle \äk-əl\ debacle • streptococcal
ocko \äk-ō\ see OCCO
ocks \äks\ see OX
ocky \äk-ē\ blocky, cocky, hockey, jockey, rocky, schlocky, stocky • disc jockey, field hockey, ice hockey, Iraqi, street hockey • jab-

berwocky, Miyazaki, Nagasaki, sukiyaki, teriyaki

ocle \ō-kəl\ see OCAL

oco \ō-kō\ coco, cocoa, loco • rococo • crème de cacao, Orinoco

ocoa \ō-kō\ see OCO

ocracy \äk-rə-sē\ autocracy, bureaucracy, democracy, hypocrisy, mobocracy, plutocracy • aristocracy

ocre \ō-kər\ see OKER

ocrisy \äk-rə-sē\ see OCRACY

oct \äkt\ see OCKED

octor \äk-tər\ doctor, proctor • spin doctor, witch doctor • family doctor

ocular \äk-yə-lər\ jocular • binocular

ocus \ō-kəs\ crocus, focus, hocus • in focus, refocus, soft-focus • autumn crocus, hocus-pocus

ocused \ō-kəst\ see OCUST

ocust \ō-kəst\ locust • unfocused

od[1] \äd\ bod, clod, cod, Fahd, god, mod, nod, odd, plod, pod, prod, quad, rod, scrod, shod, sod, squad, trod, wad • Cape Cod, death squad, dry-shod, facade, fly rod, hot-rod, jihad, lingcod, Nimrod, ramrod, Riyadh, roughshod, seedpod, slipshod, sun god, synod, tightwad, tripod, unshod, vice squad • accolade, act of God, arthropod, cattle prod, demigod, dowsing rod, esplanade, firing squad, flying squad, gastropod, goldenrod, lightning rod, man of God, Novgorod, piston rod, promenade, son of God, spinning rod • cephalopod, connecting rod, divining rod, Holy Synod, Islamabad, Scheherazade, Upanishad

od[2] \ō\ see OW[1]

od[3] \ōd\ see ODE

od[4] \u̇d\ see OOD[1]

od[5] \ȯd\ see AUD[1]

o'd \üd\ see UDE[1]

oda \ōd-ə\ coda, Rhoda, Skoda, soda • club soda, cream soda, pagoda • baking soda

odal \ōd-ᵊl\ modal, nodal, yodel

odden \äd-ᵊn\ Flodden, sodden, trodden • downtrodden, untrodden

odder \äd-ər\ dodder, fodder, odder, plodder, solder • flyrodder, hot-rodder • cannon fodder, Leningrader

oddery \äd-rē\ see AWDRY

oddess \äd-əs\ bodice, goddess • sun goddess • demigoddess

oddish \äd-ish\ cloddish, kaddish

oddle \äd-ᵊl\ coddle, model, swaddle, toddle, twaddle, waddle • remodel, role model • mollycoddle, supermodel

oddler \äd-lər\ coddler, modeler, toddler • mollycoddler

oddly \äd-lē\ see ODLY

oddy \äd-ē\ see ODY[1]

ode \ōd\ bode, bowed, code, goad, load, lode, mode, node, ode, road, rode, strode, toad, toed • abode, anode, bar code, boatload, busload, byroad, carload, cartload, caseload, cathode, commode, corrode, crossroad, decode, diode, download, dress code, encode, erode, explode, forebode, freeload, geode, high road, horned toad, implode, inroad, lymph node, Morse code, offload, outmode, payload, planeload, railroad, shipload, side road, Silk Road, spring-load, squaretoed, trainload, truckload, twotoed, unload, upload, zip code • à la mode, Comstock Lode, down the road, electrode, episode, hit the road, mother lode, overrode, penal code, pigeon-toed, service road, wagonload • area code, genetic code, rule of the road • middle-of-the-road, Underground Railroad

—*also* -ed *forms of verbs listed at* OW[1]

odeine \ōd-ē-ən\ see ODIAN

odel \ōd-ᵊl\ see ODAL

odeler \äd-lər\ see ODDLER

odeon \ōd-ē-ən\ see ODIAN

oder \ōd-ər\ loader, Oder, odor • breechloader, freeloader, offroader, railroader • middle-of-the-roader

oderate \äd-rət\ moderate • immoderate

odes \ōdz\ Rhodes
—*also* -s, -'s, *and* -s' *forms of nouns and* -s *forms of verbs listed at* ODE

odest \äd-əst\ modest, oddest • immodest

odeum \ōd-ē-əm\ see ODIUM

odge \äj\ see AGE[1]

odger \äj-ər\ codger, dodger, lodger, roger, Roger • Jolly Roger

odgy \äj-ē\ stodgy • demagogy

odian \ōd-ē-ən\ Cambodian, custodian, melodeon • nickelodeon

odic \äd-ik\ melodic, rhapsodic, spasmodic • episodic, periodic

odical \äd-i-kəl\ methodical • periodical

odice \äd-əs\ see ODDESS

odie \ō-dē\ see ODY[2]

odious \ōd-ē-əs\ odious • commodious, melodious

odity \äd-ət-ē\ oddity • commodity

odium \ōd-ē-əm\ podium, sodium

odius \ō-dē-əs\ see ODIOUS

odly \äd-lē\ godly, oddly • ungodly

odo \ōd-ō\ dodo • Quasimodo

odom \äd-əm\ shahdom, Sodom

odor \ōd-ər\ see ODER

odule \äj-ül\ module, lunar module, service module

ody[1] \äd-ē\ body, gaudy, Mahdi, shoddy, toddy • cell body, embody, homebody, nobody, somebody, wide-body • antibody, anybody, busybody, everybody,

Irrawaddy, out-of-body, student body, underbody

ody[2] \ōd-ē\ Cody, Jodie, roadie, toady

odz \üj\ see UGE[1]

oe[1] \ō\ see OW[1]

oe[2] \ō-ē\ see OWY

oe[3] \ē\ see EE[1]

oea[1] \òi-ə\ see OIA

oea[2] \ē-ə\ see IA[1]

oeba \ē-bə\ see EBA

oebe \ē-bē\ see EBE[1]

oebel \ā-bəl\ see ABLE

oed \ōd\ see ODE

oehn \ən\ see UN[1]

oeia \ē-ə\ see IA[1]

oek \ùk\ see OOK[1]

oel \ō-əl\ Joel, Lowell, Noel • bestowal • protozoal

oeless[1] \ō-ləs\ see OLUS

oeless[2] \ü-ləs\ see EWLESS

oem \ōm\ see OME[1]

oeman \ō-mən\ see OMAN

oena \ē-nə\ see INA[2]

oentgen \en-chən\ see ENSION

oer[1] \òr\ see OR[1]

oer[2] \ü-ər\ see EWER[1]

oer[3] \ùr\ see URE[1]

oer[4] \ō-ər\ blower, grower, lower, mower, rower, slower, sower, thrower • beachgoer, churchgoer, fairgoer, flamethrower, filmgoer, glassblower, lawn mower, playgoer, snowblower, winegrower • concertgoer, moviegoer, operagoer, partygoer, whistle-blower • theatergoer

o'er \òr\ see OR[1]

oes[1] \əz\ see EUSE[1]

oes[2] \ōz\ see OSE[2]

oes[3] \üz\ see USE[2]

oesia \ē-shə\ see ESIA[1]

oesn't \əz-ᵊnt\ see ASN'T

oest \ü-əst\ see OOIST

oesus \ē-səs\ see ESIS

oet \ō-ət\ poet • inchoate, prose poet

oeuf \əf\ see UFF
oeur \ər\ see EUR[1]
oeuvre \ərv\ see ERVE
oey \ō-ē\ see OWY
of[1] \äv\ see OLVE[2]
of[2] \əv\ see OVE[1]
of[3] \óf\ see OFF[2]
ofar \ō-fər\ see OFER
ofer \ō-fər\ chauffeur, gopher, loafer, shofar • penny loafer
off[1] \äf\ coif, doff, prof, quaff, scoff • carafe, pilaf • Romanov
off[2] \óf\ cough, doff, off, scoff, trough • Azov, back off, beg off, blastoff, blow off, break off, bring off, brush-off, bug off, bump off, burn off, call off, cast-off, castoff, charge off, check off, Chekhov, cook-off, cutoff, cut off, drop-off, drop off, dust off, face-off, face off, falloff, far-off, fire off, first off, fob off, get off, give off, go off, goof-off, handoff, hand off, hands-off, haul off, head off, hold off, jump-off, kickoff, kick off, kill off, kiss-off, kiss off, knock-off, knock off, Khrushchev, laugh off, layoff, lay off, leadoff, lead off, leave off, liftoff, make off, nod off, palm off, pass off, payoff, pay off, peel off, pick off, play-off, pull off, push off, put off, reel off, rip-off, rip off, rub off, runoff, sawed-off, seal off, sell off, sell-off, send-off, set off, show-off, show off, shrug off, shut off, sign off, sound off, spin-off, standoff, stave off, swear off, takeoff, take off, teed off, tee off, tell off, throw off, tick off, tip-off, touch off, trade-off, turnoff, turn off, well-off, work off, write off • better-off, cooling-off, Gorbachev, hit it off, level off, Molotov, Nabokov, polish off, Pribilof, taper off • beat the pants off, beef Stroganoff, knock one's socks off,

power take-off, Rachmaninoff • Mexican standoff, Rimsky-Korsakov
offal[1] \äf-əl\ see AFEL
offal[2] \ó-fəl\ see AWFUL
offaly \óf-ə-lē\ see AWFULLY
offee \ó-fē\ coffee, toffee • Mr. Coffee
offer[1] \äf-ər\ coffer, offer, scoffer • counteroffer
offer[2] \óf-ər\ coffer, offer, scoffer • counteroffer
offin \ó-fən\ coffin, often, soften • every so often
offle \ó-fəl\ see AWFUL
oft[1] \óft\ croft, loft, oft, soft • aloft, choir loft, hayloft • Microsoft, semisoft, undercroft
—*also* -ed *forms of verbs listed at* OFF[2]
oft[2] \äft\ see AFT[1]
often \ó-fən\ see OFFIN
ofty \óf-tē\ lofty, softy
og[1] \äg\ blog, bog, clog, cog, flog, fog, frog, grog, hog, jog, log, nog, Prague, slog, smog • agog, backlog, bullfrog, defog, eggnog, footslog, groundhog, hedgehog, ice fog, leapfrog, photog, prologue, road hog, sandhog, tree frog, unclog, warthog, whole hog, Yule log • analog, analogue, catalog, demagogue, dialogue, epilogue, leopard frog, monologue, pedagogue, pollywog, synagogue, travelogue, waterlog • card catalogue
og[2] \óg\ blog, bog, clog, dog, fog, frog, hog, jog, log, smog • backlog, bird dog, bulldog, bullfrog, corn dog, coydog, defog, groundhog, guide dog, gundog, hangdog, hedgehog, hotdog, ice fog, lapdog, leapfrog, prologue, road hog, sandhog, sheepdog, sled dog, top dog, tree frog, warthog, watchdog, whole-hog, wild dog, wolf

dog, Yule log • analog, analogue, attack dog, catalog, chili dog, dialogue, dog-eat-dog, epilogue, hearing dog, leopard frog, monologue, police dog, pollywog, prairie dog, shaggy-dog, travelogue, underdog, water dog, working dog • card catalog, Eskimo dog, Shetland sheepdog

og[3] \ōg\ see OGUE[1]

oga \ō-gə\ toga, yoga • Conestoga, hatha yoga

ogan \ō-gən\ shogun, slogan • Mount Logan

oge \üzh\ see UGE[2]

ogel \ō-gəl\ see OGLE[1]

ogeny \äj-ə-nē\ progeny • misogyny

oger[1] \äj-ər\ see ODGER

oger[2] \ȯg-ər\ see OGGER[2]

ogey[1] \ō-gē\ see OGIE

ogey[2] \ùg-ē\ see OOGIE

oggan \äg-ən\ see OGGIN

oggar \äg-ər\ see OGGER[1]

ogger[1] \äg-ər\ blogger, jogger, lager, logger • defogger • cataloger

ogger[2] \ȯg-ər\ auger, augur, jogger, logger • defogger, hotdogger • cataloger

oggin \äg-ən\ noggin • toboggan, Volkswagen • Copenhagen

oggle \äg-əl\ boggle, goggle, joggle, toggle • boondoggle • synagogal

oggy[1] \äg-ē\ boggy, foggy, groggy, smoggy, soggy

oggy[2] \ȯg-ē\ doggy, foggy, soggy

ogh[1] \ōg\ see OGUE[1]

ogh[2] \ōk\ see OKE[1]

ogh[3] \äk\ see OCK[1]

ogh[4] \ō\ see OW[1]

ogi \ō-gē\ see OGIE

ogian \ō-jən\ see OJAN

ogic \äj-ik\ logic • biologic, chronologic, demagogic, geologic, mythologic

ogical \äj-i-kəl\ logical • illogical

• astrological, biological, chronological, cosmological, ecological, geological, mythological, pathological, pedagogical, psychological, seismological, technological, theological, zoological • archaeological, dermatological, ideological, sociological

ogie \ō-gē\ bogey, bogie, dogie, fogy, hoagie, logy, stogie, yogi • pierogi

ogle[1] \ō-gəl\ Gogol, ogle

ogle[2] \äg-əl\ see OGGLE

ogna[1] \ō-nə\ see ONA[1]

ogna[2] \ō-nē\ see ONY[1]

ogna[3] \ōn-yə\ see ONIA[2]

ogne \ōn\ see ONE[1]

ogned \ōnd\ see ONED[1]

ogo \ō-gō\ go-go, logo, Togo

ographer \äg-rə-fər\ biographer, cryptographer, discographer, photographer • choreographer, oceanographer, videographer • cinematographer

ography \äg-rə-fē\ biography, cryptography, discography, filmography, geography, photography, typography • bibliography, choreography, oceanography • autobiography, cinematography

ogress \ō-grəs\ ogress, progress

ogue[1] \ōg\ brogue, rogue, vogue, Vogue

ogue[2] \äg\ see OG[1]

ogue[3] \ȯg\ see OG[2]

oguish \ō-gish\ roguish, voguish

ogun \ō-gən\ see OGAN

ogyny \äj-ə-nē\ see OGENY

oh \ō\ see OW[1]

oha \ō-ə\ see OA[1]

ohl \ōl\ see OLE[1]

ohm \ōm\ see OME[1]

ohn \än\ see ON[1]

ohns \änz\ see ONZE

ohn's \ōnz\ see ONZE

ohnson \än-sən\ Johnson • Wisconsin

ohr \ȯr\ see OR[1]

oi[1] \ä\ see A[1]

oi[2] \ȯi\ see OY

oia \ȯi-ə\ Goya, olla • sequoia, Sequoya • paranoia

oic \ō-ik\ stoic • echoic, heroic • Cenozoic, Mesozoic • Paleozoic

oice \ȯis\ choice, Joyce, voice • invoice, of choice, pro-choice, rejoice • with one voice • multiple-choice

oiced \ȯist\ see OIST

oicer \ȯi-sər\ pro-choicer, rejoicer

oid[1] \ȯid\ Floyd, Freud, void • android, avoid, deltoid, devoid, factoid, Negroid, ovoid, rhomboid, schizoid, steroid, tabloid, thyroid, typhoid • anthropoid, asteroid, celluloid, hemorrhoid, humanoid, Mongoloid, null and void, overjoyed, paranoid, planetoid, trapezoid, unalloyed, unemployed • underemployed
—*also* -ed *forms of verbs listed at* OY

oid[2] \ä\ see A[1]

oidal \ȯid-ᵊl\ adenoidal, asteroidal, trapezoidal

oie \ä\ see A[1]

oif \äf\ see OFF[1]

oign \ȯin\ see OIN[1]

oil \ȯil\ boil, broil, coil, foil, Hoyle, loyal, oil, roil, royal, soil, spoil, toil • airfoil, charbroil, coal oil, corn oil, despoil, disloyal, embroil, fish oil, fuel oil, gargoyle, hard-boil, palm oil, parboil, recoil, snake oil, subsoil, tinfoil, topsoil, trefoil, turmoil • baby oil, castor oil, desert soil, drying oil, holy oil, hydrofoil, linseed oil, London broil, mineral oil, neat's-foot oil, olive oil, peanut oil, prairie soil, quatrefoil, rapeseed oil, safflower oil, salad oil, soybean oil • canola oil, coconut oil, cod-liver oil, cottonseed oil, induction coil, sesame oil, vegetable oil • burn the midnight oil

oilage \ȯi-lij\ soilage, spoilage

oile[1] \äl\ see AL[1]

oile[2] \ȯil\ see OIL

oiled \ȯild\ oiled • hard-boiled, soft-boiled, uncoiled, well-oiled
—*also* -ed *forms of verbs listed at* OIL

oiler \ȯi-lər\ boiler, broiler, spoiler, toiler • potboiler, steam boiler • double boiler

oiling \ȯi-liŋ\ boiling, broiling
—*also* -ing *forms of verbs listed at* OIL

oilus \ȯi-ləs\ see OYLESS

oin[1] \ȯin\ coin, groin, join, loin • adjoin, Burgoyne, conjoin, Des Moines, enjoin, purloin, rejoin, sirloin • tenderloin

oin[2] \aⁿ\ see IN[4]

oine \än\ see ON[1]

oines \ȯin\ see OIN[1]

oing[1] \ō-iŋ\ Boeing, going, knowing, rowing, sewing, showing • churchgoing, foregoing, freeflowing, glassblowing, mindblowing, ongoing, outgoing, seagoing • concertgoing, easygoing, moviegoing, oceangoing, theatergoing, thoroughgoing, whistle-blowing • to-ing and froing
—*also* -ing *forms of verbs listed at* OW[1]

oing[2] \ü-iŋ\ doing • undoing, wrongdoing • evildoing, nothing doing
—*also* -ing *forms of verbs listed at* EW[1]

oing[3] \ō-ən\ see OAN[1]

o-ing \ō-iŋ\ see OING[1]

oint[1] \ȯint\ joint, point • anoint, appoint, ballpoint, butt joint, checkpoint, clip joint, dew point, end point, flash point, grade point, gunpoint, hinge joint, hip joint, juke joint, knifepoint, lap joint, match point, midpoint, pen point, pinpoint, standpoint, viewpoint • at gunpoint, at knifepoint, boiling point, breaking point, brownie point, cardinal point, case in point, counterpoint, disappoint, focal point, freezing point, knuckle joint, melting point, miter joint, Montauk Point, needlepoint, out of joint, point-to-point, pressure point, sticking point, talking point, to the point, turning point, vantage point • beside the point, decimal point, percentage point, vanishing point

oint² \ant\ see ANT⁵

ointe \ant\ see ANT⁵

ointed \òint-əd\ jointed, pointed • disjointed, loose-jointed • disappointed, double-jointed, self-appointed, well-appointed
—*also* -ed *forms of verbs listed at* OINT¹

ointing \òin-tiŋ\ disappointing, finger-pointing
—*also* -ing *forms of verbs listed at* OINT¹

ointment \òint-mənt\ ointment • anointment, appointment • disappointment • fly in the ointment

oir¹ \īr\ see IRE¹

oir² \är\ see AR³

oir³ \òir\ see OYER

oir⁴ \òr\ see OR¹

oire¹ \är\ see AR³

oire² \òir\ see OYER

oire³ \òr\ see OR¹

ois¹ \ä\ see A¹

ois² \òi\ see OY

ois³ \òis\ see OICE

oise¹ \äz\ 'twas, vase, was • vichyssoise
—*also* -s, -'s, *and* -s' *forms of nouns and* -s *forms of verbs listed at* A¹

oise² \òiz\ noise, poise • turquoise, white noise

—*also* -s, -'s, *and* -s' *forms of nouns and* -s *forms of verbs listed at* OY

oise³ \òi-zē\ see OISY

oist \òist\ foist, hoist, joist, moist, voiced • unvoiced
—*also* -ed *forms of verbs listed at* OICE

oister \òi-stər\ cloister, oyster, roister • seed oyster

oisy \òi-zē\ Boise, noisy

oit¹ \òit\ adroit, Detroit, exploit

oit² \āt\ see ATE¹

oit³ \ō-ət\ see OET

oit⁴ \ä\ see A¹

oite \ät\ see OT¹

oiter \òit-ər\ goiter, loiter • Detroiter • reconnoiter

oivre \äv\ see OLVE¹

oix¹ \ä\ see A¹

oix² \òi\ see OY

oiz \òis\ see OISE²

ojan \ō-jən\ Trojan • theologian

ok¹ \äk\ see OCK¹

ok² \ək\ see UCK¹

ok³ \òk\ see ALK

oka \ō-kə\ see OCA

oke¹ \ōk\ bloke, broke, choke, cloak, coke, Coke, croak, folk, joke, oak, poke, Polk, smoke, soak, spoke, stoke, stroke, woke, yoke, yolk • ad hoc, awoke, backstroke, baroque, breaststroke, brushstroke, chain-smoke, convoke, cowpoke, downstroke, evoke, heatstroke, in-joke, invoke, keystroke, kinfolk, kinsfolk, live oak, menfolk, pin oak, presoak, provoke, red oak, revoke, scrub oak, sidestroke, slowpoke, sunstroke, townsfolk, upstroke, white oak • artichoke, Bolingbroke, fisherfolk, go for broke, masterstroke, okeydoke, poison oak, Roanoke, thunderstroke, womenfolk

oke² \ō-kē\ see OKY

oke[3] \ō\ see OW[1]

oke[4] \ùk\ see OOK[1]

okee \ō-kē\ see OKY

okel \ō-kəl\ see OCAL

oken \ō-kən\ broken, oaken, spoken, token, woken • awoken, betoken, heartbroken, housebroken, outspoken, plainspoken, soft-spoken, unbroken • by the same token

oker \ō-kər\ broker, croaker, joker, ocher, poker, smoker, stoker • chain-smoker, draw poker, pawnbroker, stockbroker, stud poker • mediocre, power broker, red-hot poker

okey \ō-kē\ see OKY

oki \ō-kē\ see OKY

oko \ō-kō\ see OCO

oky \ō-kē\ croaky, folkie, hokey, jokey, Loki, poky, smoky • Great Smoky • hokeypokey, karaoke • Okefenokee

ol[1] \ōl\ see OLE[1]

ol[2] \äl\ see AL[1]

ol[3] \ȯl\ see ALL[1]

ola \ō-lə\ cola, Lola • Angola, canola, Ebola, gondola, granola, Tortola, Victrola, viola, Viola • ayatollah, gladiola, Gorgonzola, Hispaniola, Osceola, Pensacola

olable \ō-lə-bəl\ see OLLABLE

olace \äl-əs\ see OLIS

olan \ō-lən\ see OLON

oland \ō-lənd\ see OWLAND

olar[1] \ō-lər\ see OLLER

olar[2] \äl-ər\ see OLLAR

olas \ō-ləs\ see OLUS

old[1] \ōld\ bold, bowled, cold, fold, gold, hold, mold, mould, old, scold, sold, soled, told • age-old, ahold, all told, behold, billfold, blindfold, blue mold, bread mold, choke hold, controlled, cuckold, eightfold, enfold, fivefold, fool's gold, foothold, foretold, fourfold, green mold, handhold, head cold,

household, ice-cold, knock cold, leaf mold, ninefold, on hold, potholed, scaffold, sheepfold, sixfold, slime mold, stone-cold, stronghold, take hold, tenfold, threefold, threshold, toehold, twofold, unfold, untold, uphold, withhold • centerfold, common cold, fingerhold, hundredfold, manifold, marigold, scissors hold, sevenfold, stranglehold, thousand-fold, throttlehold • as good as gold, blow hot and cold, lo and behold, marsh marigold, out in the cold

—*also* -ed *forms of verbs listed at* OLE[1]

old[2] \ȯld\ see ALD[1]

oldan \ōl-dən\ see OLDEN

olden \ōl-dən\ golden, olden • beholden, embolden

older[1] \ōl-dər\ boulder, folder, holder, shoulder, smolder • beholder, bondholder, cardholder, householder, jobholder, landholder, leaseholder, penholder, placeholder, pot holder, shareholder, slaveholder, stockholder, toolholder • officeholder, titleholder

—*also* -er *forms of adjectives listed at* OLD[1]

older[2] \äd-ər\ see ODDER

oldie \ōl-dē\ see OLDY

olding \ōl-diŋ\ folding, holding, molding, scolding • hand-holding, landholding, scaffolding, slaveholding

—*also* -ing *forms of verbs listed at* OLD[1]

oldster \ōl-stər\ see OLSTER

oldt \ōlt\ see OLT[1]

oldy \ōl-dē\ moldy, oldie • golden oldie

ole[1] \ōl\ bowl, coal, Cole, dole, droll, foal, goal, hole, knoll, mole, pole, Pole, poll, role, roll, scroll,

Seoul, shoal, sol, sole, soul, stole, stroll, toll, troll, vole, whole • airhole, armhole, atoll, bankroll, beanpole, bedroll, black hole, blowhole, bunghole, cajole, charcoal, console, control, creole, Creole, drumroll, egg roll, enroll, extol, eyehole, field goal, fishbowl, flagpole, foxhole, hard coal, half sole, hellhole, insole, keyhole, knothole, loophole, manhole, maypole, Mongol, Nicolle, North Pole, parole, patrol, payroll, peephole, pinhole, porthole, pothole, ridgepole, Sheol, ski pole, South Pole, spring roll, tadpole, unroll, washbowl, wormhole • buttonhole, camisole, casserole, coffee roll, cubbyhole, Dover sole, escarole, exit poll, finger hole, fumarole, honor roll, innersole, in the hole, Jackson Hole, jelly roll, kaiser roll, lemon sole, methanol, on the whole, oriole, ozone hole, pigeonhole, protocol, rabbit hole, rigmarole, rock and roll, Seminole, totem pole, water hole • ace in the hole, cholesterol, Costa del Sol, Haitian Creole, magnetic pole

ole² \ō-lē\ see OLY[1]

ole³ \ól\ see ALL[1]

olean \ō-lē-ən\ see OLIAN

oled \ōld\ see OLD[1]

oleful \ōl-fəl\ doleful, soulful

olely \ō-lē\ see OLY[1]

olemn \äl-əm\ see OLUMN

oleon \ō-lē-ən\ see OLIAN

oler¹ \ō-lər\ see OLLER

oler² \äl-ər\ see OLLAR

oless \ō-ləs\ see OLUS

oleum \ō-lē-əm\ see OLIUM

oley \ō-lē\ see OLY[1]

olf¹ \älf\ golf, Rolf • Adolph, Randolph, Rudolph, Lake Rudolf • miniature golf

olf² \əlf\ see ULF

olga \äl-gə\ Olga, Volga

oli \ō-lē\ see OLY[1]

olia \ō-lē-ə\ Mongolia • Anatolia, melancholia • Inner Mongolia, Outer Mongolia

olian \ō-lē-ən\ aeolian, Mongolian, napoleon, Napoleon, Tyrolean

olic \äl-ik\ colic, frolic, rollick • bucolic, symbolic, systolic • alcoholic, apostolic, chocoholic, diabolic, hyperbolic, melancholic, shopaholic, vitriolic, workaholic

olicking \ä-lik-iŋ\ frolicking, rollicking

olid \äl-əd\ solid, squalid, stolid • semisolid

olin¹ \äl-ən\ see OLLEN[5]

olin² \ō-lən\ see OLON

olis \äl-əs\ braless, solace, Wallace, Wallis • Cornwallis

olish \äl-ish\ polish • abolish, demolish • apple-polish, spit-and-polish

olity \äl-ət-ē\ see ALITY[1]

olium \ō-lē-əm\ linoleum, petroleum

olk¹ \elk\ see ELK[1]

olk² \ōk\ see OKE[1]

olk³ \əlk\ see ULK

olk⁴ \ók\ see ALK

olkie \ō-kē\ see OKY

olky \ō-kē\ see OKY

oll¹ \ōl\ see OLE[1]

oll² \äl\ see AL[1]

oll³ \ól\ see ALL[1]

olla¹ \äl-ə\ see ALA[2]

olla² \ói-ə\ see OIA

ollable \ō-lə-bəl\ controllable • inconsolable, uncontrollable

ollack \äl-ək\ see OLOCH

ollah¹ \ō-lə\ see OLA

ollah² \äl-ə\ see ALA[2]

ollah³ \əl-ə\ see ULLAH

ollar \äl-ər\ collar, dollar, holler, Mahler, scholar, squalor • bluecollar, dog collar, flea collar, halfdollar, sand dollar, shawl collar, top dollar, white-collar • Eurodollar, petrodollar • clerical collar

ollard \äl-ərd\ collard, collared, hollered

olled \ōld\ see OLD[1]

ollee \ō-lē\ see OLY[1]

ollege \äl-ij\ see OWLEDGE

ollen[1] \ō-lən\ see OLON

ollen[2] \əl-ə\ see ULLAH

ollen[3] \əl-ən\ see ULLEN

ollen[4] \ö-lən\ see ALLEN

ollen[5] \äl-ən\ Colin, pollen

oller \ō-lər\ bowler, molar, polar, poller, roller, solar, stroller • bankroller, comptroller, controller, high roller, logroller, steamroller • rock and roller

ollet \äl-ət\ wallet • whatchamacallit

ollett \äl-ət\ see OLLET

olley \äl-ē\ see OLLY[1]

ollick \äl-ik\ see OLIC

ollicking \ä-lik-iŋ\ see OLICKING

ollie \äl-ē\ see OLLY[1]

ollin \äl-ən\ see OLLEN[5]

olling \ō-liŋ\ bowling • highrolling, logrolling • exit polling —*also* -ing *forms of verbs listed at* OLE[1]

ollis \äl-əs\ see OLIS

ollity \äl-ət-ē\ see ALITY[1]

ollo \äl-ō\ see OLLOW[1]

ollop \äl-əp\ dollop, polyp, scallop, trollop, wallop • bay scallop, sea scallop

ollow[1] \äl-ō\ follow, hollow, swallow, wallow • Apollo, barn swallow, cliff swallow, tree swallow

ollow[2] \äl-ə\ see ALA[2]

ollower \äl-ə-wər\ follower, wallower • camp follower

ollster \ōl-stər\ see OLSTER

olly[1] \äl-ē\ Bali, Cali, collie, Dalí, dolly, folly, golly, Halle, holly, jolly, Mali, Molly, Ollie, Polly, Raleigh, trolley, volley • Denali, finale, Kigali, Nepali, Somali,

Svengali, tamale • melancholy, Mexicali

olly[2] \ō-lē\ see AWLY

olm \ōm\ see OME[1]

olman \ōl-mən\ dolmen • patrolman

olmen \ōl-mən\ see OLMAN

olmes \ōmz\ Holmes —*also* -s, -'s, *and* -s' *forms of nouns and* -s *forms of verbs listed at* OME[1]

olo \ō-lō\ bolo, polo, solo • Marco Polo, water polo

oloch \äl-ək\ Moloch, rowlock

ologist \äl-ə-jəst\ biologist, ecologist, gemologist, geologist, mythologist, neurologist, oncologist, psychologist, seismologist, zoologist • anthropologist, archaeologist, cardiologist, climatologist, cosmetologist, dermatologist, Egyptologist, entomologist, immunologist, musicologist, ophthalmologist, ornithologist

ology \äl-ə-jē\ anthology, apology, astrology, biology, chronology, cosmology, doxology, ecology, geology, mythology, pathology, psychology, seismology, technology, theology, zoology • anthropology, archaeology, cardiology, climatology, cosmetology, criminology, dermatology, Egyptology, etymology, genealogy, ideology, immunology, methodology, mineralogy, musicology, numerology, ophthalmology, ornithology, pharmacology, physiology, Scientology, sociology, terminology • microbiology, nanotechnology, paleontology

olon \ō-lən\ bowline, Colin, colon, Nolan, stolen, swollen • semicolon

olonel \ərn-əl\ see ERNAL

olonist \äl-ə-nəst\ colonist, Stalinist

olor[1] \ō-lər\ see OLLER

olor[2] \äl-ər\ see OLLAR

olored \əl-ərd\ colored, dullard • tricolored

olp \ōp\ see OPE

olph \älf\ see OLF[1]

olster \ōl-stər\ bolster, holster, oldster, pollster • upholster

olt[1] \ōlt\ bolt, colt, dolt, jolt, molt, volt • dead bolt, revolt, spring bolt, unbolt • thunderbolt

olt[2] \ólt\ see ALT

olta \äl-tə\ see ALTA

oltish \ōl-tish\ coltish, doltish

oluble \äl-yə-bəl\ soluble, voluble • insoluble • indissoluble

olumn \äl-əm\ column, slalom, solemn • fifth column • giant slalom, spinal column, steering column

olus \ō-ləs\ snowless, toeless • gladiolus

olve[1] \älv\ salve, solve • absolve, devolve, dissolve, evolve, involve, resolve, revolve

olve[2] \äv\ of, salve, Slav, suave • Gustav, thereof, whereof • Stanislav, unheard-of, well-thought-of, Yugoslav

oly[1] \ō-lē\ goalie, holy, lowly, mole, slowly, solely • cannoli, frijole, unholy • guacamole, ravioli, rolypoly

oly[2] \äl-ē\ see OLLY[1]

olyp \äl-əp\ see OLLOP

om[1] \äm\ balm, bomb, calm, from, Guam, mom, palm, prom, psalm, qualm, tom • A-bomb, aplomb, ashram, becalm, bee balm, buzz bomb, car bomb, dive-bomb, dotcom, embalm, firebomb, grande dame, H-bomb, imam, Islam, napalm, noncom, phenom, pogrom, pom-pom, salaam, sitcom, stink bomb, therefrom, time bomb, tom-tom, wigwam • atom bomb, cardamom, CD-ROM, cherry bomb, cluster bomb, diatom, intercom, lemon balm, letter bomb, neutron bomb, Peeping Tom, royal palm, sago palm, soccer mom, supermom, telecom, Uncle Tom, Vietnam • atomic bomb, coconut palm, Dar es Salaam, hydrogen bomb, Omar Khayyám

om[2] \ōm\ see OME[1]

om[3] \üm\ see OOM[1]

om[4] \əm\ see UM[1]

om[5] \ùm\ see UM[2]

om[6] \óm\ see AUM[1]

oma \ō-mə\ chroma, coma, Roma • aroma, diploma, glaucoma, lymphoma, Tacoma • carcinoma, melanoma, Oklahoma[2]

omac \ō-mik\ see OMIC[2]

omace \äm-əs\ see OMISE

omaly \äm-ə-lē\ homily • anomaly

oman \ō-mən\ bowman, foeman, omen, Roman, showman, snowman, yeoman

omany \äm-ə-nē\ see OMINY

omas \äm-əs\ see OMISE

omb[1] \ōm\ see OME[1]

omb[2] \üm\ see OOM[1]

omb[3] \äm\ see OM[1]

omb[4] \əm\ see UM[1]

omba \äm-bə\ see AMBA

ombe[1] \ōm\ see OME[1]

ombe[2] \üm\ see OOM[1]

ombe[3] \äm\ see OM[1]

ombed \ümd\ see OOMED

omber[1] \äm-ər\ bomber • divebomber, embalmer

omber[2] \ō-mər\ see OMER[1]

ombic \ō-mik\ see OMIC[2]

ombie \äm-bē\ zombie • Abercrombie

ombing \ō-miŋ\ see OAMING

ombo[1] \äm-bō\ combo, mambo

ombo[2] \əm-bō\ see UMBO

ombre \äm-bər\ see OMBER[2]

ome[1] \ōm\ chrome, comb, dome, foam, gnome, home, loam, ohm, poem, roam, Rome, tome • at-home, beachcomb, bring home, Cape Nome, down-home, genome, hot comb, Jerome, rest home, rhizome, shalom, Stockholm, syndrome • catacomb, chromosome, close to home, Down syndrome, fine-tooth comb, foster home, funeral home, honeycomb, metronome, mobile home, monochrome, motor home, nursing home, onion dome, polychrome, Reye's syndrome, soldiers' home, stay-at-home, Styrofoam • detention home, Mercurochrome, X chromosome, Y chromosome

ome² \ō-mē\ see OAMY

ome³ \əm\ see UM¹

omely \əm-lē\ see UMBLY²

omen \ō-mən\ see OMAN

omenal \äm-ən-ᵊl\ see OMINAL

omene \äm-ə-nē\ see OMINY

omer¹ \ō-mər\ homer, Homer, roamer • beachcomber, misnomer

omer² \əm-ər\ see UMMER

omery \əm-ə-rē\ see UMMERY

omet \äm-ət\ comet, grommet, vomit

ometer \äm-ət-ər\ barometer, chronometer, kilometer, micrometer, odometer, pedometer, speedometer, tachometer, thermometer

ometry \äm-ə-trē\ geometry, optometry • plane geometry, trigonometry

omey \ō-mē\ see OAMY

omi \ō-mē\ see OAMY

omic¹ \äm-ik\ comic • atomic, Islamic • anatomic, diatomic, economic, ergonomic, gastronomic, metronomic, subatomic, tragicomic

omic² \ō-mik\ gnomic • Potomac

omical \äm-i-kəl\ comical

• anatomical, astronomical, economical

omics \äm-iks\ comics • economics, ergonomics • home economics

omily \äm-ə-lē\ see OMALY

ominal \äm-ən-ᵊl\ nominal • abdominal, phenomenal

ominance \äm-nəns\ dominance, prominence • predominance

ominant \äm-nənt\ dominant, prominent • predominant

omine \äm-ə-nē\ see OMINY

ominence \äm-nəns\ see OMINANCE

ominent \äm-nənt\ see OMINANT

oming¹ \əm-iŋ\ coming, numbing, plumbing • becoming, forthcoming, have coming, homecoming, incoming, mind-numbing, oncoming, shortcoming, upcoming • Second Coming, unbecoming, up-and-coming
—*also* -ing *forms of verbs listed at* UM¹

oming² \ō-miŋ\ see OAMING

omini \äm-ə-nē\ see OMINY

ominy \äm-ə-nē\ hominy • ignominy • anno Domini

omise \äm-əs\ pomace, promise, Thomas • Saint Thomas • breach of promise, doubting Thomas • lick and a promise

omit \äm-ət\ see OMET

omma \äm-ə\ see AMA²

ommel¹ \äm-əl\ pommel, Rommel

ommel² \əm-əl\ pommel, pummel • Beau Brummell

ommet \äm-ət\ see OMET

ommie \äm-ē\ see AMI¹

ommon \äm-ən\ Brahman, common, shaman • in common • Tutankhamen

ommy¹ \äm-ē\ see AMI¹

ommy² \əm-ē\ see UMMY

omo \ō-mō\ Como, promo • major-domo

omon \ō-mən\ see OMAN

omp¹ \ämp\ champ, chomp, clomp,

pomp, romp, stamp, stomp,
swamp, tramp, tromp, whomp
omp² \əmp\ see UMP
ompass \əm-pəs\ compass, rumpus
• encompass
omper \äm-pər\ romper, stamper,
stomper
ompey \äm-pē\ see OMPY
ompt \aûnt\ see OUNT²
ompy \äm-pē\ Pompey, swampy
on¹ \än\ ban, Bonn, con, dawn,
don, Don, drawn, faun, fawn,
gone, John, Jon, khan, on, pawn,
prawn, Ron, spawn, swan, wan,
yawn, yon, yuan • aeon, add-on,
Amman, anon, Anton, argon,
Argonne, Aswan, Avon, bank on,
baton, big on, bonbon, boron,
bouillon, bring on, build on,
bygone, caisson, call on, catch on,
Ceylon, chevron, chew on, chif-
fon, chignon, clip-on, come-on,
cordon, coupon, crampon,
crayon, crouton, Dacron, dead-
on, Dear John, doggone, dog-
goned, Don Juan, eon, far-gone,
foregone, Freon, futon, Gibran,
Golan, go on, hand on, hands-on,
hang on, head-on, high on, hit on,
hogan, hold on, Hunan, icon,
Inchon, ion, Ivan, jargon, keen
on, krypton, Leon, let on, lock
on, log on, look on, Luzon, Milan, moron, neon, neuron, neutron, Nippon, nylon, odds-on,
Oman, Orlon, pecan, peon, pho-
ton, pick on, piton, plankton,
pompon, proton, Pusan, put-on,
pylon, python, Qur'an, radon, rag
on, rayon, right-on, Saint John,
Saipan, salon, San Juan, shaman,
sign on, sit on, slip-on, snap-on,
solon, spot on, stand on, stuck on,
sweet on, Szechwan, Taiwan, take
on, Teflon, Tehran, toucan, Tristan, try on, Tucson, turned-on,
turn on, upon, wait on, walk-on,

wonton, work on, Yukon,
Yvonne, zircon • Abidjan, aileron,
amazon, Amazon, and so on,
Aragon, autobahn, Avalon, Baby-
lon, Barbizon, bear down on, beat
up on, biathlon, call upon, caril-
lon, carry-on, carry on, check up
on, come upon, cyclotron, decathlon, early on, echelon, elec-
tron, epsilon, fall back on,
Fuji-san, Genghis Khan, go back
on, going on, goings-on, Grand
Teton, hanger-on, helicon, hexa-
gon, hold out on, Kazakhstan,
Kublai Khan, Kyrgyzstan, Lake
Huron, lay eyes on, Lebanon,
leprechaun, lexicon, liaison, load
up on, make good on, marathon,
marzipan, mastodon, miss out on,
myrmidon, octagon, off and on,
omicron, Oregon, Pakistan, pan-
theon, paragon, Parmesan,
Parthenon, pentagon, pentathlon,
Phaethon, pick up on, polygon,
put-upon, Ramadan, ride herd on,
Rubicon, run low on, set eyes on,
set foot on, silicon, sneak up on,
talkathon, Teheran, telethon,
triathlon, undergone, upsilon,
walkathon, walk out on, whereupon, woebegone • Agamemnon,
automaton, Azerbaijan,
Bellerophon, emoticon, get a
move on, keep an eye on, oxy-
moron, phenomenon, pteran-
odon, Saskatchewan, set one's
heart on, set one's sights on, sine
qua non, t'ai chi ch'uan, take it
out on, turn one's back on, zoo-
plankton • a leg to stand on, put
one's finger on, throw cold water
on, ultramarathon
on² \ō^n\ fond, ton • baton, bouillon, Dijon, Gabon, Lyon, salon
• filet mignon
on³ \ȯn\ Bonn, brawn, dawn,
Dawn, drawn, faun, fawn, gone,

lawn, on, pawn, prawn, Sean, spawn, Vaughn, won, yawn • add-on, Argonne, begone, bygone, clip-on, come-on, dead-on, dog-gone, far-gone, foregone, hands-on, head-on, odds-on, put-on, Quezon, run-on, slip-on, snap-on, turned-on, turn-on, turn on, upon, walk-on, whereon, with-drawn • Ben-Gurion, carry-on, goings-on, hanger-on, leprechaun, put-upon, undergone, whereupon, woebegone

on⁴ \ōn\ see ONE¹

on⁵ \ən\ see UN¹

ona¹ \ō-nə\ Jonah, Mona • bologna, Bologna, corona, kimono, Leona, Pamplona, persona, Pomona, Ramona, Verona • Arizona, Barcelona, Desdemona

ona² \än-ə\ see ANA¹

oña \ōn-yə\ see ONIA²

onachal \än-i-kəl\ see ONICAL

onae \ō-nē\ see ONY¹

onah \ō-nə\ see ONA¹

onal \ōn-ᵊl\ tonal, zonal • hormonal

onald \än-ᵊld\ Donald, Ronald • MacDonald

onant \ō-nənt\ see ONENT

onas \ō-nəs\ see ONUS²

onc \äŋk\ see ONK¹

once¹ \äns\ see ANCE²

once² \əns\ see UNCE

onch¹ \äŋk\ see ONK¹

onch² \änch\ see AUNCH¹

oncha \äŋ-kə\ see ANKA

oncho \än-chō\ honcho, poncho, rancho

onco \äŋ-kō\ bronco, Franco

ond¹ \änd\ blond, bond, fond, frond, pond, wand • abscond, ash-blond, beyond, fishpond, gourmand, junk bond, millpond, respond • bottle blond, corre-spond, savings bond, vagabond, Walden Pond • back of beyond,

slough of despond, strawberry blond
—*also* -ed *forms of verbs listed at* ON¹

ond² \ōⁿ\ see ON²

ond³ \ȯnt\ see AUNT¹

onda \än-də\ Fonda, Honda, Rhonda, Wanda • Golconda, Rwanda, Uganda • anaconda

ondant \än-dənt\ see ONDENT

onday \ən-dē\ see UNDI

ondays \ən-dēz\ see UNDAYS

ondda \än-də\ see ONDA

onde \änd\ see OND¹

ondeau \än-dō\ see ONDO

ondent \än-dənt\ despondent, respondent • correspondent

onder¹ \än-dər\ condor, maunder, ponder, squander, wander, yonder • responder, transponder
—*also* -er *forms of adjectives listed at* OND¹

onder² \ən-dər\ see UNDER

ondly \än-lē\ see ANLY

ondo \än-dō\ condo, rondo • glissando • accelerando

ondor \än-dər\ see ONDER¹

ondrous \ən-drəs\ see UNDEROUS

one¹ \ōn\ blown, bone, clone, cone, crone, drone, flown, groan, grown, hone, Joan, known, loan, lone, moan, mown, own, phone, prone, Rhône, roan, Saône, scone, sewn, shone, shown, sown, stone, throne, thrown, tone, zone • alone, atone, backbone, be-moan, birthstone, bloodstone, bluestone, breastbone, brimstone, brownstone, calzone, Capone, cell phone, cheekbone, cologne, Cologne, colon, Colón, condone, corn pone, curbstone, cyclone, dethrone, dial tone, disown, drop zone, earphone, earth tone, end zone, enthrone, fieldstone, fire-stone, flagstone, flyblown, full-blown, gallstone, gemstone, gravestone, grindstone, hailstone, handblown, headphone, headstone, hearthstone, high-flown, hip bone, homegrown, hormone, ingrown, in stone, intone, jawbone, keystone, limestone, lodestone, long bone, milestone, millstone, moonstone, nose cone, outgrown, outshone, ozone, pay phone, pinecone, postpone, Ramon, rhinestone, sandstone, shinbone, Shoshone, snow cone, soapstone, strike zone, T-bone, tailbone, thighbone, time zone, tombstone, touchstone, touchtone, trombone, turnstone, twotone, Tyrone, unknown, war zone, well-known, whalebone, whetstone, windblown, wishbone • anklebone, Barbizon, baritone, buffer zone, Canal Zone, chaperon, cinder cone, cobblestone, collarbone, comfort zone, cornerstone, cortisone, crazy bone, cuttlebone, Dictaphone, free-fire zone, frigid zone, funny bone, gramophone, growth hormone, herringbone, hold one's own, ice-cream cone, kidney stone, knucklebone, leave alone, let alone, megaphone, microphone, minestrone, monotone, neutral zone, on one's own, overblown, overgrown, overthrown, overtone, Picturephone, provolone, saxophone, silicone, sousaphone, speakerphone, stand-alone, stepping-stone, telephone, temperate zone, torrid zone, traffic cone, twilight zone, undertone, vibraphone, xylophone, Yellowstone • accident-prone, Asunción, close to the bone, eau de cologne, fire-and-brimstone, radiophone, Rosetta stone, sine qua non, strawberry roan, testosterone, videophone • philosopher's stone, Ponce de León, Sierra Leone

one[2] \ō-nē\ see ONY[1]

one[3] \än\ see ON[1]

one[4] \ən\ see UN[1]

one[5] \ón\ see ON[3]

onean \ō-nē-ən\ see ONIAN[1]

oned[1] \ōnd\ boned, toned • earth-toned, high-toned, pre-owned, rawboned, two-toned • cobble-stoned
—*also* -ed *forms of verbs listed at* ONE[1]

oned[2] \än\ see ON[1]

onely \ōn-lē\ lonely, only • eyes-only

onement \ōn-mənt\ atonement, postponement • Day of Atonement

onent \ō-nənt\ component, exponent, opponent, proponent

oneous \ō-nē-əs\ see ONIOUS

oner[1] \ō-nər\ boner, cloner, donor, groaner, loaner, loner, owner, stoner • landowner, shipowner • telephoner

oner[2] \ón-ər\ see AWNER[1]

onerous \än-ə-rəs\ onerous, sonorous

ones \ōnz\ Jones • bare-bones, Dow Jones • Davy Jones, lazy-bones, make no bones • skull and crossbones
—*also* -s, -'s, *and* -s' *forms of nouns and* -s *forms of verbs listed at* ONE[1]

oney[1] \ō-nē\ see ONY[1]

oney[2] \ən-ē\ see UNNY

oney[3] \ü-nē\ see OONY

ong[1] \äŋ\ gong, prong, tong • Da Nang, Hong Kong, Mah-Jongg, Mekong, ping-pong, sarong • billabong, Pyongyang, Sturm und Drang, Vietcong

ong[2] \óŋ\ bong, gong, long, prong, song, strong, thong, throng, tong, wrong • along, Armstrong, belong, birdsong, chaise longue, daylong, ding-dong, dugong, fight

song, folk song, furlong,
Haiphong, headlong, headstrong,
Hong Kong, hour-long, lifelong,
livelong, Mekong, monthlong,
nightlong, oblong, part-song,
Ping-Pong, prolong, sarong, side-
long, singsong, so long, swan
song, theme song, torch song,
weeklong, work song, yearlong
• all along, before long, billabong,
come along, cradlesong, drinking
song, get along, go along, run
along, sing-along, siren song,
string along, summerlong, taga-
long, Vietcong

ong³ \əŋ\ see UNG¹

ong⁴ \ùng\ see UNG²

onga \äŋ-gə\ conga, Tonga
• chimichanga

onge \ənj\ see UNGE

onged \òŋd\ pronged, wronged
• multipronged
—*also* -ed *forms of verbs listed at*
ONG²

onger¹ \əŋ-gər\ hunger, younger
• fearmonger, fishmonger, scare-
monger, warmonger • gossipmon-
ger, rumormonger,
scandalmonger

onger² \ən-jər\ see UNGER¹

ongery \əŋ-grē\ hungry • ironmon-
gery

ongful \òŋ-fəl\ wrongful, songful

ongish \òŋ-ish\ longish, strongish

ongo \äŋ-gō\ bongo, Congo • Belgian Congo, Pago Pago

ongous \əŋ-gəs\ see UNGOUS

ongue¹ \əŋ\ see UNG¹

ongue² \òŋ\ see ONG²

ongy \ən-jē\ see UNGY

onhomous \än-ə-məs\ see ONYMOUS

oni \ō-nē\ see ONY¹

onia¹ \ō-nē-ə\ Estonia, Franconia,
Laconia, Slavonia, zirconia
• Amazonia, Babylonia, Caledonia, Catalonia, Macedonia, Patagonia • New Caledonia

onia² \ō-nyə\ doña, Sonia • ammo-
nia, begonia, Bologna, Estonia,
Franconia, Laconia, pneumonia,
Slavonia • Babylonia, Caledonia,
Catalonia, Macedonia, Patagonia
• double pneumonia, New Caledonia, walking pneumonia

onial \ō-nē-əl\ baronial, colonial
• ceremonial, Dutch Colonial,
matrimonial, testimonial

onian¹ \ō-nē-ən\ Bostonian, dra-
conian, Estonian, Houstonian,
Jacksonian, Miltonian, Newtonian, Wilsonian • Amazonian,
Arizonian, Babylonian, calypson-
ian, Catalonian, Ciceronian,
Emersonian, Hamiltonian, Jeffersonian, Macedonian, Oregonian,
Patagonian, Washingtonian

onian² \ō-nyən\ Bostonian, Eston-
ian, Franconian, Houstonian,
Miltonian, Newtonian, Nixonian,
Slavonian • Amazonian, Arizon-
ian, Babylonian, Ciceronian,
Emersonian, Jeffersonian, Mace-
donian, Oregonian, Patagonian,
Washingtonian

onic \än-ik\ chronic, conic, phonic,
sonic, tonic • bionic, bubonic,
cyclonic, demonic, harmonic,
iconic, Ionic, ironic, laconic,
Masonic, mnemonic, moronic,
planktonic, platonic, sardonic,
Slavonic, subsonic, symphonic,
tectonic, Teutonic • catatonic,
electronic, embryonic, histrionic,
Housatonic, philharmonic, poly-
phonic, quadraphonic, super-
sonic, ultrasonic • stereophonic

onica \än-i-kə\ Monica • harmonica, Veronica • electronica, glass
harmonica, Santa Monica, Thes-
salonica

onical \än-i-kəl\ chronicle, conical,
monocle • canonical

onicle \än-i-kəl\ see ONICAL

onics \än-iks\ onyx, phonics

• bionics, tectonics • electronics,
plate tectonics
—*also* -s, -'s, *and* -s' *forms of
nouns listed at* ONIC
onika \än-i-kə\ see ONICA
oning[1] \än-iŋ\ awning
—*also* -ing *forms of verbs listed at*
ON[1]
oning[2] \ō-niŋ\ jawboning,
landowning
—*also* -ing *forms of verbs listed at*
ONE[1]
onion \ən-yən\ see UNION
onious \ō-nē-əs\ Antonius, erro-
neous, felonious, harmonious,
Petronius, Polonius • acrimo-
nious, ceremonious, parsimo-
nious, sanctimonious
• unceremonious
onis[1] \ō-nəs\ see ONUS[2]
onis[2] \än-əs\ see ONUS[1]
onish \än-ish\ admonish, astonish
• leprechaunish
onishment \än-ish-mənt\ admon-
ishment, astonishment
onium \ō-nē-əm\ euphonium,
plutonium • pandemonium, Pandemonium
onius \ō-nē-əs\ see ONIOUS
onja \ō-nyə\ see ONIA[2]
onk[1] \äŋk\ bonk, bronc, conch,
conk, honk, plonk, wonk, zonk
• honky-tonk
onk[2] \əŋk\ see UNK
onkey[1] \äŋ-kē\ see ONKY
onkey[2] \əŋ-kē\ see UNKY
onky \äŋ-kē\ donkey, wonky,
yanqui
onless \ən-ləs\ see UNLESS
only \ōn-lē\ see ONELY
onment \ōn-mənt\ see ONEMENT
onn[1] \än\ see ON[1]
onn[2] \ȯn\ see ON[3]
onna[1] \ȯn-ə\ Donna, fauna, sauna
• prima donna
onna[2] \än-ə\ see ANA[1]
onne[1] \än\ see ON[1]

onne[2] \ən\ see UN[1]
onne[3] \ȯn\ see ON[3]
onner \än-ər\ see ONOR[1]
onnet \än-ət\ bonnet, sonnet
• bluebonnet, sunbonnet, warbon-
net • bee in one's bonnet
onnie \än-ē\ see ANI[1]
onnish \än-ish\ see ONISH
onnor \än-ər\ see ONOR[1]
onny[1] \än-ē\ see ANI[1]
onny[2] \ən-ē\ see UNNY
ono[1] \ō-nō\ kimono, pro bono
ono[2] \ō-nə\ see ONA[1]
ono[3] \än-ō\ see ANO[1]
onocle \än-i-kəl\ see ONICAL
onomist \än-ə-məst\ agronomist,
economist • home economist
onomous \än-ə-məs\ see ONYMOUS
onomy \än-ə-mē\ agronomy, as-
tronomy, autonomy, economy,
gastronomy, taxonomy
• Deuteronomy
onor[1] \än-ər\ goner, honor, yawner
• dishonor, O'Connor • Afrikaner,
maid of honor, marathoner, point
of honor, weimaraner • Legion of
Honor, matron of honor, Medal
of Honor
onor[2] \ō-nər\ see ONER[1]
onorous \än-ə-rəs\ see ONEROUS
ons[1] \änz\ see ONZE
ons[2] \ō^n\ see ON[2]
onsil \än-səl\ see ONSUL
onsin \än-sən\ see OHNSON
onson \än-sən\ see OHNSON
onsul \än-səl\ consul, tonsil • pro-
consul
ont[1] \ənt\ blunt, brunt, bunt, front,
grunt, hunt, punt, runt, shunt,
stunt, want • affront, beachfront,
cold front, confront, forefront,
home front, lakefront, manhunt,
shorefront, storefront, up-front,
warm front, witch hunt • battle-
front, oceanfront, riverfront,
waterfront • scavenger hunt
ont[2] \änt\ see ANT[2]

ont[3] \ònt\ see AUNT[1]

on't \ōnt\ don't, won't

ontal[1] \änt-ᵊl\ horizontal • periodontal

ontal[2] \ǝnt-ᵊl\ see UNTLE

ontas \änt-ǝs\ see ONTUS

onte[1] \änt-ē\ see ANTI[1]

onte[2] \än-tā\ see ANTE[1]

onted \ònt-ǝd\ vaunted, wonted
• undaunted
—*also* -ed *forms of verbs listed at*
AUNT[1]

onter \ǝnt-ǝr\ see UNTER

onth \ǝnth\ month • billionth,
millionth, trillionth, twelvemonth
• gazillionth

ontil \änt-ᵊl\ see ONTAL[1]

onto \än-tō\ see ANTO

ontra \än-trǝ\ contra, mantra

ontre \änt-ǝr\ see AUNTER[1]

ontus \änt-ǝs\ Pontus • Pocahontas

onty \änt-ē\ see ANTI[1]

onus[1] \än-ǝs\ Cronus, Faunus
• Adonis

onus[2] \ō-nǝs\ bonus, Cronus,
Jonas, onus, slowness • Adonis

ony[1] \ō-nē\ bony, coney, crony,
phony, pony, Sony, stony, Toni,
Tony • baloney, bologna, cow
pony, Giorgione, Marconi, Moroni, Shoshone, spumoni, tortoni
• abalone, acrimony, alimony,
ceremony, hegemony, macaroni,
matrimony, minestrone, one-trick
pony, patrimony, pepperoni,
provolone, sanctimony, Shetland
pony, testimony, zabaglione
• phony-baloney • dramatis personae

ony[2] \än-ē\ see ANI[1]

onya \ō-nyǝ\ see ONIA[2]

onymist \än-ǝ-mǝst\ see ONOMIST

onymous \än-ǝ-mǝs\ anonymous,
autonomous, synonymous

onymy \än-ǝ-mē\ see ONOMY

onyon \ǝn-yǝn\ see UNION

onyx \än-iks\ see ONICS

onze \änz\ bronze • long johns,
Saint John's • Afrikaans
—*also* -s, -'s, *and* -s' *forms of
nouns and* -s *forms of verbs listed
at* ON[1]

oo[1] \ü\ see EW[1]

oo[2] \ō\ see OW[1]

oob \üb\ see UBE

oober \ü-bǝr\ see UBER

ooby \ü-bē\ booby, ruby, Ruby

ooch[1] \üch\ brooch, mooch,
pooch, smooch

ooch[2] \ōch\ see OACH

oocher \ü-chǝr\ see UTURE

oochy \ü-chē\ smoochy • penuche,
Vespucci

ood[1] \ùd\ good, hood, should,
stood, wood, would • basswood,
boxwood, boyhood, brushwood,
childhood, cordwood, corkwood,
deadwood, dogwood, driftwood,
falsehood, feel-good, firewood,
for good, girlhood, greenwood,
hardwood, heartwood, ironwood,
knighthood, make good, manhood, Mount Hood, no-good,
pinewood, plywood, priesthood,
pulpwood, redwood, rosewood,
sainthood, Sherwood, softwood,
statehood, stinkwood, Talmud,
Wedgwood, wifehood, withstood,
wormwood • adulthood, bachelorhood, brotherhood, candlewood, cedarwood, cottonwood,
fatherhood, Hollywood, knock on
wood, likelihood, livelihood,
maidenhood, motherhood, neighborhood, parenthood, Robin
Hood, sandalwood, sisterhood, to
the good, tulipwood, understood,
widowhood, womanhood • blood
brotherhood, grandparenthood,
misunderstood, second childhood,
unlikelihood

ood[2] \ōd\ see ODE

ood[3] \üd\ see UDE[1]

ood[4] \ǝd\ see UD[1]

ooded[1] \əd-əd\ blue-blooded, cold-blooded, full-blooded, half-blooded, hot-blooded, pure-blooded, red-blooded, star-studded, warm-blooded
—*also* -ed *forms of verbs listed at* UD[1]

ooded[2] \ùd-əd\ hooded, wooded

ooder[1] \üd-ər\ see UDER

ooder[2] \əd-ər\ see UDDER

oodle \üd-ᵊl\ doodle, feudal, noodle, poodle, strudel • caboodle, canoodle, toy poodle • Yankee-Doodle

oodoo \üd-ü\ doo-doo, hoodoo, kudu, voodoo • in deep doo-doo

oods \ùdz\ hoods • backwoods, dry goods, piece goods, white goods • bill of goods, piney woods • consumer goods, Lake of the Woods • deliver the goods
—*also* -s, -'s, *and* -s' *forms of nouns listed at* OOD[1]

oodsman \ùdz-mən\ woodsman • backwoodsman, ombudsman

oody[1] \üd-ē\ broody, Judy, moody, Rudy, Trudy

oody[2] \ùd-ē\ goody, hoody, woody

oody[3] \əd-ē\ see UDDY[1]

ooer \ü-ər\ see EWER[1]

ooey \ü-ē\ see EWY

oof[1] \üf\ goof, hoof, poof, proof, roof, spoof, woof • aloof, bombproof, childproof, crushproof, fireproof, flameproof, foolproof, forehoof, germproof, greaseproof, heatproof, leakproof, lightproof, moonroof, pickproof, rainproof, reproof, rustproof, shockproof, soundproof, stainproof, sunroof, windproof • bulletproof, burglarproof, gable roof, gambrel roof, hit the roof, ovenproof, shatterproof, tamperproof, through the roof, waterproof, weatherproof • burden of proof, idiotproof

oof[2] \ùf\ hoof, poof, roof, woof

• moon roof • cloven hoof, gable roof, gambrel roof, hit the roof, through the roof

oof[3] \ōf\ see OAF

oof[4] \üv\ see OVE[3]

oofer[1] \ü-fər\ roofer, twofer

oofer[2] \ùf-ər\ roofer, woofer

oofy \ü-fē\ goofy, Sufi

ooga \ü-gə\ see UGA

ooge \üj\ see UGE[1]

ooger \ùg-ər\ see UGUR

oogie \ùg-ē\ bogey, boogie • boogie-woogie

oo-goo \ü-gü\ see UGU

ooh \ü\ see EW[1]

ooi \ü-ē\ see EWY

ooist \ü-əst\ doest • tattooist, voodooist
—*also* -est *forms of adjectives listed at* EW[1]

ook[1] \ùk\ book, brook, cook, Cook, crook, hook, look, nook, rook, shook, took • bankbook, checkbook, cookbook, e-book, forsook, fishhook, guidebook, handbook, hymnbook, Innsbruck, logbook, matchbook, mistook, Mount Cook, notebook, outlook, partook, phrase book, pothook, prayer book, schoolbook, scrapbook, sketchbook, songbook, stylebook, textbook, unhook, wordbook, workbook, yearbook • buttonhook, comic book, donnybrook, grappling hook, inglenook, off the hook, overlook, overtook, picture book, pocketbook, pocket book, pressure-cook, pruning hook, Sandy Hook, storybook, talking book, tenterhook, undertook • audiobook, coloring book, gobbledygook, ring off the hook, telephone book • by hook or by crook

ook[2] \ük\ see UKE

ooka \ü-kə\ yuca • bazooka, palooka

ooke \ùk\ see OOK[1]

ooker \ùk-ər\ booker, cooker, looker, snooker • good-looker, onlooker • pressure cooker

ookery \ùk-ə-rē\ cookery, rookery

ookie \ùk-ē\ bookie, cookie, hooky, rookie • fortune cookie

ooking \ùk-iŋ\ booking, cooking • good-looking • forward-looking, solid-looking
—also -ing forms of verbs listed at OOK[1]

ooklet \ùk-lət\ booklet, brooklet

ooks[1] \üks\ deluxe
—also -s, -'s, and -s' forms of nouns and -s forms of verbs listed at UKE

ooks[2] \ùks\ Brooks, crux, looks • deluxe • on tenterhooks
—also -s, -'s, and -s' forms of nouns and -s forms of verbs listed at OOK[1]

ooky[1] \ü-kē\ kooky, spooky • bouzouki, Kabuki

ooky[2] \ùk-ē\ see OOKIE

ool[1] \ül\ cool, drool, fool, fuel, ghoul, mule, pool, rule, school, spool, stool, tool, you'll, yule • air-cool, B-school, carpool, church school, cesspool, day school, edge tool, footstool, gene pool, grade school, high school, homeschool, Kabul, misrule, Mosul, old school, prep school, preschool, refuel, retool, self-rule, step stool, synfuel, tide pool, toadstool, trade school, uncool, unspool, whirlpool • April fool, blow one's cool, boarding school, charter school, ducking stool, grammar school, Istanbul, Liverpool, machine tool, magnet school, middle school, minuscule, molecule, motor pool, nursery school, overrule, private school, public school, reform school, ridicule, summer school, Sunday school, training school, vestibule, wading pool • finishing school, junior high school, parochial school, primary school, senior high school • alternative school, secondary school

ool[2] \ùl\ see UL[1]

oola \ü-lə\ see ULA

oole \ül\ see OOL[1]

oolean \ü-lē-ən\ see ULEAN

ooled \üld\ bejeweled, unschooled
—also -ed forms of verbs listed at OOL[1]

ooler \ü-lər\ cooler, ruler • carpooler, grade-schooler, high schooler, homeschooler, preschooler, wine cooler • middle schooler, watercooler

oolie \ü-lē\ see ULY

oolish \ü-lish\ foolish, ghoulish, mulish

oolly[1] \ü-lē\ see ULY

oolly[2] \ùl-ē\ see ULLY[2]

oom[1] \üm\ bloom, boom, broom, doom, flume, fume, gloom, groom, loom, plume, room, spume, tomb, vroom, whom, womb, zoom • abloom, assume, backroom, ballroom, barroom, bathroom, bedroom, boardroom, bridegroom, chat room, checkroom, classroom, cloakroom, coatroom, consume, costume, courtroom, darkroom, entomb, exhume, greenroom, guardroom, headroom, heirloom, homeroom, Khartoum, legroom, legume, lunchroom, men's room, mushroom, perfume, playroom, poolroom, pressroom, presume, restroom, resume, schoolroom, showroom, sickroom, stateroom, stockroom, storeroom, sunroom, throne room, washroom, weight room, whisk broom, workroom • baby boom, banquet room, birthing room, elbow room, family room, ladies' room, living room, locker-room, nom de plume, powder room, rumpus room, sitting room, sonic boom, standing room, waiting room, women's room • lower the boom, master bedroom, recovery room • emergency room, recreation room

oom² \ûm\ see UM²

oomed \ümd\ plumed • well-groomed
—*also* -ed *forms of verbs listed at* OOM¹

oomer \ü-mər\ see UMER

oomily \ü-mə-lē\ doomily, gloomily

ooming¹ \ü-mən\ see UMAN

ooming² \ü-miŋ\ see UMING

oomy \ü-mē\ bloomy, boomy, doomy, gloomy, roomy • costumey

oon¹ \ün\ boon, Boone, coon, croon, dune, goon, hewn, June, loon, moon, noon, prune, rune, soon, spoon, swoon, strewn, tune • attune, baboon, balloon, bassoon, blue moon, buffoon, Calhoun, Cancún, cartoon, cocoon, commune, doubloon, dragoon, festoon, fine-tune, forenoon, full moon, half-moon, harpoon, high noon, immune, impugn, Kowloon, lagoon, lampoon, maroon, monsoon, Neptune, new moon, Pashtun, platoon, pontoon, raccoon, rough-hewn, saloon, soupspoon, teaspoon, tribune, tycoon, typhoon, Walloon • afternoon, Brigadoon, Cameroon, dessertspoon, greasy spoon, harvest moon, honeymoon, importune, macaroon, opportune, picayune, Saskatoon, silver spoon, tablespoon • contrabassoon, inopportune, over the moon, trial balloon

oon² \ōn\ see ONE¹

oona \ü-nə\ see UNA

oonal \ün-ᵊl\ see UNAL

oone \ün\ see OON¹

ooner \ü-nər\ crooner, lunar, schooner, tuner • harpooner • honeymooner, prairie schooner

oonery¹ \ün-rē\ buffoonery, lampoonery

oonery² \ü-nə-rē\ see UNARY

ooney \ü-nē\ see OONY

oonie \ü-nē\ see OONY

ooning \ü-niŋ\ ballooning, cartooning, cocooning
—*also* -ing *forms of verbs listed at* OON¹

oonish \ü-nish\ buffoonish, cartoonish

oonless \ün-ləs\ moonless, tuneless

oons \ünz\ afternoons, loony tunes
—*also* -s, -'s, *and* -s' *forms of nouns and* -s *forms of verbs listed at* OON¹

oony \ü-nē\ loony, Moonie, moony, puny, Zuni • cartoony

oop \üp\ coop, coupe, croup, droop, dupe, goop, group, hoop, loop, poop, scoop, sloop, snoop, soup, stoop, swoop, troop, troupe, whoop • age-group, blood group, duck soup, in-group, newsgroup, pea soup, playgroup, recoup, regroup, war whoop • alley-oop, Betty Boop, bird's-nest soup, for a loop, Guadeloupe, Hula Hoop, nincompoop, paratroop, pressure group, support group • alphabet soup, knock for a loop, mock turtle soup

o-op \üp\ see OOP

oopee \ü-pē\ see OOPY

ooper \ü-pər\ blooper, Cooper, looper, scooper, stupor, super, trooper, trouper • storm trooper • party pooper, paratrooper, pooper-scooper, super-duper

oops \ûps\ oops, whoops

oopy \ü-pē\ droopy, groupie,
loopy, snoopy, Snoopy, soupy,
whoopee
oor[1] \ȯr\ see OR[1]
oor[2] \ür\ see URE[1]
oorage[1] \ur-ij\ moorage • sewerage
oorage[2] \ȯr-ij\ see ORAGE[2]
oore[1] \ȯr\ see OR[1]
oore[2] \ür\ see URE[1]
oored \ȯrd\ see OARD
oorer \ȯr-ər\ see ORER
oori \ur-ē\ see URY[1]
ooring[1] \ȯr-iŋ\ see ORING
ooring[2] \ur-iŋ\ see URING
oorish \ur-ish\ boorish, Moorish
oorly \ur-lē\ see URELY
oorman \ȯr-mən\ see ORMAN
oors \ȯrz\ drawers, yours • Azores,
indoors, outdoors • out-of-doors
—*also* -s, -'s, *and* -s' *forms of nouns
and* -s *forms of verbs listed at* OR[1]
oorsman \ȯrz-mən\ see OARSMAN
oort \ȯrt\ see ORT[1]
oosa \ü-sə\ see USA[1]
oose[1] \üs\ see USE[1]
oose[2] \üz\ see USE[2]
ooser[1] \ü-sər\ see UCER
ooser[2] \ü-zər\ see USER
oosey \ü-sē\ see UICY
oosh[1] \üsh\ see OUCHE
oosh[2] \ush\ see USH[2]
oost \üst\ boost, juiced, roost
• self-induced
—*also* -ed *forms of verbs listed at*
USE[1]
oosy \ü-zē\ see OOZY
oot[1] \ut\ foot, put, root, soot
• afoot, barefoot, bigfoot, Black-
foot, board foot, clubfoot, cube
root, hard put, input, kaput, on
foot, output, Rajput, shot put,
square root, taproot, trench foot,
uproot • arrowroot, athlete's foot,
hand and foot, pussyfoot, tender-
foot, underfoot
oot[2] \üt\ see UTE
oot[3] \ət\ see UT[1]

ooted[1] \üt-əd\ booted, fruited,
muted • deep-rooted, jackbooted,
reputed
—*also* -ed *forms of verbs listed at*
UTE
ooted[2] \ut-əd\ clubfooted, deep-
rooted, flat-footed, fleet-footed,
four-footed, heavy-footed, light-
footed, slow-footed, surefooted,
web-footed • cloven-footed
—*also* -ed *forms of verbs listed at*
OOT[1]
ooter[1] \ut-ər\ footer, putter • shot-
putter • pussyfooter
ooter[2] \üt-ər\ see UTER
ooth[1] \üth\ smooth, soothe
ooth[2] \üth\ booth, Booth, Ruth,
sleuth, tooth, truth, youth • buck-
tooth, dogtooth, Duluth, eye-
tooth, half-truth, in truth, milk
tooth, sweet tooth, tollbooth,
uncouth, untruth • baby tooth,
snaggletooth, wisdom tooth • mo-
ment of truth, projection booth,
telephone booth
oothe \üth\ see OOTH[1]
oothed \ütht\ sleuthed, toothed
• bucktoothed, gap-toothed
• saber-toothed, snaggletoothed
oothless \üth-ləs\ see UTHLESS
ootie \üt-ē\ see OOTY[1]
ooting[1] \ut-iŋ\ footing • off-put-
ting, war footing
—*also* -ing *forms of verbs listed at*
OOT[1]
ooting[2] \üt-iŋ\ see UTING
ootle \üt-ᵊl\ see UTILE
ootless \üt-ləs\ fruitless, rootless
oots \üts\ grassroots, Vaduz
—*also* -s, -'s, *and* -s' *forms of
nouns and* -s *forms of verbs listed
at* UTE
ootsie \ut-sē\ footsie, tootsie
ooty[1] \üt-ē\ beauty, booty, cootie,
cutie, duty, fruity, snooty, sooty
• agouti, Djibouti • Funafuti,
heavy-duty, tutti-frutti

ooty[2] \ət-ē\ see UTTY
oove \üv\ see OVE[3]
oover \ü-vər\ see OVER[3]
oovy \ü-vē\ groovy, movie • B movie
ooze \üz\ see USE[2]
oozer \ü-zər\ see USER
oozle \ü-zəl\ see USAL
oozy \ü-zē\ choosy, floozy, newsy, oozy, Susie, woozy • Jacuzzi
op[1] \äp\ bop, chop, clop, cop, crop, drop, flop, fop, glop, hop, lop, mop, plop, pop, prop, shop, slop, sop, stop, swap, top, whop • Aesop, airdrop, a pop, atop, backdrop, backstop, bakeshop, bebop, bellhop, benchtop, big top, blacktop, bookshop, cartop, cash crop, clip-clop, coin-op, cooktop, co-op, cough drop, desktop, dewdrop, doorstop, doo-wop, dry mop, dust mop, eavesdrop, field crop, flattop, flip-flop, gumdrop, hardtop, high-top, hilltop, hiphop, hockshop, housetop, laptop, name-drop, nonstop, one-stop, palmtop, pawnshop, pit stop, poptop, post-op, pre-op, ragtop, raindrop, rooftop, root crop, sharecrop, shortstop, snowdrop, sweatshop, sweetshop, tank top, teardrop, thrift shop, tip-top, treetop, truck stop, workshop • barbershop, beauty shop, belly flop, blow one's top, body shop, carrottop, channel-hop, coffee shop, countertop, cover crop, drag-and-drop, island-hop, lollipop, machine shop, mom-and-pop, mountaintop, photo op, set up shop, soda pop, tabletop, techno-shop, teenybop, turboprop, union shop, whistle-stop, window-shop • comparison shop
op[2] \ō\ see OW[1]
opal \ō-pəl\ opal • Constantinople
ope \ōp\ cope, dope, grope, hope, Hope, lope, mope, nope, ope, pope, Pope, rope, scope, slope, soap, taupe • downslope, elope, fly dope, jump rope, North Slope, skip rope, tightrope, towrope • antelope, cantaloupe, envelope, forlorn hope, gyroscope, horoscope, interlope, isotope, microscope, misanthrope, periscope, slippery slope, stethoscope, telescope • Cape of Good Hope, kaleidoscope, oscilloscope, pay envelope, stereoscope
opean \ō-pē-ən\ see OPIAN
opee \ō-pē\ see OPI
opence \əp-əns\ see UPPANCE
oper \ō-pər\ coper, soaper • eloper • interloper
opey \ō-pē\ see OPI
oph \ōf\ see OAF
ophe[1] \ō-fē\ see OPHY
ophe[2] \òf\ see OFF[2]
opher \ō-fər\ see OFER
ophie \ō-fē\ see OPHY
ophir \ō-fər\ see OFER
ophy \ō-fē\ Sophie, strophe, trophy
opi \ō-pē\ dopey, Hopi, mopey, ropy, soapy
opia \ō-pē-ə\ myopia, utopia • cornucopia, Ethiopia
opian \ō-pē-ən\ Aesopian, utopian • Ethiopian
opic[1] \äp-ik\ topic, tropic • Aesopic, myopic, subtropic • gyroscopic, microscopic, misanthropic, philanthropic, semitropic, telescopic • kaleidoscopic, stereoscopic
opic[2] \ō-pik\ tropic • myopic • Ethiopic
opical \äp-i-kəl\ topical, tropical • subtropical
oplar \äp-lər\ see OPPLER
ople \ō-pəl\ see OPAL
opol \ō-pəl\ see OPAL
opolis \äp-ə-ləs\ acropolis, metropolis, necropolis • megalopolis

opoly \äp-ə-lē\ choppily, floppily, sloppily • monopoly, Monopoly, vox populi

opped \äpt\ see OPT

opper \äp-ər\ chopper, copper, dropper, hopper, proper, shopper, stopper, swapper, whopper • clodhopper, eavesdropper, eyedropper, eyepopper, grasshopper, heart-stopper, hip-hopper, improper, jaw-dropper, job-hopper, leafhopper, name-dropper, sharecropper, showstopper, woodchopper • teenybopper, window-shopper

oppily \äp-ə-lē\ see OPOLY

oppiness \äp-ē-nəs\ choppiness, sloppiness

opping \äp-iŋ\ hopping, sopping, topping, whopping • eye-popping, heart-stopping, jaw-dropping, job-hopping, name-dropping, outcropping, showstopping • channel-hopping
—*also* -ing *forms of verbs listed at* OP[1]

oppler \äp-lər\ Doppler, poplar

oppy \äp-ē\ choppy, copy, floppy, gloppy, poppy, sloppy, soppy • jalopy, serape • photocopy

ops \äps\ chops, copse, tops • Cheops, cyclops, Cyclops, eyedrops, Pelops • lick one's chops • from the housetops, triceratops
—*also* -s, -'s, *and* -s' *forms of nouns and* -s *forms of verbs listed at* OP[1]

opse \äps\ see OPS

opsy \äp-sē\ autopsy, biopsy

opt \äpt\ opt, topped • adopt, close-cropped, co-opt • carrot-topped
—*also* -ed *forms of verbs listed at* OP[1]

opter \äp-tər\ copter • adopter, helicopter

optic \äp-tik\ Coptic, optic • fiber-optic

option \äp-shən\ option • adoption

opuli \äp-ə-lē\ see OPOLY

opus \ō-pəs\ opus • Canopus, Mount Scopus • magnum opus

opy[1] \ō-pē\ see OPI

opy[2] \äp-ē\ see OPPY

oque[1] \ōk\ see OKE[1]

oque[2] \äk\ see OCK[1]

oque[3] \ōk\ see ALK

or[1] \ór\ boar, Boer, bore, chore, core, corps, door, drawer, floor, for, fore, four, gore, Gore, lore, Moore, more, nor, o'er, oar, or, ore, poor, pore, pour, roar, score, shore, snore, soar, sore, spoor, spore, store, swore, Thor, tor, tore, war, wore, yore, your, you're • abhor, adore, and/or, as for, ashore, backdoor, Bangor, bedsore, before, bookstore, box score, call for, candor, captor, centaur, chain store, closed-door, cold sore, condor, decor, deplore, dime-store, Dior, done for, donor, downpour, drugstore, Dutch door, encore, explore, eyesore, fall for, Fillmore, flexor, folklore, footsore, fourscore, French door, full-bore, galore, go for, ground floor, hard-core, ignore, implore, indoor, in for, in-store, Lahore, lakeshore, Lenore, look for, Luxor, memoir, mentor, Mysore, Nestor, next-door, offshore, onshore, outdoor, phosphor, rancor, rapport, raptor, Realtor, restore, savior, seafloor, seashore, sector, señor, sensor, Seymour, smoothbore, s'more, sophomore, stand for, storm door, subfloor, Tagore, take for, temblor, tensor, therefore, threescore, Timor, topdrawer, trapdoor, uproar, vendor, what's more, wherefore, wild boar, woodlore • albacore, allosaur, alongshore, anymore, archosaur, at death's door, at one's door, Baltimore, Bangalore, bargain for, Barrymore, canker sore, carnivore, close the door, come in for, commodore, corridor, dinosaur, door-to-door, double door, Eastern shore, East Timor, Ecuador, either-or, Eleanor, elector, evermore, except for, forest floor, from the floor, furthermore, general store, go in for, guarantor, herbivore, heretofore, in line for, Labrador, man-of-war, matador, metaphor, meteor, Minotaur, more and more, Mount Rushmore, Mount Tabor, nevermore, omnivore, picador, pinafore, pompadour, predator, reservoir, saddle sore, Salvador, semaphore, Singapore, stand up for, stevedore, stick up for, struggle for, superstore, sycamore, take the floor, Theodore, to die for, troubadour, tug-of-war, two-by-four, uncalled-for, underscore • ambassador, conquistador, conservator, convenience store, Corregidor, department store, El Salvador, esprit de corps, foot in the door, forevermore, go to bat for, have it in for, insectivore, legislator, national seashore, revolving door, San Salvador, toreador, tyrannosaur • administrator, lobster thermidor, variety store

or² \ər\ see EUR¹

ora \ȯr-ə\ aura, Cora, Dora, flora, Flora, hora, Laura, Lora, Nora, Torah • Andorra, angora, aurora, fedora, Gomorrah, Lenora, menorah, Pandora, remora, señora, Sonora • Bora-Bora, Leonora, Simchas Torah

orable \ȯr-ə-bəl\ horrible, pourable, storable • adorable, deplorable, restorable

orace \ȯr-əs\ see AURUS

orage¹ \är-ij\ forage, porridge

orage² \ȯr-ij\ forage, porridge, storage • cold storage

orah \ȯr-ə\ see ORA

oral \ȯr-əl\ aural, choral, coral, floral, laurel, Laurel, moral, oral, quarrel • amoral, immoral, mayoral, monaural • electoral

oram \ȯr-əm\ see ORUM

orative \ȯr-ət-iv\ pejorative, restorative

oray \ə-rē\ see URRY

orb \ȯrb\ orb • absorb • reabsorb

orc \ȯrk\ see ORK²

orca \ȯr-kə\ orca • Majorca

orce \ȯrs\ see ORSE¹

orced \ȯrst\ see ORST¹

orceful \ȯrs-fəl\ see ORSEFUL

orcement \ȯr-smənt\ see ORSEMENT

orcer \ȯr-sər\ coarser, hoarser • enforcer

orch \ȯrch\ porch, scorch, torch • blowtorch, sunporch • sleeping porch

orcher \ȯr-chər\ scorcher, torture

orchid \ȯr-kəd\ forked, orchid

ord¹ \ȯrd\ see OARD

ord² \ərd\ see IRD

ord³ \ȯr\ see OR¹

ordan \ȯrd-ᵊn\ see ARDEN²

ordant \ȯrd-ᵊnt\ mordant • discordant

orde \ȯrd\ see OARD

orded \ȯrd-əd\ see ARDED²

ordent \ȯrd-ᵊnt\ see ORDANT

order \ȯrd-ər\ boarder, border, hoarder, order • back order, court order, disorder, gag order, in order, keyboarder, mail-order, on order, recorder, reorder, sailboarder, short-order, skateboarder, snowboarder, surfboarder, transborder, word order • flight recorder, holy order, in short order, law-and-order, made-to-order, money order, mood disorder, pecking order, tape recorder, wire recorder • eating disorder, panic disorder, restraining order

ordered \ȯrd-ərd\ bordered, ordered • disordered, well-ordered
—*also* -ed *forms of verbs listed at* ORDER

orders \ȯrd-ərz\ marching orders
—*also* -s, -'s, *and* -s' *forms of nouns and* -s *forms of verbs listed at* ORDER

ordid \ȯrd-əd\ see ARDED²

ording¹ \ȯrd-iŋ\ hoarding • recording, rewarding, skateboarding • tape recording, weatherboarding
—*also* -ing *forms of verbs listed at* OARD

ording² \ərd-iŋ\ see ERDING

ordion \ȯrd-ē-ən\ accordion, Edwardian

ordon \ȯrd-ᵊn\ see ARDEN²

ordure \ȯr-jər\ see ORGER

ordy \ərd-ē\ see URDY

ore¹ \ȯr-ē\ see ORY

ore² \ur\ see URE¹

ore³ \ər-ə\ see OROUGH¹

ore⁴ \ȯr\ see OR¹

oreal \ȯr-ē-əl\ see ORIAL

orean \ȯr-ē-ən\ see ORIAN

oreas \ȯr-ē-əs\ see ORIOUS

ored \ȯrd\ see OARD

orehead \ȯr-əd\ see ORRID

oreign¹ \är-ən\ see ARIN

oreign² \ȯr-ən\ see ORIN¹

oreigner \ȯr-ə-nər\ see ORONER

orem \ȯr-əm\ see ORUM

oreman \ȯr-mən\ see ORMAN

orence \ȯr-ən(t)s\ see AWRENCE

oreous \ȯr-ē-əs\ see ORIOUS

orer \ȯr-ər\ borer, corer, floorer, horror, poorer, pourer, scorer, snorer, sorer • adorer, corn borer, explorer • Sea Explorer

ores¹ \ȯr-əs\ see AURUS

ores² \ȯrz\ see OORS

orest \ȯr-əst\ see ORIST

orester \ȯr-ə-stər\ see ORISTER

oreum \ȯr-ē-əm\ see ORIUM

oreward \ȯr-wərd\ see ORWARD

oreword \ȯr-wərd\ see ORWARD

orey \ȯr-ē\ see ORY

orf \ȯrf\ see ORPH

org¹ \ȯrg\ Borg, morgue • cyborg

org² \ȯr-ē\ see ORY

organ \ȯr-gən\ gorgon, Morgan, organ • hand organ, house organ, mouth organ, pipe organ, reed organ, sense organ • barrel organ

orge \ȯrj\ forge, George, gorge • disgorge, engorge, Fort George, Lake George, Lloyd George • Royal Gorge • Olduvai Gorge

orger \ȯr-jər\ forger, ordure

orgi \ȯr-gē\ see ORGY

orgia \ȯr-jə\ Borgia, Georgia

orgon \ȯr-gən\ see ORGAN

orgue \ȯrg\ see ORG¹

orgy \ȯr-gē\ corgi, porgy

ori \ȯr-ē\ see ORY

oria \ȯr-ē-ə\ Gloria • euphoria, Peoria, Pretoria, Victoria • Lake Victoria • phantasmagoria

orial \ȯr-ē-əl\ boreal, oriole • arboreal, armorial, authorial, corporeal, factorial, manorial, marmoreal, memorial, pictorial, sartorial, tutorial • curatorial, dictatorial, editorial, equatorial, immemorial, janitorial, professorial, senatorial, territorial • ambassadorial, conspiratorial, gubernatorial, prosecutorial, time immemorial

oriam \ȯr-ē-əm\ see ORIUM

orian \ȯr-ē-ən\ Dorian • Azorean, Gregorian, historian, praetorian, stentorian, Victorian • dinosaurian, Ecuadorean, Labradorean, Salvadorean, Singaporean • salutatorian, valedictorian

oric \ȯr-ik\ caloric, euphoric, folkloric, historic, phosphoric • metaphoric, meteoric,

noncaloric, prehistoric, sopho-
moric • phantasmagoric

orical \ȯr-i-kəl\ historical, rhetori-
cal • allegorical, categorical,
metaphorical, oratorical

orid \ȯr-əd\ see ORRID

oriel \ȯr-ē-əl\ see ORIAL

orin[1] \ȯr-ən\ chlorine, foreign,
Lauren, Orrin, warren, Warren
• Andorran

orin[2] \är-ən\ see ARIN

orine \ȯr-ən\ see ORIN[1]

oring \ȯr-iŋ\ boring, flooring,
roaring • outpouring, rip-roaring,
wood-boring
—also -ing forms of verbs listed at
OR[1]

öring \ər-iŋ\ see URRING

oriole \ȯr-ē-əl\ see ORIAL

orious \ȯr-ē-əs\ Boreas, glorious
• censorious, laborious, notori-
ous, uproarious, uxorious, vain-
glorious, victorious • meritorious

oris \ȯr-əs\ see AURUS

orish \ur-ish\ see OORISH

orist \ȯr-əst\ florist, forest, poorest,
sorest • Black Forest, deforest,
folklorist, reforest • Petrified
Forest

orister \ȯr-ə-stər\ chorister,
forester

ority \ȯr-ət-ē\ authority, majority,
minority, priority, seniority,
sonority, sorority • inferiority,
superiority

orium \ȯr-ē-əm\ emporium • audi-
torium, cafetorium, crematorium,
in memoriam, moratorium, sana-
torium

ork[1] \ȯrk\ clerk, Dirk, irk, jerk,
Kirk, lurk, murk, perk, quirk,
shirk, smirk, Turk, work • art-
work, at work, beadwork,
berserk, brickwork, brushwork,
casework, clockwork, Dunkirk,
earthwork, file clerk, firework,
footwork, framework, Grand
Turk, groundwork, guesswork,
handwork, homework, house-
work, ironwork, knee-jerk, leg-
work, lifework, make-work,
network, outwork, patchwork,
piecework, rework, roadwork,
salesclerk, schoolwork, Selkirk,
stonework, teamwork, town
clerk, waxwork, woodwork,
young Turk • Atatürk, basket-
work, bodywork, busywork,
cabinetwork, city clerk, clean-
and-jerk, handiwork, leather-
work, masterwork, metalwork,
needlework, out of work, over-
work, paperwork, piece of work,
shipping clerk, social work, soda
jerk, wickerwork

ork[2] \ȯrk\ cork, Cork, dork, fork,
pork, quark, stork, torque, York
• bulwark, Cape York, New York,
North York, pitchfork, salt pork,
uncork, wood stork

orked \ȯr-kəd\ see ORCHID

orker[1] \ər-kər\ lurker, shirker,
worker • caseworker,
dockworker, farmworker, field-
worker, ironworker, networker,
pieceworker, steelworker, tear-
jerker, woodworker
• autoworker, metalworker, social
worker, wonder-worker

orker[2] \ȯr-kər\ corker, porker
• New Yorker

orkie \ȯr-kē\ see ORKY

orking \ər-kiŋ\ hardworking, net-
working, tear-jerking, woodwork-
ing • metalworking,
wonder-working
—also -ing forms of verbs listed at
ORK[1]

orky \ȯr-kē\ dorky, Gorky, porky,
Yorkie

orl \ərl\ see IRL

orld \ərld\ world • dreamworld,
free world, New World, old-
world, Old World, real-world,

third world • afterworld, brave new world, Disney World, in the world, netherworld, otherworld, underworld • for all the world, man of the world, out of this world • on top of the world
—*also* -ed *forms of verbs listed at* IRL

orled \ərld\ see ORLD

orm¹ \ərm\ firm, germ, perm, squirm, term, worm • affirm, bookworm, budworm, confirm, cutworm, deworm, earthworm, flatworm, glowworm, heartworm, hookworm, hornworm, inchworm, infirm, long-term, midterm, pinworm, ringworm, roundworm, short-term, silkworm, tapeworm, webworm • pachyderm, reconfirm

orm² \ȯrm\ dorm, form, norm, storm, swarm, warm • aswarm, barnstorm, brainstorm, by storm, conform, deform, dust storm, firestorm, free-form, hailstorm, ice storm, inform, landform, lifeform, lukewarm, perform, platform, preform, rainstorm, re-form, reform, sandstorm, snowstorm, transform, waveform, windstorm • chloroform, cruciform, land reform, thunderstorm, uniform • cuneiform, dress uniform, magnetic storm, quadratic form

ormal \ȯr-məl\ formal, normal • abnormal, informal, subnormal • paranormal, semiformal

ormally \ȯr-mə-lē\ formally, formerly, normally, stormily • abnormally, informally • paranormally

orman \ȯr-mən\ doorman, foreman, Foreman, Mormon, Norman • longshoreman

ormant \ȯr-mənt\ dormant • informant

ormative \ȯr-mət-iv\ formative, normative • informative, transformative

orme \ȯrm\ see ORM²

ormed \ȯrmd\ deformed, informed, malformed, unformed • well-informed
—*also* -ed *forms of verbs listed at* ORM²

ormer \ȯr-mər\ dormer, former, warmer • barnstormer, benchwarmer, brainstormer, heartwarmer, informer, performer, reformer, transformer

ormerly \ȯr-mə-lē\ see ORMALLY

ormily \ȯr-mə-lē\ see ORMALLY

orming \ȯr-miŋ\ brainstorming, heartwarming, housewarming, performing • habit-forming
—*also* -ing *forms of verbs listed at* ORM²

ormity \ȯr-mət-ē\ conformity, deformity, enormity • nonconformity, uniformity

ormless \ȯrm-ləs\ formless, gormless

ormon \ȯr-mən\ see ORMAN

ormy \ər-mē\ see ERMY

orn¹ \ȯrn\ born, borne, corn, horn, morn, mourn, scorn, shorn, sworn, thorn, torn, warn, worn • acorn, adorn, airborne, bighorn, blackthorn, blue corn, boxthorn, broomcorn, buckthorn, bullhorn, Cape Horn, careworn, Dearborn, dehorn, earthborn, field corn, firethorn, firstborn, flint corn, foghorn, forewarn, forlorn, freeborn, French horn, greenhorn, hawthorn, Hawthorne, highborn, inborn, longhorn, lovelorn, newborn, outworn, popcorn, pronghorn, ramshorn, reborn, saxhorn, seaborne, shipborne, shoehorn, shopworn, shorthorn, skyborne, soilborne, stillborn, sweet corn, tick-borne, timeworn, tinhorn, tricorne, unborn, unworn, well-born, well-worn, wind-borne • barleycorn, Capricorn, English horn, flügelhorn, foreign-born, hunting horn, Matterhorn, peppercorn, powder horn, saddle horn, unicorn, waterborne, weatherworn • Indian corn, Little Bighorn, Texas longhorn • to the manner born, to the manor born

orn² \ərn\ see URN

ornament \òr-nə-mənt\ ornament, tournament

orne \òrn\ see ORN¹

orned \òrnd\ horned, thorned • unadorned
—*also* -ed *forms of verbs listed at* ORN¹

orner \òr-nər\ corner, scorner, Warner • kitty-corner

orney \ər-nē\ see OURNEY¹

ornful \òrn-fəl\ mournful, scornful

orning \òr-niŋ\ morning, mourning, warning
—*also* -ing *forms of verbs listed at* ORN¹

ornment \ərn-mənt\ see ERNMENT

orny \òr-nē\ corny, thorny

oro \ər-ə\ see OROUGH¹

oroner \òr-ə-nər\ coroner, foreigner

orough¹ \ər-ə\ borough, burro, burrow, furrow, ore, thorough • Gainsborough, Greensboro • Edinburgh, kookaburra

orough² \ər-ō\ see URROW¹

orous \òr-əs\ see AURUS

orp \òrp\ gorp, warp

orpe \òrp\ see ORP

orph \òrf\ dwarf, morph • Düsseldorf

orphan \òr-fən\ orphan • endorphin

orpheus \òr-fē-əs\ Morpheus, Orpheus

orphin \òr-fən\ see ORPHAN

orpoise \òr-pəs\ see ORPUS

orps \òr\ see OR¹

orpsman \òr-mən\ see ORMAN

orpus \òr-pəs\ porpoise • habeas corpus

orque \òrk\ see ORK²

orquer \òr-kər\ see ORKER²

orr \òr\ see OR¹

orra¹ \är-ə\ see ARA¹

orra² \òr-ə\ see ORA

orrah¹ \òr-ə\ see ORA

orrah² \är-ə\ see ARA¹

orran¹ \är-ən\ see ARIN

orran² \òr-ən\ see ORIN¹

orrence \òr-əns\ see AWRENCE

orrel \òr-əl\ see ORAL

orrent \òr-ənt\ torrent, warrant • abhorrent, death warrant, search warrant

orrer \òr-ər\ see ORER

orres \òr-əs\ see AURUS

orrest \òr-əst\ see ORIST

orrible \òr-ə-bəl\ see ORABLE

orrid \òr-əd\ florid, horrid, torrid

orridge¹ \är-ij\ see ORAGE¹

orridge² \òr-ij\ see ORAGE²

orrie¹ \är-ē\ see ARI¹

orrie² \òr-ē\ see ORY

orrier \òr-ē-ər\ see ARRIOR

orrin¹ \är-en\ see ARIN

orrin² \òr-ən\ see ORIN¹

orris¹ \är-əs\ Juárez, Maurice, morris, Morris • Benares, Polaris

orris² \òr-əs\ see AURUS

orror \òr-ər\ see ORER

orrow¹ \är-ō\ borrow, morrow, sorrow, taro • bizarro, Pizarro, saguaro, tomorrow • Kilimanjaro

orrow² \är-ə\ see ARA¹

orry¹ \är-ē\ see ARI¹

orry² \ər-ē\ see URRY

ors \òrz\ see OORS

orsal \òr-səl\ see ORSEL

orse¹ \òrs\ coarse, course, force, hoarse, horse, Morse, Norse, source • clotheshorse, concourse, crash course, dark horse, dead horse, discourse, divorce, en-

dorse, enforce, golf course, gut
course, high horse, iron horse,
midcourse, of course, one-horse,
packhorse, racecourse, racehorse,
recourse, remorse, resource,
sawhorse, sea horse, unhorse,
warhorse, Whitehorse, workhorse
• charley horse, Crazy Horse,
harness horse, hobbyhorse, mini-
course, pommel horse, quarter
horse, reinforce, rocking horse,
saddle horse, stalking horse,
telecourse, tour de force, Trojan
horse, vaulting horse,
watercourse • collision course,
matter of course, obstacle course,
par for the course • Arabian
horse

orse² \ərs\ see ERSE

orseful \ȯrs-fəl\ forceful • remorse-
ful, resourceful

orsel \ȯr-səl\ dorsal, morsel

orseman \ȯr-smən\ horseman,
Norseman

orsement \ȯr-smənt\ endorsement,
enforcement • reinforcement

orsen \ərs-ᵊn\ see ERSON

orset \ȯr-sət\ corset, Dorset

orsion \ȯr-shən\ see ORTION

orst¹ \ȯrst\ forced
—also -ed forms of verbs listed at
ORSE¹

orst² \ərst\ see URST

ort¹ \ȯrt\ court, fort, forte, port,
quart, short, snort, sort, sport,
thwart, tort, torte, wart • abort,
airport, athwart, Bridgeport,
carport, cavort, cohort, comport,
consort, contort, deport, disport,
distort, effort, escort, exhort,
export, extort, fall short, for short,
Gulfport, home port, in short,
Newport, passport, presort, pur-
port, report, re-sort, resort, retort,
seaport, sell short, Shreveport,
spaceport, spoilsport, support,
transport • davenport, heliport,

hold the fort, life-support, non-
support, of a sort, worrywart
• pianoforte, the long and short

ort² \ȯr\ see OR¹

ort³ \ərt\ see ERT¹

ortage \ȯrt-ij\ portage, shortage
• reportage

ortal \ȯrt-ᵊl\ chortle, mortal, portal
• immortal

ortar \ȯrt-ər\ see ORTER

orte¹ \ȯrt\ see ORT¹

orte² \ȯrt-ē\ see ORTY

orted \ȯrt-əd\ assorted, purported
• self-supported
—also -ed forms of verbs listed at
ORT¹

orter \ȯrt-ər\ mortar, porter,
Porter, quarter, shorter, sorter
• exporter, headquarter, importer,
reporter, supporter, transporter
• brick-and-mortar • athletic
supporter

orteur \ȯrt-ər\ see ORTER

orth¹ \ȯrth\ forth, fourth, north,
North • bring forth, call forth,
thenceforth • and so forth, back
and forth, Firth of Forth

orth² \ərth\ see IRTH

orthless \ərth-ləs\ see IRTHLESS

orthy \ər-thē\ earthy, worthy • air-
worthy, blameworthy, crashwor-
thy, newsworthy, noteworthy,
praiseworthy, roadworthy, sea-
worthy, trustworthy, unworthy
• creditworthy

ortie \ȯrt-ē\ see ORTY

orting \ȯrt-iŋ\ sporting • nonsport-
ing • self-supporting
—also -ing forms of verbs listed at
ORT¹

ortion \ȯr-shən\ portion, torsion
• apportion, contortion, distor-
tion, extortion, proportion • dis-
proportion, in proportion,
reapportion

ortionate \ȯr-shnət\ extortionate,
proportionate • disproportionate

ortionist \ȯr-shnist\ contortionist, extortionist

ortis \ȯrt-əs\ mortise, tortoise • rigor mortis

ortise \ȯrt-əs\ see ORTIS

ortive \ȯrt-iv\ abortive, supportive

ortle \ȯrt-ᵊl\ see ORTAL

ortly \ȯrt-lē\ courtly, portly, shortly

ortment \ȯrt-mənt\ assortment, comportment, deportment

ortoise \ȯrt-əs\ see ORTIS

orts \ȯrts\ quartz, shorts, sports • boxer shorts, out of sorts, undershorts • Bermuda shorts, bicycle shorts
—also -s, -'s, and -s' forms of nouns and -s forms of verbs listed at ORT[1]

ortunate \ȯrch-nət\ fortunate • importunate, unfortunate

orture \ȯr-chər\ see ORCHER

orty \ȯrt-ē\ forty, shorty, sporty • pianoforte

orum \ȯr-əm\ forum, quorum • decorum • indecorum • sanctum sanctorum

orus \ȯr-əs\ see AURUS

orward \ȯr-wərd\ forward, foreword, shoreward • bring forward, fast-forward, flash forward, henceforward, look forward, put forward, set forward, straightforward, thenceforward

ory \ȯr-ē\ dory, glory, gory, Laurie, Lori, quarry, sorry, story, Tory • backstory, fish story, ghost story, Old Glory, short story, sob story • allegory, auditory, bedtime story, category, cover story, crematory, desultory, dilatory, dormitory, horror story, hunky-dory, inventory, Lake Maggiore, laudatory, lavatory, mandatory, migratory, Montessori, morning glory, offertory, oratory, predatory, prefatory, promissory, promon-

tory, purgatory, repertory, statutory, territory, transitory • accusatory, ambulatory, celebratory, compensatory, conservatory, dedicatory, defamatory, depository, derogatory, exculpatory, explanatory, exploratory, inflammatory, laboratory, masturbatory, obligatory, observatory, preparatory, reformatory, regulatory, repository, revelatory, respiratory • anticipatory, discriminatory, hallucinatory

orze \ȯrz\ see OORS

os[1] \äs\ boss, dross, floss, gloss, toss • Argos, chaos, cosmos, Delos, emboss, en masse, Eros, kudos, Lagos, Laos, Madras, Naxos, pathos, Patmos, Pharos, ringtoss • albatross, coup de grâce, demitasse, dental floss, gravitas, semigloss

os[2] \ō\ see OW[1]

os[3] \ōs\ see OSE[1]

os[4] \ȯs\ see OSS[1]

osa \ō-sə\ Xhosa • Formosa, mimosa

osable \ō-zə-bəl\ disposable, opposable, reclosable

osal \ō-zəl\ Mosel • disposal, proposal

osch \äsh\ see ASH[2]

oschen \ō-shən\ see OTION

osco \äs-kō\ see OSCOE

oscoe \äs-kō\ Bosco, Roscoe • fiasco

ose[1] \ōs\ Bose, close, dose, gross • Carlos, cosmos, dextrose, engross, fructose, glucose, lactose, maltose, morose, pathos, sucrose, Sukkoth, up close, verbose • adios, bellicose, cellulose, comatose, diagnose, grandiose, Helios, lachrymose, megadose, overdose, varicose • metamorphose

ose[2] \ōz\ chose, close, clothes, doze, froze, hose, nose, pose,

prose, rose, Rose • Ambrose, arose, bedclothes, bulldoze, compose, depose, dextrose, disclose, dispose, dog rose, enclose, expose, foreclose, fructose, glucose, impose, Mount Rose, nightclothes, oppose, plainclothes, primrose, propose, pug nose, repose, rockrose, suppose, transpose, tuberose • Berlioz, cabbage rose, cellulose, China rose, Christmas rose, damask rose, decompose, diagnose, indispose, interpose, juxtapose, on the nose, panty hose, predispose, presuppose, shovelnose, swaddling clothes, thumb one's nose, underclothes • evening primrose, follow one's nose, look down one's nose, metamorphose, overexpose, pay through the nose, superimpose, under one's nose
—*also* -s, -'s, *and* -s' *forms of nouns and* -s *forms of verbs listed at* OW[1]

ose[3] \üz\ *see* USE[2]

osed \ōzd\ closed • composed, exposed, hard-nosed, opposed, pug-nosed, supposed • indisposed, shovel-nosed, well-disposed
—*also* -ed *forms of verbs listed at* OSE[2]

osee \ō-zē\ *see* OSY

osel \ō-zəl\ *see* OSAL

osen \ōz-ᵊn\ chosen, frozen • deep-frozen, quick-frozen

oser[1] \ō-zər\ brownnoser, bulldozer, composer, disposer

oser[2] \ü-zər\ *see* USER

oset \äz-ət\ *see* OSIT

osey \ō-zē\ *see* OSY

osh[1] \òsh\ *see* ASH[2]

osh[2] \ōsh\ *see* OCHE[2]

oshed[1] \äsht\ galoshed
—*also* -ed *forms of verbs listed at* ASH[1]

oshed[2] \òsht\ *see* ASHED[1]

oshen \ō-shən\ *see* OTION

osher \äsh-ər\ *see* ASHER[1]

osible \ō-zə-bəl\ *see* OSABLE

osier \ō-zhər\ *see* OSURE

osily \ō-zə-lē\ cozily, nosily, rosily

osing \ō-ziŋ\ closing • disclosing, imposing, self-closing, supposing
—*also* -ing *forms of verbs listed at* OSE[2]

osion \ō-zhən\ corrosion, erosion, explosion, implosion

osis \ō-səs\ cirrhosis, hypnosis, meiosis, mitosis, neurosis, osmosis, prognosis, psychosis, sclerosis • diagnosis, halitosis, symbiosis • cystic fibrosis, tuberculosis • mononucleosis

osit \äz-ət\ closet, posit • composite, deposit

osite \äz-ət\ *see* OSIT

osius \ō-shəs\ *see* OCIOUS

osive \ō-siv\ corrosive, explosive, implosive, purposive • high explosive

osk \äsk\ mosque • kiosk

oso[1] \ō-sō\ mafioso, virtuoso • concerto grosso

oso[2] \ü-sō\ *see* USOE

osophy \äs-ə-fē\ philosophy, theosophy

osque \äsk\ *see* OSK

oss[1] \òs\ boss, cross, floss, gloss, loss, moss, Ross, sauce, toss • across, Blue Cross, brown sauce, club moss, crisscross, emboss, Greek cross, lacrosse, pathos, peat moss, Red Cross, ringtoss, tau cross, uncross, white sauce • albatross, applesauce, at a loss, béarnaise sauce, Celtic cross, chili sauce, come across, dental floss, double-cross, get across, hoisin sauce, Iceland moss, Irish moss, Latin cross, Maltese cross, Mornay sauce, motocross, Navy Cross, Northern Cross, papal cross, reindeer moss, run across, semigloss, Southern Cross, Spanish moss, tartar sauce, underboss • pectoral cross, sign of the cross, Worcestershire sauce • stations of the cross

oss² \ōs\ see OSE¹

oss³ \äs\ see OS¹

ossa \äs-ə\ see ASA¹

ossal \äs-əl\ docile, fossil, jostle, tassel, wassail • apostle, colossal

osse¹ \äs\ see OS¹

osse² \äs-ē\ see OSSY¹

osse³ \ȯs\ see OSS¹

ossed \ȯst\ see OST³

osser \ȯ-sər\ Chaucer, saucer • double-crosser, flying saucer

ossil \äs-əl\ see OSSAL

ossity \äs-ət-ē\ atrocity, ferocity, monstrosity, pomposity, precocity, velocity, verbosity, viscosity • animosity, curiosity, generosity, grandiosity, reciprocity, virtuosity • religiosity

ossly \ȯs-lē\ costly, crossly

osso \ō-sō\ see OSO¹

ossos \äs-əs\ see OCESS

ossum \äs-əm\ blossom, possum • opossum, play possum

ossus \äs-əs\ see OCESS

ossy¹ \äs-ē\ Aussie, bossy, glossy, posse, quasi

ossy² \ȯ-sē\ Aussie, bossy, mossy

ost¹ \äst\ accost • Pentecost
—*also* -ed *forms of verbs listed at* OS¹

ost² \ōst\ boast, coast, ghost, host, most, post, roast, toast • almost, at most, bedpost, compost, doorpost, endmost, foremost, French toast, gatepost, goalpost, Gold Coast, lamppost, milepost, pot roast, rearmost, rib roast, seacoast, signpost, Slave Coast, topmost, utmost • at the most, Barbary Coast, bottommost, coast-to-coast, command post, easternmost, Holy Ghost, innermost, Ivory Coast, melba toast, northernmost, outermost, parcel post, southernmost, trading post, uppermost, uttermost, whipping post • from coast to coast, give up the ghost, Mosquito Coast, Washington Post
—*also* -ed *forms of verbs listed at* OSE¹

ost³ \ȯst\ cost, frost, lost • accost, defrost, exhaust, hoarfrost, Jack Frost, star-crossed • holocaust, Pentecost, permafrost,
—*also* -ed *forms of verbs listed at* OSS¹

ost⁴ \əst\ see UST¹

ostal¹ \ōs-tᵊl\ coastal, postal • bicoastal

ostal² \äs-tᵊl\ see OSTEL

oste \ōst\ see OST²

ostel \äs-tᵊl\ hostile • youth hostel • Pentecostal

oster¹ \äs-tər\ foster, Foster, roster • impostor • paternoster

oster² \ȯs-tər\ foster, Foster, roster

oster³ \ō-stər\ see OASTER

ostic \äs-tik\ acrostic, agnostic • diagnostic

ostile \äs-tᵊl\ see OSTEL

ostle \äs-əl\ see OSSAL

ostly¹ \ōst-lē\ ghostly, mostly

ostly² \ȯs-lē\ see OSSLY

oston \ȯs-tən\ Austen, Austin, Boston

ostor \äs-tər\ see OSTER¹

ostrum \äs-trəm\ nostrum, rostrum

osure \ō-zhər\ closure, crosier • composure, disclosure, enclosure, exposure, foreclosure • time exposure • overexposure, underexposure

osy \ō-zē\ cozy, dozy, mosey, nosy, posy, prosy, rosy • ring-around-the-rosy

osz \ȯsh\ see ASH²

oszcz \ȯsh\ see ASH²

ot¹ \ät\ blot, bot, clot, cot, dot, got,

hot, jot, knot, lot, Lot, naught,
not, plot, pot, rot, Scot, Scott,
shot, slot, sot, spot, squat, swat,
tot, trot, watt, Watt, what, yacht
• Alcott, allot, a lot, a shot, big
shot, blind spot, bloodshot, boy-
cott, buckshot, cannot, cheap
shot, crackpot, despot, dogtrot,
dovecote, dry rot, dunk shot,
earshot, feedlot, fiat, forgot, foul
shot, fox-trot, gunshot, have-not,
hotshot, jackpot, jump shot,
kumquat, long shot, mascot, mug
shot, Pequot, Pol Pot, potshot,
Rabat, red-hot, reef knot, robot,
root rot, Sadat, sandlot, sexpot,
Shabbat, shallot, sheepcote, slap
shot, slingshot, slipknot, snapshot,
soft spot, somewhat, square knot,
stinkpot, stockpot, subplot,
sunspot, sweet spot, teapot, tin-
pot, upshot, wainscot, whatnot,
white-hot, woodlot • aeronaut,
apricot, aquanaut, argonaut,
astronaut, booster shot, Camelot,
caveat, chamber pot, chimney
pot, coffeepot, cosmonaut, coun-
terplot, diddley-squat, flowerpot,
granny knot, hit the spot, Hotten-
tot, Huguenot, juggernaut, kilo-
watt, Lancelot, like a shot, like as
not, lobster pot, megawatt, melting pot, microdot, monocot,
ocelot, on the spot, parking lot,
patriot, Penobscot, piping hot,
polka dot, scattershot, tie the
knot, touch-me-not, Windsor
knot • as like as not, by a long
shot, compatriot, forget-me-not,
Gordian knot, hit the jackpot,
penalty shot, stevedore knot,
whether or not • all over the lot
• Johnny-on-the-spot

ot² \ō\ see OW¹

ot³ \ōt\ see OAT

ot⁴ \ȯt\ see OUGHT¹

ôt \ō\ see OW¹

ota \ōt-ə\ quota • Carlota, Dakota,
iota, Lakota, Toyota • Minnesota,
North Dakota, Sarasota, South
Dakota

otable \ōt-ə-bəl\ notable, potable,
quotable

otal \ōt-ᵊl\ total • subtotal, sum
total • anecdotal

otany \ät-ᵊn-ē\ botany, cottony
• monotony

otary \ōt-ə-rē\ coterie, rotary

otas \ō-təs\ see OTUS

otch \äch\ blotch, botch, crotch,
notch, scotch, Scotch, splotch,
swatch, watch • bird-watch,
deathwatch, hopscotch,
Sasquatch, stopwatch, top-notch,
wristwatch • butterscotch

otchman \äch-mən\ Scotchman,
watchman

otchy \äch-ē\ blotchy, boccie,
splotchy • hibachi, Karachi • Lib-
erace, mariachi

ote¹ \ōt-ē\ throaty • coyote, peyote
• Don Quixote

ote² \ōt\ see OAT

ote³ \ät\ see OT¹

oted \ōt-əd\ see OATED

oten \ōt-ᵊn\ see OTON

oter \ōt-ər\ see OATER

oterie \ōt-ə-rē\ see OTARY

oth¹ \ȯth\ broth, cloth, froth,
moth, sloth, swath • breechcloth,
clothes moth, dishcloth, face-
cloth, ground cloth, ground sloth,
hawk moth, loincloth, oilcloth,
sailcloth, scotch broth, silk moth,
sphinx moth, washcloth • gypsy
moth, luna moth, Ostrogoth,
tablecloth, three-toed sloth, tiger
moth, two-toed sloth

oth² \äth\ Goth, sloth, swath • Ostrogoth, Visigoth

oth³ \ōs\ see OSE¹

oth⁴ \ōt\ see OAT

oth⁵ \ōth\ see OWTH

othe \ōth\ clothe, loathe • unclothe

other[1] \əth-ər\ brother, mother, other, rather, smother • another, big brother, blood brother, den mother, each other, godmother, grandmother, half brother, queen mother, stepbrother, stepmother • fairy godmother

other[2] \äth-ər\ see ATHER[1]

otherly \əth-ər-lē\ brotherly, motherly, southerly • grandmotherly

othes \ōz\ see OSE[2]

othing \ō-thiŋ\ clothing, loathing • betrothing, unclothing • underclothing • wolf in sheep's clothing

otho \ō-tō\ see OTO

oti[1] \ōt-ē\ see OTE[1]

oti[2] \ȯt-ē\ see AUGHTY[1]

otiable \ō-shə-bəl\ see OCIABLE

otic \ät-ik\ aquatic, chaotic, despotic, erotic, exotic, hypnotic, narcotic, neurotic, psychotic, quixotic, robotic • idiotic, patriotic, symbiotic • antibiotic

otice \ōt-əs\ see OTUS

otics \ät-iks\ robotics • aeronautics, astronautics
—also -s, -'s, and -s' forms of nouns listed at OTIC

otid \ät-əd\ see OTTED

otile \ōt-ᵊl\ see OTAL

oting[1] \ōt-iŋ\ see OATING

oting[2] \ät-iŋ\ see OTTING

otinous \ät-ᵊn-əs\ see OTONOUS

otion \ō-shən\ Goshen, lotion, motion, notion, ocean, potion • commotion, demotion, devotion, emotion, Laotian, promotion, slow-motion • Arctic Ocean, locomotion, Nova Scotian, set in motion, Southern Ocean • Antarctic Ocean, Atlantic Ocean, Indian Ocean, Pacific Ocean

otional \ō-shnəl\ devotional, emotional, promotional • unemotional

otis \ōt-əs\ see OTUS

otive \ōt-iv\ motive, votive • emotive • automotive, locomotive

otl \ät-ᵊl\ see OTTLE

otle \ät-ᵊl\ see OTTLE

otley \ät-lē\ see OTLY

otly \ät-lē\ hotly, motley

oto \ō-tō\ photo • de Soto, in toto, Kyoto, Lesotho • telephoto, Yamamoto

otomy \ät-ə-mē\ dichotomy, lobotomy

oton \ōt-ᵊn\ oaten • Lofoten, verboten

otonous \ät-ᵊn-əs\ rottenness • monotonous

otor \ōt-ər\ see OATER

otory \ōt-ə-rē\ see OTARY

ots \äts\ Graz, lots, Scots • age spots, ersatz • call the shots • connect-the-dots, hit the high spots
—also -s, -'s, and -s' forms of nouns and -s forms of verbs listed at OT[1]

otsman \ät-smən\ Scotsman, yachtsman

ott \ät\ see OT[1]

otta \ät-ə\ see ATA[1]

ottage \ät-ij\ cottage, wattage

ottal \ät-ᵊl\ see OTTLE

otte[1] \ät\ see OT[1]

otte[2] \ȯt\ see OUGHT[1]

otted \ät-əd\ knotted, potted, spotted • besotted, unspotted • polka-dotted
—also -ed forms of verbs listed at OT[1]

otten \ät-ᵊn\ cotton, gotten, rotten • au gratin, forgotten, ill-gotten • misbegotten, sauerbraten

ottenness \ät-ᵊn-əs\ see OTONOUS

otter \ät-ər\ blotter, daughter, hotter, otter, plotter, potter, Potter, Qatar, rotter, spotter, squatter, swatter, Tatar, totter, trotter, water • backwater, bathwater, boycotter, breakwater, Clearwater, deepwater, dishwater, floodwater, flyswatter, freshwater, globe-trotter, groundwater, headwater, hot water, ice water, jerkwater, meltwater, rainwater, saltwater, sea otter, seawater, tap water, tidewater, tread water, white-water • above water, alma mater, holy water, in deep water, mineral water, river otter, running water, soda water, teeter-totter, tonic water, underwater • dead in the water, fish out of water, hell or high water

ottery \ät-ə-rē\ lottery, pottery, tottery, watery

ottid \ät-əd\ see OTTED

ottie \ät-ē\ see ATI[1]

otting \ät-iŋ\ jotting • globe-trotting, wainscoting
—also -ing forms of verbs listed at OT[1]

ottle \ät-ᵊl\ bottle, mottle, throttle, wattle • squeeze bottle • Aristotle, at full throttle, spin the bottle, vacuum bottle • Quetzalcoatl

otto[1] \ät-ō\ see ATO[1]

otto[2] \ȯt-ō\ see AUTO[1]

ottom \ät-əm\ see ATUM[1]

otty \ät-ē\ see ATI[1]

otun \ōt-ᵊn\ see OTON

oture \ō-chər\ see OACHER

otus \ōt-əs\ lotus, notice, Otis

oty \ȯt-ē\ see AUGHTY[1]

otyl \ät-ᵊl\ see OTTLE

ou[1] \ō\ see OW[1]

ou[2] \ü\ see EW[1]

ou[3] \au̇\ see OW[2]

oubled \əb-əld\ see UBBLED

ouble \əb-əl\ see UBBLE

oubly \əb-lē\ see UBBLY[1]

oubt \au̇t\ see OUT[3]

oubted \au̇t-əd\ see OUTED

oubter \au̇t-ər\ see OUTER[2]

ouc[1] \ü\ see EW[1]

ouc[2] \ük\ see UKE

ouc[3] \u̇k\ see OOK[1]

ouce \üs\ see USE[1]

oucester[1] \äs-tər\ see OSTER[1]

oucester[2] \ȯs-tər\ see OSTER[2]

ouch[1] \üch\ see OOCH[1]

ouch[2] \üsh\ see OUCHE

ouch[3] \əch\ see UTCH

ouch[4] \au̇ch\ couch, crouch, grouch, ouch, pouch, slouch, vouch • studio couch

ouche \üsh\ swoosh, whoosh

ouchy[1] \əch-ē\ see UCHY

ouchy[2] \au̇-chē\ grouchy, pouchy, slouchy

oud[1] \üd\ see UDE[1]

oud[2] \au̇d\ boughed, bowed, cloud, crowd, loud, proud, shroud • aloud, becloud, do proud, enshroud, out loud, Saint Cloud, unbowed • funnel cloud, mushroom cloud, overcloud, overcrowd, thundercloud
—also -ed forms of verbs listed at OW[2]

ou'd \üd\ see UDE[1]

ouda \üd-ə\ see UDA

oudy \au̇d-ē\ see OWDY

oue \ü\ see EW[1]

ouf \üf\ see OOF[1]

ouffe \üf\ see OOF[1]

oug \əg\ see UG

ouge[1] \üj\ see UGE[1]

ouge[2] \üzh\ see UGE[2]

ough[1] \ō\ see OW[1]

ough[2] \ü\ see EW[1]

ough[3] \au̇\ see OW[2]

ough[4] \äk\ see OCK[1]

ough[5] \əf\ see UFF

ough[6] \ȯf\ see OFF[2]

ougham[1] \ōm\ see OME[1]

ougham[2] \üm\ see OOM[1]

oughed \au̇d\ see OUD[2]

oughen \əf-ən\ see UFFIN

ougher \əf-ər\ see UFFER

oughie \əf-ē\ see UFFY

oughly \əf-lē\ see UFFLY

oughs \ōz\ see OSE[2]

ought[1] \ȯt\ bought, brought, caught, dot, fought, fraught, naught, ought, sought, taught, taut, thought, wrought

• distraught, forethought, hand-wrought, onslaught, self-taught, store-bought, unsought, untaught • aeronaut, afterthought, aquanaut, argonaut, astronaut, cosmonaut, juggernaut, overwrought, second thought

ought² \aut\ see OUT³

oughy¹ \ō-ē\ see OWY

oughy² \ü-ē\ see EWY

ouie \ü-ē\ see EWY

ouille \ü-ē\ see EWY

ouis \ü-ē\ see EWY

ouk \ük\ see UKE

ouki \ü-kē\ see OOKY¹

oul¹ \ōl\ see OLE¹

oul² \ül\ see OOL¹

oul³ \aul\ see OWL²

ould¹ \ōld\ see OLD¹

ould² \ud\ see OOD¹

oulder \ōl-dər\ see OLDER¹

ouldered \ōl-dərd\ shouldered • round-shouldered
—*also* -ed *forms of verbs listed at* OLDER¹

ouldest \ud-əst\ couldest, shouldest, wouldest

ouldn't \ud-ᵊnt\ couldn't, shouldn't, wouldn't

oule¹ \ü-lē\ see ULY

oule² \ül\ see OOL¹

ouled \ōld\ see OLD¹

oulee \ü-lē\ see ULY

ouleh¹ \ü-lə\ see ULA

ouleh² \ü-lē\ see ULY

ouli \ü-lē\ see ULY

oulie \ü-lē\ see ULY

ouling \au-liŋ\ see OWLING²

oulish \ü-lish\ see OOLISH

ou'll¹ \ül\ see OOL¹

ou'll² \ul\ see UL¹

oulle \ül\ see OOL¹

oulli \ü-lē\ see ULY

oully \au-lē\ see OWLY²

oult \ōlt\ see OLT¹

oum \üm\ see OOM¹

oun¹ \aun\ see OWN²

oun² \ün\ see OON¹

ounce \auns\ bounce, flounce, ounce, pounce, trounce • announce, denounce, pronounce, renounce • dead-cat bounce, fluid ounce, mispronounce

ouncer \aun-sər\ bouncer • announcer

ound¹ \ünd\ wound • flesh wound
—*also* -ed *forms of verbs listed at* OON¹

ound² \aund\ bound, crowned, found, ground, hound, mound, pound, round, sound, wound • abound, aground, all-round, around, astound, background, bloodhound, campground, chowhound, compound, confound, coonhound, dachshund, deerhound, dumbfound, earthbound, eastbound, elkhound, expound, fairground, fogbound, foot-pound, foreground, foxhound, gain ground, greyhound, Greyhound, hardbound, high ground, homebound, housebound, icebound, impound, inbound, lose ground, newfound, northbound, outbound, playground, profound, rebound, redound, renowned, resound, rockbound, rock hound, snowbound, southbound, spellbound, staghound, stone-ground, stormbound, surround, unbound, unsound, westbound, wolfhound, year-round • aboveground, Afghan hound, all-around, basset hound, battleground, been around, belowground, break new ground, breeding ground, bring around, common ground, dumping ground, fool around, get around, go around, hang around, horse around, kick around, mess around, muscle-bound, Nootka Sound, off the ground, on the

ground, outward-bound, paper-bound, proving ground, Puget Sound, push around, runaround, screw around, spiral-bound, staging ground, stand one's ground, stick around, stomping ground, surround sound, turnaround, turn around, ultrasound, underground, wraparound • Albemarle Sound, English foxhound, Irish wolfhound, Long Island Sound, McMurdo Sound, merry-go-round, Prince William Sound, run rings around, Russian wolfhound, Scottish deerhound • happy hunting ground, run circles around, throw one's weight around
—*also* -ed *forms of verbs listed at* OWN[2]

oundary \aùn-drē\ see OUNDRY

ounded \aùn-dəd\ bounded, grounded, rounded • confounded, unbounded, unfounded, well-founded, well-grounded, well-rounded
—*also* -ed *forms of verbs listed at* OUND[2]

ounder \aùn-dər\ bounder, flounder, founder, grounder, pounder, sounder

ounding \aùn-diŋ\ grounding, sounding • astounding, high-sounding, resounding
—*also* -ing *forms of verbs listed at* OUND[2]

oundless[1] \ün-ləs\ see OONLESS

oundless[2] \aùn-ləs\ boundless, groundless

oundly \aùnd-lē\ roundly, soundly • profoundly

oundness \aùn-nəs\ roundness, soundness

oundry \aùn-drē\ boundary, foundry

ounds[1] \ünz\ see OONS

ounds[2] \aùnz\ zounds • out-of-bounds • by leaps and bounds

—*also* -s, -'s, *and* -s' *forms of nouns and* -s *forms of verbs listed at* OUND[2]

oundsman \aùnz-mən\ see OWNSMAN

ounge \aùnj\ lounge, scrounge • cocktail lounge

ounger[1] \aùn-jər\ lounger, scrounger

ounger[2] \əŋ-gər\ see ONGER[1]

ounker \əŋ-kər\ see UNKER

ount[1] \änt\ see ANT[2]

ount[2] \aùnt\ count, fount, mount • account, amount, discount, dismount, recount, remount, surmount, viscount • body count, catamount, paramount, Rocky Mount, tantamount • call to account, checking account, expense account, on no account, savings account • Sermon on the Mount, take into account

ountable \aùnt-ə-bəl\ countable • accountable, discountable, surmountable • insurmountable, unaccountable

ountain \aùnt-ᵊn\ fountain, mountain • drinking fountain, soda fountain

ountie \aùnt-ē\ see OUNTY

ounting \aùnt-iŋ\ mounting • accounting
—*also* -ing *forms of verbs listed at* OUNT[2]

ounty \aùnt-ē\ bounty, county, Mountie

oup[1] \ōp\ see OPE

oup[2] \ü\ see EW[1]

oup[3] \üp\ see OOP

oupe[1] \ōp\ see OPE

oupe[2] \üp\ see OOP

ouper \ü-pər\ see OOPER

oupie \ü-pē\ see OOPY

ouple \əp-əl\ see UPLE[1]

ouplet \əp-lət\ see UPLET

oupy \ü-pē\ see OOPY

our[1] \ȯr\ see OR[1]

our[2] \úr\ see URE[1]

our[3] \aúr\ see OWER[2]

our[4] \är\ see AR[3]

our[5] \ər\ see EUR[1]

oura \úr-ə\ see URA

ourable \òr-ə-bəl\ see ORABLE

ourbon \ər-bən\ see URBAN

ource \órs\ see ORSE[1]

ourceful \órs-fəl\ see ORSEFUL

ourd \órd\ see OARD

ourde \úrd\ see URED[1]

ou're[1] \òr\ see OR[1]

ou're[2] \ü-ər\ see EWER[1]

ou're[3] \úr\ see URE[1]

ou're[4] \ər\ see EUR[1]

oured \órd\ see OARD

ourer[1] \òr-ər\ see ORER

ourer[2] \úr-ər\ see URER

ourg \úr\ see URE[1]

ourge[1] \ərj\ see URGE

ourge[2] \órj\ see ORGE

ourger \ər-jər\ see ERGER

ouri \úr-ē\ see URY[1]

ourier[1] \úr-ē-ər\ courier • couturier

ourier[2] \ər-ē-ər\ see URRIER

ouring[1] \òr-iŋ\ see ORING

ouring[2] \úr-iŋ\ see URING

ourish \ər-ish\ flourish, nourish • amateurish

ourist \úr-əst\ see URIST

ourly \aúr-lē\ dourly, hourly, sourly • half-hourly

ourn[1] \órn\ see ORN[1]

ourn[2] \ərn\ see URN

ournal \ərn-ᵊl\ see ERNAL

ournament \òr-nə-mənt\ see ORNAMENT

ourne \órn\ see ORN[1]

ourney[1] \ər-nē\ Bernie, Ernie, gurney, journey, tourney • attorney • district attorney

ourney[2] \òr-nē\ see ORNY

ournful \órn-fəl\ see ORNFUL

ourning \òr-niŋ\ see ORNING

ournment \ərn-mənt\ see ERNMENT

ours[1] \órz\ see OORS

ours[2] \ärz\ see ARS

ours[3] \aúrz\ ours • all hours • after-hours —*also* -s, -'s, *and* -s' *forms of nouns and* -s *forms of verbs listed at* OWER[2]

ours[4] \úr\ see URE[1]

ourse \órs\ see ORSE[1]

ourt[1] \órt\ see ORT[1]

ourt[2] \úrt\ see URT[1]

ourth \órth\ see ORTH[1]

ourtier \òr-chər\ see ORCHER

ourtly \órt-lē\ see ORTLY

oury \aúr-ē\ see OWERY

ous[1] \ü\ see EW[1]

ous[2] \üs\ see USE[1]

ousa[1] \ü-sə\ see USA[1]

ousa[2] \ü-zə\ see USA[2]

ousal \aú-zəl\ spousal, tousle • arousal, carousal

ouse[1] \üs\ see USE[1]

ouse[2] \aús\ blouse, douse, grouse, house, Klaus, Laos, louse, mouse, souse, spouse, Strauss • alehouse, bathhouse, Bauhaus, birdhouse, boathouse, book louse, bunkhouse, clubhouse, courthouse, crab louse, deer mouse, delouse, doghouse, dollhouse, dormouse, espouse, farmhouse, field house, field mouse, firehouse, flophouse, full house, fun house, greenhouse, guardhouse, guesthouse, head louse, hothouse, house mouse, icehouse, jailhouse, keep house, lighthouse, longhouse, madhouse, nuthouse, outhouse, penthouse, playhouse, poorhouse, ranch house, roadhouse, roughhouse, roundhouse, row house, ruffed grouse, schoolhouse, smokehouse, statehouse, steak house, storehouse, teahouse, titmouse, tollhouse, Toll House, town house, tree house, warehouse, wheelhouse, White House, wood louse, workhouse • boardinghouse, body louse, cat and mouse, coffee-house, countinghouse, country house, customhouse, halfway house, house-to-house, manor house, meetinghouse, Mickey Mouse, motherhouse, on the house, open house, opera house, pocket mouse, powerhouse, rooming house, slaughterhouse, station house, sugarhouse, sum-merhouse, Westinghouse • bring down the house, man of the house

ouse³ \aủz\ blouse, browse, douse, dowse, drowse, house, mouse, rouse, spouse • arouse, carouse, delouse, espouse, rehouse, rough-house, warehouse
—*also* -s, -'s, *and* -s' *forms of nouns and* -s *forms of verbs listed at* ow²

ouse⁴ \üz\ see USE²

ousel \aủ-zǝl\ see OUSAL

ouser \aủ-zǝr\ mouser, schnauzer, trouser, wowser • carouser • rab-ble-rouser

ousin \ǝz-ᵊn\ see OZEN¹

ousing \aủ-ziŋ\ housing, rousing • rabble-rousing
—*also* -ing *forms of verbs listed at* OUSE³

ousle¹ \ü-zǝl\ see USAL

ousle² \aủ-zǝl\ see OUSAL

ousse \üs\ see USE¹

ousseau \ü-sō\ see USOE

oust¹ \aủst\ Faust, joust, oust, roust
—*also* -ed *forms of verbs listed at* OUSE²

oust² \üst\ see OOST

ouste \üst\ see OOST

ousy \aủ-zē\ see OWSY

out¹ \ü\ see EW¹

out² \üt\ see UTE

out³ \aủt\ bout, clout, doubt, drought, flout, gout, grout, lout, out, pout, rout, route, scout,

shout, snout, spout, sprout, stout, tout, trout • about, act out, all-out, back out, bailout, bail out, bawl out, bear out, beat out, blackout, black out, blot out, blowout, bombed-out, bow out, Boy Scout, breakout, break out, breechclout, bring out, brook trout, brownout, brown trout, bug out, burned-out, burnout, burn out, butt out, buy-out, buy out, campout, cast out, checkout, check out, chill out, clear out, closeout, come out, cookout, cop out, Cub Scout, cutout, cut out, devout, die out, dig out, dine out, dish out, dole out, downspout, draw out, dropout, drop out, dry out, dugout, eke out, en route, fade-out, fake out, fallout, fall out, farm out, far-out, fill out, find out, flake out, flameout, flame out, flat-out, flunk out, foldout, foul out, freak-out, freaked-out, get out, Girl Scout, give out, go out, grind out, gross-out, gross out, handout, hand out, hangout, hide-out, holdout, hold out, iron out, kick out, knockout, knock out, lake trout, layout, lights-out, line out, lock out, lookout, look out, lose out, make out, max out, miss out, no doubt, nose out, opt out, pan out, pass out, payout, phase-out, phase out, pick out, pig out, printout, print out, psych-out, pull out, punch out, put out, roll out, rub out, rule out, run out, sack out, Sea Scout, sea trout, sellout, sell out, set out, shell out, shoot-out, shout-out, shutout, shut out, sick-out, sign out, sit out, sleep out, smoke out, sold-out, spaced-out, space out, speak out, spell out, stakeout, stake out, standout, stand out, step out, stick out, stressed-out, strikeout, strike out, strung out, sweat out, takeout, take out, talk out, thought-out, throughout, throw out, time-out, trade route, tryout, try out, tune out, turnout, turn out, veg out, wait out, walkout, walk out, washout, wash out, watch out, way-out, wear out, weird out, whiteout, wigged-out, wimp out, wiped out, wipeout, wipe out, without, workout, work out, worn-out, write out, zone out, zonked-out • autoroute, bring about, brussels sprout, Cape Lookout, carryout, carry out, cast about, come about, cutthroat trout, down-and-out, duke it out, Eagle Scout, falling-out, figure out, gadabout, go about, hammer out, have it out, how about, just about, long-drawn-out, odd man out, out-and-out, rainbow trout, roustabout, runabout, rural route, sauerkraut, set about, speckled trout, spit it out, talent scout, waterspout • day in day out, eat one's heart out, knock-down dragout, stick one's neck out • technical knockout

oute[1] \üt\ see UTE

oute[2] \aut\ see OUT[3]

outed \aut-əd\ snouted • undoubted

—*also* -ed *forms of verbs listed at* OUT[3]

outer[1] \üt-ər\ see UTER

outer[2] \aut-ər\ doubter, outer, shouter, stouter • devouter

outh[1] \üth\ see OOTH[2]

outh[2] \auth\ mouth, south • badmouth, Deep South, loudmouth, trench mouth • blabbermouth, cottonmouth, hand-to-mouth, motormouth, word-of-mouth • down in the mouth • from the horse's mouth • put one's foot in one's mouth

outherly \əth-ər-lē\ see OTHERLY

outhful \üth-fəl\ see UTHFUL

outi \üt-ē\ see OOTY[1]

outing \aut-iŋ\ outing, scouting
—*also* -ing *forms of verbs listed at* OUT[3]

outre \üt-ər\ see UTER

outrement \ü-trə-mənt\ see UTRIMENT

outs \auts\ bean sprouts • hereabouts, on the outs, thereabouts, whereabouts
—*also* -s, 's, *and* -s' *forms of nouns and* -s *forms of verbs listed at* OUT[3]

ou've \üv\ see OVE[3]

ouver \ü-vər\ see OVER[3]

oux \ü\ see EW[1]

ouy \ē\ see EE[1]

ouzel \ü-zəl\ see USAL

ov[1] \äf\ see OFF[1]

ov[2] \óf\ see OFF[2]

ova \ō-və\ nova • Jehovah • Casanova, supernova • Navratilova

ovable \ü-və-bəl\ movable, provable • disprovable, immovable, improvable, removable

ovah \ō-və\ see OVA

oval \ü-vəl\ approval, removal • disapproval

ove[1] \əv\ dove, glove, love, of, shove • above, as of, dream of, foxglove, in love, kind of, make love, out of, rock dove, short of, tough love, truelove • afoul of, ahead of, all kinds of, all sorts of, because of, become of, boxing glove, by means of, by way of, dispose of, get wind of, have none of, in case of, in light of, in place of, inside of, in spite of, instead of, in terms of, in view of, ladylove, make fun of, make use of, mourning dove, on top of, outside of, puppy love, turtledove, unheard-of, well-thought-of • alongside of, at the hands of, in

advance of, in behalf of, in favor
of, in the face of, in the light of,
in the wake of, make the most of,
on account of, on behalf of, on
the heels of, push comes to shove,
regardless of • at the mercy of, in
defiance of, irrespective of

ove² \ōv\ clove, cove, dove, drove,
grove, Jove, mauve, rove, stove,
strove, trove, wove • alcove,
cookstove, mangrove, woodstove
• Franklin stove, interwove, treasure trove • potbellied stove

ove³ \üv\ groove, move, prove,
you've • approve, disprove, im-
prove, remove, reprove • disap-
prove, on the move

ovel¹ \äv-əl\ grovel, novel • graphic
novel

ovel² \əv-əl\ grovel, hovel, shovel
• steam shovel • power shovel

ovement \üv-mənt\ movement
• improvement

oven \ō-vən\ cloven, coven, woven
• Beethoven, handwoven, plain-
woven • interwoven

over¹ \əv-ər\ cover, hover, lover,
plover • bedcover, discover, dust-
cover, gill cover, ground cover,
hardcover, recover, slipcover,
softcover, uncover • blow one's
cover, undercover

over² \ō-vər\ clover, Dover,
Grover, over, rover • all over,
blow over, boil over, bowl over,
chew over, comb-over, crossover,
flyover, get over, go over, hand
over, hangover, holdover, hold
over, in clover, knock over, lay-
over, lay over, leftover, look over,
moreover, once-over, Passover,
pass over, pick over, popover,
pullover, pull over, pushover, put
over, red clover, rollover, run
over, sea rover, spillover,
stopover, strikeover, sweet clover,
takeover, take over, talk over,

tide over, turnover, turn over,
voice-over, walk over, warmed-
over, watch over, work over
• carryover, Strait of Dover • over
and over

over³ \ü-vər\ Hoover, louver,
mover • earthmover, maneuver,
remover, Vancouver • people
mover

over⁴ \äv-ər\ see AVER¹

overt \ō-vərt\ covert, overt

overy \əv-rē\ discovery, recovery

ovey \ə-vē\ covey • lovey-dovey

ovie \ü-vē\ see OOVY

ovo \ō-vō\ Provo • de novo

ow¹ \ō\ beau, blow, bow, bro,
crow, do, doe, dough, floe, flow,
foe, fro, glow, go, grow, hoe, Jo,
joe, Joe, know, lo, low, mow, no,
o, O, oh, owe, Poe, pro, roe, row,
schmo, sew, show, slow, snow, so,
sow, stow, Stowe, though, throe,
throw, toe, tow, whoa, woe, yo
• aglow, ago, airflow, air show,
although, archfoe, argot, a throw,
backhoe, Bardot, below, bestow,
big toe, Bordeaux, bravo, callow,
chateau, cockcrow, cornrow,
corn snow, crossbow, Cousteau,
Day-Glo, death row, Defoe,
deathblow, elbow, fencerow,
forego, forgo, freak show, free
throw, game show, Glasgow, go-
slow, gung ho, Hankow, heave-
ho, hedgerow, hello, horse show,
ice floe, ice show, inflow, in tow,
Io, Jane Doe, jim crow, Joe Blow,
John Doe, Juneau, kayo, KO, lie
low, light show, longbow, Lu-
chow, macho, mallow, Marlowe,
marrow, merlot, minnow, mojo,
Monroe, Moscow, mudflow, no-
no, no-show, nouveau, oboe,
outflow, outgrow, oxbow,
plateau, pronto, quiz show, rainbow, red snow, regrow, repo,
road show, Rousseau, scarecrow,

sideshow, skid row, ski tow, Soho, so-so, sourdough, stone's throw, tableau, talk show, tiptoe, Thoreau, trade show, trousseau, uh-oh, van Gogh, wallow, widow, willow, winnow, yarrow • afterglow, aikido, Angelo, apropos, art deco, art nouveau, audio, barrio, bay window, Bilbao, black widow, blow-by-blow, bone marrow, Borneo, buffalo, Buffalo, bungalow, calico, cameo, centimo, CEO, Cicero, curio, do-si-do, domino, dynamo, embryo, Eskimo, French window, hammer throw, hammertoe, high and low, HMO, horror show, Idaho, in a row, indigo, in the know, Jericho, Lake Tahoe, little toe, long-ago, Longfellow, Mario, medico, Mexico, mistletoe, Monaco, Navajo, NCO, oleo, on tiptoe, overflow, overgrow, overthrow, patio, piccolo, Point Barrow, polio, pompano, portico, quid pro quo, radio, ratio, rococo, rodeo, Romeo, rose window, Scorpio, semipro, show window, sloppy joe, so-and-so, status quo, stereo, stop-and-go, studio, tallyho, tangelo, tic-tac-toe, TKO, to-and-fro, Tokyo, touch-and-go, tupelo, UFO, undergo, undertow, vertigo, video, zydeco • Antonio, Arapaho, arpeggio, at one's elbow, bull's-eye window, centesimo, clock radio, Geronimo, get-up-and-go, go with the flow, Guantánamo, home video, lothario, magnifico, medicine show, New Mexico, oregano, Ozark Plateau, picture window, politico, portfolio, pussy willow, Rosario, Sarajevo, scenario, simpatico, talk radio, tennis elbow • archipelago, braggadocio, dog and pony show, ex officio, gener-

alissimo, impresario, oratorio, Paramaribo, variety show

ow² \aù\ bough, bow, brow, chow, ciao, cow, Dow, how, Howe, Lao, Mao, now, ow, plow, pow, prow, row, scow, slough, sow, Tao, thou, vow, wow • allow, and how, as how, avow, bowwow, cacao, cash cow, chowchow, chow chow, Cracow, Dachau, endow, eyebrow, Hankow, highbrow, hoosegow, Jungfrau, know-how, kowtow, Kraków, lowbrow, luau, Macao, mau-mau, meow, Moscow, nohow, Palau, powwow, sea cow, snowplow, somehow, Spandau • anyhow, cat's meow, disallow, disavow, here and now, Hu Jintao, Krakatau, middlebrow, sacred cow • crème de cacao, Guinea-Bissau • holier-than-thou, Oberammergau

ow³ \òv\ see OFF²

owa \ō-və\ see OVA

owable¹ \ō-ə-bəl\ knowable, showable • unknowable

owable² \aù-ə-bəl\ plowable • allowable

owal¹ \ō-əl\ see OEL

owal² \aùl\ see OWL²

owan \ō-ən\ see OAN¹

oward¹ \òrd\ see OARD

oward² \aùrd\ see OWERED

owd¹ \üd\ see UDE¹

owd² \aùd\ see OUD

owdah \aùd-ə\ see AUDE³

owder \aùd-ər\ chowder, louder, powder, prouder • black powder, gunpowder, tooth powder • chili powder, curry powder, talcum powder

owdown \ō-daùn\ lowdown, showdown, slowdown

owdy \aùd-ē\ Audi, cloudy, dowdy, howdy, rowdy • cum laude • magna cum laude, summa cum laude

owe \ō\ see OW[1]
owed[1] \ōd\ see ODE
owed[2] \aud\ see OUD[2]
owel \aul\ see OWL[2]
oweling \au-liŋ\ see OWLING[2]
owell[1] \aul\ see OWL[2]
owell[2] \ō-əl\ see OEL
owen \ō-ən\ see OAN[1]
ower[1] \or\ see OR[1]
ower[2] \aur\ bower, cower, dour, flour, flower, glower, hour, our, plower, power, scour, shower, sour, tower • air power, bellflower, bell tower, black power, brainpower, coneflower, cornflower, devour, disk flower, empower, firepower, fire tower, Glendower, great power, half hour, horsepower, man-hour, manpower, mayflower, moonflower, pasqueflower, ray flower, rush hour, safflower, sea power, starflower, state flower, strawflower, sunflower, wallflower, watchtower, wildflower, willpower, world power • candlepower, cauliflower, conning tower, cooling tower, Devils Tower, disempower, Eisenhower, flower power, gillyflower, happy hour, hydropower, ivory tower, overpower, passionflower, person-hour, quarter hour, staying power, superpower, sweet-and-sour, thundershower, trumpet flower, waterpower, water tower, whisky sour, zero hour • balance of power, eleventh hour, kilowatt-hour
ower[3] \ō-ər\ see OER[4]
owered \aurd\ coward, flowered, Howard, powered • high-powered • ivory-towered, underpowered
    —also -ed forms of verbs listed at OWER[2]
owering \au-riŋ\ flowering, towering • nonflowering

—also -ing forms of verbs listed at OWER[2]
owery \aur-ē\ dowry, floury, flowery, Maori, showery
owhee \ō-ē\ see OWY
owie \au-ē\ Maui, zowie
owing \ō-iŋ\ see OING[1]
owl[1] \ōl\ see OLE[1]
owl[2] \aul\ bowel, foul, fowl, growl, howl, jowl, owl, prowl, scowl, towel, trowel, vowel, yowl • avowal, barn owl, barred owl, beach towel, befoul, horned owl, night owl, peafowl, screech owl, tea towel, wildfowl • disavowal, disembowel, guinea fowl, jungle fowl, on the prowl, snowy owl, spotted owl, Turkish towel, waterfowl • throw in the towel • neither fish nor fowl
owland \ō-lənd\ lowland, Poland, Roland
owledge \äl-ij\ college, knowledge • acknowledge
owler[1] \ō-lər\ see OLLER
owler[2] \au-lər\ growler, howler, prowler, scowler
owless \ō-ləs\ see OLUS
owline \ō-lən\ see OLON
owling[1] \ō-liŋ\ see OLLING
owling[2] \au-liŋ\ growling, howling, toweling
    —also -ing forms of verbs listed at OWL[2]
owlock \äl-ək\ see OLOCH
owly[1] \ō-lē\ see OLY[1]
owly[2] \au-lē\ foully, growly, jowly
owman \ō-mən\ see OMAN
ow-me \ō-mē\ see OAMY
own[1] \ōn\ see ONE[1]
own[2] \aun\ Braun, brown, clown, crown, down, drown, frown, gown, noun, town • back down, bear down, boil down, boomtown, breakdown, break down, bring down, Cape Town, Charlestown, clampdown, clamp

down, closedown, comedown, come down, cooldown, countdown, count down, cow town, crackdown, crack down, crosstown, cut down, downtown, dress down, dumb down, facedown, first down, Freetown, Georgetown, ghost town, go down, hand down, hands-down, hold down, hometown, Jamestown, knockdown, knock down, lay down, letdown, let down, lie down, live down, look down, lowdown, markdown, mark down, meltdown, melt down, midtown, nightgown, nutbrown, phase down, pipe down, play down, pronoun, pull-down, renown, rubdown, rundown, set down, shakedown, shake down, shoot down, showdown, shutdown, shut down, slap down, slowdown, splashdown, splash down, strike down, strippeddown, sundown, swansdown, take down, tear down, thumbs-down, top-down, touchdown, touch down, trade down, turndown, turn down, uptown, Von Braun, wear down, weigh down, wind down, write down, Youngstown • Allentown, broken-down, Chinatown, common noun, dressing gown, eiderdown, go to town, hand-me-down, proper noun, shantytown, simmer down, thistledown, Tinseltown, trickledown, Triple Crown, tumbledown, up and down, upand-down, upside down, water down, watered-down • bring the house down, let one's hair down, man-about-town, nervous breakdown, put one's foot down

ownded \aùn-dəd\ see OUNDED

ownding \aùn-diŋ\ see OUNDING

owned[1] \ōnd\ see ONED[1]

owned[2] \aùnd\ see OUND[2]

owner[1] \ō-nər\ see ONER[1]

owner[2] \ü-nər\ see OONER

owner[3] \aù-nər\ downer • downtowner

owness \ō-nəs\ see ONUS[2]

ownia \ō-nē-ə\ see ONIA[1]

ownie \aù-nē\ see OWNY

owning \ō-niŋ\ see ONING[2]

ownish \aù-nish\ brownish, clownish

ownsman \aùnz-mən\ groundsman, townsman

owny \aù-nē\ brownie, browny, downy, townie

owper \ü-pər\ see OOPER

owry \aùr-ē\ see OWERY

owse \aùz\ see OUSE[3]

owser \aù-zər\ see OUSER

owster \ō-stər\ see OASTER

owsy \aù-zē\ blousy, blowsy, drowsy, frowsy, lousy, mousy

owth \ōth\ both, growth, loath, oath, quoth • old-growth, outgrowth • overgrowth, undergrowth • Hippocratic oath

owy \ō-ē\ blowy, Chloe, doughy, Joey, showy, snowy • echoey

owys \ō-əs\ see OIS[3]

ox \äks\ box, fox, Fox, Knox, lox, ox, pox • bandbox, black box, boom box, boondocks, Botox, cowpox, detox, dreadlocks, firebox, Fort Knox, gearbox, gray fox, hatbox, icebox, in-box, jewel box, jukebox, lockbox, mailbox, matchbox, musk ox, out-box, outfox, red fox, sandbox, smallpox, soapbox, squawk box, strongbox, toolbox, unbox, voice box, workbox, Xerox • arctic fox, ballot box, bobby socks, chatterbox, chicken pox, equinox, flying fox, music box, orthodox, Orthodox, paradox, sentry box, shadowbox, silver fox, tinderbox, window box, witness-box • dialog

box, Greek Orthodox, heterodox, idiot box, jack-in-the-box, Pandora's box, penalty box, unorthodox • Eastern Orthodox, safe-deposit box
—*also* -s, -'s, *and* -s' *forms of nouns and* -s *forms of verbs listed at* OCK[1]

oxer \äk-sər\ boxer, Boxer • kickboxer • bobby-soxer

oxie \äk-sē\ see OXY

oxy \äk-sē\ boxy, foxy, moxie, proxy • epoxy • orthodoxy • unorthodoxy

oy \òi\ boy, buoy, cloy, coy, joy, Joy, koi, oy, ploy, poi, Roy, soy, toy, Troy • ahoy, alloy, annoy, ball boy, batboy, B-boy, beachboy, bellboy, bell buoy, bok choy, borzoi, busboy, carboy, choirboy, convoy, cowboy, decoy, deploy, destroy, doughboy, employ, enjoy, envoy, Hanoi, homeboy, houseboy, killjoy, Leroy, life buoy, McCoy, newsboy, pageboy, page boy, playboy, plowboy, po'boy, Quemoy, Saint Croix, schoolboy, stock boy, Tolstoy, tomboy, viceroy • Adonai, altar boy, attaboy, bullyboy, cabin boy, corduroy, hoi polloi, Illinois, Iroquois, mama's boy, office boy, overjoy, paperboy, poster boy, Tinkertoy, whipping boy • delivery boy, Helen of Troy

oya \òi-ə\ see OIA

oyable \òi-ə-bəl\ employable, enjoyable • unemployable

oyal[1] \ī l\ see ILE[1]

oyal[2] \òil\ see OIL

oyalist \òi-ə-ləst\ loyalist, royalist

oyalty \òil-tē\ loyalty, royalty • disloyalty

oyance \òi-əns\ annoyance, clairvoyance, flamboyance
—*also* -s, -'s, *and* -s' *forms of nouns listed at* OYANT

oyant \òi-ənt\ buoyant • clairvoyant, flamboyant

oyce \òis\ see OICE

oyd \òid\ see OID[1]

oyed \òid\ see OID[1]

oyer \òir\ foyer • destroyer

oyes \òiz\ see OISE[2]

oying \òiŋ\ see AWING

oyle \òil\ see OIL

oyless \òi-ləs\ joyless, Troilus

oyment \òi-mənt\ deployment, employment, enjoyment • redeployment, self-employment, unemployment

oyne \òin\ see OIN[1]

oyo \òi-ə\ see OIA

oyster \òi-stər\ see OISTER

oz[1] \əz\ see EUSE[1]

oz[2] \òz\ see AUSE[1]

oz[3] \ōz\ see OSE[2]

oze \ōz\ see OSE[2]

ozen[1] \əz-ᵊn\ cousin, dozen • first cousin • baker's dozen, second cousin • a dime a dozen

ozen[2] \ōz-ᵊn\ see OSEN

ozer \ō-zər\ see OSER[1]

ozily \ō-zə-lē\ see OSILY

ozo[1] \ō-sō\ see OSO[1]

ozo[2] \ō-zō\ see OSO[2]

ozy \ō-zē\ see OSY

ozzle \äz-əl\ Basel, Basil, nozzle, schnozzle

U

u \ü\ see EW[1]

ua \ä\ see A[1]

uable \ü-ə-bəl\ chewable, doable, viewable • renewable, undoable • nonrenewable

ual \ü-əl\ see UEL[1]

uan \ü-ən\ bruin, ruin, yuan

uancy \ü-ən-sē\ see UENCY

uant \ü-ənt\ see UENT

uart \u̇rt\ see URT[1]

ub \əb\ chub, club, cub, drub, dub, flub, grub, hub, nub, pub, rub, schlub, scrub, shrub, snub, stub, sub, tub • bathtub, book club, brew pub, glee club, health club, hot tub, hubbub, nightclub, war club, washtub, yacht club • billy club, country club, overdub, service club, syllabub • Beelzebub

uba \ü-bə\ Cuba, scuba, tuba • Aruba, saxtuba

ubal \ü-bəl\ nubile, ruble, tubal

uban \ü-bən\ see EUBEN

ubbard \əb-ərd\ cupboard • Mother Hubbard

ubber \əb-ər\ blubber, rubber, scrubber • foam rubber, landlubber, nightclubber • moneygrubber

ubbery \əb-rē\ blubbery, rubbery, shrubbery

ubbily \əb-ə-lē\ bubbly, grubbily

ubbing \əb-iŋ\ drubbing, rubbing • *also* -ing *forms of verbs listed at* UB

ubble \əb-əl\ bubble, double, Hubble, rubble, stubble, trouble • abubble, redouble, soap bubble • body double, borrow trouble, daily double, on the double

ubbled \əb-əld\ bubbled, doubled, troubled • redoubled, untroubled

ubbly[1] \əb-lē\ bubbly, doubly, stubbly

ubbly[2] \əb-ə-lē\ see UBBILY

ubby \əb-ē\ chubby, clubby, grubby, hubby, scrubby, shrubby, stubby, tubby

ube \üb\ boob, cube, lube, rube, tube • boob tube, Danube, flashcube, jujube, test tube • bouillon cube, breathing tube, down the tube, inner tube

uben \ü-bən\ see EUBEN

ubens \ü-bənz\ Rubens —*also* -s, -'s, *and* -s' *forms of nouns listed at* EUBEN

uber \ü-bər\ goober, tuber

uberance \ü-brəns\ exuberance, protuberance

uberant \ü-brənt\ exuberant, protuberant • overexuberant

uberous \ü-brəs\ see UBRIS

ubic \ü-bik\ cubic • cherubic

ubile \ü-bəl\ see UBAL

uble \ü-bəl\ see UBAL

ubric \ü-brik\ Kubrick, rubric

ubrious \ü-brē-əs\ lugubrious, salubrious

ubris \ü-brəs\ hubris, tuberous

ubtile \ət-ᵊl\ see UTTLE

uby \ü-bē\ see OOBY

uca \ü-kə\ see OOKA

ucat \ək-ət\ see UCKET

ucca[1] \ü-kə\ see OOKA

ucca[2] \ək-ə\ see UKKA

uccal \ək-əl\ see UCKLE

ucci \ü-chē\ see OOCHY

uccor \ək-ər\ see UCKER

ucculence \ək-yə-ləns\ see UCULENCE

uce \üs\ see USE[1]

uced \üst\ see OOST

ucence \üs-ᵊns\ nuisance • translucence

ucer \ü-sər\ juicer • producer, seducer

uch[1] \ich\ see ITCH

uch[2] \ük\ see UKE

uch[3] \əch\ see UTCH

uche[1] \ü-chē\ see OOCHY

uche[2] \üch\ see OOCH[1]

uche[3] \üsh\ see OUCHE

ucher \ü-chər\ see UTURE

uchin \ü-shən\ see UTION

uchy \əch-ē\ duchy, touchy • archduchy, grand duchy

ucian \ü-shən\ see UTION

ucible \ü-sə-bəl\ crucible • deducible, inducible, producible, reducible • irreducible, reproducible

ucifer \ü-sə-fər\ crucifer, Lucifer

ucive \ü-siv\ see USIVE

uck[1] \ək\ buck, Buck, chuck, cluck, duck, guck, luck, muck, pluck, puck, Puck, schmuck, shuck, snuck, struck, stuck, suck, truck, tuck, yuck • awestruck, dead duck, dumbstruck, dump truck, fire truck, hard luck, lameduck, moonstruck, mukluk, potluck, roebuck, sawbuck, shelduck, stagestruck, starstruck, sunstruck, unstuck, upchuck, woodchuck • Daffy Duck, Habakkuk, horror-struck, Keokuk, ladder truck, megabuck, motortruck, muckamuck, nip and tuck, pass the buck, Peking duck, pickup truck, push one's luck, sitting duck, thunderstruck

uck[2] \ùk\ see OOK[1]

ukar \ək-ər\ see UCKER

ucker \ək-ər\ pucker, shucker, succor, sucker, trucker, tucker • bloodsucker, goatsucker, sapsucker, seersucker, shark sucker

ucket \ək-ət\ bucket, ducat • lunch-bucket, Nantucket, Pawtucket, rust bucket • kick the bucket • drop in the bucket

uckle \ək-əl\ buckle, chuckle, knuckle, suckle, truckle • bareknuckle, pinochle, swashbuckle, unbuckle • honeysuckle

uckled \ək-əld\ cuckold, knuckled • bare-knuckled
—also -ed forms of verbs listed at UCKLE

uckling \ək-liŋ\ duckling, suckling • swashbuckling • ugly duckling
—also -ing forms of verbs listed at UCKLE

uckold \ək-əld\ see UCKLED

ucks \əks\ see UX[1]

uckus \ùk-əs\ ruckus, Sukkoth

ucky \ək-ē\ ducky, lucky, mucky, plucky, sucky, yucky • Kentucky, unlucky • happy-go-lucky

uct \əkt\ duct • abduct, bile duct, conduct, construct, deduct, destruct, induct, instruct, obstruct • aqueduct, deconstruct, reconstruct, self-destruct, viaduct
—also -ed forms of verbs listed at UCK[1]

uctable \ək-tə-bəl\ see UCTIBLE

uctible \ək-tə-bəl\ deductible, destructible • indestructible, nondeductible

uction \ək-shən\ suction • abduction, conduction, construction, deduction, destruction, induction, instruction, obstruction, production, reduction, seduction • coproduction, deconstruction, introduction, liposuction, mass production, reconstruction, reproduction, self-destruction

uctive \ək-tiv\ conductive, constructive, deductive, destructive, inductive, instructive, obstructive, productive, reductive, seductive • nonproductive, reconstructive, reproductive, self-destructive,

unconstructive, unproductive
• counterproductive

uctor \ək-tər\ conductor, instructor • nonconductor • semiconductor, superconductor

uculence \ək-yə-ləns\ succulence, truculence

ucy \ü-sē\ see UICY

ud¹ \əd\ blood, bud, crud, cud, dud, flood, Judd, mud, scud, spud, stud, thud • bad blood, blue blood, earbud, full-blood, half-blood, leaf bud, lifeblood, new blood, oxblood, pure-blood, redbud, rosebud, shed blood, smell blood, sweat blood • dragon's blood, flesh and blood, flower bud, in cold blood, in the bud • stick-in-the-mud

ud² \üd\ see UDE¹

ud³ \u̇d\ see OOD¹

uda \üd-ə\ Buddha, Gouda, Judah • Barbuda, Bermuda • barracuda

udah \üd-ə\ see UDA

udal \üd-ᵊl\ see OODLE

udd¹ \u̇d\ see OOD¹

udd² \əd\ see UD¹

udded \əd-əd\ see OODED¹

udder \əd-ər\ rudder, shudder, udder

uddha \üd-ə\ see UDA

uddhist \üd-əst\ see UDIST¹

uddie \əd-ē\ see UDDY¹

udding \əd-iŋ\ budding,
—also -ing forms of verbs listed at UD¹

uddle \əd-ᵊl\ cuddle, fuddle, huddle, muddle, puddle • befuddle

uddly \əd-lē\ cuddly, Dudley

uddy¹ \əd-ē\ bloody, buddy, Buddy, cruddy, muddy, ruddy, study • case study, work-study • buddy-buddy, fuddy-duddy, understudy

uddy² \u̇d-ē\ see OODY²

ude¹ \üd\ brood, crude, dude, feud, food, hued, Jude, lewd, mood, nude, prude, rude, shrewd, snood, 'tude, who'd, you'd • allude, blood feud, collude, conclude, delude, denude, elude, exclude, exude, fast-food, Gertrude, health food, include, intrude, junk food, nonfood, plant food, postlude, preclude, prelude, protrude, seafood, seclude, subdued, unglued • altitude, amplitude, aptitude, attitude, certitude, comfort food, finger food, fortitude, frankenfood, gratitude, interlude, lassitude, latitude, longitude, magnitude, multitude, platitude, rectitude, servitude, solitude • beatitude, ineptitude, ingratitude, natural food, vicissitude

ude² \üd-ə\ see UDA

udel \üd-ᵊl\ see OODLE

udeness \üd-nəs\ see UDINOUS

udent \üd-ᵊnt\ prudent, student • imprudent, nonstudent

uder \üd-ər\ brooder, Tudor • intruder
—also -er forms of adjectives listed at UDE¹

udge¹ \əj\ budge, drudge, fudge, grudge, judge, nudge, sludge, smudge, trudge • adjudge, begrudge, misjudge, prejudge

udge² \üj\ see UGE¹

udgeon \əj-ən\ bludgeon • curmudgeon

udgie \əj-ē\ see UDGY

udgy \əj-ē\ budgie, pudgy, sludgy, smudgy

udi \ü-dē\ see OODY¹

udie \ü-dē\ see OODY¹

udinous \üd-nəs\ crudeness, rudeness, shrewdness • multitudinous

udist¹ \üd-əst\ Buddhist, nudist
—also -est forms of adjectives listed at UDE¹

udist² \u̇d-əst\ see OULDEST

udity \üd-ət-ē\ crudity, nudity

udley \əd-lē\ see UDDLY
udly \əd-lē\ see UDDLY
udo \üd-ō\ judo, pseudo
udor \üd-ər\ see UDER
udsman \ùdz-mən\ see OODSMAN
udu \üd-ü\ see OODOO
udy[1] \ü-dē\ see OODY[1]
udy[2] \əd-ē\ see UDDY[1]
ue[1] \ü\ see EW[1]
ue[2] \ā\ see AY[1]
ued \üd\ see UDE[1]
ueghel \ü-gəl\ see UGAL
uel[1] \ü-əl\ crewel, cruel, dual, duel, fuel, gruel, jewel, Jewel • accrual, refuel, renewal, synfuel • biofuel, diesel fuel, fossil fuel
uel[2] \ül\ see OOL[1]
uely \ü-lē\ see ULY
uence \ü-əns\ affluence, confluence, congruence, influence, pursuance • incongruence
—*also* -s, -'s *and* -s' *forms of nouns listed at* UENT
uency \ü-ən-sē\ fluency, truancy • congruency
ueness \ü-nəs\ see EWNESS
uent \ü-ənt\ fluent, truant • affluent, congruent, effluent • incongruent
uer \ü-ər\ see EWER[1]
uerile \ùr-əl\ see URAL
ues \üz\ see USE[2]
uesman \üz-mən\ see EWSMAN
uesome \ü-səm\ gruesome, twosome
uesy \ü-zē\ see OOZY
uet \ü-ət\ bluet, cruet, suet • conduit, intuit
uette \et\ see ET[1]
uey \ü-ē\ see EWY
uff \əf\ bluff, buff, cuff, duff, fluff, gruff, guff, huff, luff, muff, puff, rough, ruff, scruff, scuff, slough, snuff, stuff, tough • cream puff, earmuff, enough, feedstuff, foodstuff, french cuff, handcuff, hang tough, hot stuff, kid stuff, Pine Bluff, rebuff • blindman's buff,

call one's bluff, off-the-cuff, overstuff, powder puff, strut one's stuff, up to snuff
uffe[1] \üf\ see OOF[1]
uffe[2] \ùf\ see OOF[2]
uffed \əft\ tuft
—*also* -ed *forms of verbs listed at* UFF
uffel \əf-əl\ see UFFLE
uffer \əf-ər\ bluffer, buffer, duffer, puffer, suffer • candlesnuffer, stocking stuffer
—*also* -er *forms of adjectives listed at* UFF
uffet \əf-ət\ buffet, tuffet
uffin \əf-ən\ muffin, puffin, roughen, toughen • English muffin, ragamuffin
uffle \əf-əl\ duffel, muffle, ruffle, scuffle, shuffle, snuffle, truffle • kerfuffle, reshuffle
uffled \əf-əld\ unruffled
—*also* -ed *forms of verbs listed at* UFFLE
uffly \əf-lē\ gruffly, roughly
uffy \əf-ē\ fluffy, huffy, puffy, scruffy, stuffy, toughie
ufi \ü-fē\ see OOFY
ufous \ü-fəs\ doofus, Rufus
uft \əft\ see UFFED
ufus \ü-fəs\ see UFOUS
ug \əg\ bug, chug, Doug, drug, dug, hug, jug, lug, mug, plug, pug, rug, shrug, slug, smug, snug, thug, tug, ugh • bear hug, bedbug, debug, earplug, firebug, fireplug, humbug, june bug, nondrug, prayer rug, sea slug, spark plug, stinkbug, throw rug, unplug, wall plug • antidrug, doodlebug, gateway drug, jitterbug, ladybug, lightning bug, litterbug, mealybug, pull the plug, scatter rug, shutterbug, toby jug, water bug, wonder drug • miracle drug, prescription drug • oriental rug
uga \ü-gə\ beluga, Tortuga • Chattanooga

ugal \ü-gəl\ Brueghel, bugle, frugal

ugar \ug-ər\ see UGUR

uge[1] \üj\ huge, scrooge, stooge • deluge, refuge • centrifuge, subterfuge

uge[2] \üzh\ Bruges, luge, rouge • deluge, refuge • Baton Rouge

ugel \ü-gəl\ see UGAL

uges \üzh\ see UGE[2]

ugger[1] \əg-ər\ bugger, mugger, plugger, slugger, smugger, snugger • debugger, tree hugger

ugger[2] \ug-ər\ see UGUR

uggery \əg-rē\ thuggery • skulduggery

uggie \əg-ē\ see UGGY

uggish \əg-ish\ sluggish, thuggish

uggle \əg-əl\ juggle, smuggle, snuggle, struggle

uggler \əg-lər\ juggler, smuggler

uggy \əg-ē\ buggy, muggy • beach buggy, dune buggy, swamp buggy • baby buggy, horse-and-buggy

ugh[1] \əg\ see UG

ugh[2] \ü\ see EW[1]

ughes \üz\ see USE[2]

ugle \ü-gəl\ see UGAL

ugli \ə-glē\ see UGLY

uglia \ul-yə\ see ULIA

ugly \əg-lē\ smugly, snugly, ugly

ugn \ün\ see OON[1]

ugner \ü-nər\ see OONER

ugu \ü-gü\ fugu, goo-goo

ugur \ug-ər\ booger, sugar • blood sugar, brown sugar, cane sugar • maple sugar

uhl \ül\ see OOL[1]

uhr[1] \ər\ see EUR[1]

uhr[2] \ur\ see URE[1]

ührer \ur-ər\ see URER

ui[1] \ā\ see AY[1]

ui[2] \ē\ see EE[1]

uice \üs\ see USE[1]

uiced \üst\ see OOST

uicer \ü-sər\ see UCER

uicy \ü-sē\ juicy, Lucy • Watusi

uid \ü-id\ druid, fluid

uidance \īd-ᵊns\ see IDANCE

uide \īd\ see IDE[1]

uided \īd-əd\ see IDED

uider \īd-ər\ see IDER[1]

uidon \īd-ᵊn\ see IDEN

uiker \ī-kər\ see IKER

uild \ild\ see ILLED

uilder \il-dər\ see ILDER[1]

uilding \il-diŋ\ see ILDING

uile \īl\ see ILE[1]

uiler \ī-lər\ see ILAR

uilleann \i-lən\ see ILLON

uilt \ilt\ see ILT

uimpe \amp\ see AMP[3]

uin[1] \ü-ən\ see UAN

uin[2] \ən\ see UN[1]

uin[3] \aⁿ\ see IN[4]

uing \ü-iŋ\ see OING[2]

uint \ü-ənt\ see UENT

uir \ur\ see URE[1]

uirdly \ur-lē\ see URELY

uisance \üs-ᵊns\ see UCENCE

uise[1] \üz\ see USE[2]

uise[2] \īz\ see IZE[1]

uiser \ü-zər\ see USER

uish \ü-ish\ see EWISH

uisne \ü-nē\ see OONY

uiste \is-tē\ see ICITY[2]

uit[1] \ü-ət\ see UET

uit[2] \üt\ see UTE

uitable \üt-ə-bəl\ see UTABLE

uite \üt\ see UTE

uited \üt-əd\ see OOTED[1]

uiter \üt-ər\ see UTER

uiting \üt-iŋ\ see UTING

uitless \üt-ləs\ see OOTLESS

uitor \üt-ər\ see UTER

uitous \ü-ət-əs\ circuitous, fortuitous, gratuitous

uits \üts\ see OOTS

uittle[1] \üt-ᵊl\ see UTILE

uittle[2] \ət-ᵊl\ see UTTLE

uity[1] \ü-ət-ē\ acuity, annuity, congruity, gratuity • ambiguity, continuity, incongruity, ingenuity • discontinuity

uity[2] \üt-ē\ see OOTY[1]

uk[1] \ük\ see UKE

uk[2] \ůk\ see OOK[1]

uk[3] \ək\ see UCK[1]

ukar \ə-kər\ see UCKER

uke \ük\ cuke, duke, fluke, kook, Luke, nuke, Nuuk, puke, snook, spook, uke • archduke, Chinook, Dubuque, Farouk, grand duke, Kirkuk, rebuke • antinuke, Penta-teuch

uki[1] \ü-kē\ see OOKY[1]

uki[2] \ů-kē\ see OOKIE

ukka \ək-ə\ pukka, yucca

ukker \ək-ər\ see UCKER

ukkoth \ůk-əs\ see UCKUS

ul[1] \ůl\ bull, full, pull, wool, you'll • armful, bagful, bellpull, brimful, carful, chock-full, cupful, earful, eyeful, fistful, forkful, glassful, handful, houseful, in full, John Bull, mouthful, pailful, pit bull, plateful, potful, roomful, spoon-ful, steel wool, tankful, truckful, trunkful • barrelful, basketful, bellyful, bucketful, closetful, cock-and-bull, Istanbul, shovelful, Sitting Bull, tableful • dyed-in-the-wool

ul[2] \ül\ see OOL[1]

ul[3] \əl\ see ULL[1]

ula \ü-lə\ Beulah, hula, moola • Missoula • Ashtabula, Pascagoula

ular \ü-lər\ see OOLER

ulch \əlch\ gulch, mulch

ule[1] \ü-lē\ see ULY

ule[2] \ül\ see OOL[1]

ulean \ü-lē-ən\ Julian • Herculean

uled \üld\ see OOLED

ulep \ü-ləp\ see ULIP

uler \ü-lər\ see OOLER

ules \ülz\ Jules
—also -s, -'s, and -s' forms of nouns and -s forms of verbs listed at OOL[1]

ulet \əl-ət\ see ULLET[1]

uley[1] \ü-lē\ see ULY

uley[2] \ůl-ē\ see ULLY[2]

ulf \əlf\ golf, gulf, Gulf • engulf • Beowulf

ulgar \əl-gər\ see ULGUR

ulge \əlj\ bulge • divulge, indulge • overindulge

ulgur \əl-gər\ bulgur, vulgar

ulhas \əl-əs\ see ULLUS

uli \ůl-ē\ see ULLY[2]

ulia \ül-yə\ Julia • Apulia

ulie \ü-lē\ see ULY

ulip \ü-ləp\ julep, tulip • mint julep

ulish \ü-lish\ see OOLISH

ulk \əlk\ bulk, hulk, skulk, sulk, yolk

ulky \əl-kē\ bulky, sulky

ull[1] \əl\ cull, dull, gull, hull, lull, mull, null, scull, skull • annul, mogul, numskull, seagull • her-ring gull, laughing gull, monohull, multihull, Sitting Bull

ull[2] \ůl\ see UL[1]

ulla[1] \ü-lə\ see ULA

ulla[2] \əl-ə\ see ULLAH

ullah \əl-ə\ Gullah, mullah, Sulla • medulla • ayatollah

ullan \əl-ən\ see ULLEN

ullard \əl-ərd\ see OLORED

ullate \əl-ət\ see ULLET[1]

ulle \ül\ see OOL[1]

ullein \əl-ən\ see ULLEN

ullen \əl-ən\ mullein, sullen

uller \əl-ər\ see OLOR[1]

ulles \əl-əs\ see ULLUS

ullet[1] \əl-ət\ bullet, gullet, mullet • dodge a bullet, magic bullet, silver bullet

ullet[2] \ůl-ət\ bullet, pullet

ulley \ůl-ē\ see ULLY[2]

ullis \əl-əs\ see ULLUS

ullitt \ůl-ət\ see ULLET[2]

ullus \əl-əs\ Dulles • Catullus

ully[1] \əl-ē\ gully, sully

ully[2] \ůl-ē\ bully, fully, gully, pul-ley, woolly

ulp \əlp\ gulp, pulp • wood pulp

ulse \əls\ dulse, pulse • convulse, impulse, repulse

ulsion \əl-shən\ compulsion, convulsion, emulsion, expulsion, impulsion, propulsion, repulsion, revulsion • jet propulsion, self-propulsion

ulsive \əl-siv\ compulsive, convulsive, impulsive, propulsive, repulsive • anticonvulsive

ult \əlt\ cult • adult, consult, exult, insult, occult, result, subcult, tumult • catapult, difficult •

ultant \əlt-³nt\ consultant, exultant, resultant

ultch \əlch\ see ULCH

ultery \əl-trē\ see ULTRY

ultry \əl-trē\ sultry • adultery

ulture \əl-chər\ culture, vulture • subculture • agriculture, aquaculture, counterculture, horticulture, turkey vulture

ulu \ü-lü\ lulu, Sulu, Zulu • Honolulu

uly \ü-lē\ coolie, coolly, duly, Julie, newly, Thule, truly • Grand Coulee, unduly, unruly, yours truly

um¹ \əm\ bum, chum, come, crumb, drum, dumb, from, glum, gum, hum, mum, numb, plum, plumb, rum, scum, slum, some, strum, sum, swum, them, thrum, thumb, yum • bass drum, bay rum, beach plum, become, dumdum, eardrum, green thumb, hohum, how come, humdrum, income, outcome, pond scum, side drum, snare drum, steel drum, succumb, therefrom, to come, Tom Thumb, tom-tom, yum-yum • apart from, aside from, bubblegum, chewing gum, kettledrum, kingdom come, overcome, rule of thumb, sugarplum, Tweedledum •

um² \ùm\ broom, groom, room • ballroom, barroom, bathroom, bedroom, chat room, checkroom, classroom, cloakroom, coatroom, courtroom, darkroom, headroom, homeroom, lunchroom, men's room, mushroom, push broom, rec room, restroom, schoolroom, stateroom, sunroom, washroom, weight room, workroom • breathing room, dining room, dressing room, elbow room, family room, ladies' room, locker room, sitting room, standing room, waiting room, wiggle room

um³ \üm\ see OOM¹

uma \ü-mə\ puma, Yuma • Montezuma, Petaluma

uman \ü-mən\ crewman, human, Newman, Truman, Yuman • acumen, illumine, inhuman, nonhuman, prehuman, subhuman • superhuman

umanous \ü-mə-nəs\ see UMINOUS

umb \əm\ see UM¹

umbar \əm-bər\ see UMBER¹

umbed \əmd\ unplumbed
—*also* -ed *forms of verbs listed at* UM¹

umbel \əm-bəl\ see UMBLE

umber¹ \əm-bər\ Humber, lumbar, lumber, number, slumber, umber • call number, cucumber, encumber, outnumber, prime number • sea cucumber • atomic number, 800 number, serial number

umber² \əm-ər\ see UMMER

umbered \əm-bərd\ numbered • unnumbered
—*also* -ed *forms of verbs listed at* UMBER¹

umberland \əm-bər-lənd\ Cumberland • Northumberland

umbing \əm-iŋ\ see OMING¹

umble \əm-bəl\ bumble, crumble, fumble, grumble, humble, jumble, mumble, rumble, stumble, tumble • rough-and-tumble

umbler \əm-blər\ bumbler, grumbler, tumbler

umbling \əm-bliŋ\ tumbling
—*also* -ing *forms of verbs listed at*
UMBLE
umbly[1] \əm-blē\ crumbly, grumbly,
humbly, mumbly, rumbly
umbly[2] \əm-lē\ dumbly, numbly
umbness \əm-nəs\ numbness
• alumnus
umbo \əm-bō\ gumbo, jumbo
• Colombo • mumbo jumbo
umbria \əm-brē-ə\ Cumbria
• Northumbria
ume \üm\ see OOM[1]
umed \ümd\ see OOMED
umely \ü-mə-lē\ see OOMILY
umen \ü-mən\ see UMAN
umer \ü-mər\ bloomer, Bloomer,
boomer, humor, roomer, rumor,
Sumer, tumor • consumer, cos-
tumer • baby boomer, gallows
humor
umerous \üm-rəs\ see UMOROUS
umerus \üm-rəs\ see UMOROUS
umey \ü-mē\ see OOMY
umf \əmf\ see UMPH
umi \ü-mē\ see OOMY
umin \ü-mən\ see UMAN
umine \ü-mən\ see UMAN
uming \ü-miŋ\ blooming
• everblooming, time-consuming,
unassuming
—*also* -ing *forms of verbs listed at*
OOM[1]
uminous \ü-mə-nəs\ luminous
• bituminous, voluminous
ummary \əm-ə-rē\ see UMMERY
ummate \əm-ət\ see UMMET
ummel \əm-əl\ see OMMEL[2]
ummell \əm-əl\ see OMMEL[2]
ummer \əm-ər\ bummer, drummer,
mummer, plumber, strummer,
summer • latecomer, midsummer,
newcomer • Indian summer
—*also* -er *forms of adjectives listed*
at UM[1]
ummery \əm-ə-rē\ summary, sum-
mery • Montgomery

ummet \əm-ət\ plummet, summit
ummie \əm-ē\ see UMMY
ummit \əm-ət\ see UMMET
ummox \əm-əks\ flummox, lum-
mox
ummy \əm-ē\ chummy, crummy,
dummy, gummy, mommy,
mummy, rummy, scummy,
slummy, tummy, yummy • gin
rummy
umness \əm-nəs\ see UMBNESS
umnus \əm-nəs\ see UMBNESS
umor \ü-mər\ see UMER
umorous \üm-rəs\ humerus, hu-
morous, numerous
umous \ü-məs\ humus • posthu-
mous
ump \əmp\ bump, chump, clump,
dump, grump, hump, jump, lump,
plump, pump, rump, slump,
stump, sump, thump, trump, ump
• air pump, broad jump, heat
pump, high jump, long jump, ski
jump, speed bump, sump pump
• bungee jump, vacuum pump
• hop skip and jump
umper \əm-pər\ bumper, dumper,
jumper, pumper, stumper • broad
jumper, high jumper, long
jumper, ski jumper, smoke
jumper, tub-thumper • bungee
jumper • bumper-to-bumper
umph \əmf\ humph • galumph,
harrumph
umpish \əm-pish\ lumpish, plump-
ish
umpkin \əŋ-kən\ see UNKEN
umple \əm-pəl\ crumple, rumple
umps \əms\ dumps, mumps
• goose bumps
—*also* -s, -'s, *and* -s' *forms of*
nouns and -s *forms of verbs listed*
at UMP
umption \əm-shən\ gumption
• assumption, consumption, pre-
sumption, resumption
umptious \əm-shəs\ bumptious,

scrumptious, sumptuous • presumptuous

umptuous[1] \əm-chəs\ sumptuous • presumptuous

umptuous[2] \əm-shəs\ see UMPTIOUS

umpus \əm-pəs\ see OMPASS

umpy \əm-pē\ bumpy, dumpy, grumpy, jumpy, lumpy, stumpy

umus \ü-məs\ see UMOUS

umy \ü-mē\ see OOMY

un[1] \ən\ bun, done, Donne, fun, gun, hon, Hun, none, nun, one, pun, run, shun, son, spun, stun, sun, ton, won • A-1, air gun, begun, big gun, blowgun, Bull Run, burp gun, Chaplin, dry run, earned run, end run, first-run, flashgun, godson, grandson, handgun, hard-won, hired gun, home run, homespun, long run, outdone, outgun, outrun, popgun, redone, rerun, short run, shotgun, six-gun, speargun, spray gun, squirt gun, stepson, stun gun, top gun, trial run, undone, V-1, welldone, zip gun • Algonquin, antigun, Bofors gun, Browning gun, Gatling gun, hit-and-run, jump the gun, kiloton, machine-gun, machine gun, megaton, midnight sun, one-on-one, one-to-one, on the run, overdone, overrun, pellet gun, radar gun, ride shotgun, riot gun, smoking gun, squirrel gun, tommy gun, underdone, water gun • son of a gun, submachine gun

un[2] \ün\ see OON[1]

una \ü-nə\ Luna, tuna • Altoona, kahuna, vicuña

uña[1] \ü-nə\ see UNA

uña[2] \ün-yə\ see UNIA

unal \ün-ᵊl\ communal, tribunal

unar \ü-nər\ see OONER

unary \ü-nə-rē\ buffoonery, festoonery, lampoonery

unc \ənk\ see UNK

uncan \əŋ-kən\ see UNKEN

unce \əns\ dunce, once
—also -s, -'s, and -s' forms of nouns and -s forms of verbs listed at ONT[1]

unch \ənch\ brunch, bunch, crunch, hunch, lunch, munch, punch, scrunch • box lunch, free lunch, keypunch • counterpunch, one-two punch, out to lunch, rabbit punch, sucker punch

unche \ənch\ see UNCH

uncher \ən-chər\ cowpuncher, keypuncher • counterpuncher, number cruncher

unchy \ən-chē\ crunchy, punchy

uncle \əŋ-kəl\ uncle • carbuncle, granduncle, great-uncle, say uncle

unct \əŋt\ adjunct, defunct
—also -ed forms of verbs listed at UNK

unction \əŋ-shən\ function, junction • compunction, conjunction, dysfunction, injunction, malfunction

uncture \əŋ-chər\ juncture, puncture • acupuncture

und[1] \ənd\ fund • dachshund, hedge fund, refund, rotund, slush fund, trust fund • cummerbund, underfund • mutual fund
—also -ed forms of verbs listed at UN[1]

und[2] \aund\ see OUND[2]

undae \ən-dē\ see UNDI

undant \ən-dənt\ abundant, redundant • overabundant, superabundant

unday \ən-dē\ see UNDI

undays \ən-dēz\ Mondays, Sundays, undies
—also -s and -s' forms of nouns listed at UNDI

under \ən-dər\ blunder, funder, plunder, thunder, under, wonder • asunder, down under, go under, plow under, snow under

• knuckle under, steal one's thunder • build a fire under

underous \ən-drəs\ thunderous, wondrous

undi \ən-dē\ Monday, sundae, Sunday • Bay of Fundy, salmagundi • coatimundi

undies \ən-dēz\ see UNDAYS

undle \ən-d°l\ bundle, trundle

undy \ən-dē\ see UNDI

une \ün\ see OON¹

uneau \ü-nō\ see UNO

uneless \ün-ləs\ see OONLESS

uner \ü-nər\ see OONER

unes \ünz\ see OONS

ung¹ \əŋ\ clung, dung, flung, hung, lung, rung, slung, sprung, strung, stung, sung, swung, tongue, wrung, young • among, black lung, far-flung, forked tongue, hamstrung, high-strung, iron lung, low-slung, unsung, with young • Aqua-Lung, bite one's tongue, egg foo yong, hold one's tongue, mother tongue

ung² \u̇ŋ\ Jung, Sung

ungal \ən-gəl\ see UNGLE

unge \ənj\ grunge, lunge, plunge, sponge • expunge • take the plunge

unger¹ \ən-jər\ plunger, sponger

unger² \əŋ-gər\ see ONGER¹

ungle \əŋ-gəl\ bungle, fungal, jungle • asphalt jungle

ungous \əŋ-gəs\ fungus • humongous

ungry \ən-grē\ see ONGERY

ungus \əŋ-gəs\ see UNGOUS

ungy \ən-jē\ grungy, spongy

unha \ü-nə\ see UNA

uni \ü-nē\ see OONY

unia \ün-yə\ petunia, vicuña

unic \ü-nik\ eunuch, Munich, Punic, runic, tunic

unich \ü-nik\ see UNIC

union \ən-yən\ bunion, onion • Paul Bunyan

unis \ü-nəs\ see EWNESS

unish¹ \ən-ish\ Hunnish, punish

unish² \ü-nish\ see OONISH

unity \ü-nət-ē\ unity • community, disunity, immunity, impunity • opportunity

unk \əŋk\ bunk, chunk, clunk, drunk, dunk, flunk, funk, gunk, hunk, junk, monk, plunk, punk, shrunk, skunk, slunk, spunk, stunk, sunk, thunk, trunk • chipmunk, debunk, Podunk, preshrunk, punch-drunk, slam dunk • cyberpunk, steamer trunk

unked \əŋt\ see UNCT

unken \əŋ-kən\ Duncan, drunken, pumpkin, shrunken, sunken

unker \əŋ-kər\ bunker, clunker, hunker, junker • debunker, spelunker

unkie \əŋ-kē\ see UNKY

unkin \əŋ-kəm\ see UNCAN

unky \əŋ-kē\ chunky, clunky, donkey, flunky, funky, gunky, hunky, junkie, junky, monkey, skunky, spunky • grease monkey

unless \ən-ləs\ runless, sunless

unn \ən\ see UN¹

unned \ənd\ see UND¹

unnel \ən-°l\ funnel, tunnel • wind tunnel

unner \ən-ər\ gunner, runner, stunner • base runner, forerunner, front-runner, gunrunner, roadrunner, rumrunner • machine gunner

unnery \ən-rē\ gunnery, nunnery

unning \ən-iŋ\ cunning, running, stunning • baserunning, gunrunning, rum-running • blockade-running, in the running • hit the ground running, out of the running

—*also* -ing *forms of verbs listed at* UN¹

unnion \ən-yən\ see UNION

unnish \ən-ish\ see UNISH¹

unny \ən-ē\ bunny, funny, honey,
money, runny, sonny, sunny
• blood money, Bugs Bunny, dust
bunny, pin money, prize money,
seed money, smart money, un-
funny • for one's money, funny
money, on the money, pocket
money, spending money • run for
one's money

uno \ü-nō\ Bruno, Juneau, Juno
• numero uno

unt \ənt\ see ONT[1]

untal \ənt-ᵊl\ see UNTLE

unter \ənt-ər\ bunter, hunter,
punter • foxhunter, headhunter,
witch-hunter • bounty hunter,
fortune hunter

unting \ənt-iŋ\ bunting • foxhunt-
ing, head-hunting, witch-hunting
—*also* -ing *forms of verbs listed at*
ONT[1]

untle \ənt-ᵊl\ frontal • disgruntle

unwale \ən-ᵊl\ see UNNEL

uny \ü-nē\ see OONY

unyan \ən-yən\ see UNION

uoy[1] \ü-ē\ see EWY

uoy[2] \òi\ see OY

uoyance \ü-əns\ see OYANCE

uoyant \òi-ənt\ see OYANT

up \əp\ cup, pup, sup, up, yup • act
up, add up, backup, back up,
bang-up, bear up, beat-up, beat
up, blowup, blow up, bone up,
bound up, breakup, break up,
bring up, brush up, buck up,
buildup, build up, built-up, bulk
up, buy up, catch-up, chalk up,
checkup, choose up, clam up,
cleanup, clean up, close-up, close
up, come up, cough up, crack-up,
curl up, cut up, dial-up, dial up,
dig up, doll up, do up, draw up,
dream up, dress up, dried-up,
drive-up, drum up, dry up,
dustup, face up, fed up, fill up, fix
up, flare-up, foul-up, foul up,
frame-up, gang up, gear up,

getup, get up, giddap, give up,
grown-up, grow up, hang-up,
hang up, hard up, heads-up, hic-
cup, hitch up, holdup, hold up,
hole up, hookup, hook up, hung
up, hyped-up, juice up, keep up,
lay-up, lead-up, leg up, letup, let
up, line up, linkup, lockup, look
up, louse up, made-up, makeup,
make up, markup, matchup, mix-
up, mixed-up, mop-up, one-up,
pass up, pay up, pickup, pick up,
pileup, pinup, play up, pop-up,
pull-up, pump up, push-up, rack
up, rake up, ramp up, re-up, ring
up, roll up, roundup, round up,
run-up, scare up, screwup, screw
up, setup, set up, sew up, shake-
up, shape up, shook-up, show up,
shut up, sign up, sit-up, size up,
slipup, slip up, smashup, souped-
up, speak up, speedup, spiffed-up,
spit up, stack up, stand-up, start-
up, steam up, step up, stepped-up,
stickup, stick up, strike up, sum
up, sunup, take up, talk up,
teacup, throw up, thumbs-up, tie-
up, toss-up, touch-up, trade up,
trumped-up, tune-up, turn up,
use up, wait up, wake up, warm-
up, washed-up, windup, work up,
wrap-up • belly-up, bottom-up,
buckle up, bundle up, buttercup,
butter up, cover-up, cover up,
Dixie cup, double up, follow-up,
giddyup, higher-up, hurry up,
lighten up, live it up, measure up,
open up, pick-me-up, power up,
runner-up, shoot-'em-up, suction
cup • sunny-side up

upboard \əb-ərd\ see UBBARD

upe \üp\ see OOP

upel \ü-pəl\ see UPLE[2]

uper \ü-pər\ see OOPER

upi \ü-pē\ see OOPY

upid \ü-pəd\ Cupid, stupid

upil \ü-pəl\ see UPLE[2]

uple[1] \əp-əl\ couple, supple • quadruple, quintuple, sextuple, uncouple

uple[2] \ü-pəl\ pupil, scruple • quadruple, quintuple, sextuple

uplet \əp-lət\ couplet • quadruplet, quintuplet, sextuplet

uplicate \ü-pli-kət\ duplicate • quadruplicate

upor \ü-pər\ see OOPER

uppance \əp-əns\ threepence, twopence

upper \əp-ər\ supper, upper • Last Supper, Lord's Supper • builder-upper, fixer-upper

uppie \əp-ē\ see UPPY

upple[1] \üp-əl\ see UPLE[2]

upple[2] \əp-əl\ see UPLE[1]

uppy \əp-ē\ guppy, puppy, yuppie • hush puppy, mud puppy

upt \əpt\ abrupt, bankrupt, corrupt, disrupt, erupt • developed, interrupt

—*also* -ed *forms of verbs listed at* UP

uq \ük\ see UKE

uque \ük\ see UKE

ur[1] \o̊r\ see OR[1]

ur[2] \u̇r\ see URE[1]

ur[3] \ər\ see EUR[1]

ura \u̇r-ə\ Jura, Kura • bravura, tempura • coloratura

urable \u̇r-ə-bəl\ curable, durable • endurable, incurable, insurable • unendurable, uninsurable

urae \u̇r-ē\ see URY[1]

urah \u̇r-ə\ see URA

ural \u̇r-əl\ mural, neural, plural, puerile, rural, Ural • extramural, intramural, semirural

urance \u̇r-əns\ assurance, endurance, insurance • health insurance, life insurance, reassurance, self-assurance

urate \u̇r-ət\ curate, turret

urb \ərb\ see ERB

urban \ər-bən\ bourbon, Durban, turban, turbine, urban • steam turbine, suburban, wind turbine

urber \ər-bər\ Berber • disturber

urbia \ər-bē-ə\ Serbia • exurbia, suburbia

urbine \ər-bən\ see URBAN

urble \ər-bəl\ see ERBAL

urch \ərch\ birch, church, lurch, perch, search • Christchurch, research

urchly \ərch-lē\ churchly, virtually

urd[1] \u̇rd\ see URED[1]

urd[2] \ərd\ see IRD

urder \ərd-ər\ see ERDER

urdle \ərd-ᵊl\ curdle, girdle, hurdle

urdy \ərd-ē\ birdie, sturdy, wordy • hurdy-gurdy, Mesa Verde, Monteverdi

ure[1] \u̇r\ Boer, boor, cure, dour, ewer, fewer, lure, moor, Moore, poor, pure, Ruhr, sewer, skewer, sure, tour, your, you're • abjure, allure, amour, assure, brochure, cocksure, conjure, contour, demure, detour, dirt-poor, endure, ensure, Exmoor, for sure, grandeur, impure, insure, landpoor, manure, mature, obscure, procure, secure, tenure, unmoor, unsure, velour • amateur, aperture, connoisseur, curvature, epicure, forfeiture, haute couture, immature, insecure, manicure, overture, pedicure, portraiture, premature, reassure, saboteur, signature, sinecure, soup du jour, temperature, to be sure, troubadour, Yom Kippur • caricature, entrepreneur, expenditure, imprimatur, investiture, literature, miniature, musculature, nomenclature

ure[2] \u̇r-ē\ see URY[1]

urean \u̇r-ē-ən\ see URIAN

ureau \u̇r-ō\ see URO

ured[1] \u̇rd\ gourd, Kurd • assured, steward • self-assured • out of one's gourd, underinsured

—*also* -ed *forms of verbs listed at* URE[1]

ured[2] \ərd\ see IRD

urely \uṙ-lē\ poorly, purely, surely • securely • prematurely

ureous \uṙ-ē-əs\ see URIOUS

urer \uṙ-ər\ führer, furor, juror • insurer

—*also* -er *forms of adjectives listed at* URE[1]

urety \uṙ-ət-ē\ see URITY

urey \uṙ-ē\ see URY[1]

urf \ərf\ serf, surf, turf • windsurf • Astroturf, bodysurf, channel surf, surf and turf

urgative \ər-gə-tiv\ see URGATIVE

urge \ərj\ dirge, merge, purge, splurge, surge, urge, verge • converge, diverge, emerge, resurge, submerge, upsurge • reemerge

urgence \ər-jəns\ see ERGENCE

urgency \ər-jən-sē\ see ERGENCY

urgent \ər-jənt\ urgent • convergent, detergent, divergent, emergent, insurgent, resurgent • counterinsurgent

urgeon \ər-jən\ burgeon, sturgeon, surgeon, virgin • tree surgeon • plastic surgeon

urger[1] \ər-gər\ burger, burgher • cheeseburger, hamburger, Limburger • Luxembourger, veggie burger

urger[2] \ər-jər\ see ERGER

urgery \ərj-rē\ see ERJURY

urgh[1] \ər-ə\ see OROUGH[1]

urgh[2] \ər-ō\ see URROW[1]

urgher \ər-gər\ see URGER[1]

urgic \ər-jik\ see ERGIC

urgical \ər-ji-kəl\ surgical • liturgical • metallurgical

urgor \ər-gər\ see URGER[1]

urgy \ər-jē\ clergy • dramaturgy, metallurgy

uri \uṙ-ē\ see URY[1]

urial \er-ē-əl\ see ARIAL

urian \uṙ-ē-ən\ Arthurian, centu-

rion, Manchurian, Missourian • Canterburian, epicurean

urible \uṙ-ə-bəl\ see URABLE

urie \uṙ-ē\ see URY[1]

urier[1] \er-ē-ər\ see ERRIER

urier[2] \uṙ-ē-ər\ see OURIER[1]

uriere \uṙ-ē-ər\ see OURIER[1]

uring \uṙ-iŋ\ during, mooring, touring • alluring, enduring

—*also* -ing *forms of verbs listed at* URE[1]

urion \uṙ-ē-ən\ see URIAN

urious \uṙ-ē-əs\ curious, furious, spurious • incurious, injurious, luxurious

uris \uṙ-əs\ see URUS

urist \uṙ-əst\ jurist, purist, tourist • manicurist, pedicurist • caricaturist

—*also* -est *forms of adjectives listed at* URE[1]

urity \uṙ-ət-ē\ purity • impurity, maturity, obscurity, security • immaturity, insecurity • Social Security

urk \ərk\ see ORK[1]

urka \ər-kə\ burka, circa, Gurkha

urke \ərk\ see ORK[1]

urker \ər-kər\ see ORKER[1]

urkey \ər-kē\ see ERKY

urkha \ər-kə\ see URKA

urki \ər-kē\ see ERKY

urky \ər-kē\ see ERKY

url \ərl\ see IRL

urled \ərld\ see ORLD

urlin \ər-lən\ see ERLIN

urling \ər-liŋ\ hurling, sterling

—*also* -ing *forms of verbs listed at* IRL

urlish \ər-lish\ churlish, girlish

urly \ər-lē\ burly, curly, early, pearly, squirrely, surly, swirly, twirly, whirly

urman \ər-mən\ see ERMAN

urn \ərn\ Bern, burn, churn, earn, fern, learn, spurn, stern, tern, turn, urn, yearn • adjourn, astern,

concern, discern, downturn,
heartburn, Hepburn, intern, in
turn, kick turn, Lucerne, noc-
turne, return, sojourn, sunburn,
unlearn, upturn, U-turn, wind-
burn • Arctic tern, in return, out
of turn, overturn, slash-and-burn,
taciturn, unconcern • at every
turn, from stem to stern • point
of no return

urnable \ər-nə-bəl\ burnable • dis-
cernible, returnable
• indiscernible, nonreturnable

urnal \ərn-ᵊl\ see ERNAL

urne \ərn\ see URN

urned \ərnd\ burned • concerned,
sunburned, unearned, unlearned,
windburned
—*also* -ed *forms of verbs listed at*
URN

urner \ər-nər\ burner, earner • af-
terburner

urney \ər-nē\ see OURNEY[1]

urnian \ər-nē-ən\ see ERNIAN

urnish \ər-nish\ burnish, furnish

urnt \ərnt\ see EARNT

uro \ur-ō\ bureau, euro, Euro
• politburo, travel bureau,
weather bureau

uror \ur-ər\ see URER

urore \ur-ər\ see URER

urous \ur-əs\ see URUS

urp \ərp\ burp, chirp, perp, slurp,
twerp • Antwerp, usurp

urr \ər\ see EUR[1]

urra[1] \ur-ə\ see URA

urra[2] \ər-ə\ see OROUGH[1]

urragh \ər-ə\ see OROUGH[1]

urral \ər-əl\ see ERRAL

urrant \ər-ənt\ see URRENT

urray \ər-ē\ see URRY

urre \ər\ see EUR[1]

urred \ərd\ see IRD

urrence \ər-əns\ deterrence, occur-
rence, recurrence, transference
—*also* -s, -'s, *and* -s' *forms of*
nouns listed at URRENT

urrent \ər-ənt\ currant, current,
weren't • concurrent, crosscur-
rent, deterrent, recurrent, rip
current • countercurrent, under-
current

urret \ur-ət\ see URATE

urrey \ər-ē\ see URRY

urrian \ur-ē-ən\ see URIAN

urrie \ər-ē\ see URRY

urrier \ər-ē-ər\ blurrier, courier,
furrier, worrier

urring \ər-iŋ\ stirring
—*also* -ing *forms of verbs listed at*
EUR[1]

urrish \ər-ish\ see OURISH

urro[1] \ər-ə\ see OROUGH[1]

urro[2] \ər-ō\ see URROW[1]

urrow[1] \ər-ō\ borough, burgh,
burro, burrow, furrow, thorough
• Marlborough

urrow[2] \ər-ə\ see OROUGH[1]

urry \ər-ē\ blurry, curry, flurry,
furry, hurry, Murray, scurry,
surrey, Surrey, worry • in a hurry

ursary \ərs-rē\ cursory, nursery
• day nursery • anniversary

urse \ərs\ see ERSE

ursed \ərst\ see URST

ursery \ərs-rē\ see URSARY

ursion \ər-zhən\ see ERSION[1]

ursive \ər-siv\ see ERSIVE

ursory \ərs-rē\ see URSARY

urst \ərst\ burst, cursed, first,
Hearst, thirst, worst • accursed, at
first, cloudburst, feetfirst, head-
first, knockwurst, outburst, star-
burst, sunburst • liverwurst,
microburst
—*also* -ed *forms of verbs listed at*
ERSE

ursy[1] \ər-sē\ see ERCY

ursy[2] \əs-ē\ see USSY

urt[1] \urt\ Frankfurt

urt[2] \ərt\ see ERT[1]

urtain \ərt-ᵊn\ see ERTAIN

urtal \ərt-ᵊl\ see ERTILE

urter \ərt-ər\ see ERTER

urtive \ərt-iv\ see ERTIVE
urtle \ərt-ᵊl\ see ERTILE
urton \ərt-ᵊn\ see ERTAIN
urus \u̇r-əs\ Arcturus, sulfurous
• Epicurus
urve \ərv\ see ERVE
urved \ərvd\ see ERVED
urvy \ər-vē\ curvy, nervy, scurvy
• topsy-turvy
ury¹ \u̇r-ē\ Curie, fury, jury • grand
jury, Missouri
ury² \er-ē\ see ARY¹
urze \ərz\ see ERS¹
urzy \ər-zē\ see ERSEY
us¹ \əs\ bus, cuss, fuss, Gus, muss,
plus, pus, Russ, thus, truss, us
• airbus, discuss, school bus,
surplus • blunderbuss, minibus,
motor bus, trolleybus
us² \ü\ see EW¹
us³ \u̇sh\ see OUCHE
us⁴ \üz\ see USE²
usa¹ \ü-sə\ Sousa • Medusa • Ap-
paloosa, Tuscaloosa
usa² \ü-zə\ Sousa • Medusa
• Arethusa
usable \ü-zə-bəl\ usable • excusa-
ble, reusable, unusable • inexcus-
able, nonreusable
usae \ü-sē\ see UICY
usal \ü-zəl\ bamboozle, perusal,
refusal
usc \əsk\ see USK
uscan \əs-kən\ Tuscan • Etruscan
uscle \əs-əl\ see USTLE
use¹ \üs\ Bruce, deuce, goose,
juice, loose, moose, mousse,
noose, puce, ruse, Russ, schuss,
Seuss, sluice, spruce, truce, use,
Zeus • abstruse, abuse, adduce,
blue spruce, burnoose, caboose,
chartreuse, conduce, cut loose,
deduce, diffuse, disuse, excuse,
footloose, hang loose, induce,
misuse, mongoose, obtuse, Orpheus, papoose, Perseus, produce,
profuse, Proteus, recluse, reduce,

refuse, reuse, Sanctus, seduce,
slip noose, snow goose, Theseus,
turn loose, vamoose • Belarus,
Betelgeuse, cook one's goose, fast
and loose, flag of truce, intro-
duce, mass-produce, Mother
Goose, Odysseus, overuse,
Prometheus, reproduce, Syracuse
• Canada goose, hypotenuse
use² \üz\ blues, booze, bruise,
choose, cruise, Druze, fuse,
Hughes, lose, Meuse, muse, news,
ooze, ruse, schmooze, snooze,
use, whose • abuse, accuse,
amuse, bad news, chartreuse,
confuse, defuse, diffuse, enthuse,
excuse, infuse, masseuse, misuse,
peruse, refuse, reuse, short fuse,
suffuse, transfuse • Betelgeuse,
disabuse, Newport News, overuse,
p's and q's, Santa Cruz, Syracuse,
Veracruz • Goody Two-shoes,
hypotenuse
—*also* -s, -'s, *and* -s' *forms of*
nouns and -s *forms of verbs listed*
at EW¹
used \üzd\ used • confused • un-
derused
—*also* -ed *forms of verbs listed at*
USE²
user \ü-zər\ boozer, bruiser,
cruiser, loser, user • abuser, ac-
cuser, end user • battle cruiser,
cabin cruiser
ush¹ \əsh\ blush, brush, crush,
flush, gush, hush, lush, mush,
plush, rush, shush, slush, squush,
thrush • bulrush, bum's rush,
gold rush, hairbrush, hush-hush,
nailbrush, onrush, paintbrush,
sagebrush, scrub brush, song
thrush, straight flush, toothbrush,
wood thrush • Hindu Kush, royal
flush, underbrush
ush² \u̇sh\ bush, Bush, mush, push,
shush, squoosh, swoosh, whoosh
• ambush, bell push, rosebush,

spicebush, thornbush • burning bush, Hindu Kush • beat around the bush

usher¹ \əsh-ər\ crusher, gusher, usher
—also -er *forms of adjectives listed at* USH¹

usher² \úsh-ər\ pusher • ambusher

ushi \úsh-ē\ see USHY²

ushing \əsh-iŋ\ onrushing, un-blushing
—also -ing *forms of verbs listed at* USH¹

ushy¹ \əsh-ē\ brushy, gushy, mushy, plushy, slushy

ushy² \úsh-ē\ bushy, cushy, mushy, pushy, sushi

usi \ü-sē\ see UICY

usian \ü-zhən\ see USION

usible¹ \ü-sə-bəl\ see UCIBLE

usible² \ü-zə-bəl\ see USABLE

usie \ü-zē\ see OOZY

usil \ü-zəl\ see USAL

using \əs-iŋ\ busing • antibusing
—also -ing *forms of verbs listed at* US¹

usion \ü-zhən\ fusion • allusion, collusion, conclusion, confusion, contusion, delusion, exclusion, illusion, inclusion, infusion, intrusion, profusion, protrusion, seclusion, transfusion, Venusian • Andalusian, disillusion, malocclusion • foregone conclusion • optical illusion

usive \ü-siv\ abusive, allusive, conclusive, conducive, delusive, effusive, elusive, exclusive, inclusive, intrusive, reclusive • all-inclusive, inconclusive, unobtrusive

usk \əsk\ brusque, dusk, husk, musk, tusk

usker \əs-kər\ busker • cornhusker

uskie \əs-kē\ see USKY

uskin \əs-kən\ see USCAN

usky \əs-kē\ dusky, husky, musky

uso \ü-sō\ see USOE

usoe \ü-sō\ Rousseau, trousseau, whoso • Caruso • Robinson Crusoe

usque \əsk\ see USK

uss¹ \ús\ puss, wuss • chartreuse, sourpuss • glamour-puss, octopus, platypus

uss² \üs\ see USE¹

uss³ \əs\ see US¹

ussate \əs-ət\ see USSET

usse \üs\ see USE¹

ussel \əs-əl\ see USTLE

ussell \əs-əl\ see USTLE

usset \əs-ət\ gusset, russet

ussia \əsh-ə\ Prussia, Russia • Belorussia

ussian \əsh-ən\ see USSION

ussing \əs-iŋ\ see USING

ussion \əsh-ən\ Prussian, Russian • concussion, discussion, percussion • Belorussian, repercussion

ussle \əs-əl\ see USTLE

ussy \əs-ē\ fussy, mussy

ust¹ \əst\ bust, crust, dust, gust, just, lust, must, rust, thrust, trust • adjust, august, bloodlust, disgust, distrust, encrust, entrust, in trust, leaf rust, mistrust, moondust, piecrust, robust, sawdust, stardust, unjust • antitrust, bite the dust, cosmic dust, readjust, upper crust, wanderlust
—also -ed *forms of verbs listed at* US¹

ust² \əs\ see US¹

ust³ \üst\ see OOST

ustable \əs-tə-bəl\ see USTIBLE

ustard \əs-tərd\ custard, mustard
—also -ed *forms of verbs listed at* USTER

usted \əs-təd\ busted • disgusted • maladjusted, well-adjusted
—also -ed *forms of verbs listed at* UST¹

uster \əs-tər\ bluster, buster, cluster, Custer, duster, fluster, luster, muster • adjuster, blockbuster, crop duster, gangbuster, lackluster, pass muster • broncobuster, filibuster

ustful \əst-fəl\ lustful, trustful • distrustful, mistrustful

usth \əst\ see UST[1]

ustible \əs-tə-bəl\ adjustable, combustible • incombustible

ustin \əs-tən\ Justin • Augustine

ustine \əs-tən\ see USTIN

ustle \əs-əl\ bustle, hustle, muscle, mussel, Russell, rustle, trestle, tussle • corpuscle, outhustle, outmuscle

ustor \əs-tər\ see USTER

ustrious \əs-trē-əs\ illustrious, industrious

usty \əs-tē\ busty, crusty, dusty, gusty, lusty, musty, rusty, trusty

usy \iz-ē\ see IZZY

ut[1] \ət\ but, butt, cut, glut, gut, hut, jut, mutt, nut, putt, rut, shut, smut, soot, strut, what • abut, all but, beechnut, brush cut, buzz cut, catgut, chestnut, clean-cut, clear-cut, crew cut, crosscut, doughnut, haircut, jump cut, kick butt, lug nut, peanut, pignut, pine nut, precut, putt-putt, rebut, shortcut, somewhat, walnut, wing nut, woodcut • betel nut, brazil nut, butternut, coconut, hazelnut, lychee nut, scuttlebutt, undercut, uppercut • director's cut, open-and-shut

ut[2] \ü\ see EW[1]

ut[3] \üt\ see UTE

ut[4] \u̇t\ see OOT[1]

utable \üt-ə-bəl\ suitable • immutable, inscrutable • executable, indisputable, irrefutable, substitutable

utal \üt-ᵊl\ see UTILE

utan \üt-ᵊn\ gluten, Newton, Putin, Teuton • Rasputin • highfalutin

utant \üt-ᵊnt\ mutant • disputant, pollutant

utch \əch\ clutch, crutch, dutch, Dutch, hutch, much, such, touch • and such, as such, retouch, soft touch, so much, too much • a bit much, common touch, Midas touch, overmuch, pretty much, such and such

utchy \əch-ē\ see UCHY

ute \üt\ boot, brute, butte, chute, coot, cute, flute, fruit, hoot, jute, Jute, loot, lute, moot, mute, newt, root, rout, route, scoot, shoot, snoot, soot, suit, toot, Ute • acute, astute, bear fruit, Beirut, breadfruit, Canute, commute, compute, cube root, deaf-mute, dilute, dispute, en route, flight suit, grapefruit, hip boot, hirsute, impute, jackboot, jumpsuit, lawsuit, minute, offshoot, Paiute, pantsuit, playsuit, pollute, pursuit, reboot, recruit, refute, salute, Silk Route, snowsuit, spacesuit, sport-ute, square root, star fruit, statute, strong suit, sunsuit, sweat suit, swimsuit, take root, taproot, to boot, tracksuit, trade route, transmute, tribute, uproot, wet suit • absolute, Aleut, arrowroot, attribute, autoroute, bathing suit, birthday suit, bitterroot, bodysuit, business suit, constitute, contribute, destitute, disrepute, dissolute, execute, follow suit, gingerroot, hot pursuit, institute, kiwifruit, leisure suit, malamute, overshoot, parachute, passion fruit, persecute, point-and-shoot, prosecute, resolute, rural route, substitute, troubleshoot • electrocute, forbidden fruit, reconstitute, redistribute, telecommute

uted \üt-əd\ see OOTED[1]

utee \üt-ē\ see OOTY[1]

utely \üt-lē\ acutely, minutely • absolutely, resolutely

uten \üt-ᵊn\ see UTAN
uteness \üt-nəs\ cuteness, mutinous
utenous \üt-nəs\ see UTENESS
uteous \üt-ē-əs\ beauteous, duteous
uter \üt-ər\ cuter, neuter, hooter, looter, pewter, scooter, suitor, tutor • commuter, computer, freebooter, jump shooter, peashooter, polluter, recruiter, sharpshooter, six-shooter, straight shooter, trapshooter • motor scooter, persecutor, prosecutor, troubleshooter • microcomputer, minicomputer, telecommuter
utes \üts\ see OOTS
uteus \üt-ē-əs\ see UTEOUS
uth[1] \üt\ see UTE
uth[2] \üth\ see OOTH[2]
uther \ə-ther\ see OTHER[1]
uthful \üth-fəl\ truthful, youthful • untruthful
uthless \üth-ləs\ ruthless, toothless
uti \üt-ē\ see OOTY[1]
utian \ü-shən\ see UTION
utical \üt-i-kəl\ cuticle • pharmaceutical
uticle \üt-i-kəl\ see UTICAL
utie \üt-ē\ see OOTY[1]
utiful \üt-i-fəl\ beautiful, dutiful
utile \üt-ᵊl\ brutal, futile, tootle
utin \üt-ᵊn\ see UTAN
utine \üt-ᵊn\ see UTAN
uting \üt-iŋ\ sharpshooting, trapshooting
—also -ing *forms of verbs listed at* UTE
utinous[1] \üt-ᵊn-əs\ glutinous, mutinous
utinous[2] \üt-nəs\ see UTENESS
utiny \üt-ᵊn-ē\ mutiny, scrutiny
ution \ü-shən\ Aleutian, Confucian, dilution, locution, pollution, solution • absolution, attribution, constitution, contribution, destitution, dissolution, distribution, elocution, evolution, execution, institution, persecution, prosecution, resolution, restitution, retribution, revolution, substitution • electrocution, joint resolution, redistribution
utionary \ü-shə-ner-ē\ evolutionary, revolutionary
utist \üt-əst\ cutest, flutist • absolutist
utl \ü-t³l\ see UTILE
utland \ət-lənd\ Jutland, Rutland
utlass \ət-ləs\ cutlass, gutless
utless \ət-ləs\ see UTLASS
utney \ət-nē\ chutney, gluttony
uton \üt-ⁿ\ see UTAN
utor \üt-ər\ see UTER
utriment \ü-trə-mənt\ nutriment • accoutrement
uts \əts\ see UTZ
utsy \ət-sē\ gutsy, klutzy
utt \ət\ see UT[1]
uttal \ət-³l\ see UTTLE
utte \üt\ see UTE
uttee \ət-ē\ see UTTY
utter[1] \ət-ər\ butter, clutter, cutter, flutter, gutter, mutter, putter, shutter, splutter, sputter, stutter, utter • aflutter, haircutter, stonecutter, woodcutter • bread and butter, cookie-cutter, paper cutter
utter[2] \ut-ər\ see OOTER[1]
uttery \ət-ə-rē\ buttery, fluttery
utti[1] \üt-ē\ see OOTY[1]
utti[2] \ut-ē\ see OOTY[2]
utting \ut-iŋ\ see OOTING[1]
uttle \ət-³l\ scuttle, shuttle, subtle • rebuttal, space shuttle
utton \ət-ᵊn\ button, glutton, mutton, Sutton • hot-button, pushbutton, unbutton • belly button, on the button, panic button
uttony \ət-nē\ see UTNEY
utty \ət-ē\ gutty, nutty, putty, rutty, smutty
uture \ü-chər\ future, moocher, suture • wave of the future

uty \üt-ē\ see OOTY[1]

utz \əts\ klutz, nuts • blood-and-guts, spill one's guts
—*also* -s, -'s, *and* -s' *forms of nouns and* -s *forms of verbs listed at* UT[1]

utzy \ət-sē\ see UTSY

uu \ü\ see EW[1]

uvian \ü-vē-ən\ Peruvian, Vesuvian • antediluvian

uvion \ü-vē-ən\ see UVIAN

ux[1] \əks\ crux, flux, tux • big bucks, deluxe, influx • Benelux, megabucks,
—*also* -s, -'s, *and* -s' *forms of nouns and* -s *forms of verbs listed at* UCK[1]

ux[2] \ůks\ see OOKS[2]

uxe[1] \üks\ see OOKS[1]

uxe[2] \ůks\ see OOKS[2]

uxe[3] \əks\ see UX[1]

uxion \ək-shən\ see UCTION

uy \ī\ see Y[1]

uygur \ē-gər\ see EAGER

uyot \ē-ō\ see IO[2]

uyp \īp\ see IPE

uz[1] \üts\ see OOTS

uz[2] \ůz\ see USE[2]

uze \üz\ see USE[2]

uzz \əz\ see EUSE[1]

uzzi \ü-zē\ see OOZY

uzzle \əz-əl\ guzzle, muzzle, nuzzle, puzzle • crossword puzzle, jigsaw puzzle

uzzler \əz-lər\ guzzler, muzzler, puzzler • gas-guzzler

uzzy \əz-ē\ fuzzy, muzzy, scuzzy

Y

y[1] \ī\ aye, Bligh, buy, by, bye, chai, cry, die, dry, dye, eye, fie, fly, fry, guy, Guy, hi, high, i, I, lie, lye, my, nigh, pi, pie, ply, pry, rye, scythe, shy, sigh, sky, Skye, sly, spry, spy, sty, Thai, thigh, thy, tie, try, vie, why, wry, wye, Y • air-dry, ally, anti, apply, awry, aye-aye, Bacchae, Baha'i, banzai, Belgae, belie, black eye, blackfly, black tie, blow-dry, blowfly, bone-dry, bonsai, botfly, Brunei, buckeye, bull?s-eye, bye-bye, cockeye, come by, comply, cow pie, crane fly, cream pie, cross-eye, decry, deep-fry, deerfly, defy, Delphi, deny, drip-dry, drive-by, drop by, Dubai, Eli, espy, face fly, firefly, flyby, fly high, freeze-dry, fruit fly, gadfly, get by, GI, glass eye, go by, good-bye, gun-shy, Haggai, Hawkeye, hereby, hi-fi, hog-tie, horn fly, horsefly, house-fly, imply, jai alai, July, Karzai, Kaui, Kenai, knee-high, Lehigh, let fly, Levi, magpie, Masai, mayfly, medfly, mind's eye, Mumbai, nearby, necktie, outcry, panfry, pigsty, pinkeye, Popeye, pop fly, potpie, put by, quasi, rabbi, red-eye, rely, reply, retry, rib eye, run dry, sand fly, sci-fi, screw eye, semi, shanghai, Shanghai, shut-eye, Sinai, sky-high, small-fry, stand by, standby, stir-fry, string tie, supply, swear by, test-fly, thereby, tie-dye, tongue-tie, Transkei, twist tie, two-ply, untie, vat dye, Versailles, whereby, whitefly, white tie, wise guy • abide by, Adonai, alibi, alkali, amplify, beautify, bolo tie, butterfly, by-and-by, by the bye, calcify, certify, Chou En-lai, citify, clarify, classify, codify, crucify, cut-and-dry, cutie-pie, DIY, damselfly, dandify, deify, dignify, do-or-die, dragonfly, eagle eye, edify, evil eye, falsify, fortify, Gemini, gentrify, glorify, gratify, Haggai, high and dry, horrify, junior high, justify, kiss good-bye, liquefy, Lorelei, lullaby, magnify, Malachi, misapply, modify, mollify, mortify, Mount Sinai, multi-ply, multiply, mummify, mystify, nazify, notify, nuclei, nullify, occupy, on standby, on the fly, ossify, overbuy, overfly, overlie, pacify, Paraguay, passerby, petrify, preachify, prettify, private eye, prophesy, purify, putrefy, qualify, quantify, ratify, RBI, reapply, rectify, resupply, robber fly, runner's high, Russify, samurai, sanctify, satisfy, scarify, Seeing Eye, senior high, shepherd's pie, shoofly pie, signify, simplify, specify, speechify, stratify, stultify, stupefy, sweetie pie, Tenebrae, terrify, testify, tsetse fly, tumble dry, typify, uglify, underlie, unify, Uruguay, verify, vilify, vivify, yuppify, zombify • aniline dye, a priori, beatify, decertify, declassify, demystify, detoxify, disqualify, dissatisfy, diversify, electric eye, electrify, exemplify, Helvetii, humidify, identify, intensify, misclassify, money supply, oversupply, personify, preoccupy, revivify, see eye to eye, solidify, undersupply, water supply • dehumidify, misidentify, oversimplify • in the blink of an eye, modus operandi

y² \ē\ see EE[1]

yable \ī-ə-bəl\ see IABLE[1]

yad \ī-əd\ dryad, naiad, triad • jeremiad

yan \ī-ən\ see ION[1]

yant \ī-ənt\ see IANT

yatt \ī-ət\ see IET

yber \ī-bər\ see IBER

ybia \i-bē-ə\ see IBIA

yce \īs\ see ICE[1]

yche \ī-kē\ see IKE[1]

ycin \īs-ᵊn\ see ISON[1]

ycle¹ \ī-kəl\ cycle, Michael • cell cycle, life cycle, recycle, song cycle • business cycle, carbon cycle, Exercycle, kilocycle, megacycle, motorcycle, unicycle

ycle² \ik-əl\ see ICKLE

ycler \ik-lər\ see ICKLER

yde \īd\ see IDE[1]

ydia \i-dē-ə\ see IDIA

ydian \id-ē-ən\ see IDIAN

ydney \id-nē\ see IDNEY

ye \ī\ see Y[1]

yeable \ī-ə-bəl\ see IABLE[1]

yed \īd\ see IDE[1]

yer \īr\ see IRE[1]

yeth \ī-əth\ see IATH[1]

yfe \īf\ see IFE[1]

yg \ig\ see IG

ygamous \ig-ə-məs\ see IGAMOUS

ygamy \ig-ə-mē\ see IGAMY

ygian \i-jən\ Phrygian, pidgin, pigeon, smidgen • clay pigeon, religion, rock pigeon, stool pigeon, wood pigeon • homing pigeon • carrier pigeon, passenger pigeon

ying \ī-iŋ\ crying, flying, lying, trying • high-flying, low-lying, outlying, undying • terrifying, underlying
—also -ing *forms of verbs listed at* Y[1]

yke \īk\ see IKE[2]

ylan \il-ən\ see ILLON

yle \īl\ see ILE[1]

ylem \ī-ləm\ see ILUM
yler \ī-lər\ see ILAR
ylet \ī-lət\ see ILOT
ylic \il-ik\ see ILIC
yling \ī-liŋ\ see ILING[1]
yllable \il-ə-bəl\ see ILLABLE
yllic \il-ik\ see ILIC
yllis \il-əs\ see ILLUS
yllo[1] \ē-lō\ see ILO[2]
yllo[2] \ī-lō\ see ILO[1]
ylum \ī-ləm\ see ILUM
ylus \ī-ləs\ see ILUS
yly \ī-lē\ dryly, highly, shyly, slyly,
  smiley, Wiley, wily, wryly
ym \im\ see IM[1]
ymbal \im-bəl\ see IMBLE
ymbol \im-bəl\ see IMBLE
yme \īm\ see IME[1]
ymen \ī-mən\ see IMEN
ymer \ī-mər\ see IMER[1]
ymic \im-ik\ gimmick, mimic
ymie \ī-mē\ see IMY
ymion \im-ē-ən\ see IMIAN
ymity \im-ət-ē\ see IMITY
ymn \im\ see IM[1]
ymph \imf\ lymph, nymph
ynah \ī-nə\ see INA[1]
ynast \ī-nəst\ see INIST[1]
ynch[1] \inch\ see INCH
ynch[2] \iŋk\ see INK
yness \ī-nəs\ see INUS[1]
ynic \in-ik\ see INIC
ynical \in-i-kəl\ see INICAL
ynn \in\ see IN[1]
ynth \inth\ see INTH
ynx \iŋs\ see INX
yp \ip\ see IP
ypal \ī-pəl\ disciple • archetypal,
  prototypal
ype \īp\ see IPE
yper \ī-pər\ see IPER
yph \if\ see IFF
yphen \ī-fən\ hyphen, siphon
yphic \if-ik\ see IFIC
yphony \if-ə-nē\ see IPHONY
yping \ī-piŋ\ see IPING
ypo \ī-pō\ hypo, typo

ypse \ips\ see IPS
ypsy \ip-sē\ gypsy, Gypsy, tipsy
ypt \ipt\ see IPT
yptian \ip-shən\ see IPTION
yptic \ip-tik\ cryptic, triptych
  • ecliptic, elliptic • apocalyptic
yra \ī-rə\ Ira, Lyra, Myra • Elmira,
  Elvira, hegira, Palmyra
yrant \ī-rənt\ see IRANT
yre \īr\ see IRE[1]
yria \ir-ē-ə\ see ERIA[1]
yriad \ir-ē-əd\ see ERIOD
yric \ir-ik\ see ERIC[2]
yrical \ir-i-kəl\ see ERICAL[2]
yrie \ir-ē\ see EARY
yril \ir-əl\ see ERAL[1]
yrna \ər-nə\ see ERNA
yro[1] \ī-rō\ Cairo, gyro, Gyro, tyro
yro[2] \ir-ō\ see ERO[3]
yron \īr-ən\ see IREN
yros \ī-rəs\ see IRUS
yrrh \ər\ see EUR[1]
yrrhic \ir-ik\ see ERIC[2]
yrrhus \ir-əs\ see EROUS
yrtle \ərt-ᵊl\ see ERTILE
yrup \ər-əp\ see IRRUP
yrupy \ər-ə-pē\ see IRRUPY
yrus \ī-rəs\ see IRUS
ysch \ish\ see ISH[1]
ysia \ish-ə\ see ITIA[1]
ysian[1] \is-ē-ən\ Odyssean
  • Dionysian
ysian[2] \ish-ən\ see ITION
ysian[3] \izh-ən\ see ISION
ysian[4] \ī-sē-ən\ see ISCEAN[1]
ysical \iz-i-kəl\ physical, quizzical
  • nonphysical • metaphysical
ysm \iz-əm\ see ISM
ysmal \iz-məl\ dismal • abysmal,
  baptismal • cataclysmal
yson \īs-ᵊn\ see ISON[1]
yss \is\ see ISS
yssean \is-ē-ən\ see YSIAN[1]
yst \ist\ see IST[2]
ystal \is-tᵊl\ see ISTAL
yster \ī-stər\ see EISTER[1]
ystery \is-trē\ see ISTORY

ystic \is-tik\ see ISTIC
ystical \is-ti-kəl\ see ISTICAL
ysus[1] \ē-səs\ see ESIS
ysus[2] \ī-səs\ see ISIS
yte \īt\ see ITE[1]
ythe[1] \ī\ see Y[1]

ythe[2] \īth̲\ see ITHE[1]
ytic \it-ik\ see ITIC
ytical \it-i-kəl\ see ITICAL
ytton \it-ᵊn\ see ITTEN
yx \iks\ see IX[1]
yze \īz\ see IZE[1]